Whom We Shall Welcome

Critical Studies in Italian America

Nancy C. Carnevale and Laura E. Ruberto, *series editors*

This series publishes works on the history and culture of Italian Americans by emerging as well as established scholars in fields such as anthropology, cultural studies, folklore, history, and media studies. While focusing on the United States, it also includes comparative studies with other areas of the Italian diaspora. The books in this series engage with broader questions of identity pertinent to the fields of ethnic studies, gender studies, and migration studies, among others.

Series Board:

Simone Cinotto

Thomas J. Ferraro

Donna Gabaccia

Edvige Giunta

Joseph Sciorra

Pasquale Verdicchio

# Whom We Shall Welcome

**Italian Americans and Immigration Reform, 1945–1965**

*Danielle Battisti*

FORDHAM UNIVERSITY PRESS
NEW YORK 2019

Fordham University Press has no responsibility for the persistence or accuracy of URLs for external or third-party internet websites referred to in this publication and does not guarantee that any content on such websites is, or will remain, accurate or appropriate.

Fordham University Press also publishes its books in a variety of electronic formats. Some content that appears in print may not be available in electronic books.

Visit us online at www.fordhampress.com.

Library of Congress Cataloging-in-Publication Data available online at https://catalog.loc.gov.

Printed in the United States of America
21 20 19   5 4 3 2 1
First edition

CONTENTS

As is the case for many students of immigration history, my project began at home. When I was growing up in a self-styled Italian American household, questions about immigration, ethnicity, and identity were ever present. Both my paternal grandfather and grandmother immigrated to the United States (separately) from villages in the province of Frosinone in the 1950s. They both settled in Rochester, New York, where they met and married. In Rochester, they joined extended family members who had come before; and they would later send for other family members still in Italy, as well as those who took a more circuitous route to the United States, migrating first through Canada. In work places, social settings, devotional sites, schools, and other spaces, my *nonni* sought out other Italian Americans (both American-born and other newcomers). The task was not difficult. Both chain migration patterns and industrial employment opportunities helped foster Rochester's Italian American community in the years before and after World War II.

Sunday lunch (a loose term since "lunch" lasted almost all day long) was the focal point of the week. The entire extended family gathered at my great-grandparents' house—again an easy task since their house was flanked by my *nonni*'s house on the right and my great-uncle's house on the left. My *nonna* and other women scurried around the kitchen preparing a typically over-abundant meal that now takes on a greater significance to me as I juxtapose it to the scenes of scarcity commonly recalled by my *nonni* when they talked about their own childhood experiences. In later years when Sunday lunch moved to my own *nonni*'s house, I remember both being an active and enthusiastic participant in those gatherings but also, even then, critically thinking about what it all meant. I had plenty of friends at school who, after all, didn't choose to spend multiple days of the week with their cousins, and who didn't devote a whole weekend every September to camping out in their *nonni*'s basement in order to make a stockpile of tomato sauce for the year. At family gatherings, I was probably most deeply affected by my *nonno*, seated at the head of the table, glass of homemade wine in one hand, a deck of Italian playing cards for a game of scopa or briscola in the other. Week after week, one heard him singing along with one of his favorite singers, Nicola Di Bari. While swaying in place, he would echo the refrain of his favorite song, "paese dove si nasce," I imagine as he nostalgically remembered his homeland even while simultaneously reflecting upon his own place in America.* At almost every family gathering, my *nonno* was also likely to find a reason to utter his favorite catchphrase, "Nice country this America," which he used to express a wide range of emotions from genuine appreciation for the abundance in his life to a sarcastic commentary on what he presumably thought were the unrealistic expectations of his American-born grandchildren.

As I became a student of history, I had a deep desire to better understand the experiences of my grandparents and the ways in which their experiences and worldviews in turn shaped my own identity. I decided to write their story—the story of Italian immigration to the United States after World War II. Plenty had been written about turn-of-the-century immigrants, but what about those who came, as my grandparents had, much later and under different circumstances? In that professional pursuit, I learned that their immigration experiences were much more complicated than I had previously understood them to be—for both of my grandparents came to the United States during a period in which immigrant entry was governed by the highly restrictive National Origins System. I discovered that my *nonno* was only able to immigrate in 1954 as a refugee tailor sponsored by a distant relative and Bond Clothing Company (but ultimately finding employment at the Hickey Freeman Corporation) under the 1953 Refugee Relief Act (a fact my *nonna* felt carried such a stigma that she only recently gave me permission to share that information). I also learned that my *nonna*, along with her mother and her brother, were able to immigrate in 1954 by joining her father, who had already immigrated to Rochester in 1949. Like so many other southern Italian peasants in the late nineteenth and early twentieth centuries, my

---

* In the context of the song, it makes more sense to translate this phrase as "hometown where you were born," but *paese* could also mean "country" or "nation."

great-grandfather's parents periodically worked as migrant laborers, in their case, in France. Although it seems my great-grandfather held Italian citizenship, he was born in France and was able to use his French birth to circumvent the long backlogs for Italian immigrant visas in 1949. The lengths my grandparents went to in order to immigrate to the United States, the laws that complicated their entry, the efforts of Italian Americans to change those laws, and the motivations of their coethnics for pursuing those policy changes ultimately became the focus of this book as the project evolved. I would not have started that line of inquiry without my *nonno*, *nonna*, and all of the ways they touched my life. For that, this book is dedicated to them.

Of course, this book would not have been possible without other sources of personal and professional support as well. David Gerber belongs at the top of that list. David, your tutelage and guidance have affected my work in countless ways. You nurtured the questions I had, and you challenged me to think about new ones. I have been continuously pushed by your own intellectual curiosity, deep analytical thinking, and willingness to cross boundaries. More personally, I aspire daily (and often fail) to emulate your quiet confidence, independence of thought, and self-discipline. Perhaps this comes as a surprise, since we tend to speak from the perspective of one curmudgeon to another, but I have, and continue to value, your advisement and friendship in ways that cannot be properly articulated here. I am also indebted to the dedicated cohort of archival directors and staff that I have had the pleasure to work with over the years. Over the course of a nearly ten-year period of work at the Immigration History Research Center Archives, I was fortunate enough to cross paths with Rudy Vecoli, Joel Wurl, Donna Gabaccia, Erika Lee, and Ellen Engseth. A special thanks also to Daniel Necas, whose knowledge, labor, and camaraderie especially helped to advance this project. At the Center for Migration Studies I was aided by Maria Del Giudice, Diana J. Zimmerman, and most especially Mary Brown, whose herculean labors to keep the archive accessible to researchers like myself is much appreciated. This book was also made possible by the assistance of a number of people at New York University's Tamiment Library, Columbia University's Rare Book and Manuscript Library, Syracuse University's Special Collections Research Center, the University of Michigan's Bentley Historical Library, the University of Minnesota's Social Welfare Archives, and the Eisenhower Presidential Library.

A long list of scholars has also had a hand in this project. Portions of this manuscript were improved through critiques offered by mentors and peers including Wendy Wall, Thomas Guglielmo, Torrie Hester, Christopher Capozzola, Susan Cahn, Sasha Pack, Erik Seeman, Tamara Thornton, Perry Beardsley, David Head, Simone Cinotto, Roger Waldinger, Adam Goodman, and a number of interdisciplinary scholars from the Rethinking International Migration 2011 NEH Summer Seminar. Conference participation in conjunction with scholars working on similar projects, including Maddalena Marinari and Grainne McEvoy, have also enriched my work. Portions of this work were previously published in the *Journal of American Ethnic History* and *Making Italian America* (Fordham University Press), where the review and publication process strengthened my arguments and writing. Finally, feedback and support from scholars at Fordham University Press, including Nancy Carnevale, Laura Ruberto, and thoughtful peer reviewers, have made the book stronger.

I was also able to complete this project with financial assistance from a number of sources. The State University of New York at Buffalo supported early versions of this research with the College of Arts and Sciences Presidential Fellowship, the Department of History's Milton Plesur Fellowship, and a number of research grants. Other grants supporting this research came from the Immigration History Research Center Archives (University of Minnesota) Grant-in-Aid award, the Bentley Historical Library (University of Michigan) Bordin/Gillette Researcher Travel Fellowship, the Eisenhower Foundation's research grant for work at the Dwight D. Eisenhower Presidential Library, and the New-York Historical Society's Gilder Lehrman Fellowship. Finally, this research was honored with awards from the Immigration and Ethnic History Society and the Italian American Studies Association. My home institution, the University of Nebraska Omaha, has also been a great source of support. I have been lucky enough to benefit from the financial support of the Department of History's Charles and Mary Caldwell Martin Fund. Portions of this book have been workshopped with my colleagues Kent Blansett, Elaine Nelson, Martina Saltamacchia, and Sharon Wood. I have also been able to rely upon Jim Shaw for research assistance and Derek Fister for help in securing permissions. Finally, all of my colleagues in the History Department and beyond at UNO have helped to create an environment that has fostered my scholarship.

To my mom, dad, sisters, and other extended family members, I would not have made it this far without your love, support, and humor. Rudrama, your courageous life choices, devotion to family, and welcoming embrace have also been important to me. I have made it through the long days of solitude that consume the writing process because of the friendships in my life. My Colgate cohort of strong and successful friends, especially Amy Berman, have spurred me on. The many laughs and memories supplied by the Finnerty's/Union Hall crowd (yes, I did just put that in print) were a welcome break from days of research and writing. Finally, Harsha, for many years you have supported my life choices and have made great sacrifices for my professional ambitions. More than anyone else, you have provided me reassurance during my frequent moments of self-doubt, and you have endured it all with the love, laughs, and strategically timed shenanigans that have kept it all in perspective. Meena and Raina, although you can't read these words yet, I am sure you will be able to soon because you are both brilliant. You're also hilarious, strong-willed, and caring young women and I look forward to seeing each of you make your mark on the world.

Whom We Shall Welcome

## Boundaries of Inclusion and Exclusion in Postwar America

> An outstanding characteristic of the United States is its great cultural diversity within an overriding national unity. The American story proves, if proof were needed, that such differences do not mean the existence of superior and inferior classes.
>
> — "WHAT WE BELIEVE," FROM *Whom We Shall Welcome: Report of the President's Commission on Immigration and Naturalization,* 1953

On June 11, 1963, some two hundred and fifty Italian American members of the American Committee on Italian Migration (ACIM) congregated in Washington, D.C., for their organization's third annual symposium on Italian immigration. The foremost concern on the group's agenda that year was the passage of a comprehensive immigration reform bill to overturn the National Origins System and to create, to their mind, a more egalitarian system of governing American immigration policies.[1] According to ACIM, and many other organizations that were critical of the nation's immigration policies, the National Origins System helped sustain antiquated and unjust categories of inclusion and exclusion based on a supposed hierarchy of desirable racial, ethnic, and religious traits that had no place in the world's foremost democracy.[2]

As the leading organization representing Italian Americans concerned with issues of immigration in the postwar period, ACIM delegates regularly worked with American lawmakers to influence American immigration laws.

In 1963 they had secured an audience with President Kennedy. Gathered in a colonnade by the White House Rose Garden after rain forced them from their original location, ACIM delegates swarmed the president, imploring him to lend his full support to large-scale immigration reform efforts proposed by some of the more liberal members of Congress. ACIM members had put a great deal of faith in President Kennedy. Kennedy had, after all, been an outspoken proponent of cultural pluralism throughout his public career and as a senator he actively supported a variety of immigration reform proposals. Once referring to the National Origins System as "the most blatant piece of discrimination in the nation's history," Kennedy shared ACIM's vision that the United States was "a nation of immigrants."[3]

But the affinity many Italian Americans felt with President Kennedy went beyond policy considerations. As both a self-identifying ethnic American and the first Catholic president elected in the United States, President Kennedy was a personal beneficiary of progressive social and cultural shifts regarding race, ethnicity, and religion in the United States in the postwar period on which Italian Americans also capitalized.[4] President Kennedy, indeed the entire Kennedy family, represented the ultimate immigrant success story to many Italian Americans. In their eyes, generations of Kennedys had made good in America, overcoming past prejudices through hard work, perseverance, and ambition, to now boast not only high political and economic achievements but also a level of social acceptance from their fellow Americans that some Italian Americans continued to consider elusive—even in 1963.[5]

Although Italian Americans could identify with President Kennedy on many levels, there was one major difference between their situation and his. Whereas the Irish had arguably made the transition into the ranks of "older-stock" Americans by the postwar period, immigration laws still codified Italians and other peoples from southern and eastern Europe (to say nothing of nonwhites) as inferior, less desirable, or less fit for citizenship than older-stock whites.[6] Indeed, the very same year that ACIM pressed Kennedy for action on immigration, Leonard Pasqualicchio, an Order Sons of Italy in America lobbyist, proclaimed, "We Italians are still confronted with a racial problem; limited discrimination and numerical restrictions, compared to other foreign nationalities."[7]

This book examines the nature and significance of Italian American immigration reform campaigns that emerged in the years after World War II

FIGURE I. ACIM delegates meet with President Kennedy, Washington, D.C., June 1963. Source: box 2, folder L, Giuseppe D. Procopio Papers, Immigration History Research Center Archives, University of Minnesota.

and culminated with the abolishment of the National Origins System in 1965. It focuses on the variety of reasons Italian Americans embraced immigration reform as a movement and what their motivations for doing so tell us about Italian American identity, the broader immigration reform movement, and American society more generally in the postwar period. I argue that although Italian Americans did make up an important part of the coalition of reformers that was responsible for replacing the National Origins System with a regulatory system based on the theoretically more equitable criteria of selecting immigrants on the basis of occupational needs and family reunification in 1965, there were significant limitations to their brand of liberalism and their vision of social reform for the nation. It is true that like other immigration liberals, Italian Americans considered the National Origins System problematic because it was a symbol of racial and ethnic inequality in a democratic, pluralist, and Judeo-Christian nation. But those ideological strains of a broad postwar movement for immigration reform were not always the principal motivators for large numbers of Italian American activists. There is much evidence to suggest that Italian Americans primarily sought a level of respectability and full membership in the nation through immigration reform initiatives that they saw as more befitting of their status as whites in the 1940s, 1950s, and 1960s.

When President Kennedy met with ACIM representatives that day in June, he was receptive to the group's pleas and did indeed promise to send a proposal to Congress to "improve and modernize" the nation's immigration laws the following week.[8] Kennedy kept true to his word and endorsed a major immigration reform bill shortly after ACIM's visit to the White House. It would, however, be two more years before ACIM members, and other advocates of liberal immigration reforms, would see Congress abolish the National Origins System and adopt many of their proposals for governing immigration. Slow movement in passing immigration legislation was hardly a surprise though, particularly for Americans who had long grappled with the issue of "whom we shall welcome." That question, posed ten years earlier by President Truman's administration, was perhaps the central issue of the postwar period. During World War II and the years following it, Americans had reconstructed their national identity around the idea that their form of government and their way of life best protected peoples' natural rights to political equality, social freedom, and cultural autonomy. As such, Americans proclaimed, in voices louder than ever before, a commitment to social equality and cultural pluralism. But although Americans appeared to share a consensus on these issues, they were, in fact, highly problematic and hotly contested subjects.[9] The state continued to divide the population into "superior and inferior classes" in a number of ways. As a result, many groups of Americans hardly believed themselves to be welcomed or even tolerated in America at midcentury. Jim Crow laws in the American South were perhaps the most notorious and harmful example of the disjuncture between the nation's ideology and the realities of American life. But they were by no means anomalous in their character. A range of laws, including those governing immigration and naturalization, also helped create and sustain distinctions between those believed by many Americans to be superior and inferior in character.

Just as African American civil rights activists sought to undo Jim Crow laws in the postwar period, others set their sight on dismantling the National Origins System. Adopted in 1924, the Johnson-Reed Act was a comprehensive immigration and naturalization law that set annual limits on immigration for the first time in the nation's history and established annual quotas for the number of immigrants that each country could send to the United States during any given year. Under the new system, non-Western nations were all but entirely barred from entry, and the nations of Western Europe, which had historically sent immigrants to the United States, were granted the lion's share of quotas. In allocating quotas in this manner, lawmakers purposefully sought to select for future immigrants with similar racial, ethnic, and cultural characteristics to those that were thought to be held by the nation's older-stock immigrants. This move, however, was hardly a departure from the past. The new law merely expanded and more sharply codified long-established practices. Since the nation's inception, immigration and citizenship laws created categories of inclusion for some groups and exclusion for others. A number of factors, including one's gender, sexual orientation, economic status, mental acuity, or physical bearing, could mark one as inferior, undesirable, and excludable from the benefits of full membership in the nation.[10]

Racial and ethnic distinctions had always been the most important factors that marked some individuals as fit for membership and others as inferior. One need look no further than the experiences of peoples of African or Native American descent who had been largely excluded from full political, social, and cultural inclusion in the United States since the nation's founding. That was also the case for Asian immigrants who were systematically restricted from entering the United States and naturalizing over the course of the late nineteenth and early twentieth centuries. The only major exception to the general principle that immigration and naturalization privileges were reserved for whites was the relatively open access migrants from the Western Hemisphere enjoyed. But the comparatively unfettered access historically bestowed upon Western Hemisphere migrants was only grudgingly permitted because of the nation's complicated history with Mexico, the historic labor needs of the Southwest, and the futility of trying to regulate migration along the nation's vast southern border.[11] If racial and ethnic selection in American immigration policies were standard practices then, the National Origins System was mostly notable mainly for the way it *systematized* state selection of immigrants (and therefore potential citizens) on the basis of supposedly desirable racial and cultural traits.[12]

In addition to reaffirming existing barriers to immigration and naturalization privileges for nonwhites, the new law was also noteworthy for its codification of exclusionary sentiments toward southern and eastern European peoples for the first time.[13] Debates surrounding the passage of the law suggest that Catholic, Jewish, and Orthodox immigrants from the countries of southern and eastern Europe who had swarmed American shores in the decades before the act's passage were the primary targets of new annual caps placed on immigration and the use of national origins quotas to regulate the distribution of immigration visas. Several underlying concerns led to the increased stigmatization of these groups in the late nineteenth and early twentieth centuries. Some, but certainly not a comprehensive list, of those factors include increases in industrial labor and class conflict, problems associated with urbanization, anxieties about loyalty and national security in the wake of World War I, and longtime concerns about the religious and cultural traditions of these groups that were thought to undermine the quality of democratic citizenship in the United States. Added to those long-standing fears was the emergence of new racial theories that posited that Mediterranean, Slavic, Jewish, and other racial groups were less biologically fit for democratic citizenship than Anglo-Saxon, Teutonic, or Nordic races—which cast new doubt on even the whiteness of the former groups.[14]

Southern and eastern European immigrants and their American-born children were virtually powerless to stop the National Origins System's implementation. They were simply without the political, social, and economic capital to mount any viable opposition to such a measure in the interwar period.[15] Moreover, potential progressive allies who were critical of prevailing racial theories and who advocated new models of cultural pluralism were only beginning to come together in meaningful ways—and even they faced considerable obstacles to working together.[16] A generation later, while much had changed, much stayed the same. Over the objections of social reformers who raised concerns about discriminatory immigration policies in the interwar period, as well as those whose concerns emerged out of foreign policy considerations during World War II and the Cold War, Congress largely reaffirmed the National Origins System with the passage of the 1952 Immigration and Nationality Act. The McCarran-Walter Act, as it was more commonly known, did eliminate barred zones in the Asia-Pacific triangle and allocated minimal quotas to all countries, thereby allowing its defenders to claim that the new law eliminated race-based exclusion. But in effect, the legislation continued to overwhelmingly favor older-stock whites and to heavily discriminate against nonwhites and against southern and eastern European immigrant groups who were still permitted only a small fraction of annual quota allocations. Critics therefore argued that the legislation continued to reflect popular anxiety over the racial and cultural character of those that were welcomed into the boundaries of the nation and its citizenry.[17]

But the passage of the McCarran-Walter Act spurred many Americans to actively campaign for the abolition of the National Origins System and to replace it with a more equitable system of governing immigration. Liberal internationalists in the White House, Congress, the media, and other elite institutions generally believed that national origins quotas tarnished America's democratic image abroad and restricted the nation's ability to achieve its foreign policy goals—particularly in the context of waging Cold War battles in the developing world. Religious and ethnic groups had long noted the discriminatory and unjust nature of the National Origins System and labored to overturn it with renewed vigor in the 1950s and 1960s. Their motivations were varied, ranging from desires to be reunited with family members abroad, concerns stemming from the Cold War (both at home and abroad), human rights issues, and anxieties about their own group's political and social standing in the United States. Labor organizations (composed of many second- and third-generation ethnic Americans) and minority groups who advocated for racial equality and civil rights reforms rounded out calls for immigration reform.[18]

Despite the emergence of a diverse and dramatic coalition that successfully worked to topple the National Origins System for two decades after World War II, this movement remains relatively unexamined and occupies only minimal space in narratives of postwar American history. Perhaps one reason that narrative has been obscured stems from the emphasis scholars have placed on the results of the National Origins System's abolishment. The effects of dismantling national origins quotas were nothing short of revolutionary. Its elimination created opportunities for immigrants from more diverse racial and ethnic backgrounds than ever before to come to the

United States—which they did, in record numbers. Their arrival and subsequent incorporation have indeed changed both the face and the identity of the nation.[19] However, in focusing on the effects of ending the National Origins System, scholars have tended to overlook the actors and forces that contributed to its demise. This emphasis has cast a long shadow over critically important questions about how the National Origins System fell, the groups that took it down, and the nature of their campaigns to do so.

Until recently, when historians did talk about efforts to achieve immigration reforms in the postwar period, they generally characterized the movement in one of two ways. In one narrative, the abolition of the National Origins System was seen primarily as an outgrowth of American foreign policy needs during the Cold War. In this view, reforms were largely accomplished at the urging of internationally oriented liberal policymakers in the White House and Congress who wanted more flexibility in responding to contemporary migration problems and who needed to win over the hearts, minds, and stomachs of the largely nonwhite inhabitants of developing nations.[20] In another, sometimes interlocking narrative, the undoing of racial and ethnic quotas gets clumsily tacked onto the history of the civil rights movement with only the briefest of explanations that the National Origins System was ultimately an unsustainable remnant of past injustices that could no longer survive in an era of equal rights and American international leadership.[21]

Neither of these explanations are entirely adequate. Immigration reforms that came about in 1965 were not just an inevitable byproduct of a liberal elite Cold War consensus. One of the most underappreciated aspects of postwar immigration reform efforts was the grassroots organizing of ethnic and religious groups that formed the backbone of the movement.[22] Moreover, these groups' concerns were not exclusively linked to either civil rights reforms or foreign policy issues. Many reformers appropriated anticommunist rhetoric or civil rights posturing in their campaigns, but their motivations and actions deserve deeper investigation. In examining the political and social activism of Italian Americans, this book does not aim to provide a comprehensive history of the broad postwar immigration reform movement, but it does posit that only by examining the individual groups of this liberal reform coalition can we better understand the nature of the movement, the forces that undergirded it, and the impact of ethnic interests on broader forces in American politics and culture in the postwar period.

Italian Americans were critical participants in debates about "whom we shall welcome." Matched only by Jewish Americans in their activism on the subject, Italian Americans led a concerted push for liberalizing the nation's immigration and refugee policies in the postwar period. Italian Americans embraced immigration reform as a defining issue for a number of reasons. Practical concerns such as desire to reunite with separated family members or concern for Italy and its people in the wake of World War II and the Cold War were important issues to a great many participants. But immigration reform campaigns were about something deeper than individual family needs or transnational attachments. Campaign rhetoric and goals reveal how many Italian Americans saw the nation's immigration policies as a critical marker for defining the boundaries of inclusion and exclusion in America for themselves and for others. This point may have been most aptly stated by Mae Ngai, who observes that even though quota laws technically discriminated against aliens, and not American citizens, white ethnics like Italian Americans saw the nation's reaffirmation of the National Origins System in 1952 as "a badge of their inferior status" or alternatively as "a proxy for their status" as still less desirable citizens than older-stock whites.[23]

Italian American activists therefore took up immigration reform as part of a broader movement to extend political and social rights to more peoples in the nation. In that respect, their campaigns reflected a wave of postwar political liberalism and, something scholars have less frequently observed, religious (or, even more precisely, Catholic) worldviews that advanced political ideas and practices based on divinely granted human rights.[24] In this regard, white ethnic activism to liberalize American immigration policies paralleled African American campaigns for racial equality in the civil rights era in many ways. Anticommunist discourse (particularly a renewed emphasis on political liberalism) and Cold War foreign policy concerns propelled both the civil rights movement and the immigration reform movement forward by allowing reformers to call upon the state to live up to its own liberal ideology. According to Ngai, "immigration reformers were deeply influenced by the civil rights movement, both by its broad appeals for social justice and human freedom and by its more specific conception of formal equal rights."[25] The shared ideological basis of the two movements is also evident in the ways that Catholic and Jewish groups capitalized on consensus-era cultural pluralism campaigns and the nation's corresponding shift toward a tri-faith identification to actively challenge lingering forces of ethnic and religious discrimination in housing, education, and social clubs in the 1940s and 1950s. In doing so, white ethnic and religious groups created real political and social changes that liberalized the power structure of the nation and the boundaries of inclusion and exclusion in American life.[26]

White ethnic groups such as Italian Americans did indeed have a stake in, and participate in, broad movements for social equality in the postwar period that may have been as much about ethnic and religious equality as they were about racial equality. We must not overlook that fact, and it is just one reason postwar immigration reform campaigns deserve more scholarly attention. But a narrative of liberal political and social reform is not the whole story. There are important limitations in characterizing white ethnic activism in such a manner. If we do not understand those limitations, the full scope of Italian American (and perhaps other white ethnic) activism in this period is lost. As much as Italian Americans saw themselves as expanding the boundaries of liberalism in America, their campaigns were also about quests for respectability and full membership in the nation. Despite the changing political climate of the period, those constructs remained highly racialized.[27]

The nature of Italian American immigration reform campaigns demonstrates that, in many instances, participants seemed less concerned with extending equality to all peoples than with securing a privileged status for peoples of Italian ethnicity on par with the position already enjoyed by older-stock whites in the United States.[28] Since the National Origins System's adoption in 1924, Italian Americans had made great strides in completing their voyage "from steerage to suburbs."[29] Yet, even while new immigrant groups were at once increasingly included within the boundaries of the American mainstream, many of these newcomers still believed that they remained marginalized in significant ways. For Italian Americans this was no more so apparent than in the immigration opportunities opened or, more aptly, denied to them. The legislative goals and social campaigns endorsed by Italian Americans and their representative organizations in the postwar period suggest that many individuals mobilized against the National Origins System because Italians were not accorded the same privileges as older-stock whites under its matrix. If Italian Americans had achieved full membership in the nation by the 1950s, why then did they not enjoy *all* the benefits of that status? Like older-stock whites, Italian Americans were privileged in their relatively unfettered access to suburban homeownership, higher education, social clubs, job advancement, and the right to marry almost whomever they chose. Should not they also have the right to bring their relatives to the United States? Were not they, too, entitled to the legal classification of "desirable" immigrants and citizens? They had, after all, proven that Italians were indeed "good" Americans—which of course remained a racialized distinction throughout much of the postwar period as it had been for many years before then. In this regard then, Italian Americans may have been less concerned with overhauling racial and cultural stratifications in American society then they were with moving Italians up within the hierarchy of existing classification schemes.

The tactics and rhetoric employed by Italian American immigration reform advocates in the postwar period give us the best evidence to understand the meaning Italian Americans ascribed to the immigration reform movement. In the late 1940s and early 1950s, Italian Americans tended to focus rather narrowly on American immigration policies as they affected Italian Americans and Italian immigrants specifically. In part, this inward focus reflected Italian American claims to the privileges of membership in the white mainstream for their group. The primary reform strategy of Italian Americans was thus to secure special legislation for Italian immigrants by successfully manipulating American concerns about Italy's political and economic stability during the Cold War. When new immigrants arrived under those special provisions, Italian Americans tended to emphasize the ease with which new immigrants were able to assimilate to life in America. In these campaigns, Italian Americans essentially claimed Italian fitness for American citizenship and for increased immigration opportunities without really challenging hierarchies of racial privilege embedded in laws and customs.

In one sense, those maneuvers reflected pragmatic strategies to whittle away at the effectiveness of the National Origins System in an era in which reformers did not have either the political capital or mass public support to drastically amend American immigration laws. In that regard, Italian American campaigns for special legislation specifically benefitting Italian immigrants should be understood as part of a broader liberal campaign to weaken the National Origins System through side-door channels. But there is also something fundamentally conservative about those strategies. Italian American tactics legitimated and even strengthened the very racial constructions and hierarchies they claimed to challenge. Italian Americans likewise tended to accept and advance traditional assimilationist narratives as well. Their campaigns thus ultimately demonstrate that for much of the postwar period the most prominent and active Italian American organizations were not so much concerned with reforming a system of racial and ethnic selection in America but sought to reposition the place of Italian peoples within those established frameworks.

By the end of the 1950s, a distinct shift does appear in Italian American immigration reform campaigns. As liberal reform movements gained momentum and as the strategies Italian Americans had previously campaigned on became less effective, Italian Americans adopted new tactics. From about 1960 onward, Italian Americans joined other liberals in waging a more direct attack against the National Origins System by advocating for the regulation of immigration based on what they considered to be a more equitable and humane principle of family reunification. Italian Americans advanced arguments based on both secular (democratic) liberalism and Catholic social thought to make their case.

But even as Italian Americans took greater part in campaigns for liberal immigration reforms, we are again confronted with racial limitations to their liberalism. One is struck by Italian American reformers' seemingly reluctant and incomplete adoption of family reunification arguments, despite the enormous benefits Italians were positioned to reap from a policy shift in that direction. Most notably, Italian American activists continued to use of the rhetoric of contributionism to justify immigration reform.[30] Contributionist narratives argued that various immigrant or ethnic groups should be rewarded with greater immigration opportunities for past meritorious behavior that conformed to highly racialized standards of inclusion in the nation. But those arguments hardly challenged racially charged paradigms of inclusion and exclusion, suggesting the need to qualify understandings of white ethnic liberalism, even at its height in the early 1960s.

It is not at all problematic to acknowledge that two somewhat contradictory impulses were at operation at once in Italian American and perhaps other immigration reform campaigns. Groups or coalitions rarely operate in a monolithic fashion. Nor are the end goals of constituent members always driven by a single ideological impulse. This study therefore tries to uncover the full complexity of both Italian American liberalism and the forces that ultimately led to the undoing of the National Origins System in 1965.[31] Moreover, liberals—Italian American or otherwise—are not being held to some unattainable standard when we examine the limitations of their movement. Scholars often note the racial limitations of American liberalism without fully exploring the significance of those constraints. There were, however, white ethnic liberals who did not let racialized boundaries or concerns hem in their rhetoric or activism.[32] Like African Americans who would not conform to consensus-era definitions of liberalism, their voices sometimes became politically marginalized in the postwar period.[33] In the case of the Italian American lobby, there were actors and ideas present within the network (particularly those influenced by Catholic social thought on migration) that could have pushed the movement toward a more egalitarian and racially liberal position. But at the end of the day, more conservative views and tactics remained dominant. Political circumstances might therefore explain why liberal currents were not stronger among white ethnic activists, but they should not keep us from discussing the full implications of liberalism's limits.

By simply qualifying liberal activism as limited by racial constraints, we do not fully understand the ideological impulses behind immigration reform campaigns, and we fail to grasp how white ethnic activism on immigration reflected broader political and cultural trends during the period. Take, for example, the evolution of white ethnic politics in the late twentieth century. Studying how white ethnics understood their place in the nation at midcentury can more fully explain how some of the same individuals and groups that were foundational members of the New Deal coalition and who sought to liberalize the racially discriminatory National Origins System in the 1950s and 1960s could simultaneously take part in white flight and, just a few years later, respond to, and even help construct, the politics and culture of white backlash to the civil rights movement. By considering the limitations to white ethnic liberalism in the postwar period, we can better understand conservative shifts in white ethnic politics that had already begun even as immigration reform legislation was finally passed in 1965.[34] Doing so may also help contextualize the nature of nonwhite, namely Japanese American and Chinese American immigration reform efforts in the postwar period.

Those once-marginalized groups made the transition to model minorities by adopting decidedly nonblack identity markers and largely embraced a model of Anglo-American conformity. The result was a more inclusionary position for themselves in American society, demonstrated by, among other things, greater immigration opportunities for members of their national groups.[35] In this regard, white and nonwhite ethnic repositioning of their groups' status in American society appears similarly conservative and deserves further attention.

Another point that calls for further scrutiny is that while ethnic groups were indeed at the forefront of campaigns to amend the nation's immigration laws, they may have operated as members of a coalition in only the loosest sense.[36] Most of the time, Italian Americans worked within their own ethnic organizations. When they did collaborate with other groups, they did not stray far from their comfort zone—most often collaborating with Catholic organizations. Herein we see a slight retreat from the interethnic and interfaith cooperation that had gained momentum in the interwar period and during World War II.[37] If there was relatively little interaction between Italian Americans and other ethnic or religious groups, there was even less collaboration between Italian Americans and racial minorities, suggesting links between the civil rights movement and the immigration reform movement may have been superficial at best.[38] Although white ethnics paid tribute to the idea of racial equality in their campaigns, they were largely ambivalent regarding issues of racial equality (other than immigration) in practice. Similarly, the NAACP and other African American organizations did not take great interest in the battle over the nation's immigration policies and only connected the immigration reform movement to the civil rights movement in equally rhetorical ways. At the very least, this trend suggests the need to better acknowledge the competing interests, strategies, and beliefs of the various members of this liberal coalition that worked to undo the National Origins System. For more definitive answers, scholars must continue to examine the actions of other immigrant groups that also campaigned for changes to American immigration policies after World War II.[39]

Italian Americans do, however, provide an important case study for several reasons. Along with Jewish Americans, Italian Americans were one of the most active groups that supported immigration reforms after World War II, and yet we know little about the specific nature of their campaigns.[40]

Furthermore, as one of the largest self-identifying ethnic groups at midcentury, Italian Americans occupied an important social and political position in America. Influential Italian American organizations claimed to speak for over thirteen million Americans of Italian descent, and in cities, states, and regions where they were heavily concentrated, Italian Americans wielded significant political influence.[41] The same was true on a national level. In 1948 alone, there were eight Italian Americans elected to Congress, and for a brief period in the 1960s there was even a congressional Italian American caucus.[42] Furthermore, millions of Italian Americans identified as Catholics and worked closely with American Catholic organizations. By studying their actions, we are thus able to examine the intersection of Catholic social thought with Italian American immigration reform campaigns.

Finally, European immigrants and their ethnic-identifying children and grandchildren remain relevant to the American narrative in the twentieth century. The relative inclusion of Ellis Island immigrants and their children into the American mainstream in the postwar period has masked the ways in which many members of these groups could, and often did, continue to identify and mobilize in ethnic terms (and how many older-stock Americans sometimes perceived them as ethnics).[43] European immigration to the United States in the late twentieth century also continued to affect the country. Compared to periods of relatively high immigration that took place at the turn of the century, and in more recent years, the postwar period appears, at least on the surface, as one of relative inactivity. A closer examination of immigration trends, however, reveals that while immigration rates were relatively low at midcentury, immigration and refugee policies evolved in dynamic ways—and in large part because of the activities of self-identifying ethnic Americans.[44] In the case of Italians, more than 325,000 people immigrated to the United States from 1945 to 1965. About 300,000 more followed in the decade or so after 1965.[45] These figures pale in comparison to the much larger and more familiar turn-of-the-century waves of Italian migrations in which upward of four million Italians arrived to the United States, but considering Italy's annual immigration quota was only about five thousand, the numbers appear more impressive.[46] Postwar Italian immigration rates are also significant for how many peoples they did not include. From 1946 to 1976, more than seven million Italians emigrated from Italy to continental Europe, Oceania, North America, and South America.[47]

Those who made the United States their home as part of Italy's postwar migrations were able to do so, in large part, because of the advocacy and assistance provided to them by Italian American organizations dedicated to both opening opportunities for Italian immigrants and reforming American immigration policies more generally. This work forms a small part of that transnational history of postwar Italian emigration.

The construction of immigration and citizenship policies can be fundamentally understood as an exercise in identity construction. If immigration laws are, at their core, an expression of what we imagine the nation to be, Italian Americans were critical participants in debates about the meaning of Americanism and how groups could lay claim to it in the postwar period.[48] In their attempts to shape "whom we shall welcome," Italian Americans sought to expand access to that tent, but they did so in profoundly limited ways. Their activism was, in large part, shaped by their desire to solidify their own group's inclusionary status in the American mainstream. This book, therefore, explores the nature of Italian American immigration reform campaigns in order to better understand both Italian American identity and broader political and social trends in the nation at midcentury.

# Italian American Identity and Politics: World War II to the Cold War

John Basilone's name might have been one of the most recognizable to emerge from the ranks of the servicemen who fought in World War II. Noted for his dedication and bravery at Guadalcanal, his continuing service to the country during highly publicized tours to sell war bonds, and ultimately his death in combat at Iwo Jima, Basilone was the only enlisted marine to receive both the Medal of Honor and the Navy Cross in World War II. Italian Americans took great pride in commemorating Basilone's exemplary service, both during his lifetime and after his death.[1] But as striking as Basilone's story was, it was also in keeping with a much more familiar narrative. Hundreds of thousands of Italian Americans joined the army, worked in home front industries, purchased war bonds, and took part in patriotic displays during World War II. Their participation in such activities was driven by many factors, but demonstrations of loyalty, Americanism, and fitness for citizenship were important motivating forces for a number of Italian Americans (including both recent immigrants and American-born self-identifying ethnics). Nevertheless, all too many Italian Americans understood that while every American recognized John Basilone's name, they also knew the names of Al Capone, Nicola Sacco, Bartolomeo Venzetti, and Benito Mussolini.

While Italian Americans had made great strides toward achieving political and social equality with older-stock Americans by the start of the war, Italian Americans still experienced certain stigmas at midcentury. Italian peoples (in the United States and Italy) continued to be viewed by some Americans as inferior—as evidenced by the nation's immigration laws and more informal acts of discrimination. Many Italian Americans also saw the rise of Italian fascism and, later, the appeal of communist advances in Italy (which reached their zenith in 1948) as threatening developments. Fears that foreign radicals would corrupt American democracy shored up the restrictionary immigration regime that the country adopted in 1924. Aware of the improving but ultimately precarious position they occupied during and after the war, many Italian Americans were understandably concerned that continued associations with totalitarianism in Italy might tarnish their group's position in the United States and undo the significant gains they had made in American society.

It is therefore no surprise that during and after the war, Italian Americans invested a great deal of energy in public campaigns aimed at demonstrating their group's loyalty to the nation and their fitness as democratic citizens. With World War II and the onset of the Cold War reaffirming the interconnected nature of the world, Italian American elites inherently understood that those displays necessitated engagement with American perceptions of both Italian Americans at home and Italians abroad. The result was Italian Americans actively crafting a new group identity through wartime loyalty displays, international engagement premised on the utility of ethnic ambassadorship, and even attempts to reframe the boundaries of Italian identity and citizenship. It was also in their involvement with Italian reconstruction initiatives that immigration concerns again bubbled to the surface. Italian Americans, many of whom were already personally aware of their relatives' ambitions to seek economic security through migration, also came to believe that the successful democratization of Italy (and therefore their own standing in the United States) was dependent upon relieving population pressures that they had come to see as a threat to the reconstruction of Italy along democratic lines. Those conclusions amplified existing anxieties about Italian Americans' place in the nation and contributed to political mobilization on immigration and other issues.

### *Italian American Fitness for Citizenship in World War II–Era America*

Following Japan's attack on Pearl Harbor in December 1941, any lingering debates about American involvement in World War II abruptly ended. American officials and the public alike almost unanimously called for a declaration of war in the wake of the attack, and the nation quickly mobilized its resources for the fight. The war effort drew upon the support and labor of Americans from all backgrounds. For Italian Americans, much was at stake. Along with fighting for their nation's security, political ideals, and international interests, Italian Americans also understood that the war had the potential to affect them in deeply personal ways. Hanging in the balance for Italian Americans was the fate of their homeland, the lives of family members or other associates still in Italy, and their future relationships with both Italy and its people. But the nation's fight with fascist regimes in Japan, Germany, and Italy also provoked concerns among many Italian Americans about their group's perceived identity and loyalty at home.

Italian Americans had made considerable political, economic, and social gains in the years leading up to World War II. Only twenty years earlier Americans had considered southern and eastern European peoples so problematic, even menacing, that the National Origins System was passed to mitigate against their impact on the country. Early twentieth-century racial constructions were paramount in shaping those attitudes. Compared to "Nordic" whites, members of southern and eastern European "races" were thought to be inferior on several fronts. From a physical standpoint, the latter groups were commonly found to be less intelligent, smaller in stature or strength, and disease-ridden. Inferior behavioral traits such as displays of criminal deviancy, moral weakness, and political radicalism were also associated with newcomers. These relatively new beliefs about the rational or scientific basis for the existence of racial hierarchies only added to long-held fears among Americans that the cultural traditions of Catholics or Jews made certain immigrant groups unfit for democratic citizenship. The 1924

Immigration Act codified the idea that Italian peoples (and many other racial or ethnic groups) were of inferior racial stock to older-stock whites in America.[2]

Yet even at the height of anti-immigrant sentiments and the ascendancy of scientific racism, social scientists began to challenge the validity of scientific determinations of racial categories by positing that constructed notions of both racial and ethnic differences were determined primarily by cultural factors instead of biological ones.[3] Those new ideas helped to fuel a cultural gifts movement that rejected theories and policies based on scientific racism—including not only the National Origins System but the assimilation paradigm itself. Therefore, even while conservatives looked backward toward older constructions of an American national identity, liberal social reformers promoted programs based on cultural pluralism and tolerance for ethnic, if not racial, diversity in the country. At the same time that those ideological changes were underway, Ellis Island immigrants and their children increasingly experienced degrees of political, economic, and social inclusion in the nation. Their color (if not their race) generally afforded newcomers access to relatively high-paying manufacturing jobs, union membership, machine politics, and ultimately social welfare programs made available by New Deal legislation in the interwar years.[4] It was also during this time that ethnic Americans began to more closely mirror older-stock groups in their domestic household arrangements, gender roles, and consumption patterns as they took part in mainstream American culture and as sustained immigrations from their home countries declined.[5]

But World War II offered a true sea change for new immigrant groups and their children in the United States. The atrocities perpetrated by Nazi Germany's use of pseudoscientific racial theories and its ensuing eugenics programs sounded scientific racism's death rattle.[6] When combined with the rhetoric and ideology of the war at home, the results were dramatic. Messages from both public and private sectors during the war proclaimed America's commitment to fighting for the freedoms and equalities that liberal democratic regimes helped to protect and that fascist ones helped to destroy. As a result, Americans reimagined the American way as embodying political equality and social tolerance for all classes, races, ethnicities, and religions. Part of that shift was practical. Americans were told that racial, ethnic, and religious discord on the home front would hurt the war effort by distracting them from their ultimate goal of winning the war. But tolerance and unity campaigns were also the outcome of more complex cultural projects that Americans had been grappling with throughout the twentieth century.

Such campaigns were, of course, not without problems. Race-based discrimination continued to remain the most formidable barrier to American unity and the promises of the liberal state. However, white ethnics were clearly the primary beneficiaries of wartime messages. Throughout the war, Americans widely embraced the notion that the contributions of immigrants and their children had made the nation stronger. They likewise rejected the "100 percent Americanism" philosophy of the last war in favor of ideology that enabled Americans to retain, and even embrace, their ethnic identities as sources of pride and strength. Diversity, as the argument went, made the nation stronger at home even while ethnic ambassadors could help promote the nation's mission abroad.[7] Wartime liberalism also provided a boon to white ethnics in its transformation of the country into a tri-faith nation. Messages from both the state and the private sector increasingly underscored the idea that the nation's identity and values were derived not just from its Protestant heritage but from its Catholic and Jewish ones as well. This shift had begun with liberal social reformers in the 1920s and 1930s who had promoted interfaith cooperation and the acceptance of Catholic and Jewish Americans into what was once considered a Protestant nation. Wartime tolerance and unity campaigns heightened and institutionalized that trend already underway. As a result, anti-Catholic and anti-Semitic sentiments did not completely disappear, but they did recede significantly.[8]

Wartime ideological changes were accompanied by economic and social shifts that signaled the inclusionary status of Ellis Island ethnics. Revitalized union strength and work in war production industries created better paying jobs for millions of white ethnic working-class men and women. Furthermore, the social mobility that flowed from those opportunities was accompanied by physical mobility. Italian Americans and other recent newcomers began to move out of ethnic enclaves into more ethnically diverse neighborhoods as they sought employment in wartime industries. Service in the army mirrored trends at home. In the army, new immigrant groups often left their ethnic neighborhoods for the first time and experienced unprecedented levels of social interaction with Americans from (almost) all walks of life. The same could not be said for African Americans, who continued to experience segregation in the army and at home.[9]

For these and other reasons, new immigrant groups could lay reasonable claims to both whiteness and social inclusion in the American mainstream by World War II. Yet despite the unprecedented levels of acceptance and integration achieved by the Ellis Island cohort, white ethnics could and did still experience discrimination, stigmatization, or exclusion on the basis of their ethnicity or religion.[10] Above all else, the nation's immigration laws continued to reflect the perceived inferiority of Italian peoples. In a few circles, Italian American whiteness even continued to be called into question.[11] Such experiences were surely less frequent than in earlier periods, and they may have stung less deeply, but they were not altogether absent or even considered altogether unacceptable behaviors. It is not surprising then that many Italian Americans fiercely guarded the gains their group had made and actively worked to combat any developments that may have threatened that tenuous upward mobility.

For many Italian Americans, their group's association with Italian fascism threatened to do just that. While it is difficult to quantify the exact number and the degree to which Italian Americans supported Mussolini and his regime in the interwar period, it is safe to say that the community's enthusiasm was not insignificant, and their activities left their mark on the group's image in America. The most vocal support for Mussolini and his government came from Italian American elites and the ethnic institutions they dominated.[12] The Italian-language press, led by *Il Progresso Italo-Americano*, the largest circulating Italian-language newspaper in the United States, actively promoted Mussolini's regime and its accomplishments throughout the interwar period. The Order Sons of Italy in America (the largest Italian American fraternal organization, with hundreds of chapters nationwide), the Dante Alighieri Society, and other ethnic organizations also frequently celebrated fascist Italy's accomplishments publicly in the 1920s and early 1930s. Business elites engaged in trade with Italy also gave a public face to Italian American admiration for the fascist state, even if they did so primarily out of necessity.[13] These groups were generally responsive to Mussolini's calls for action on behalf of the Italian state. Conceptualizing of Italian communities abroad as informal colonies, Mussolini exploited transnational connections among "Italiani all'estero" (Italians abroad) to promote his government's foreign policy goals overseas. Those elite members of the pro-Italy lobby, wielding the threat of the Italian American vote and other forms of influence, engaged in "parallel diplomacy" for Mussolini's government during the interwar years by advocating for Italian interests on issues such as debt payments, tariff reductions, and American neutrality during both Italy's invasion of Ethiopia and the Spanish Civil War.[14]

At the grassroots level, hundreds of thousands of Italian Americans had expressed admiration for Benito Mussolini and the accomplishments of his regime in the 1920s and early 1930s. Most working-class Italian Americans supported Mussolini in broad terms but never really held deep ideological commitments to fascism as a political ideology. They did, however, revel in the sense of nationalism, or *Italianita*, that Mussolini promoted worldwide, and they were captivated by Il Duce's quest to restore Italy's international prestige.[15] Reflecting those sentiments, one Italian American from southwestern Pennsylvania, Ralph Arlotti, later recalled:

> I was very upset as an American, an Italian American, at Mussolini. Because I used to love Mussolini, I used to respect Mussolini. Anyhow I respected him as a great leader, I thought he was a savior of Italy. I thought all of this as a young kid. . . . But when he got with Hitler and he and being our enemy I hated him. He betrayed me as an Italian and that fed me. I was very proud to be an American because I was fighting the lousy Mussolini that double crossed me, that let me down.[16]

Like many other Italian Americans, Arlotti's position hardly suggested an attachment to fascism as a political ideology but instead reflected veneration for a leader who could potentially modernize and glorify a nation and its people. However, those kinds of distinctions may have been lost upon American audiences, who were less concerned with parsing out the intricacies of Italian American politics than identifying potential security threats. It was more likely that Americans would remember public displays of fasci in the streets (small and fleeting as they were) or the heightened tensions that emerged between Italian Americans and African Americans in cities like New York and Chicago during the Ethiopian conflict.[17] To American spectators, it could certainly appear that Italian Americans had easily fallen prey to a foreign government and its propaganda.

Italian American support for Mussolini's regime, in whatever form, declined steadily throughout the interwar period and fell drastically with the country's invasion of Ethiopia in 1935. At that point, Italian Americans increasingly perceived Italy's real threat to American interests abroad and responded to shifts in public opinion from their fellow citizens. But the transition did not happen overnight. A number of Italian Americans still held rallies and raised considerable sums of money to send to Mussolini's government in support of the Ethiopian campaign in 1935, and conflict over America's condemnation of the invasion prompted friction between some community members and the Roosevelt administration in 1936.[18] The Ethiopian War was a turning point though for the Order Sons of Italy in America (OSIA) and other important ethnic groups.[19] Likewise, most formerly pro-Mussolini Italian-language papers shifted gears. Generoso Pope, the owner of *Il Progresso* and arguably the leading power broker among Italian Americans, who had been backed by Mussolini in several of his business ventures, was much more reluctant to cut ties with the regime. Pope faced increasing pressure from President Roosevelt to do so in the late 1930s, but it was not until the Axis powers' attack on France in 1940 that he gradually began to distance the paper from Italy's government. It took Japan's attack on Pearl Harbor and America's formal entry into the war on the side of the Allies for *Il Progresso* to firmly pivot to an antifascist position.[20]

Despite Italian Americans' repudiation of Il Duce by the outbreak of the war, veneration for Mussolini and his brand of Italian nationalism had been public and widespread in many Italian American communities throughout the country. So much so that some Americans continued to fear Italian Americans as a potential fifth column force as the nation inched toward war. Anxiety about domestic subversion was at a high point after Japan's attack on Pearl Harbor in 1941, which prompted the federal government to take action against individuals it deemed enemy aliens. Although peoples of Japanese ancestry, both aliens and citizens alike, bore the brunt of American hysteria and prejudices in ways that other groups did not, Italian and German aliens were also targets of suspicion.[21] The same executive order that authorized the internment of Japanese peoples also allowed for the detention of Italian and German nationals considered threats to national security. Even though fewer than two thousand Italians were ever detained and their classification as "enemy aliens" was lifted in October 1942, the stigma was hard to shake.[22] The Italian-language press and radio came under intense scrutiny from the government and faced pressure from the public to use English and to clearly endorse antifascist, pro-American positions throughout the war. Ethnic organizations and institutions were subject to similar pressures.[23] The army even interrogated Italian American recruits about their willingness to fight in Italy and engage in combat against fellow Italians.[24]

A number of Italian Americans were old enough to remember the anti-immigrant sentiments that had thrived during the last war when so-called hyphenated-Americans were encouraged to shed attachments to their homelands, completely abandon their use of foreign languages, and renounce un-American political ideas in order to become "100 percent American." Many feared that those currents could resurface despite the government's more moderate posture the second time around.[25] The state's decision to promote cultural pluralism through "tolerance and unity" campaigns during World War II offered opportunities for new immigrant groups to combat the forces at work against them and to further their ascent into the social and cultural mainstream.[26] Therefore, many Italian Americans proactively set out to remake their group's public image as the United States entered into the war. In a desire to show that they were not merely "Pearl Harbor Democrats," as some critics charged, Italian Americans took care to reaffirm their belief in democracy and other liberal political ideals. They did this by joining the army in record numbers, supporting the war effort at home, and by crafting public displays that highlighted their patriotism and commitment to democracy.[27] To that end, ethnic leaders were quick to establish organizations expressly dedicated to that purpose.

The Italian American Victory Council (IAVC) was one such organization. Founded in Chicago by George Quilici, a community leader and long-time antifascist, the IAVC touted the twin goals of "victory for America" and "freedom for Italy."[28] Branches soon sprung up all over the country. Like other wartime organizations, the IAVC advanced its former objective primarily through the sale of war bonds.[29] For Italian Americans, contributions were vital to the American war effort and, in the words of George Quilici, to "the restoration of a free and democratic republic" in Italy as well.[30] He and others in the IAVC maintained throughout the war that the Italian people were, at their core, a democratic people. In their telling, it was Garibaldi and Mancini, the great Italian freedom fighters of the Risorgimento, who more appropriately embodied true Italian political traditions than its current illegitimate leaders. Quilici likewise claimed that Mussolini had only come to power by lying to and betraying the otherwise well-intentioned Italian people. As the war went on, he and other Italian American leaders cited the Italian peoples' acceptance of the Allied occupation and their participation in partisan activities as evidence of their shallow commitment to fascism and desire to restore a liberal government in Italy.[31] These sentiments were reinforced in the ethnic press as well. In 1944, the antifascist (communist) paper *L'Unità del Popolo* proclaimed that Italian resistance fighters proved that "the seeds of democracy and liberty never died in the hearts of Italian people even under fascism."[32]

These arguments reflected Italian American concerns about their group's political image during the war. For Italian Americans, it was important that Americans view all Italian peoples, be they in Italy or the United States, as a democratic and freedom-loving people. In its charter, the IAVC outlined one of its goals as the restoration of "dignity and respect to the Italian name and to every honest person of Italian origin all over the world."[33] It also said the organization should be used as "the public expression of our loyalty to the cause of freedom."[34] Thus, ethnic leaders tried to shed all associations between themselves and fascism by reaffirming their commitment to democracy. When pressed to explain his community's previous support for fascist Italy, Quilici argued that "there were those in our community who were confused—good people who believed in the principles and traditions of the American form of government. They confused the blatant misrepresentations of Mussolini and the black shirts [*sic*] with the strength, growth, and importance of Italy."[35]

Central to these narratives was the idea that, at their core, Italians were an inherently democratic people. This argument came to be a staple in Italian American wartime displays of loyalty and patriotism—even though this logic, ironically, reflected antiquated notions that racial or national groups possessed certain immutable traits or characteristics. This was, of course, the very same reasoning that formed the basis for restricting Italian immigration to the United States since the 1920s. In this respect, Italian Americans (who were perhaps more comfortable with the racialized logic that afforded them claims to whiteness) took a very different tactic than racial minorities also concerned with wartime loyalty displays. Both Chinese American and Japanese American loyalty campaigns during the war tended to focus on evidence of their groups' records of "good" behavior in the United States rather than claims to immutable racial or national characteristics that made one a desirable citizen.[36]

Even as Italian Americans sought to prove their loyalty to the United States and their ability to be good democratic citizens (on battle lines and at home), they did not completely cut their ties to their homeland. Progressive interwar campaigns to promote cultural pluralism and an emerging spirit of internationalism inspired wartime leaders to encourage ethnic Americans to retain ties to their homelands—so long as those attachments did not conflict with American interests. To both manage ethnic loyalties and transform homeland ties into American assets, ethnic Americans were encouraged by public messages and private advocates to become "ambassadors" who could bridge links between the United States and their countries of origin.[37] Italian Americans answered this call to action by engaging in public diplomacy that promised not only to help bring democracy to Italy but to reinforce their image as fit and active citizens at home as well. Ethnic ambassadorship could take many forms. A rally for the sale of war bonds might combine displays of American patriotism with ethnic markers like folk dancing, games of bocce, and Italian-language music, as one such rally in 1942 Chicago did.[38] Such displays proclaimed to a larger American audience Italian Americans' hopes that the triumph of democracy in Europe might preserve freedom of expression for Italians that Italian Americans already enjoyed in the United States. The Foreign Language Division of the Office of War Information also worked with Italian American organizations like the IAVC to broadcast Italian-language messages to Italians about the virtues of democracy and the American way in an effort to persuade their Italian counterparts to join the Allied liberation of Italy.[39]

But the most significant way ethnic ambassadors had traditionally promoted American interests abroad was by demonstrating tangible examples of the fruits of democracy, capitalism, and liberal freedoms to their counterparts back home. The war disrupted normal flows of information and exchanges such as letter writing, return visits home, and the transmission of remittances. So midway through the American war effort, Italian Americans began pressing high-ranking members of the State Department that they be allowed to form an organization to oversee the collection and distribution of relief materials to Italians suffering from the deprivations of war.[40] Quilici and other ethnic elites leading the charge believed that reopening those channels would be a means to restore lost connections with their countrymen and women and promote an American victory in Italy by demonstrating the superiority of the American way of life. Given the complications of waging war on the Italian peninsula and elsewhere, government officials were understandably reluctant to grant such requests. Relief shipments posed potential security risks in a warzone and managing them was judged to be an inefficient use of limited military and civilian manpower. But by the end of 1944, as an American victory in Europe loomed on the horizon, the State Department acquiesced and sanctioned the creation of American Relief for Italy, Inc. (ARI) and other organizations that similarly connected a number of American ethnic groups to their homelands. Drawing from the National War Fund, which had collected roughly $115 million by 1945 to be distributed to war-torn areas in Europe and Asia, ARI received approximately $3 million annually to provide relief to Italians.[41] Although ARI was officially under the auspices of the State Department, it was headed by Italian American community leaders, and hundreds of thousands of Italian Americans mobilized behind its mission. The organization functioned as an umbrella uniting war-relief organizations, Italian American community-based organizations (including mutual benefit aid societies, ethnic clubs, and labor unions), and Catholic lay groups that added to ARI's coffers with millions of dollars' worth of material and monetary donations from 1944 to 1946.[42]

During the war, ARI collected and shipped nearly six million pounds of new and used clothing, about one million pounds of new and used shoes, over one million pounds of powdered milk, over one million pounds of food, and roughly thirty thousand pounds of medicine and vitamins to Italy. Other donations included blankets, bolts of cloth, soap, sewing tools, toys, and automotive parts. All told, nearly $10 million of materials were sent to the country, with most shipments destined for southern provinces hit hardest by the war.[43] The following year, *Il Progresso* kept ARI's relief campaign visible after the war ended and Italian Americans responded with an additional $2 million in cash and material donations.[44] Similar organizations contributed to the effort in other forms. Italian American doctors led the group Medical Relief for Italy, which collected medicine, medical supplies, and vitamins for distribution to individuals and to hospitals damaged or destroyed by the war.[45] Hometown or regional associations such as American Aid to Calabria, for example, raised thousands of dollars to help rebuild the infrastructure of towns or regions of their members' origin.[46] Other organizations earmarked their donations specifically for Italian orphans and children.[47] The OSIA, for example, collected half a million dollars in the years after the war to construct an orphanage at Monte Cassino in the name of Italian American soldiers who fought and died there.[48] The Catholic charity Boys' Town likewise established an Italian subsidiary that became a popular organization for Italian American donors during and immediately after the war. Boys' Town of Italy donations helped to finance the construction and maintenance of orphanages and supported the organization's educational programs, which taught children democratic and free market values through such initiatives as the introduction of savings programs in community banks and the staging of mock governing bodies where children learned lessons in citizenship.[49] These relief efforts were not lost upon American policymakers and educational professionals who increasingly thought about childhood in new ways and sought to promote American foreign policy objectives by remaking the next generation of global citizens in the postwar period.[50]

Italian Americans understood that shipments of food, clothing, medicine, and money were components of humanitarian aid and that these forms of diplomacy made a multifaceted political statement relevant to both Italian and American audiences. Like the remittances they had long sent back home, war relief packages demonstrated the abundance and prosperity that flourished in the United States. American resources helped to provide some small sense of economic and, therefore, political stability in a country that was struggling to re-establish liberal political institutions after the collapse of the fascist regime. In this regard, Italian American actions supported American ambitions to play a greater role in reconstructing Italy's postwar political and economic order by demonstrating the superiority of the American way. These relief efforts thus aided in the construction of a new spirit of internationalism emerging as a hallmark of Americanism during World War II and the immediate postwar years. As such, ethnic Americans were not merely responding to, or coopted by, consensus-era politics, they were formative actors in constructing the political culture of the period.

Unlike remittances, large-scale charitable donations acted as a very public substitute for the private and individual exchanges that Italian Americans had regularly sent to family members before the war. Public recognition from their fellow Americans was just as important for ethnic elites who spearheaded and widely publicized their campaigns in both ethnic and mainstream media outlets. The last time Americans saw such a public transfer of resources from Italian Americans to Italy, not ten years earlier, it took the shape of women sending their wedding bands to be melted down to finance Mussolini's invasion of Ethiopia. These shipments, and their purpose, served as a stark contrast to that previous image of Italian Americans. It was not enough that Italian Americans privately help family members overseas; the public and community-based nature of these programs were a mode of revamping their group's image at home through expressions of active and engaged democratic citizenship in promoting American reconstruction goals abroad.

Italian American war relief activities were also the first manifestations of a broad-based, loosely organized Italy lobby in the United States that took form during and immediately after the war. Italian American relief efforts were significant in establishing important networks between Italian American organizations, the United States government, and public and private Italian institutions that received aid. From 1945 to 1947, participants were generally united by little more than a shared concern for Italy and its people. However, as groups matured, campaigns shifted, and the battle lines of the Cold War took shape, Italian American organizations would build on wartime networks to launch campaigns that spoke more directly to their concerns not as ethnic ambassadors but as ethnic Americans.

### *Italian Reconstruction and Italian American Internationalism*

American war relief efforts declined by the end of 1946, but Italian American involvement in Italian affairs did not. Concerns for family and friends, as well as sentimental attachments to an ancestral homeland, did not disappear. Nor did the spirit of internationalism that had motivated Italian Americans suddenly wane. In fact, those attitudes intensified as events in 1946 and early 1947 prompted some Americans, particularly Italian Americans, to believe that their own political and economic security was increasingly linked to the stability of postwar Europe. As the dividing lines of the Cold War took shape, Italy emerged as one of the early battlegrounds of that conflict. For Italian Americans, the stakes were high. Certainly, the fate of Italy and their connections to it hung in the balance. But having just struggled to prove their commitment to democracy and the American way of life during the war, Italian Americans were also quick to understand how another ideological conflict might, once again, affect their group's standing at home. By 1947, many Italian Americans had concluded that it was in their own best interest to promote Italy's long-term economic recovery because they believed it would help shore up the country's new democratic government and affect their group's position in the United States as well.

The collapse of fascism in Italy created a political and economic vacuum. Recognizing this fact, and affirming the United States' new foreign policy orientations, American officials immediately became involved in Italian reconstruction. In conjunction with Great Britain and antifascist leaders in Italy, the United States helped establish an Allied Military Government in the country in 1944 and a fledgling parliamentary democracy began to take shape. Both American and British officials wanted to see Italy become a republic once again. To facilitate that transition, the Allies insisted that Italians create new popularly elected local governments, that the state hold a referendum on the future of the Italian monarchy, and that an interim government write a new republican constitution. A broad-based six-party antifascist coalition government emerged to meet these challenges in 1945. At the same time, American and international aid channeled through the new United Nations Relief and Rehabilitation Administration (UNRRA) kept the Italian economy functioning. All of these moves were crafted to curtail the influence of the Left, whom Americans (accurately or not) calculated was the largest threat to a parliamentary democracy at the end of the war.[51]

The Anglo-American vision for Italian reconstruction yielded early and promising results. By 1946, Italians had adopted a new democratic constitution, abolished the monarchy, and formed a parliamentary government led by the Christian Democratic (Democrazia Cristinia, DC) party.[52] However, the DC-led coalition included Catholics, socialists, communists, and others, which meant that it was fragile and united behind little more than antifascism and the need for national unity. Parties were divided over foreign policy concerns, social issues, and, most importantly, how to reconstruct the nation's postwar economy. The most pressing of those economic problems included stabilizing the lira and reversing spiraling inflation, restoring employment in the industrial North, and addressing deep-rooted sectional disparities that had long kept the Italian South, or Mezzogiorno, underdeveloped. The "Southern question," which had plagued the country since unification, was only exacerbated by Allied military campaigns that caused physical destruction to southern landscapes, displaced people, and disrupted local economies. Factional divisions over how to move forward on these policy issues kept this loose coalition from taking significant action.[53]

But slow movement was not an option for the United States. With American liberals embracing neo-Wilsonian ideals that envisioned long-term international peace accomplished through the free flow of ideas, goods, and people around the world, American intervention in Italian politics stressed the need for pro-Western, anticommunist policies from 1946 forward.[54] Although Italy's postwar coalition government was headed by Alcide De Gasperi of the DC, the Christian Democrats by no means dominated Italian politics. The Italian Communist Party (Partito Comunista Italiano, PCI) was the largest communist party in western Europe and enjoyed considerable, and growing, support. That changed in January 1947 when De Gasperi embarked on a ten-day trip to the United States in which he sought to negotiate amended terms to the Italian peace treaty and secure immediate economic assistance. De Gasperi and the Truman administration used the state visit, during which time De Gasperi secured a $100 million loan from the United States, as an opportunity to solidify their relationship. Assured by promises and displays of American support, De Gasperi followed up his visit by expelling members of the PCI from his government. In doing so, De Gasperi committed his government to what one scholar calls "a passive, even servile, pro-American foreign policy" and guaranteed the Left's exclusion from power.[55]

Despite the deepening relationship between the Truman administration and DC leaders, there were still significant hurdles both governments would have to confront for their partnership to prevail. Italy would need more than $100 million in aid to rebuild northern industry, develop the South, and keep the currency stabilized. Moreover, the DC party could not expect to maintain its position of power without delivering on its policy promises in a timely fashion. But Truman and, more to the point, the American public were not yet prepared to provide long-term and massive financial aid for reconstruction in Italy and elsewhere in Europe in 1946 and early 1947. In fact, Italian Americans were one of the few groups at the time who favored and spoke out for sustaining American aid to Italy.[56]

The DC government lost face early in 1947 when the final version of Italy's peace settlement fell short of the Italian public's expectations. The peace settlement largely reflected competing American and Soviet interests when it came to settling issues such as reparations and UN membership. But the most contentious point of all, where American interests outweighed those of Italy or any other nation, had to do with territorial concessions. American policymakers envisioned the dismantling of European imperial systems and the institution of a global network of free-trading liberal states. That end goal ultimately prevailed as the United States pressed Italy to give over its African colonies (Ethiopia, Eritrea, Libya, and Somalia) to a UN trusteeship for an undetermined period before those territories were granted independence. Although Italy would play a role in administering these trusteeships, those losses, considered by many Italians as important sources of economic growth, outlets for population pressures, and symbols of international prestige, hardly shored up the government's position and signaled an early point of friction between Italy and the United States.[57]

Even more damaging to the Christian Democrats was the loss of certain mainland territories. De Gasperi's government fought aggressively to keep one economically and symbolically important territory, Venezia-Giulia. Located due east of Venice on the Adriatic Coast, Venezia-Giulia had been home to both Italian and Slovene peoples for centuries. The territory was once part of the Austro-Hungarian Empire but had become a major focus of Italy's turn of the century irredentist movement. At the end of World War I, the dissolution of the Austro-Hungarian Empire allowed Italy to take possession of the region and throughout the 1920s the government instituted "Italianization" policies including the prohibition of Slovene languages and associations and the Italianization of Slovene and German names. At the same time, Slavic nationalists began mounting their own campaigns to redeem the territory. During World War II, Yugoslavian forces helped liberate Trieste, the region's lucrative port city, for the Allies and briefly claimed the city for itself. During peace negotiations, the United States and Soviet Union each pressed the claims of their respective client states for control of the area. In the final peace treaty, the region was divided between Italy and Yugoslavia. Trieste was declared an independent city-state under the protection of the United Nations but was also divided into two zones—one to be administered by an Anglo-American military government and loosely attached to Italy, the other to be controlled by Yugoslavia.[58] Although Italians did not suffer a complete loss in Venezia-Giulia, taken together with other mainland and colonial concessions, many Italians were deeply concerned about the impact that such losses would have on the nation's already weakened industrial and commercial centers. Moreover, the loss of territory would necessarily precipitate the movement of Italian nationals living in those areas to the Italian mainland and would compound the nation's current overpopulation problems. The result was that some Italians continued to question whether the DC's emerging partnership with the United States was in their best interests.[59]

Italian Americans were keenly aware of these concerns as well. Continuing in the new spirit of internationalism that mobilized Italian Americans to provide war relief to Italy, Italian American elites continued to involve their communities in Italian reconstruction by taking action in the peace process. In 1946, Italian Americans formed the Committee for a Just Peace with Italy, Inc. (A Just Peace). Its leaders and most active members included prominent Italian Americans such as Fiorello La Guardia, former New York City mayor; Charles Poletti, the Allied military commander of Italy; OSIA officers Felix Forte and Eugene Alessandroni; labor leader Luigi Antonini; and Edward Corsi, a former commissioner of immigration and then-current New York state industry and labor commissioner. The group lobbied State Department officials, senators, and representatives to pursue a peace treaty in line with Italian interests.[60] Although A Just Peace was not a mass-based organization, it did claim to speak for "six million Americans of Italian origin," and it enjoyed widespread support in the Italian-language press, from the OSIA, the Knights of Columbus, Italian American labor unions, and other ethnic organizations.[61]

A Just Peace laid out their goals for Italy's peace settlement in a memo to Secretary of State James Byrnes in 1946.[62] Concerns about war reparations, Italy's status in the United Nations, and other political and commercial issues were, at best, secondary points of interest for the committee. The group's primary goal was to advocate for Italy to maintain as much territory as possible, especially when it came to border disputes with Yugoslavia, France, and Austria, but the committee even went so far as to press Italian claims to African colonies. In furtherance of that agenda, the group stressed economic issues like the industrial and commercial importance of port cities, the significance of hydroelectric facilities on the French and Austrian borders, and industrial output in Venezia-Giulia. They argued that Italy would need to harness all of those assets to remain free and democratic in a time of economic crisis. Relatedly, the committee also argued that Italy must be allowed to keep Eritrea, Somalia, and Libya (acquired before Mussolini came to power) not for imperial aggrandizement or national glory but "in recognition of Italy's essential need of an outlet for the steady growth of her population." With over two hundred thousand Italians living in colonies and one hundred thousand ethnic Italians in Venezia-Giulia, committee members viewed potential migrants as burdens, not assets, to an already fragile economy.[63]

At first glance, these arguments sound strikingly similar to the nationalist and imperial rhetoric of the fascist era. And for some Italian Americans, it may have been difficult to abandon those ideas.[64] But on the whole, A Just Peace was careful to frame their arguments in a slightly different manner. The committee stressed the need for land and resources in order to foster employment and residential opportunities that an economically strained and overpopulated nation would need to remain a functioning democracy. The group reasoned that without the proper resources, Italians would be unable to resist communist appeals. A Just Peace therefore employed the new rhetoric of American internationalism and the emerging Cold War to justify its positions. Time and again, Italian American forces argued that "a free democratic Italy, in the very heart of Europe, is essential to the peace of Europe," and it was for that reason that Italy must be allowed to retain the economic resources of its territories in order to thrive. Advocates likewise argued that the international community was watching, and judging, the United States' treatment of Italy. In its appeal to Secretary of State James Byrnes, A Just Peace argued, "America cannot be indifferent to her responsibility of exercising international leadership in the rebuilding of a war-stricken world." It further added how the United States dealt with Italy "will constitute a pattern of how far and how fully solemn promises will be kept, and democratic principles translated into practice."[65]

A Just Peace, the OSIA, and other Italian American organizations continued to lobby the Truman administration and the Senate on Italy's behalf even after the final peace settlement fell short of expectations in February 1947.[66] By that point, the committee was increasingly using the rhetoric of anticommunism to urge the Senate to appeal ratification of the treaty and warned that the peace settlement would demonstrate the "dangers of following a policy of appeasement of the Soviet Union."[67] Other organizations followed suit. In a letter to President Truman appealing to him to reject the settlement, the Committee for Religious Freedom in Italy called Italy "a newly born child. . . . Our own democratic creature which we must sustain as a democracy, lest she be destroyed by the imposition of unbearable conditions . . . which places the Italian people in a state of continued economic slavery and servitude for centuries to come." The group cautioned the president that "at this moment of transition, we frown at the *inroads of Communism in Italy and all over the world*. In our considered opinion, Communism is an exotic plant, which can only thrive and grow among people who have lost faith in their future." Committee members asserted a similar argument as A Just Peace's organizers in positing:

> Italy today is deprived, in the name of liberty, of the essentials of life, such as food, clothing, shelter, and the pursuit of happiness. Within the borders of her overcrowded land, the Italian people live today, as in a prison with no visible avenue of escape. In the very name of liberty and honor, so dear to our free America, as so well established by the forefathers and founders of this glorious Republic, we beg you Mr. President, to save Italy from Communism by interposing all your good offices with our Senate against the ratification of a Treaty which spells misery and disgrace for Italy.[68]

While ultimately Italian American campaigns did not yield changes in the terms of the final peace settlement, their efforts were significant nonetheless.[69] Italian American labor unions, businesses, religious groups, relief organizations, and fraternal orders all voiced support for A Just Peace because they believed a favorable peace settlement would help further Italian reconstruction along democratic lines.[70] A Just Peace also commanded recognition from American policymakers who could not afford to ignore Italian American concerns. This was particularly true for President Truman, who needed ethnic voters in the notoriously close 1948 presidential election. Furthermore, in their participation in Italian reconstruction campaigns, Italian Americans were demonstrating a growing anticommunist consensus that stemmed from concerns for their homeland and its people, as well as from concerns at home. The connections that Italian Americans made between aiding Italian reconstruction and advancing an anticommunist agenda predated President Truman's now famous Truman Doctrine of March 1947. This is an important distinction that suggests that ethnic Americans were key participants in building and shaping the anticommunist coalition, rhetoric, and policies that began to dominate American politics and culture in the following decades.

Finally, A Just Peace with Italy's campaigns were significant in that they showed the first manifestations of an argument that one scholar terms the "communists of the stomach" approach that Italian Americans (and American policymakers, for that matter) preferred to take in regard to Italian communism.[71] Rather than acknowledge the legitimate ideological appeal of Italian communism, or concede the real strength and organizational abilities of the PCI, Italian Americans began to formulate the argument that communism in Italy could be easily combatted if only the Italian people were ably employed, properly housed, and sufficiently fed. In short, if Americans allowed Italy to be deprived of the land and resources it needed to rebuild its economy, an already weakened and war-weary population could easily fall prey to communist propaganda. This logic suggested that Italian peoples were naturally inclined to support liberal regimes, it was only circumstances of extreme crises that prompted them to act against their nature. Although A Just Peace would soon dissolve, its argument would remain one of the most important weapons Italian Americans would repeatedly wield in their quest to remake their group's image and to secure policies that benefitted both Italians and themselves in the postwar period.

## Italian "Democratization" at Home and Abroad

The pivotal years of 1947 and 1948 were when the boundaries of the Cold War in Europe were drawn. In March 1947, President Truman announced in a speech before Congress and the nation that his administration would pursue a new policy of containment toward the Soviet Union by pledging American support for anticommunist governments in Greece and Turkey. In what came to be known as the Truman Doctrine, President Truman advocated that the United States provide financial assistance and potential military action in defense of anticommunist allies facing communist aggression—presumably backed by Soviet machinations. Months later, Secretary of State George Marshall built on Truman's position by calling on Americans to approve unprecedented levels of foreign aid to help speed economic recovery in Europe. The European Recovery Program, or Marshall Plan, would demonstrate to the world that containment could be achieved through American aid and generosity, not just through military threats. It also reaffirmed the idea that the United States advocated policies that helped to build international free trade and liberalism. Together, the Truman Doctrine and the Marshall Plan became the bedrocks of American foreign policy initiatives that would shape American responses to Cold War threats for decades to come.[72]

A wide spectrum of Americans responded to their government's call to action with a degree of consensus rarely seen in American politics. Liberal internationalists who wanted to see the United States take a greater role in fostering liberalism abroad through cooperative action endorsed the new activist orientation of American foreign policy. Conservatives could likewise support containment at home and abroad in the name of national security interests. Disparate groups ranging from American business organizations, labor groups, religious institutions, and ethnic organizations all had their own reasons for embracing anticommunism. For Italian Americans and other ethnic groups concerned with homeland politics, the political and cultural concerns of the Cold War spoke directly to their own interests.[73]

The volatile situation in Italy in 1948 provided an important testing ground for both American containment policies abroad and anticommunist politics at home. By 1948, many Italians had lost confidence in the pro-Western Christian Democratic government that had been in power since 1946. Disappointment over the nation's peace settlement, continued economic hardships, and the slow pace of recovery all contributed to the DC's declining popularity. Meanwhile, the Italian people expressed increasing support for the PCI and the Italian Socialist Party (Partito Socialista Italiano, PSI)—both of which joined together in a Popular Front coalition in 1948. With roughly 40 percent of Italians likely to vote for one of those two opposition parties, the Popular Front posed a serious to challenge DC rule in April 1948, when national elections were scheduled to take place. But Italian voters knew that the decision they would make in April was not just about domestic leadership and policies. In the context of the Cold War, Italy's 1948 elections became a referendum for the Italian people to choose between democracy and communism, capitalism or a command economy, an American or Soviet alliance.[74]

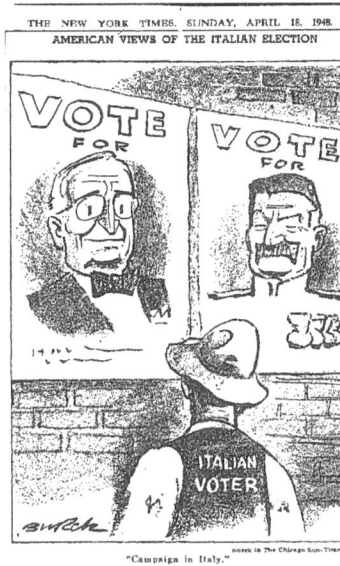

FIGURE 2. "American Views of the Italian Election," *New York Times*, April 18, 1948.

American policymakers feared a PCI-led victory would put Italy on the road to communism and directly into the hands of Moscow—where the strings were being pulled. American officials generally viewed the 1948 elections as part of an orchestrated Soviet plot that, in conjunction with events in Greece, Turkey, and elsewhere, suggested a Soviet push into the Mediterranean and perhaps even Western Europe. Americans cited reports that the USSR had provided arms, funding, and tactical advice to the PCI so that it could stage a coup in Italy—either through the polls or by a popular revolt. The Truman administration further worried that a PCI victory would buttress the strength of the French Communist Party, the second largest communist presence in Western Europe, behind the PCI. As such, the situation in Italy was a critical battleground in the emerging Cold War and warranted active involvement from the United States.[75] In the spring of 1948, the State Department therefore began to work with American labor union leaders, particularly Luigi Antonini of the International Ladies' Garment Workers' Union, to try to curb communist influence in Italian labor unions. The rationale was that PCI dominance over Italy's unions provided the party with an organized and mobilized base and an organ to disseminate ideology. At the behest of the American government, Antonini and others tried to strengthen Catholic or social democratic leadership and thought in the Italian trade union movement from the end of World War II through the early 1950s. Their efforts were moderately successful. By channeling funds and causing a rift in socialist leadership, American influence helped encouraged a split in the PSI before the critical 1948 election. But in the long term, Catholic or liberal democratic trade unionism never supplanted communist dominance in Italian unions.[76]

Even more important, the US government also wielded its considerable economic and ideological weapons. The Truman administration was intent on getting the European Recovery Program passed by Congress early in 1948 (before Italy's elections) and began sending shipments of supplies to Italy and elsewhere in Europe. Through a rapid and massive infusion of American aid to Italy, American officials hoped to stimulate economic recovery and shore up confidence in the DC government. The program also played into liberals' long-term goals to foster American patterns of consumption, which they believed would also stabilize democratic regimes and culture.[77] In the months preceding the Italian elections, American diplomats, government officials, and the media also bombarded Italians with propaganda denouncing the Soviet Union, communism, and command economies. At the same time, Americans portrayed the United States as an ideologically just ally and as an economic and social model for Italy to emulate. Finally, to be sure American intentions were understood, in March 1948 the State Department threatened to immediately withdraw Marshall Plan aid to Italy in the event of a PCI victory at the polls the following month.[78]

Italy's elections also provided an opportunity for Italian Americans to intervene in their homeland's affairs once again and to project their group's political and cultural messages at home as well. In the Spring of 1948, hundreds of thousands of Italian Americans engaged in a movement that came to be known as the Letters to Italy Campaign in which they wrote to family members and friends in Italy encouraging them to vote democratic in the elections on April 18. Letters were accompanied by remittances, gifts, and other materials in an attempt to demonstrate the fruits of a democratic and capitalistic way of life (as well as to symbolize the benefits of American friendship to the Italian people).[79] By all assessments, a combination of foreign aid and diplomatic pressure from the United States, as well as the Vatican's efforts to mobilize anticommunist Catholic voters, were the most influential factors in shaping voter outcomes.[80] Nevertheless, the Letters to Italy Campaign does deserve significant mention. In the Letters to Italy Campaign, regular correspondence and exchanges, visits to Italy, and in their remittances and charity, Italian Americans helped convince Italians that American political and economic models generated prosperity, a high standard of living, and a better way of life. Under these circumstances, Italians could more fully understand the consequences of losing American aid, guidance, and trade. In short, the collective efforts of Italian Americans since the end of World War II had helped raise Italian expectations about appropriate standards of living and consumption patterns. The Letters to Italy Campaign was part of a wider project in which Italian Americans, even if unintentionally, were instrumental in fostering the development mass consumption in postwar Italy. By helping to change Italian worldviews about mass consumption, Italian Americans contributed to the transformation of Europeans into mass consumers and became critical agents in carrying out American Cold War foreign policy messages.[81]

But Italian American intervention in Italian democratization was not only meaningful abroad. The Letters to Italy Campaign's greatest impact was in the United States, and it must be understood as a domestic project as well as an Italian one. In one regard, the campaign reflected a continuation of ethnic ambassadorship and the spirit of internationalism that Italian Americans had embraced during the war and postwar years. But it also reflected Italian American desires to prove their anticommunist credentials to their fellow Americans and to affirm their status as members of the American mainstream. Individual and mass-produced form letters were not only sent to Italy. They were widely circulated and discussed in the United States. Letters sent to Italy (and positive response letters from Italians) were published in American newspapers, entered into the Congressional Record, distributed among ethnic and religious organizations, broadcast over the radio, and accompanied by public demonstrations ranging from parades in major cities to prayer vigils in Catholic parishes.[82] When the Christian Democrats ultimately won the election, Italian Americans received a great deal of praise from their fellow Americans for their efforts.[83] Following the elections, an American correspondent in Rome reported to the Associated Press, "probably no single factor weighted the scales as heavily as [the letters]. Whole villages read these letters. They were discussed in cafes. They were the witnesses that a confused and groping people believed."[84] That reporter may have captured what was ultimately most meaningful about the campaign though when he observed, "There is something very moving in the way these immigrants of yesterday rose to the opportunity of testifying for America and American intentions. In an hour of rest, this is the best gauge of the strength of the great union we have made out of the people of Europe."[85] In their campaign, Italian Americans had gained domestic recognition as immigrants "of yesterday" and rose to the rank of full-fledged American citizens with their efforts. In becoming anticommunist crusaders, one scholar argues that Italian Americans found "a short-cut into 'mainstream' American society" and that "Cold War anticommunism allowed many ethnics to reconcile their religious and Old World allegiances" with a newly emerging definition of Americanism in the postwar period.[86]

Certain themes were critical in conveying letter writers' intended message to both Italian and American readers. The first point that typical letter writers made was the indemnification of communist ideas and policies; closely followed by a defense of democratic institutions and values. Letter writers denounced the Soviet Union, its ideological underpinnings, and its aggressive foreign policies. Like American officials, they implored Italians to protect freedom, liberty, and world peace by halting the spread of communism at the polls. They also stressed the idea that the United States was a true friend to Italy and to all the "freedom-loving" peoples of the world. But Italian Americans also framed the issue in broader terms. Italian American Cold War crusaders also reminded Italians of Italy's central role in fostering a transatlantic Western cultural heritage that Italians and Americans shared. From Christianity to the Renaissance, from Columbus to Enrico Fermi, Italian Americans argued that their two peoples shared not only a cultural history but a heritage or brotherhood. Italians now had the responsibility to keep this historic flow of ideas, people, and goods that brought Italians and Americans together open by not closing their nation off from the West. One publically circulated letter even went so far as to claim that it was an Italian, Christopher Columbus, who was responsible for the origins of the American nation and the democratic cultural traditions that would follow his voyages to the Americas.[87] Other letter writers reminded their American and Italian readers of the influence of Italian Renaissance culture on all of Western civilization.[88]

A major part of the cultural identity Italians and Americans shared was their Christian heritage. During the Cold War, religious identification and displays of religiosity became a marker of anticommunism, providing a stark contrast to the atheism and secular materialism of the communist credo.[89] Italy was not only a Catholic nation but, for Catholics around the world, the home of the Holy See at the Vatican. One form letter publicized in American newspapers pointed out to readers that "We look to Rome as the cradle of our civilizations and, for many of us, the eternal citadel of our religious faith."[90] A quarter million copies of one form letter penned and circulated by politician Victor Anfuso reminded Italians of their duty to God and to their families to maintain Christian traditions, as well as of their obligation to their Christian brethren in the United States and elsewhere to maintain the openness and safety of Rome and the Vatican.[91]

Most important, Italian American cold warriors stressed economic and material arguments. Letter writers extolled capitalism, free trade, and the high standard of living that such a way of life could offer Italians. One way they did so was in their focus on the importance of Marshall Plan aid. Countless letters reminded Italians that American raw materials and financial aid had already begun to revitalize Italian industries and discussed how the absence of Marshall Plan aid would hurt the ordinary Italian worker and consumer. Without the Marshall Plan, they cautioned, much needed basic foodstuffs and in-demand manufactured goods would disappear almost immediately.[92]

Italian Americans also argued that the higher standard of living promised by the PCI, and that the Soviet Union boasted its citizens enjoyed, was a farce.[93] Letter writers denounced "false promises" for material wealth that were made by communists and focused on America's "material plenty."[94] They spoke of abundant jobs in the United States, high wages, and the copious supply of food, clothing, and other consumer goods. Italian Americans often enclosed American newspapers along with their letters so that even those who could not read English could see the many advertisements and images that showed the wide array of products readily available to consumers.[95] Testimonies of American abundance found in the campaign could be found in other exchanges as well. As noted, Italian American individuals and organizations had been providing relief money and materials to Italians since the end of the war. Their very presence in Italy suggested the surplus of goods that existed in the United States.

Since the late nineteenth century, remittances and returnees from the Americas had remade Italian landscapes, diets, and patterns of consumption.[96] Regular flows of information, goods, and people between Italian Americans and their relatives had been disrupted by the war but resumed with relative speed after 1945.[97] In private letters and personal networks, Italian Americans shared news of their lives and successes to their loved ones back home. Indications of material abundance could be found in a multitude of ways throughout these exchanges. Enclosed in a letter might be a photograph of a well-dressed, well-fed family standing in front of their new automobile or home. Images such as these carried great meaning on both sides of the Atlantic and required no lengthy explanations. Of even greater significance, however, may have been the financial remittances carried in such correspondences. Nearly $30 million in remittances was sent to Italians in 1948 alone.[98] By that year, Italian Americans had also begun to take trips back to their homeland to visit relatives and reconnect with their ancestral roots. Those trips similarly provided avenues for financial and cultural exchanges.[99]

But the Letters to Italy Campaign went beyond a simple appropriation of emerging anticommunist ideology and the rhetoric. Italian Americans also tried to recast the nature of Italian communism itself and therefore change American perceptions of the Italian people. As previously noted, some Italian Americans were fearful that a good number of Americans continued to view all Italians or, worse yet, Italian Americans as potential communist sympathizers or fifth column agents. Italians were already tainted by their association with fascism. The strength of the PCI further suggested to some Americans that Italians possessed values that made them especially prone to support totalitarian governments. Many Italian Americans were concerned that perceptions of Italians in this manner would further stigmatize the group as "undesirable" Americans. Italian Americans therefore tried to mitigate American perceptions about the nature of Italian communism itself. Arguments about consumption were central to this effort. Italian Americans were careful to argue that although the Popular Front coalition reputedly had the support of nearly 40 percent of Italian voters in the months before the election, few Italians actually possessed genuine ideological commitments to communism. Instead, Italian American letter writers further developed the "communists of the stomach" idea that they had already begun to articulate in their fight for a pro-Italian peace settlement.

In the press, from the pulpit, and on the radio, Italian Americans argued again and again that the majority of Italians were not in fact communist ideologues. In a press release on the subject, George Spatuzza, the head of the OSIA, argued that the "hungry people" of Italy, "with poverty staring in their faces," were "no match for the tireless propaganda and activity of a well-fed Communist organization."[100] In this view, people who were weary and worn down by years of war and deprivation were cast as victims of communist propaganda rather than active agents. Spatuzza went on to argue that communism only thrived in Italy because of the "confusion and chaos caused by the dire need of the people" and implored the American people to send food, clothing, and medical supplies to Italians so they would have "the physical strength to oppose communism."[101] In OSIA newsletters, letter writers were instructed to remind Italians that goods were not rationed in the United States, that there was a surplus of food and clothing in the country, and that consumer goods abounded. Thousands of letters to Italy included written pleas, canned goods, consumer baubles, and cash as well.[102] These enclosures served as symbols that democratic regimes could also deliver immediate material aid that Italians would need to resist communist promises and appeals.

One *New York Times* article chronicled the travels of an Italian immigrant priest who had recently visited a rural town in southern Italy and reported how communist agents "walk into the peasants' homes and . . . ask whether the roof of the house is leaking or the barnyard needs repair, and what agricultural implements they can use." He added that these agents go on to tell these impoverished peasants "it is up to you now to have these things." Later in the article, the priest summed up the situation in Italy by declaring how difficult it was for people in this condition "to resist the materialist appeal of the communists."[103] By spinning the appeal of communism in Italy in this manner, Italian Americans distanced themselves, and all Italians, from the stigma of being communist sympathizers. Italian Americans tried to cast Italians as a desperate people duped by promises of material abundance rather than as a people who possessed a firm ideological commitment to communism. Instead, they attempted to show that, just like Americans, Italians were primarily concerned with achieving "freedom from want." In this schema, Americans, particularly Italian Americans who sent money and materials back home, had the weapons to effectively eradicate the communist menace in Italy.

The Brooklyn-based Italian-language Catholic periodical *Il Crociato* similarly portrayed the situation in Italy. One article published on the eve of Italy's elections pointed out, "The people of Italy have gone through the experience of a total war, that for years they have gone hungry, that they are discouraged, disillusioned; that many of them have lost courage and hope. They are tired of the perennial conflict, disorganized, and weakened. In that condition they have been no match for the tireless propaganda and activity of a well-fed Communist organization which has been working with diabolical cleverness to enslave an entire people with promises of a rosy future."[104] It was only under these circumstances, this particular Italian American author argued, that "so many have been fooled by the usual Communist methods of fraud, deceit, insincerity, by their lying promises, and by the most despicable tricks imaginable. Hungry people do not advert to the fact that they are dealing with an opponent who on principle is devoid of any sentiments of fair dealing, of justice, of pity or kindness, or mercy."[105] Once again, it was not ideology but the physical and psychological burdens of war and poverty that deprived well-intentioned and naturally democratic peoples to fall prey to the trickery of communist propaganda.

As a corollary to the argument that the Italian people were at best "communists of the stomach," Italian Americans also set out to prove to their fellow Americans that Italians were an inherently democratic people. Many letters that were published in American newspapers or otherwise publicly circulated in the United States reminded both Italians and Americans that Italy, or Rome more specifically, was the cradle of republican government and citizenship. They likewise recalled the republicanism of the Italian freedom fighters Mazzini and Garibaldi. Many further argued that the liberal political traditions of Renaissance-era Italian city-states or the Risorgimento period more accurately reflected Italy's true political heritage, which had only recently been momentarily suppressed by fascism and was again threatened by another totalitarian regime.[106]

In making these arguments, Italian Americans were not only fighting communism in Italy. They were making a case to the American people that

Italians were no less capable of embracing democratic citizenship than any other Western peoples, given adequate economic conditions. This line of reasoning reinforced anticommunist rhetoric emerging in the United States, which linked political and economic freedoms. It also lent support to the Truman administration's call for large-scale economic aid to Europe and reinforced liberal ideas that by fostering material plenty abroad, Americans could protect their own security and material wealth at home. But it was also an implicit argument against increasingly antiquated, yet still meaningful racialized characterizations of Italian immigrants and their offspring as somehow less fit for democratic citizenship than other "races" who immigrated to the United States. Indeed, the Letters to Italy Campaign itself was not only evidence of ethnic Italian peoples' devotion to democracy but also a public display of civic activism and engaged citizenship on display to their fellow Americans.

All told, Italian American rhetoric and behavior in 1948 reflected a concerted effort to remake the image of Italians and Italian Americans in the United States. By 1948, Italian Americans had laid claim to an anticommunist identity and were in the process of remaking their group's public image. In the Letters to Italy Campaign, Italian Americans claimed that Italian Americans stood for liberal democratic traditions, shared Western desires for the "good life" found in a high standard of living that capitalism could furnish, and held membership in a common Western Christian heritage.

This newly defined Italian American identity was one way Italian Americans asserted their full and equal membership in the United States. Directly confronting restrictions to Italian immigration was another. Letters were not only flowing to Italy in 1948. Italian Americans' postwar activism reflected anxieties over how their fellow Americans perceived them as a group, but that concern was not their singular motivation. Almost as soon as the war ended, Italian Americans were inundated with appeals from family members, covillagers, and other associates who hoped to carve out their futures in the United States. National origins quotas almost guaranteed there was little Italian Americans could do to directly aid family and friends in their attempts to immigrate to the United States. Renewed Italian American interest in cross-border connections in the postwar period must also be understood as attempts to make Italy better for those individuals who were reaching out to their kin about their desires to immigrate. The reality was that in the years immediately after the war, Italian Americans had more influence over American foreign policy than they did over the country's immigration laws. A number of Italian Americans hoped to change that. Recognizing that their group's activism tended to coalesce around the issue of Italian "population pressures," Italian Americans would soon argue that there was a clear need for immigration reform at home.

## The Italian American Immigration Reform Lobby

As the 1940s drew to a close, the position of Italian Americans in the United States had been fundamentally altered by the events of World War II and the start of the Cold War. It became clear that the United States and the Soviet Union held unreconcilable visions for the political and economic future of Europe and, ultimately, the world. The two superpowers' ideological and strategic conflicts quickly manifested themselves on several fronts—including Italy. Italy's 1948 "crisis of democracy," as American cold warriors and anticommunists around the world framed it, created a heightened awareness among Italian Americans, particularly those with family members abroad, about the daily struggles of their former countrymen. It also reminded Italian Americans that in an increasingly interconnected world, developments abroad had the potential to greatly affect their own lives. The Christian Democratic victory in 1948 eased some anxieties but hardly signaled an end to Italian American concerns for Italy, its people, or even for themselves.

In wartime loyalty displays and in efforts to influence the nature of Italian reconstruction, Italian Americans attempted to redefine the values and public markers of Italian identity by emphasizing their national group's proclivity to embrace the ideas and behaviors associated with democratic citizenship in both Italy and the United States. Italian Americans advanced a similar position in the months and years following Italy's 1948 election. Drawing on the Letters to Italy Campaign, in which they had argued "communism of the stomach" was the only real threat to democracy in Italy, Italian Americans began to advocate for large-scale Italian immigration to the United States as a means of relieving population pressures and, thereby, fostering economic and democratic stability in Italy. In doing so, they accomplished several goals important to many Italian Americans throughout the country. They advanced policies that they generally considered to be in the interest of their ancestral homeland and in the interest of their fellow Italians (many of whom were their relatives) who sought a better quality of life in the wake of war. Italian Americans were also able to further the argument that members of their national or ethnic group were, in fact, patriotic and dutiful citizens committed to the basic tenets of American democracy and the country's anticommunist mission. Finally, Italian Americans hit upon a politically expedient platform to chip away at one of the few remaining barriers to their full membership in the nation—the strict restrictions to Italian immigration found in the National Origins System.

But if Italian Americans came to believe that increasing Italian immigration to the United States was the solution to both Italy's problems and advancing their own political and social equality at home, other Americans did not share their view. In fact, the majority of Americans favored keeping the nation's gates tightly guarded after the war. A 1946 Gallup poll found that 51 percent of Americans favored a decrease or even a temporary suspension of immigration altogether, 32 percent supported keeping immigration flows at their current rate, and only 5 percent advocated for increasing immigration to the United States.[1] Fueled by concerns for national security, economic stability, and the cultural composition of the nation, the country largely kept its gates closed to most displaced persons (DPs), refugees, and other immigrants after the war. Those restrictionary sentiments found expression in laws governing immigration and refugee admissions and in other aspects of national security in the postwar period. For Italian Americans, the nation's reaffirmation of the National Origins System in the 1952 Immigration and Nationality Act was perhaps the most problematic of these trends.[2] Better known as the McCarran-Walter Act, the 1952 legislation maintained low annual ceilings on immigration, hardly altered discriminatory national origins quotas, and even placed new restrictions on naturalized citizens.

The passage of the McCarran-Walter Act seemed to dash any Italian American hopes that the United States would provide assistance to Italy in the form of either increasing immigration opportunities for Italians specifically or liberalizing the country's immigration policies more generally. That fact alone prompted a backlash from Italian Americans. But Italian American opposition to restrictionary immigration policies was not just rooted in the group's concerns for Italy and its people. The attitudes that undergirded the McCarran-Walter Act's passage signaled another, perhaps more serious, problem to many Italian Americans. They, and other opponents of the National Origins System, considered the racial and ethnic quotas at the heart of American immigration laws discriminatory, offensive, and based on outmoded racist ideologies that did not represent the nation's professed democratic values. Nor did they believe that such quotas accurately reflected the social and political status of Italian peoples in the United States in the postwar period. Those concerns galvanized Italian Americans to dedicate themselves to advancing the interests of Italian immigrants and promoting immigration reform legislation in the United States.

Leading the charge on this front was the newly formed American Committee on Italian Migration (ACIM). Organized in 1952, ACIM's primary goal was to achieve immigration reform and advance issues of political equality by altering or even abolishing the National Origins System. As such, it functioned as a political organization through which a network of Italian American and Catholic organizations lobbied American lawmakers and other government officials to reform the nation's immigration policies. ACIM also operated as an immigrant-aid group helping Italian immigrants and their mostly Italian American sponsors navigate the intricacies of American immigration laws and the challenges of resettlement. But these two functions were not mutually exclusive. The organization's leadership believed that demonstrating the needs and even achievements of new immigrants would go a long way toward securing liberalizations to American immigration policies. Thus, even while continuing to be constrained by the National Origins

System, Italian Americans had at least begun to organize more effectively to oppose it and mitigate its effects on Italian immigration.

### Advocating for Italian Immigration in a Gatekeeping Nation

In the Letters to Italy Campaign, Italian Americans had begun to advance the idea that Italians who did not share America's vision for postwar Europe could not possibly be considered threatening because they were not, in fact, zealous ideologues but were instead only "communists of the stomach."[3] This logic certainly had its merits. In reducing potentially threatening political and social philosophies to the desperate actions of well-intentioned but misguided peoples, Italian Americans found a way to defuse any potential association between themselves and threats of subversion as the Cold War intensified both at home and abroad. The "communists of the stomach" concept also obscured the myriad challenges of Italian democratization and repackaged them into a concise and manageable paradigm that both American and Italian anticommunists could embrace: improve Italian standards of living and democracy would flourish. The appeal of this formula lay in the fact that it ignored legitimate critiques of capitalism and it was also based on policies Americans had already adopted at home in New Deal recovery programs and abroad in Cold War foreign aid strategies like the European Recovery Program.[4]

The Order Sons of Italy in America (OSIA), which had taken an interest in Italian reconstruction and democratization campaigns, took the lead in constructing a path upon which Italian Americans could base their advocacy. Reflecting the "communists of the stomach" argument embraced by the group during the peace settlement and the Letters to Italy Campaign, one spokesperson for the OSIA commented shortly after the 1948 election, "So long as there is poverty in a potentially abundant world . . . there will be some form of communism."[5] Nicholas Petruzzelli, a member of the OSIA and a foreign trade expert in the US Department of Commerce, became the unofficial voice of the OSIA in championing a position on immigration that OSIA members believed buttressed the Marshall Plan and other economic-aid programs Americans had already undertaken in Italy. Following the Letters to Italy Campaign, he laid out the OSIA's "Three Point Program" to aid Italy.[6] Petruzzelli reminded American audiences of the neo-Wilsonian ideas that were at the core of Cold War foreign exchanges. American foreign policies relied on, and fostered, "expanding trade on a multilateral and mutually advantageous basis," and those open and sustained exchanges of goods and services helped foster liberalism and a lasting peace throughout the world.[7] But Petruzzelli believed there were still great hurdles to achieving a "bona fide two-way street" between the United States and Italy, including a weak lira, an overall currency shortage in Italy, and trade imbalances. The OSIA therefore advocated for, among other points, an amendment to American immigration laws to allow an astounding one hundred thousand Italian immigrants to come to the United States each year.[8] Petruzzelli argued that Italy warranted special assistance because "it is the outstanding single example of an area where United States immigration policy is directly in conflict with its foreign policy."[9] According to Petruzzelli and the OSIA, easing Italy's surplus population problem (which the organization believed to be the country's single greatest problem) would increase trade between the United States and Italy, as well as infuse much-needed capital into Italian markets via immigrant remittances. In the OSIA's view, it was the millions of dollars of immigrant remittances that had helped to fuel industrial growth and commercial spending in Italy's recent history. Without such infusions of capital, international trade and balanced exchanges needed for economic stability would not be achieved in the near future. The OSIA believed opening the gates to Italian immigrants was essential for promoting Italian economic recovery and ensuring democratic stability in the country.[10]

Members of the OSIA frequently pointed out that liberalizing immigration for Italians would be a strategic and relatively inexpensive way to carry out American goals for Italian reconstruction. Rather than send millions of taxpayer dollars overseas in the form of loans and foreign aid, Americans could promote economic recovery while reaping the benefits themselves by increasing Italian immigration. OSIA members argued that Italian immigrants would create "a larger and more varied labor force" in the United States and would also become valued American consumers. Thus, immigration reform would add to American as well as Italian economic growth. Moreover, Italian Americans in the OSIA and other organizations argued that as a world leader, the United States "must offer its moral, material, and spiritual prestige" in leading the world to help resettle those in need.[11]

According to this rationale, other receiving nations would then follow American leadership and liberalize their own immigration policies. Once again, this course would provide a cost-effective alternative to combatting the unemployment and underconsumption that communists supposedly preyed upon in Italy.

The OSIA also pointed to "the corrupt philosophy of those who maintain that in the interest of perpetuating the 'Anglo-Saxon' strain in America, we must restrict the immigration of the 'southern European'" as standing in the way of their vision for aid to Italy.[12] What they saw as antiquated yet persistent attitudes about racial and ethnic fitness in the United States seemed to OSIA members to be perhaps the greatest challenge in bringing the nation's immigration policies in line with its foreign policies. Although wartime pluralism campaigns, the upward mobility of recent immigrant groups, the horrors of the Holocaust, and the debunking of scientific racism were certainly eroding a belief in Anglo-American Protestant superiority, those sentiments had far from disappeared. American Jewish groups similarly linked persistent anti-Semitism with the nation's poor record toward German Jews who sought entry to the United States before the war and the seeming indifference toward displaced Jews after the war by certain segments of the population.[13]

At the same time, the DC government also began to wield the "communists of the stomach" paradigm to stabilize its own position in Italy and increase its bargaining power with the United States. With a total population of approximately forty-eight million people, more than two million Italians were unemployed and approximately four million more were classified as "marginally" employed or underemployed by the end of the decade.[14] The continued, and in some cases, growing presence of displaced persons, refugees, and repatriates compounded Italy's population crisis. The war had left three and a half million Italians homeless or without a livelihood. While some turned to family members for assistance, many others looked to state or international agencies for help. At the end of the war, both displaced Italians and foreign nationals were given quarter by the Italian government and international agencies, such as the United Nations Relief and Rehabilitation Administration (UNRRA), in one of the more than one hundred refugee camps established throughout the country. By 1950, all but fifty thousand or so war refugees had left the camps, but other factors, particularly the loss of mainland and colonial territories in the 1947 peace settlement, led to a more prolonged DP crisis in the country.[15] From 1947 to 1951, over twenty-seven thousand displaced persons from just the Venezia-Giulia region (ceded to Yugoslavia) took refuge in Italian camps and almost seventy-four thousand more were given some form of assistance by the government. Moreover, refugees from that region continued to enter the country and stay (at least temporarily) in refugee camps throughout 1955 rather than assume Yugoslavian citizenship under a communist regime.[16] Hundreds of thousands of Italians who had been agents of the country's empire in North Africa and the Mediterranean also left former colonies to "return" to Italy from 1946 through the early 1960s.[17]

The Christian Democratic government actively supported the conclusion that migration was the solution to the country's population pressures and ensuing economic challenges. Although the party's victory in 1948 and burgeoning alliances with Western democracies in Europe and across the Atlantic were encouraging developments, the Christian Democrats were still quite vulnerable to attacks from a strong and organized opposition movement on the Left.[18] In the North, the Italian Communist Party used the communist-dominated labor union Confederazione Generale Italiana del Lavoro to challenge and slow DC economic policies through strategic strikes that closed ports, interrupted communication and transportation, and cut industrial production.[19] In the South, where the government was confronted with an entirely different set of challenges, the Christian Democrats promised full-scale land reform initiatives to combat historic underdevelopment, inequality, and poverty but delivered only limited reforms for fear of losing the support of conservative landowners. Moreover, the agency the state created in 1950 to oversee reform programs, La Cassa per il Mezzogiorno, almost instantly became associated with high levels of political corruption and clientelism. The PCI and the PSI therefore enjoyed considerable support from rural southern workers as well as northern laborers throughout the 1950s.[20] Thus confronted with a growing population that included millions of impoverished or displaced peoples, many of whom were at least temporarily or partially dependent on the state in the late 1940s and early 1950s, and many of whom were drawn to the Left's prescriptions for change, the Christian Democrats increasingly saw emigration as a practical and expedient solution to combat the challenging economic, social, and political challenges their government faced.[21]

Although Italian emigration began immediately after the war ended, via personal chain migration networks as it always had, it was government support for migration in the late 1940s and throughout the next decade that ultimately shaped the character of postwar Italian migration. Invoking the self-serving logic of the "communist of the stomach" paradigm, the DC government began to actively encourage and facilitate the migration of so many of its citizens that one historian characterized it a "padrone state" in the years after the war.[22] De Gasperi's government revived or created a number of state agencies that collected information on Italian workers that could be sent abroad, transferred information about foreign jobs to potential emigrants, provided financial assistance and social services to migrants, and, most importantly, negotiated bilateral agreements with foreign governments to accept Italian emigrants and guest workers into their countries. From 1946 to 1954 three-quarters of all Italian emigrants bound for continental Europe received some form of state assistance in locating employment or in traveling to their final destinations.[23] The state likewise worked with Catholic agencies that viewed migration as important for the preservation of families and more broadly as a social safety net. The government also called upon (with varying degrees of success) multilateral organizations, such as the Organization for European Economic Cooperation, the International Labor Organization, and the Intergovernmental Committee for European Migration, to name only a few, to assist in facilitating international migrations. All of these actions helped to facilitate the transfer of millions of Italians to continental Europe, North and South America, and Oceania by the mid-1950s.[24]

Efforts by the DC government to facilitate the emigration of Italian workers yielded much more success in Europe, Canada, and, later, South America and Oceania than in the United States.[25] Indeed, Americans made no special arrangements for Italian migrants even as their Italian allies and ethnic advocates at home implored them to do so. Although the Cold War prompted Americans to seriously invest in European security, Italy was the junior partner in its relationship with the United States, and Italian Americans were one of the few groups at the start of the Cold War to support the DC's position to use American immigration policies as a means to fight communism. By 1948, Americans had invested billions of dollars in UNRRA, the Marshall Plan, Export-Import Bank loans, and other programs designed to foster the reconstruction of liberal capitalism and higher rates of material consumption in Europe. But only the Italian government and Italian Americans were arguing that all those efforts would be for naught if the United States did not follow up on those policies with additional measures to ensure their effectiveness.[26] The majority of Americans expressed sympathy for European refugees, DPs, and other potential emigrants, but their anxieties over immigration generally outweighed their sympathies for migrants when it came to policy decisions. Furthermore, influential conservatives in Congress, who also expressed skepticism in opening the gates, were largely effective in checking the ambitions of internationalists to liberalize the nation's policies on immigration. As a result, the government extended only limited assistance to war refugees and maintained relatively restrictive general immigration policies in the years after the war.[27]

Anxiety over reconversion to a peacetime economy contributed to initial restrictionary impulses in the country. A great number of Americans feared that reconversion to a peacetime economy might bring a return to depression-era conditions. Those anxieties were influential in prompting Congress to pass the Servicemen's Readjustment Act in 1944. The GI Bill, as it was more commonly known, was designed to keep millions of returning soldiers temporarily out of the labor market by subsidizing higher education and technical training programs, thereby buttressing their impact on the postwar economy. Other provisions were designed to stimulate growth in the housing sector and other areas of the consumer economy by guaranteeing home and farm loans for servicemen. These measures signaled an indication that Americans worried that a drop in public spending would precipitate a steep economic decline as the war came to a close.[28] If Americans were anxious about the economy's ability to reabsorb their own citizens, it is understandable that they were wary about adding newcomers to the ranks. Although it did not pass, congressional conservatives proposed legislation to temporarily cut off immigration entirely in 1944 to protect American jobs for returning servicemen.[29] The one major exception to this trend was the continuation of the bracero program, which allowed in foreign guest workers to address labor shortages in agricultural sectors. The political clout of powerful southern and southwestern agribusiness interests helped to extend the program after the war, but it was also renewed because most Americans viewed the Mexican migrant laborers who took advantage of the program as cheap and exploitable laborers rather than immigrants who intended to permanently resettle in the United States and ultimately seek citizenship.[30]

If Americans were nervous about opening the gates to traditional economic migrants after the war, they were even more concerned about the potential economic impact of accepting refugees and displaced persons. Refugees and DPs were, by definition, people without homes and usually without the material resources and social capital to ease their resettlement in a new country.[31] American policymakers and citizens alike had long found ways to guard against the entry of those who were deemed "likely to become a public charge" because they feared the political, social, and economic costs of their presence in the country.[32] The growth of the country's social welfare state during the Great Depression and World War II compounded those longstanding concerns and was cited as a legitimate reason to block the entry of German Jews fleeing Nazi persecution.[33] After the war, many groups of Americans continued to express their unwillingness to bear the burden of subsidizing the movement and incorporation of Europe's most destitute classes into the country.

The case of Jewish refugees, before and after the war, raises another important point. Economic anxieties were not the only factors at play in the exclusion of German Jews from the country. Racial, ethnic, and religious prejudices continued to contribute to restrictions in American immigration policy during the war, as evidenced by American indifference to the appeals of Jewish refugees, the symbolic nature to the end of Chinese exclusion, and the bracero program that created, in effect, a racially distinct subclass of exploitable foreign laborers.[34]

Postwar anxieties about immigration also reflected national security concerns that took root with the onset of the Cold War. However, Americans were at odds about the best way to protect the nation. The Truman White House, liberals in Congress, and other internationalists believed that more liberal and flexible immigration laws could be used to court allies and shape the world in American interests. They saw immigration visas as one of several tools in America's arsenal to fight political instability, economic unrest, and thus the spread of communism abroad (particularly in Europe). They also recognized that the racially discriminatory character of the National Origins System both hindered the country's ability to build foreign alliances and undermined American messages that preached liberty, equality, and democracy abroad. To that end, they advocated for increasing ceilings on annual immigration, overhauling the National Origins System, opening the gates to war refugees and DPs, and giving the president wide latitude in his executive authority to extend emergency immigration benefits when necessary.[35]

While Italian Americans and several other ethnic groups wholeheartedly supported these positions, the majority of Americans and many conservative members of Congress wanted to insulate the United States from what they viewed as an increasingly unstable and dangerous world. Conservatives believed that a lasting peace would best be achieved through military dominance, the strategic protection of American national security interests abroad, and by curtailing political and cultural subversion at home. To that end, they primarily saw immigration as a national security concern. Long-held racial and cultural biases caused many Americans to fear that new and varied sources of immigration might weaken the political and cultural unity conservatives believed was necessary to stand up to Soviet aggression abroad and subversion at home. Restrictionists also reinforced their objections to immigration in economic terms. They argued that since the United States had already extended considerable resources in providing economic and military assistance for European reconstruction and to fight communist incursions in places like Greece, Turkey, Italy, and elsewhere, American allies should bear a greater financial burden in assisting and absorbing DPs, refugees, and other immigrants than the United States. Conservatives thus defended immigration restriction, supported the National Origins System, and pushed for even stricter controls in screening new immigrants and monitoring the behavior of recently naturalized citizens.[36]

With a cautious public and conservatives occupying key positions in Congress overseeing immigration policies, restrictionist attitudes largely shaped American responses to Europe's displaced persons crisis after the war. In 1945, between twenty and thirty million people had been displaced not only from their homes or workplaces but in many cases from their countries as well. In Europe, the Allied military command and UNRRA attempted to assist DPs by sheltering them in temporary camps and then assisting in their return to their homes. However, this was a daunting task with virtually no precedent. Moreover, several groups considered especially vulnerable to continued persecution would not or could not simply be repatriated. These groups included Jewish refugees from Germany and Eastern Europe, as well as Ukrainian, Polish, and Baltic nationals who now faced potential persecution from communist governments upon their return home.[37] But aside from American Jewish groups and a small group of liberals in the White House and Congress, few Americans advocated opening American gates to DPs and refugees. Reflecting that position, Congress debated but failed to pass any legislation to extend aid to Jewish refugees in 1945. It was only by President Truman's executive order, independent of Congress, that the United States extended visas from unused annual quotas to Holocaust survivors and other refugees, which ultimately enabled about forty thousand DPs to enter the country at the end of the war. Anticipating traditional sources of opposition, Truman was careful to state that the order applied to "persons of all faiths, creeds, and nationalities."[38]

American Jewish groups were not satisfied with what they believed to be an inadequate gesture and began a campaign in 1946 to push for special legislation for Jewish refugees and other DPs. They were effective in courting the support of religious and humanitarian organizations, as well as liberal politicians, particularly President Truman, by including migrants of all nationalities and faiths in their appeals for further refugee relief and by framing their arguments in terms of the geopolitical concerns of the early Cold War. Aware that nativist, particularly anti-Semitic, sentiments fueled some sources of opposition, Jewish American organizations made it a point to form interfaith coalitions such as the Citizens Committee on Displaced Persons to lead the fight and to downplay the plight of Jewish refugees in their campaigns. The lobby focused on the urgent need to confront a broad DP crisis in Europe stemming from the flow of communist escapees in the East and wartime displacements that affected peoples of a variety of nationalities and faiths.[39] The DP advocates were also careful to draw distinctions between refugees and regular immigrants, understanding that it would be easier to secure special legislation for refugees than it would be to amend the nation's general immigration policies (which contained virtually no provisions for refugee immigration). For his part, Truman, following internationalist logic and trying to establish American leadership in European reconstruction, stressed the need for immediate aid for Europe's DPs in his 1947 State of the Union address. The combined efforts of faith-based organizations and White House lobbying ultimately yielded the Stratton bill in 1947, which called for the entry of four hundred thousand DPs into the United States over a four-year period. Under its terms, the bill defined "displaced persons" as both Jewish survivors of the Holocaust and those fleeing persecution in their countries of origin (understood at the time to be those now controlled by communist regimes). Supporters of the bill strategically characterized it as an "emergency" measure that in no way altered the National Origins System or the regulation of general immigration.[40]

While the bill received backing from Jewish organizations, other ethnic groups (including Italian Americans, who saw the potential benefits of the legislation for their compatriots), liberal policymakers, religious groups, and even organized labor, there was strong opposition to the measure by restrictionist lawmakers and patriotic associations such as the American Legion and the Veterans of Foreign Wars. Opponents argued that new immigrants, regardless of their DP or refugee status, threatened to take jobs away from Americans, especially returning servicemen. They also argued that the culturally foreign beneficiaries of the legislation would threaten the homogeneity of the American people at a critical moment when political and cultural consensus was needed more than ever to counter the dangerous Soviet threat. Southern Democrats and conservative Republicans were thus able to stall the bill in 1947, but they continued to face increasing pressure in 1948 by the unrelenting liberal lobby to address the DP crisis in Europe. It was the unfolding struggle for leadership in Cold War Europe and new data reflecting the enormous cost of maintaining DP camps abroad that finally swayed conservatives to pass DP legislation the following year.[41]

The resulting Displaced Persons Act of 1948 was hardly the victory its advocates had expected. The final piece of legislation reflected considerable amendments to the original bill. Conservatives cut the number of DPs allowed entry into the United States down from the original proposal for 400,000 visas to only 202,000. Moreover, conservatives were determined to ensure that DP immigration would not increase the overall number of immigrants accepted into the country, so DP visas were to be mortgaged against future quota slots for their country of origin. Also reflecting restrictionist impulses and cultural prejudices, the final provisions of the amended bill even had the effect of making large numbers of Jewish DPs ineligible for visas by virtue of date restrictions and preferences for agricultural workers. Finally, for the first time ever, the Displaced Persons Act added the stipulation that an immigrant would have to be sponsored by an American citizen, who would help to arrange housing and employment for the new arrival and guarantee that the newcomer would not become a public charge. This unprecedented requirement created a potential roadblock for all immigrants—but especially for those without a great deal of social capital in their homelands or connections to American citizens and organizations.[42]

Jewish American organizations and dissatisfied liberals continued to campaign for a more expansive refugee policy. They managed to secure an extension of the Displaced Persons Act in 1950 for two hundred thousand additional immigrants with modest improvements in the terms of the law.[43] The amendment did not, however, reflect a liberal turn on immigration. The concerns that kept the original legislation limited continued to be a factor in the extension of the law and other pieces of legislation that were also passed that year. The Internal Security Act (1950), while not specific to immigration, placed new restrictions, including the threat of deportation, on both aliens and naturalized citizens with ties to communist or other "subversive" organizations. Rather, it was fiscal concerns over the maintenance of DP camps in Europe, the negative economic effects of a permanent displaced population on Europe, and heightened political concerns in both Europe and Asia that were more compelling in convincing Americans to demonstrate to their allies, once again, that the United States was committed to addressing migration problems and other reconstruction issues in Europe.[44]

Italian Americans lent their support to Jewish American–led campaigns for DP relief for both ideological and practical reasons. At the same time, they also began to advocate for legislation that would more directly benefit Italians. In July 1947, while Congress was still debating the Stratton bill, Italian American organizations and constituents in New York's Ninth Congressional District (Brooklyn) lobbied their representative, Eugene Keogh, to introduce a bill that would add Italy's unused immigration visas during the war (1939–1946) into its 1948 and 1949 quota allotments. The bill enjoyed the support of the OSIA and nearly one hundred Italian American political and social leaders who formed a national committee lobbying for its passage. Of all its supporters, Victor Anfuso, a leader in New York's Italian American community who had been appointed as the assistant to the commissioner of Immigration and Naturalization Services in 1946, took the lead in campaigning for the bill's passage. Mirroring Jewish Americans' strategy to highlight foreign policy issues, but also building on the narrative advanced by Italian American organizations after the war, Anfuso cited Italy's "excess population" as the primary need for the legislation—which he characterized as "in line with our foreign policy to keep Europe from becoming a communist state." Anfuso warned lawmakers that "Mussolini used this excuse [overpopulation] to lead its people to a war which they did not want" and that "communists are now using the same problem to promote discontent and spread confusion all over Italy." Accordingly, Anfuso argued the unrest that would follow if population pressures were not addressed could not be "prevented by food shipped from America" but only by "emigrant ships."[45]

The bill failed to pass for a number of reasons, including liberals' focus on the DP issue and because Italy's population pressures were not necessarily on most Americans' radar.[46] Clearly Italian Americans were trying to raise that awareness with their interventions into Italian reconstruction and in their support for legislation of this kind. But even while they could not claim victory, Italian Americans remained convinced that framing Italian immigration needs in terms of American foreign policy concerns was the right strategy. Italian Americans, once again in New York, convinced Congressman Robert Tripp Ross (R) to introduce a bill Ross called "The Emergency Italian Immigration Act," which called for the entry of an astounding three hundred thousand Italian relatives of American citizens over a four-year period. Following his constituents' lead, Ross echoed Italian American rhetoric in the Letters to Italy Campaign in stating before Congress that "overpopulation of Italy is the greatest threat to success in the Cold War," and he warned that "if the nations of western Europe are to remain free, Italy must be provided every assistance in preventing Communist domination."[47] Ross and Italian American supporters knew the bill had virtually no hope of passing, but its introduction was meant to draw attention to the problem. Although Italian Americans generally supported the Displaced Persons Act because its passage set a precedent that would help advance their interrelated goals of assisting Italy and highlighting the National Origins System's shortcomings, ethnic organizers recognized that only a small number of its visas would be issued to Italians. The Ross bill thus drew attention to Italian Americans' claim that additional immigration opportunities for Italians would effectively deliver aid to a strategic partner and would also provide a much-needed mechanism for their kin to have a realistic chance of immigrating while the National Origins System was in place.

Indeed, when the Ross bill was introduced in 1948, a critical shift in Italian immigration was taking place. In the previous two decades, Italian immigration was ground to a virtual halt by the global economic crisis of the 1930s, the war, and restrictive migration policies in both Italy and the United States.[48] But by the late 1940s, that trend was reversing. Annual quotas for Italy were regularly filled and quickly became oversubscribed. Potential immigrants soon faced increasingly long waiting lists to obtain visas. Nonquota Italian immigration also picked up in the immediate postwar period. Special legislation such as the War Brides Act (1945), the Alien Fiancées and Fiancés Act (1946), and the Displaced Persons Act (1948) afforded tens of thousands of Italians entry to the United States. Thousands of Italians also turned to unauthorized modes of entry (such as overstaying on a visitor visa or crewmen jumping ship at an American port) rather than face the challenges of legal immigration.[49] Finally, still others came to the United States as "immigrants" in all but name. Tens of thousands of people who were born in the United States, or who could derive American citizenship through their parents but who had lived in Italy most of their lives, now sought to reclaim their American citizenship and relocate to the United States.[50]

The resurgence of Italian immigration in this manner had a significant impact on Italian Americans. For the first time in decades, new immigrants were again a notable presence in neighborhoods, churches, places of work, and social spaces. Reflecting their impact on Italian American communities, *Il Progresso* ran multiple articles and photographs each week publicizing the arrival of new immigrants in these years.[51] Compounding the visibility of these newcomers were the increasingly frequent letters and other pleas from family members in Italy who desired to come to the United States and begged their American relatives for help. The result was a growing awareness among Italian Americans that Italians wanted to immigrate to the United States and a sense of urgency to do something to clear a path for their entry. Thus, the pleas of Italian migrants, continued concerns for the health of Italy's economy and democracy, and latent desires to dismantle the National Origins System all contributed to the renewed advocacy for special legislation for Italian immigration—and even broader reforms to the nation's immigration policies by the turn of the decade.[52]

Italian Americans had reason to believe that their goals were attainable. Increasing Italian immigration seemed to be on par with the Truman administration's foreign policy orientations and was also supported by the policies of Italy's Christian Democratic government. Moreover, Italian Americans enjoyed a significant degree of political influence at midcentury. They had just proven their anticommunist credentials through engaged displays of citizenship in the Letters to Italy Campaign—and in doing so helped establish an internationalist consensus in the United States that was vital in creating support for Truman's reconstruction plans and other early Cold War policies in Europe. Italian Americans and other self-identifying ethnics were also key members of the Roosevelt coalition. The most recent (and notoriously close) presidential election, in which an incumbent President Truman narrowly defeated Thomas Dewey (R-NY), demonstrated that the Democratic Party needed to maintain the allegiance of Italian Americans and other key voting blocs to maintain that base. But as second- and third-generation Italian Americans enjoyed upward mobility and the fruits of postwar prosperity, their allegiance to the Democratic Party began to dwindle. Thus, both Democrats and Republicans were careful to speak to the ethnic group's interests in the postwar years.[53] Finally, there were more Italian Americans elected to national, state, and local offices than ever before. In 1948 alone, there were eight Italian Americans elected to Congress (double the rate of any previous year), and in 1950, John Pastore (D-RI) became the first Italian American senator.[54]

The Truman administration, liberal members of Congress, other ethnic advocacy groups, and religious organizations wanted to liberalize the country's immigration system to one degree or another. Like Italian Americans, other advocates of immigration reform were primarily motivated by concerns for equality at home, the desire to extend foreign aid to allies, and the need to demonstrate to the world that American policies truly reflected liberal ideals.[55] This last point was particularly pressing in the early years of the Cold War as the Soviet Union pointed out time and again American hypocrisies to world audiences by highlighting the existence of Jim Crow laws and racist immigration policies.[56]

Emanuel Celler, a liberal Democrat who chaired the House Judiciary Committee and who had opposed the National Origins System since its inception in the 1920s, led the charge for liberal immigration reform in

Congress after World War II.[57] In 1951, Celler proposed a reform bill that included provisions to increase annual ceilings on immigration, pool unused quota slots so that oversubscribed nations could take advantage of unused quotas, recalculate quotas based on the most recent census, provide a stronger emphasis on family reunification, offer guarantees of civil liberties for aliens, and remove "all racial discriminations from American immigration laws."[58] However, once again, conservatives with nativist leanings wielded considerable influence over immigration reform efforts in Congress. Immigration restrictionists were the dominant members of key committees, especially the Judiciary, and controlled whether an immigration bill ever left committee and was opened for debate. Restrictionist senator Patrick McCarran chaired the Joint House and Senate Subcommittee on Immigration when Congress finally debated reforms to the nation's immigration system in 1951 and 1952. McCarran and conservative allies in the House of Representatives, particularly Francis Walter, largely controlled the terms of those debates moving forward.

McCarran strategically responded to internationalist calls for immigration reform by proposing his own legislation and advancing it through committee.[59] But McCarran's bill was hardly a reform effort. His legislation kept the National Origins System (and the notions of racial and ethnic hierarchy on which it was based) in place with only minor modifications. It reestablished quota levels based on the 1920 census, rather than the seemingly more logical choice of the most current census (1950), in order to continue discriminatory practices toward nonwhite and southern and eastern European groups, who continued to be underrepresented in the older census. Finally, the new legislation did not increase overall annual quota allotments. McCarran and Walter (the bill's cosponsor) could, however, make the claim, by abolishing provisions for Asian exclusion and by removing barriers to naturalization for Asian groups, that the new law was a step in the direction of liberal reform. In fact, McCarran, Walter, and their allies went so far as to argue that the legislation ended racial discrimination in American immigration policy. It could therefore be held up as a symbol of America's progress in race relations to both Americans and the rest of the world. Advocates of the new law also claimed to be making reforms by establishing a new preference system that allocated percentages of visas based on occupational skills and family reunification. Opponents, however, pointed out that these changes continued to operate within the National Origins System and therefore did not substantially liberalize immigration opportunities for many potential immigrants.[60]

However, the 1952 Immigration and Nationality Act reflected continuing nativist concerns for preserving the nation's ethnic and racial composition in significant ways.[61] While overtly racist justifications for immigration restriction did not disappear entirely from public discourse, anti-immigrant policymakers more frequently used the thinly veiled rhetoric of "cultural compatibility" to make their case for racial, ethnic, and religious homogeneity in only slightly less problematic ways in the postwar period. The Senate Judiciary subcommittee assigned to assess the nation's immigration policies in 1950 concluded Americans were fully justified in "admit[ting] immigrants considered to be more readily assimilable because of the similarity of their cultural background to those of the principal components of our population."[62] Arguments stressing the need for cultural homogeneity were particularly effective in this period when McCarthyism was at its height. But, the idea of restricting politically subversive and, especially, culturally foreign immigrants in order to strengthen the nation's defense against communism helped legitimize such discourse.

President Truman recognized nativists' coded language when he vetoed the bill. In his veto message the president called the National Origins System "discriminatory" and claimed that it reflected the ill-conceived idea that Americans with "English or Irish names were better citizens than Americans with Italian or Greek or Polish names."[63] Certainly electoral politics played a part in Truman's position, but his statements were consistent with his general advocacy for advancing issues of racial and ethnic equality. His veto also stressed how the new legislation undermined American foreign policy objectives. For Truman and other liberals, the act sent a negative message to allied nations with a precarious hold on democracy. Nations like Italy, Greece, and Turkey were cases in point. Each of these countries with population pressures and weak economies would presumably take advantage of opportunities to immigrate to the United States, and each believed that as an ally the United States should extend that option to their peoples. The implication that Italians, Greeks, and others were unfit to become citizens in the United States hurt the credibility of democratic missions in those countries. Likewise, Truman and others believed that in failing to set aside slots for refugees and communist escapees, the act failed to address a central foreign policy concern that showed no signs of abating.[64]

The disappointing terms of the Displaced Persons Act and the passage of the McCarran-Walter Act galvanized immigration liberals, especially key ethnic groups who faced continued discrimination under the law, to take part in the crusade for immigration reform and perhaps even a broader movement to promote ethnic and racial equality in the United States. Both pieces of legislation seemed to underscore the point that many Americans continued to view certain ethnicities and nationalities as undesirable relative to older-stock Americans. These laws also cast doubt on American foreign policy objectives—and the ideologies of equality, liberty, and democracy behind them. American leadership and friendship seemed suspect if it was unwilling to help Europe's most destitute, homeless, and war-ravaged peoples because they did not have the right last names, possess desirable physical or behavioral characteristics, or hold compatible religious beliefs.

Members of the OSIA and other fraternal organizations, as well as a number of other prominent Italian American political and social leaders, spoke out in opposition to the McCarran-Walter bill as it was being debated in 1951. Their objections generally focused on the tried and true tactic of emphasizing Italy's emigration needs in the context of the Cold War. Italian American testimonials also noted the inequities of national origins quotas and the resulting separation of Italian Americans from their family members abroad (as secondary concerns), but only a few witnesses offered direct attacks on what they considered the racist elements of the law.[65] Their position hardly mattered though. Congressional restrictionists firmly controlled the parameters of the debate and the resulting legislation had enough votes to withstand even President Truman's strong objections and veto. But it was not just conservative strength that doomed Italian American objections. Liberal critics of the immigration system lacked organization and consistency in their opposition to the proposed legislation.[66] For their part, a number of Italian Americans organizers were determined to do something about it.

## The American Committee on Italian Migration

As it became clear that the McCarran-Walter bill would soon become law, ethnic leaders came to understand that they would have to better organize

their base if they hoped to successfully combat the restrictionary forces behind the not-so-new immigration act. Although the OSIA had taken the
early lead in steering their community in that direction, it was ultimately
Catholic organizers that helped Italian American activists firmly focus their
community's attention on the issue of immigration reform. At the 1951 annual meeting of the National Catholic Resettlement Conference (NCRC),
an NGO that had aided in the reconstruction of Italy and other countries,
leaders in the United States Catholic hierarchy encouraged one of its members, Juvenal Marchisio, who had long been a prominent ethnic leader in
New York City's Italian American community and who had recently offered
testimony against the McCarran-Walter bill, to form an organization dedicated to representing Italian American interests in immigration policy.[67] In
doing so, Catholic leaders sought to further promote their own goal of encouraging American immigration and refugee policies that were Christian,
democratic, and internationalist in their character.[68]

Assured by the promises of both moral and logistical support from the
National Catholic Welfare Conference, Marchisio answered this call to
arms and began organizing several dozen Italian American leaders around
the country in late 1951 and early 1952. The product was the American
Committee on Italian Migration (ACIM). The organization would function
as both an immigrant-aid association and a political action group espousing
three distinct but interrelated goals. Its first mission was to facilitate Italian
immigration to the United States. To that end, ACIM would give practical
assistance to both Italian immigrants and their American sponsors in understanding and navigating the logistics of American immigration laws and
other facets of the migration experience. Organizers also planned to provide
material, legal, and social assistance to newcomers in order to help them cope
with the challenges of resettlement in the United States. Secondly, ACIM's
founders envisioned the organization as a political vehicle that could spearhead their ethnic community's appeals for immigration reform to lawmakers. The organization's founding documents indicate that the group would
work to overturn the National Origins System and replace it with a system
of governing American immigration that was more equitable for all national
groups and did not suggest there was something "undesirable" about Italian
immigrants. That quest was closely related to ACIM's third and final goal—
to assert Italian (and Italian American) political, social, and cultural equality

with older-stock ethnic groups who were not demeaned and discriminated against with such paltry immigration quotas.[69]

In many respects, ACIM looked much like other immigrant-aid organizations that had achieved prominence in the interwar period. The National Catholic Welfare Council (NCWC), the Hebrew Immigrant Aid Society, and Lutheran Immigration and Refugee Service, to name only a few examples, provided immigration and resettlement assistance to their respective constituent groups and were also committed to achieving more equitable immigration laws in the United States. Moreover, ACIM arose, at least in part, because the dislocations and instability caused by the war created more work than existing immigrant-aid agencies such as the NCWC could handle.[70] Because part of ACIM's reason for being was to help the NCWC deal with ongoing migration problems, many former NCWC personnel initially joined ACIM, and ACIM built off of the NCWC's organizational structure. However, ACIM quickly transcended the NCWC's model and became something more than just an immigrant-aid or resettlement agency. ACIM's mission was much more politicized from the start, particularly in the way it linked immigration reform and antidefamation issues. It also quickly became a clearinghouse for other Italian American (and sometimes Catholic) groups to organize under the banner of immigration reform in the two decades after World War II. In this respect, ACIM appears similar to such ethnic advocacy groups as the Anti-Defamation League of B'nai B'rith that represented Jewish Americans in a similar manner.[71]

ACIM's existence owed a great deal to its chief organizer and national chairman, Juvenal Marchisio, who headed the organization from its founding until 1968. Marchisio had a public presence in New York's Italian American community since the 1930s, but he earned national notoriety during and after the war for his service as a delegate to the Italian Red Cross and as the head of the Committee for American Relief to Italy (ARI). In leading the ARI, he gained organizing experience by helping to establish 125 committees nationwide and by working with a network of Italian American and Catholic organizations to raise over $72 million of donations for Italian war relief and reconstruction projects. It was also during that period that he contributed to the development of the Catholic charity for war orphans, Boys' Town of Italy. Marchisio coordinated with the American State Department, the Italian government, and private organizations in all of these positions.[72]

After Marchisio, Reverend Caesar Donanzan was the second most important figure in ACIM's leadership—serving as the organization's executive national secretary from 1952 to 1966. The Italian-born priest (ordained in the immigrant-focused Order of the Scalabrini Fathers) was sent to his first American assignment, St. Mary of Mount Carmel Church in Utica, New York, just after the war.[73] With recent ties to Italy, Father Donanzan became a leading voice in Italian American campaigns to assist in Italian war relief and reconstruction. Under his leadership, Father Donanzan's parish was one of the first and most active churches to participate in the Letters to Italy Campaign, garnering him national recognition for his efforts to promote the cause.[74] In ACIM, Donanzan functioned in an administrative capacity as well as served as a link between ACIM and the Church. Donanzan worked closely with Catholic hierarchy, including national and regional diocese directors, as well as with individual Catholic priests and lay organizations, in promoting the organization of ACIM chapters, raising money for the organization's activities, and assisting in individual resettlement cases.[75]

ACIM's other founding members included individuals who had been formerly active in the National Catholic Welfare Council's War Relief Services division that assisted displaced persons in Italy before they joined ACIM. Participants included NCWC displaced persons resettlement directors, as well as representatives from twenty-five major Catholic dioceses with large Italian American populations. ACIM's founders also included Italian American business and civic leaders from New York City, Chicago, Philadelphia, Detroit, Seattle, and other major cities with large Italian American populations. Among the most important of these lay leaders were those with ties to major Italian American cultural organizations and labor unions in their respective cities. But even those secular participants often enjoyed ties with their local Italian American Catholic communities, even if they did not formally represent Catholic institutions.[76]

ACIM's founders chose New York City for the organization's headquarters. New York had long been home to the nation's largest Italian American communities. Moreover, the city continued to be the most important site for immigrant entry. While ACIM's offices in New York were its most active and functioned as the hub of its network, Italian Americans quickly established over one hundred additional branches throughout the country, giving the organization a truly national reach. With an Italian American population second only to New York, ACIM's Chicago chapter was, not surprisingly, the second most active site of community organizing and political activism in the nation. The branch was headed by Joseph DeSerto, the president of the National Civic League in Chicago, and Father Luigi Donanzan (brother to Caesar Donanzan), who likewise took on important leadership roles nationwide.[77] Both men used their well-established connections within the community's ethnic and religious organizations to recruit members and establish networks that ACIM could call upon as it carried out its mission.

Similar patterns followed in chapters all over the country. Dr. Nicola Gigante, president of ACIM's Detroit chapter, was also the president of Detroit's American Medical Relief for Italy chapter. Likewise, Detroit's recording and financial secretary, Carolyn (née Sinelli) Burns, was an active member of Detroit's Piemontese Social Club, the Piemontese Ladies Club, the American-Italian Business and Professional Women's Club, the Italian Flood Relief Committee, and American Medical Relief for Italy. Burns was also an officer of Detroit's Council of Catholic Women (a subset of the NCWC), an active member of the Friends of St. Peter and Paul missionary group, and went on annual retreats with other women in her church.[78] Gigante, Burns, and other members in ACIM regularly recruited members from the ethnic, religious, social, and labor organizations of which they were a part.[79] It was these kinds of connections that made cooperation and cross-membership between ACIM, other Italian American groups, and Catholic organizations effective on both local and national levels. In city after city, ACIM's chapters grew in this manner. Local ethnic leaders who started an ACIM chapter tapped into their existing network of ethnic and religious organizations to mobilize their community. Most ACIM chapters also established a women's auxiliary group, which focused on fundraising, social functions, and providing daily relief to new immigrants.[80]

In most cases, Marchisio and Donanzan helped local chapters get underway. They frequently traveled to the city organizing a chapter and augmented the efforts of local leaders by instructing interested parties on the chapter's organizational framework, mission, and near-term plans.[81] It was not uncommon, as was the case in Detroit, for Marchisio to make appearances on local television and radio programs to promote ACIM. Of course, the Italian-language press provided publicity and served as a recruitment tool as well.[82] In Detroit, Marchisio took part in the chapter's first meeting (held in Sta. Maria Church) where he helped familiarize hundreds of new members with ACIM's mission to aid newcomers, the significance of the recent passage of the McCarran-Walter Act and the Truman administration's opposition to it, and what Italian Americans could do to change the nation's immigration policies.[83]

With over one hundred chapters established nationwide within a year and growing, ACIM had become the backbone of a concerted Italian American effort to reform American immigration laws, to facilitate Italian immigration to the United States, and to help recent Italian immigrants adjust and resettle in the country. But ACIM did not work alone. Existing Italian American organizations, including the Italian Welfare League, the OSIA and other fraternal organizations, Italian American labor unions, Catholic Churches and lay groups, and other ethnic organizations, social clubs, and mutual benefit societies, all rounded out the ethnic lobby. Without the aid of partner organizations, ACIM would not have been successful in helping immigrants find sponsors, jobs, homes, and welfare assistance and integrate into communities. Nor would ACIM have commanded the same level of political clout in its legislative campaigns.

Although they were known to contribute in other ways, the OSIA and other fraternal organizations largely aided ACIM in its legislative appeals. The OSIA and similar groups continued to represent hundreds of thousands of Italian Americans, but their influence declined markedly (with declining membership and prestige) as ACIM's rose. The OSIA's celebration of Mussolini, even if for a short time and in limited ways, was difficult for it to overcome after the war. Moreover, OSIA lodges found it difficult to attract younger members for a number of reasons having to do with both the changing nature of the ethnic community and broader cultural changes. Yet, despite its diminished role in some Italian American communities, the OSIA continued to represent Italian American voices in public politics. The OSIA had national officers who coordinated political campaigns with local chapters and a national representative in Washington, DC, who met with officials in Congress and the White House regarding important political issues throughout the postwar period, including concerns about Italian reconstruction, American immigration policy, antidefamation issues, and Columbus Day as a national holiday.[84]

Labor unions dominated by Italian Americans also played a key role in Italian American activism. During the interwar period, leadership in Italian American dominated unions (particularly in the garment trades) largely abandoned their organizations' socialist or even more radical roots for a more moderate brand of democratic socialism and a seat at the table in Roosevelt's New Deal coalition. Italian American labor elites also gained more currency in America's political landscape at midcentury owing to their fierce antifascism and criticism of Mussolini's regime. In the postwar period, Italian American labor leaders continued to argue for social democratic reforms at home, within the confines of anticommunist liberalism, but also saw themselves as members of a transnational movement and remained committed to intervening in Italian reconstruction efforts. Prominent Italian American labor leaders, most significantly Luigi Antonini, who held leadership positions in both the International Ladies' Garment Workers' Union (ILGWU) and the Italian American Labor Council (IALC), labored at the behest of the State Department to promote free trade labor unionism and diminish the influence of communists in Italy's labor movement in the late 1940s and early 1950s.[85] Antonini and other unionists believed their actions would advance social democratic reforms by diminishing communist influence in both Italy's unions and its government. Their participation in Italian reconstruction projects also helped unionists establish a healthy distance between themselves and the extreme Left during the early Cold War. Like many other Italian Americans, trade unionists supported immigration reform in large part out of concerns for Italian workers at home and abroad, because of the desire to help friends and family achieve economic stability, and in order to buttress their own standing in the United States. In the 1950s and 1960s the IALC and the ILGWU worked closely with ACIM to lobby for changes to American immigration laws. Those organizations also helped ACIM coordinate resettlement assistance for newcomers by helping immigrants secure work, join unions, and make social and political connections in the United States.[86]

The Italian Welfare League (IWL) also took part in immigrant resettlement. The IWL was founded in New York City in 1920 by a small group of Italian American women who were active in social work and other family welfare causes. The IWL's original mission was "to promote the interests of, and look over the needy Italians in New York."[87] As an ethnic-based charity, most of the organization's resources went to help struggling Italian American families buy groceries and other household items during the interwar period. It also tackled immigration and naturalization case work, but those activities were not the organization's primary focus. The IWL suspended much of its work during World War II, but when Italian immigration resumed after the war, immigration work became more central to the group's operations. Once ACIM was established, the IWL coordinated its social welfare and resettlement work with ACIM. It also devoted increasing amounts of its resources and services to aid in the immigration process itself. The IWL (working with ACIM) helped new immigrants navigate customs, disembarkation, and complete domestic travel to their final destinations. It also provided pro bono or low-cost legal representation to Italians involved in immigration and naturalization cases.[88]

Finally, Catholic Churches with Italian American priests and parishioners rounded out the core of ACIM's network of partners.[89] From the Letters to Italy Campaign forward, churches had become important sites of political activity for Italian Americans concerned with transnational issues like immigration. They were also social spaces where Italian Americans and new Italian immigrants interacted. Moreover, as ACIM and the NCWC's relationship suggested, the Church's core missions naturally went hand in hand with offering newcomers resettlement assistance. Together these groups formed a network of Italian American leaders, active members, and occasional participants that worked toward the successful resettlement of Italian newcomers, increasing opportunities for Italian immigrants, and broader immigration reform.

If ACIM's mission was to simultaneously facilitate Italian immigration to the United States, campaign for immigration reform legislation aimed at overturning the National Origins System, and assert Italian (and Italian American) equality with older-stock Americans, there was a certain tension that existed in promoting these goals. Although there was no problem in trying to carry out what many considered the mutually reinforcing aims of assisting immigrants and promoting legislative reforms simultaneously, the issue for ACIM was in deciding what kind of legislative strategy and ideological critique it should take. The central problem is best illustrated by one of its own members' comments on the subject. ACIM–Detroit's chairman, Nicola Gigante, called the nation's reaffirmation of the National Origins

System "a Christian and a moral problem which needs to be addressed," suggesting, like their founding documents stated, that he and other members believed that a system of racial and ethnic hierarchies in immigration laws sanctioned both undemocratic and immoral tiers of citizenship in the United States and that those policies could not be squared with the nation's liberal political and moral creeds.[90] The implications of this kind of critique went far beyond the grievances felt by Italian immigrants or Italian Americans. In it, ACIM recognized certain fundamental rights of all peoples for fair treatment under the law.

Yet, more often than not, ACIM members made specific mention of how American immigration laws affected Italians and Italian Americans in particular. The very same month that Gigante made the statement above, he also argued that the National Origins System had to be overturned "so that the stigma of discrimination against people of South and Eastern Europe will be erased."[91] Now these two statements are not necessarily at odds with one another, nor were those kinds of remarks made exclusively by Italian Americans. A number of ethnic groups regularly pointed out how the National Origins System negatively affected their own groups and pressed for reforms that would specifically benefit immigrants from their countries of origin.[92] They do, however, suggest a certain ambiguity over whether ACIM would be committed (and to what degree) to fighting for universal political equality for all groups of immigrants or if it would prioritize quests to secure the rights, and perhaps even privileges, enjoyed by Italian immigrants and Italian Americans. Ignoring the implications of these tensions for Italian Americans, or for any other group of immigration reform advocates, would be a mistake and would detract from our ability to understand the nature of the liberal immigration reform movement in the postwar period.

Italian Americans in ACIM and other organizations clearly opposed the National Origins System in part because it violated the core principles of political liberalism in America. Defining American liberalism can be challenging, given its changing nature throughout the nation's history.[93] However, by World War II, its central principles included the equality of all peoples under the law and, correspondingly, an ardent defense of individual rights and freedoms (particularly the freedom to choose as free market values re-emerged as the dominant force in the nation's political economy). Moreover, liberals increasingly conceived of individual rights translating

into group rights—whether they be the class-based rights that were the focus of the New Deal or the rights of social (often racial, ethnic, or religious)
groups more prominently emphasized during World War II and later.[94]

Italian Americans had much to celebrate as the country championed liberalism during the war. While liberals often fell short on delivering their
promises of freedom and equality to racial minorities, that was not the case
for white ethnic and religious groups who enjoyed unprecedented incorporation into the political, economic, and cultural mainstream.[95] Italian
Americans therefore had a significant stake in advancing policy reforms that
furthered their ideals—not least of which included the abolishment of the
National Origins System. This perspective was clearly articulated by several
of the dozen or so Italian Americans who offered testimony against the adoption of the McCarran-Walter bill in the 1951 hearings on the subject. Henry
Andreini, president of the American Chamber of Commerce for Trade with
Italy, argued national origins quotas were based on a "most un-American
philosophy in that it favors one group of immigrants to the exclusion of others" and that "ethnical [*sic*] and geographical criteria cannot determine who
is best."[96] Amerigo D'Agostino, representing the Columbian Civic Club of
New Jersey and the National Unico Clubs of America, similarly claimed that
"under the cloak of government policy, we have permitted 'nativist' enemies
in our Nation to enunciate and promulgate an unscientific and dangerous
racialist doctrine that is at its roots subversive and undemocratic."[97] ACIM's
charter statement likewise corroborated these views in stating that the organization sought "the revision of our immigration laws so that they will be in
harmony with American democratic concepts of racial equality."[98]

In a similar but distinct manner, many Italian American Catholics also
objected to the National Origins System on the grounds of what might be
called "religious liberalism." Human rights scholars generally agree that
modern constructions of human rights ideology and rhetoric coalesced
around World War II.[99] There is less agreement, however, if that moment
reflected the progressive triumph of (largely secular) liberal democratic traditions or if it emerged in large part through Christian (and, even more
specifically, Catholic) assertions of the God-given rights of man.[100] In either case, a long canon of Catholic social thought that attempted to define
man's God-given (or human) rights influenced Catholic reformers around
the world.[101] In the late 1930s and 1940s, the Catholic Church and other

Catholic institutions supplied a countervailing ideology to Europe's totalitarian regimes by endorsing a concept of governance based on the "dignity of the human person."[102] That trend continued in the postwar years. Wartime atrocities and the international community's reckoning with them, the rise of human rights rhetoric internationally, and the ideological framing of the Cold War all buoyed Catholics to continue to think about man's fundamental rights and ideal modes of Christian governance.[103] Nowhere were those concepts more relevant than in the realm of international migration.

The same year that ACIM was founded, the Catholic Church issued one of the most important social commentaries of the twentieth century—on the right of man to migrate. Pope Pius XII's apostolic constitution, *Exsul Familia* (1952), built on earlier Catholic social teachings that postulated, among other things, a man's right to a living wage and his right to adequate living space for himself and his family.[104] In many ways, *Exsul Familia* was a continuation of *Rerum Novarum*'s (1891) arguments that pointed out the moral shortcomings of liberal nation-states and their economic systems. But the treatise also emerged from the Church's concerns over postwar Europe's population crises and the reluctance of supposedly Christian nation-states, including the United States, to intercede on the behalf of displaced persons, refugees, and others in need.[105] The main purpose of the authoritative decree (an apostolic constitution represents the highest level of Church authority on any given subject) was to provide a defense of man's God-given right to migrate. According to the pope, man's right to migrate was derived from the belief in a divinely created Earth and man's purpose on it. In this view, God bestowed abundant material resources on Earth so that individuals and families may sustain themselves both temporally and spiritually. It therefore follows that man has a right to have access to a minimum amount of Earth's resources that are necessary for his and his family's prosperity. Accordingly, in areas where resources are scarce, man and his family must migrate to fulfill their basic needs. In a modern context, that logic meant that people have a right to migrate from nations with scarce amounts of arable land, natural resources, and economic opportunities to nations with abundant supplies of all three commodities.[106]

As was the case in previous Catholic commentaries, the Church's understanding of the family was a central element of the pope's argument in *Exsul Familia*. Man's God-given right to a family was of paramount importance in the pope's message. According to the Church, familial love was an expression of God's love. Individuals had both the right and the duty to experience that love through familial relationships such as motherhood and fatherhood. However, economic competency was necessary for the maintenance of modern family life. Thus, the pope reasoned, nations must recognize an individual's right to seek his or her family's economic sufficiency through migration in cases where it was warranted.[107] As a corollary to both man's right to a family and his right to migrate in support of that family, the Church argued that although the sovereignty of the state must be respected, there are limits to the modern nation-state's authority to restrict man's rights. In this worldview, the state is not completely sovereign. The state derives its authority from its ability to promote the laws of God and to ensure the common good by protecting the moral and material welfare of its members. When it ceases to do so, it loses legitimacy. Therefore, nation-states, as part of a holy family of nations on Earth, must submit to a higher natural law working toward the common good of humanity—particularly in the case of man's right to migrate. Thus, the pope reasoned in *Exsul Familia*, there are moral limitations on a state's ability to restrict international migration. According to the Church, a state can restrict migration when it is necessary to preserve society's internal order and security—all of which serves the common good. However, other concerns, such as self-serving political or economic protectionism, are illegitimate foundations for state restrictions on migration.[108]

In the eyes of the Catholic Church, the United States was one of several countries guilty of putting its own self-interests above natural or divine laws. Indeed, Pius XII singled out the United States in this regard. The pope announced his position on international migration on Christmas Day 1952, just as the McCarran-Walter Act was poised to take effect, and explicitly mentioned the United States as a nation that put undue restrictions on the movement of refugees. This was a grievous injustice considering refugees were individuals who were, in many ways, perhaps the most in need of exercising their right to migrate. The pope also suggested that as a major world power, the United States had a moral obligation to lead other nations by example on this and other issues. These were meant to be particularly stinging words, and they were received that way in the context of the Cold War. Using the rhetoric of Cold War internationalism to shame the United

States and other liberal regimes, the pope further argued that the relatively free exchange of people and materials among nations would help foster a lasting peace among nations and would promote the "the increased welfare of man and the progress of human culture." Finally, the pope warned that restrictionary policies based on economic protectionism and "exaggerated nationalism" were just as threatening to the world as were the regulations of totalitarian states.[109]

Italian American Catholics who joined ACIM and other ethnic and religious organizations were surely influenced by these ideas. Both Catholic social thought and the ideology of secular liberalism created a firm foundation for Italian Americans to press for higher ceilings on annual immigration and for the total elimination of the national origins quotas, which they argued were not democratic, equitable, or Christian in character. One Italian American who offered testimony against the McCarran-Walter bill in 1951 asserted that all immigrants have "a human and social right not to be denied any opportunity our land can offer them."[110] Following the McCarran-Walter Act's passage in 1952, ACIM's national chairman, Juvenal Marchisio, offered this multilayered critique of American immigration policies: "Unless we change our basic migration laws, unless we let the world know we practice what we preach, we cannot hope to obtain . . . confidence. . . . We must remember and let the world know that we believe that God gave the world not to any especially gifted race, but that He gave it to all people; and that we here in America believe that in addition to the fourth freedom there is a fifth freedom—the freedom to migrate."[111] Marchisio's statement suggested he and others in ACIM understood the fight for immigration reform as simultaneously part of the country's Cold War mission, a moral and religious issue, and ultimately a reflection of liberty, democracy, and equality in America. The concern for him and other Italian Americans was how to make these types of critiques translate into policy actions.

Taken to its logical conclusions, the religious moralism of *Exsul Familia* called for immigration policies based almost exclusively on human rights principles and for complete equality for all racial or national groups seeking entry into the United States.[112] These ideas were certainly in accordance with the tenets of secular or political liberalism in America. But both of these sentiments were almost certainly too progressive for most Americans at the time and therefore lacked political viability in the conservative climate of the early 1950s. Although the NCWC's Bureau of Migration officially endorsed "an educational crusade to inculcate a Christian and democratic attitude toward immigration" in 1952, even it tended not to press lawmakers too forcefully on ideological issues during debates surrounding the McCarran-Walter Act's passage, preferring instead to labor quietly for incremental and pragmatic changes.[113] However, as Marchisio suggested, Catholic social thought on immigration was not unrelated to America's Cold War mission, and that is where ACIM's leaders ultimately decided to situate, and moderate, such ideas in the early years of ACIM's operations. Religious critiques of the National Origins System therefore tended to show up indirectly or in very subtle ways in ACIM's immigration reform platforms, and the organization seems to have embraced what scholars have called "Cold War liberalism"—meaning the articulation of liberal political ideas so long as those critiques and their effects did not challenge the nation's geopolitical and economic position during the Cold War.[114]

The Cold War offered ACIM a clear and practical foundation to advance immigration reform arguments on the basis of both secular and religious liberalism that commanded the attention of American policymakers, be they liberals or conservatives. ACIM therefore positioned itself from the start as an anticommunist organization. No conversation seems to have taken place among ACIM's leaders about how to proceed; indeed, that silence in the records speaks to the hegemony of anticommunist culture. Why would ACIM take another position? The rhetoric that developed during the Letters to Italy Campaign had proven successful at home and abroad. American Jewish groups had successfully employed a similar approach when they pressed for the passage of the Displaced Persons Act. Moreover, the more liberal elements of the McCarran-Walter Act were arguably adopted out of concerns for the nation's credibility in waging the Cold War. Anticommunist positions were ubiquitous in ACIM's early years of operation. In one of his first public statements as ACIM's chairman, Marchisio argued, "It is necessary to an establishment of world peace that we extend a helping hand in solving the base problem of Italy—its unemployment—and in this cradle of civilization effect the liberation of Italy from the dangers of communism."[115] Marchisio and other Italian Americans similarly focused on American foreign policy concerns in Italy when they offered testimony against the McCarran-Walter bill in 1951.[116] Horatio Tocco, an ACIM representative who also contributed to President Truman's Commission on Immigration and Naturalization, critiqued the McCarran-Walter bill, arguing that immigration opportunities might provide more influence abroad than even foreign aid packages. Tocco asserted, "It is the immigrant who provides the only direct and personal touch with the people of his native country," and as Italian Americans demonstrated in 1948, their influence in fostering bonds of affection between the United States and its allies can be substantial.[117] Finally, in 1953 when the Italian Communist Party again seemed poised to obtain majority control of the Italian government, Marchisio (speaking for ACIM) argued, "There is only one blot in our record of assistance to the Italians—one that threatens to negate all the good we have done in the last eight years. It is the McCarran-Walter Immigration and Naturalization Act of 1952 which has shut the doors to hundreds of thousands of Italians who must emigrate or topple Italian democracy. There is no doubt that the psychological effect of this law will have its impact on the coming elections."[118]

But the rhetoric of Cold War liberalism may also have appealed to ACIM members because it allowed Italian Americans to focus their campaigns exclusively on Italy's emigration needs and increasing immigration opportunities for Italian immigrants. Those issues may have been more of a priority to many Italian American immigration reform advocates than was the cause of championing political equality or Christian human rights for all groups of immigrants. Some scholars argue that even from the start of the postwar immigration reform movement, it was not the conservative political climate of the Cold War alone that hemmed in liberals (particularly white ethnic groups such as Italian Americans). It was instead their relative ambivalence on the issue of achieving true equality or universal opportunities for immigrants from all over the world—not just for those from Europe.[119] Again, if one looks at the testimony provided by Italian Americans who opposed the passage of the McCarran-Walter Act, about half of those witnesses spoke about the specific needs of Italian immigrants or the grievances endured by Italian Americans affected by the National Origins System. Even D'Agostino, who rather aggressively used the rhetoric of secular liberalism to rail against the undemocratic nature of the National Origins System, still qualified his calls for reform by asking Congress to adopt "a more liberal policy regarding Southern European quotas."[120] Both Juvenal Marchisio and

Fortune Pope, the son and successor to *Il Progresso* media mogul Generoso Pope, took similar positions. Not only did they both voice opposition to the disparity between western and southeastern European quotas, but they discussed, at some length, the past and potential future economic and cultural contributions that Italian peoples had and would make to the nation's development.[121] These statements suggest that instead, Italian Americans sought to achieve immigration reforms that better reflected the advanced position of peoples of Italian descent in American society.

If the passage of the McCarran-Walter Act was the catalyst for formalizing Italian American resistance to restrictionary immigration laws in 1952, ACIM and other organizations needed a strategy to move forward. ACIM ultimately settled on a plan to advocate for the passage of special refugee relief legislation for Italians (and other immigrant groups). That agenda emerged, at least in part, because the events of 1952 demonstrated that immigration liberals did not have the political capital or public support to completely overhaul the nation's immigration policies. Although many Italian Americans could draw from Catholic and secular political ideologies to oppose the National Origins System on its merits, they chose to embrace another strategy. Drawing on the example set by the advocates of displaced persons legislation before them, leading Italian American immigration reformers believed that they could effectively wield the rhetoric and ideology of the Cold War to crack open the gates via side-door channels.[122] That strategy was tested the following year with the passage and implementation of the Refugee Relief Act.

# THREE

# Refugees and Relatives: Italian Americans and the Refugee Relief Act

Although calls to increase immigration opportunities for Italians had fallen short with the country's reaffirmation of the National Origins System in 1952, concerned Italian Americans did not give up on their cause. They continued to organize American Committee on Italian Migration (ACIM) chapters throughout the country and expand the network of organizations and individuals mobilizing around the issue of immigration reform. Other immigration liberals did not give up either. Realizing that most Americans remained unresponsive to progressively minded critiques of the racial and ethnic prejudices codified in the National Origins System, immigration reformers understood that they could make headway when framing their arguments in the context of Cold War foreign policy imperatives. So, in 1952 and 1953, immigration liberals pursued a campaign for the passage of "emergency" legislation that would significantly widen immigration opportunities for refugees and other special immigrant groups. Italian Americans involved in ACIM and other Italian American organizations provided important support for such legislation. They and other liberals hoped that the passage of special immigration legislation would signal the McCarran-Walter Act's inadequacy to address real-world conditions. If successful, those campaigns might offer a strategy to ultimately whittle away at the effectiveness of the McCarran-Walter Act in a piecemeal fashion and thus render it illegitimate and in need of further reform.[1]

Responding to their calls, Congress passed the Refugee Relief Act in 1953. Liberal advocates of the program justified refugee relief as an important aspect of America's Cold War crusade to keep Europe free and democratic. For their part, immigration restrictionists, primarily concerned with issues of national security, conceded the need to crack American gates open ever so slightly in order to relieve population pressures stemming from the continuing presence of displaced persons and refugees in several geopolitically strategic countries in Europe. The new legislation created a sweeping program allowing over two hundred thousand nonquota immigrants emergency entry into the United States over the course of the next three years—and Italians may have been its greatest beneficiaries. Italy received sixty thousand visas (the most assigned to any single nation under the program) that could be used by both refugees and relatives of American citizens. Furthermore, like the Displaced Persons Act before it, the passage of the Refugee Relief Act offered a practical model for liberalizing the country's immigration policies. In the wake of 1952, Italian Americans and other immigration liberals came to believe that sweeping immigration reform would only take place by highlighting the shortcomings of the McCarran-Walter Act. If handled correctly, the Refugee Relief Program might help sway members of Congress and the American people to support further reform initiatives.

With so much at stake, little was left to chance. Italian American organizations, particularly ACIM, took the lead in shaping how Italian immigrants and Italian Americans took advantage of the Refugee Relief Act. Confronted with ever-growing backlogs for regular immigration visas from Italy, ACIM made it a priority to ensure that every one of the sixty thousand visas allocated to Italy under the Refugee Relief Program was utilized. In doing so, Italian Americans in ACIM hoped to demonstrate to Congress and the American people the need to provide even more immigration opportunities for Italian immigrants. To accomplish their goals, ACIM members helped Italian American sponsors and Italian immigrants understand and navigate the many requirements of the Refugee Relief Program. Therefore, ACIM played an essential role in educating the public about the opportunities created by the new law. The Refugee Relief Act was not only a complex piece of legislation but also something of a misnomer, since it made immigration opportunities available to nonrefugees as well. So ACIM leaders had to make clear the many ways immigrants and sponsors could utilize the program. ACIM also helped negotiate the boundaries of refugee status and fought for more inclusive definitions to benefit Italian immigrants and their families in the United States. Finally, once applications were made, ACIM served as a legal resource for sponsors and immigrants. In that capacity, its members provided assistance to each of those groups in completing applications, securing necessary documentation, connecting refugees with sponsors, and working with both American and Italian government officials to complete paperwork.

All told, the collaborative efforts undertaken by ACIM, and partner organizations such as the National Catholic Welfare Congress, the Italian Welfare League, Catholic churches, Italian American social groups, and labor unions to facilitate Italian immigration under the Refugee Relief Act, as well as their efforts to assist newcomers in their resettlement in the United States, were not only acts of social welfare for their fellow ethnics but also part of a calculated political strategy to achieve both immigration policy reforms and social inclusion for peoples of Italian descent in the United States.

## ACIM and Passage of the 1953 Refugee Relief Act

By the end of 1952, ACIM's national officers and members of more than one hundred chapters had begun their mission. To help Italians immigrate to the United States, ACIM began providing assistance to immigrants who had secured one of the few immigration visas available to Italians under the National Origins System or who benefited from the Displaced Persons Act or similar acts of special immigration legislation.[2] In these cases, aid workers helped process applications, navigate laws, locate sponsors when necessary, and provide material aid to newcomers. Italian American organizations also provided assistance to Italian peoples who were, for all intents and purposes, immigrants in all but name. Thousands of individuals living in Italy but who could derive American citizenship from one or both of their parents increasingly sought entry to the United States after the war and looked to ACIM and other immigrant aid organizations for help.[3] The same went for migrants who could claim American citizenship from their own birth in the United States but who had subsequently returned to Italy (in most cases as a child traveling with parents) and now sought re-entry. However, in many cases service in the Italian army, membership in a fascist organization, or voting in an Italian election put the migrants' claims of American citizenship in jeopardy. Italian Americans saw this as an area where they could actually be effective in taking action on the behalf of migrants (including their own relatives) and intervened. They first lobbied Congress to grant wholesale exemptions for individuals who had voted in Italy's postwar elections by reminding lawmakers just how strongly the United States had urged *all* Italians to support democratic regimes at the polls. They argued that the state could not conceivably punish people for following the American government's instructions or for demonstrating their commitment to Italian democratization and anticommunism in the process. Taking into consideration the diplomatic advantages of conceding the point, as well as weighing the relatively limited number of people affected, Congress responded by passing legislation in 1951 to restore American citizenship to those who cast their ballot in Italy's 1946 and 1948 elections.[4]

But even with legislation from Congress, not all claims were systematically approved. ACIM and the Italian Welfare League provided legal assistance to petitioners contesting the loss of their citizenship by voting or taking another action in service to the Italian government. In the midst of the culture of fear and suspicion that reached its height in the early Cold War, Americans were particularly sensitive to the notion that service in the army or membership in another group associated with Mussolini was evidence that an individual was susceptible to totalitarian ideologies and inclined to support such regimes. However, ACIM and the IWL were often successful in the courts by arguing that individuals who were automatically enrolled in fascist youth organizations or who were similarly compulsorily enrolled in the army posed no threat to the nation. Immigration lawyers likewise attempted to demonstrate that in many Italian industries individuals were compelled to join state-affiliated unions to maintain job security and that many individuals did so solely for that express purpose. ACIM and IWL records show high rates of success in restoring citizenship to migrants in this fashion. If they failed, the last recourse was to petition Congress for a special relief bill for the individual in question.[5]

There were, however, only a small number of people who came to the United States from Italy as returning citizens. The vast majority of cases that came to the attention of ACIM and other immigrant-aid groups were those of prospective sponsors who wanted to help bring a family member in Italy to the country or where an Italian migrant contacted ACIM directly. In these cases, organizations were usually unable to provide any substantive assistance. With the meager annual quota of about five thousand immigration visas open to Italians, immigrants faced increasingly long backlogs, which prevented them from immigrating and made ACIM's goal to assist sponsors and immigrants an unlikely achievement. In most cases, all that ACIM members could do was help Italian Americans who were trying to bring their relatives to the United States understand the intricacies of the American immigration laws and urge them to actively join the fight to reform the nation's immigration system.[6] With the passage of the McCarran-Walter Act, this meant mobilizing Italian Americans in what all involved expected to be a long campaign to overturn the National Origins System. But it also meant garnering support for special legislation that would benefit Italian immigrants in more immediate ways. In late 1952, it looked to ACIM and other members of the immigration reform lobby that the passage of special refugee relief legislation might address both issues.

By the end of 1952, restrictive national origins quotas had been reaffirmed for most countries and extensions to the Displaced Persons Act had expired. Restrictionist attitudes dominated the halls of Congress, and much of the American public shared those sentiments. But, although in the minority, immigration liberals had significant bases of support and powerful arguments on their side. Liberal cold warriors in the White House and Congress, progressive elites concerned with racial and ethnic equality, and ethnic and religious advocacy groups continued to campaign for more open and flexible immigration and refugee policies. These groups once again argued that national origins quotas were out of step with American political ideals and messages of equality. They also stressed how the McCarran-Walter Act failed to address American foreign policy needs or provide for flexible responses to real-world crises during the Cold War—especially when it came to refugees and other special migration cases. So in 1953, immigration liberals in the White House and Congress renewed a campaign that they had begun the previous year for emergency refugee relief.

The legislative effort began with a special message from President Eisenhower to Congress requesting "emergency" legislation to admit European refugees to the United States. Although it is debatable whether Eisenhower was truly committed to liberalizing American immigration policies, he had certainly come to believe, as the preceding administration had, that national origins quotas impeded American foreign policy goals during the Cold War because they did not provide the flexibility needed to deal with crisis situations as they arose. The White House wanted the discretion to offer sanctuary for communist escapees and other refugee populations that threatened European democracy and economic stability. Eisenhower also made the case, although perhaps less forcefully than Truman before him, that the National Origins System contradicted American messages of tolerance and openness that were such a vital component of America's efforts to reach out to the developing world as the Cold War intensified.[7]

Liberals in Congress shared these views on the relationship between American immigration and Cold War foreign policy objectives, but they also saw refugee relief legislation as part of a larger battle. They thought the passage of such legislation provided an opportunity to chip away at the legitimacy of the McCarran-Walter Act. Liberal internationalists reasoned if displaced persons, refugees, and escapees were allowed to enter outside of quota limitations, exceptions might be made for other immigrant categories as well. Moreover, if enough people entered outside of the quota system, the system would eventually prove ineffective, flawed, and in need of genuine reform. Therefore, immigration liberals, including Italian Americans in ACIM, saw refugee relief legislation as the first part of a long-term strategy to attack and discredit the McCarran-Walter Act via a piecemeal dismantling of its provisions until the legislation could be completely overhauled.[8]

Religious and ethnic organizations were among the first groups to offer their support for refugee relief bills for much the same reasons. About two dozen religious organizations, including the National Catholic Welfare Conference (NCWC), Church World Services, the Hebrew Immigrant Aid Society, and other immigrant-aid organizations, took part in campaigning for refugee relief. Many of these organizations had been highly active in war relief and continued to provide aid for European refugees, escapees, orphans, and others in need. These groups believed that the United States, with its abundant land, resources, and thriving economy, had a moral obligation to offer a haven and long-term immigration opportunities to peoples who needed help the most. In that respect, these groups generally reinforced their long-held beliefs that the National Origins System violated the nation's liberal and religious values.[9]

Italian Americans were particularly invested in securing special legislation for their kinfolk. By 1953, Italians represented the largest national group seeking immigration visas each year since the end of the war. Overpopulation, unemployment, and continuing economic and political reconstruction created massive hardships for Italians. By the early 1950s, these conditions compelled hundreds of thousands of Italians to migrate annually within Europe and ultimately farther afield. But in Italy's postwar diaspora, movement to the United States was severely limited by the country's restrictive immigration policies. The result was a continually growing backlog of Italian visa applications at midcentury.[10] Under these circumstances, Italians and their Italian American counterparts sought ways around immigration barriers. For ACIM, its members, and its constituent population, the Refugee Relief Act provided one such solution.

ACIM was one of several ethnic organizations that joined in the campaign for emergency refugee relief in 1953. ACIM had already campaigned for a similar refugee relief bill proposed by Emanuel Celler the previous year.[11] Although the bill did not pass, it provided a basis for moving forward. The proposal had identified "dangerously" overcrowded areas of Europe, including Germany, Austria, Italy, Trieste, the Netherlands, and Greece. ACIM members and other Italian Americans were particularly supportive of the measure. While they had generally been dissatisfied with the 1948 Displaced Persons Act because they believed it ignored Italian needs, Celler's bill promised to address the problem of displaced persons and overpopulation in Italy. ACIM officials and congressional supporters of the bill advocated its passage in ACIM's newsletter, the *Dispatch*, in 1952. With circulation among ACIM chapters, Catholic churches, and sister organizations, ACIM leaders used the *Dispatch* to reiterate increasingly familiar arguments about the dangers of overpopulation in Italy and to rally support for the proposed legislation from Italian Americans. Senator Lehman and Congressmen Celler and Anfuso all penned guest editorials in the publication asking Italian Americans to campaign for refugee legislation.[12]

ACIM renewed its support in 1953 when refugee relief legislation again appeared on the congressional agenda. ACIM leaders worked closely with policymakers in the White House and Congress on that score. In March 1953, Juvenal Marchisio, ACIM's national chairman, and Bishop Edward Swanstrom of the NCWC met with Congressman Celler to discuss the details of his emergency migration bill that would admit 328,000 persons from Europe to the United States over the next three years. One hundred thousand of those slots were earmarked for refugees from Italy and Trieste.[13] In campaigning for the bill, ACIM leaders began to cultivate a partnership with Congressman Celler and Senator Lehman, who were the principal sponsors of the legislation and who would work for immigration reform throughout the 1950s and 1960s.[14] One month later, Marchisio and other ACIM leaders obtained an audience with President Eisenhower and Senator Irving Ives of New York at the White House, where they also endorsed the emergency refugee legislation.[15] They also pressed their case that Congress pass a measure that would allow the president to use his emergency powers to reallocate unused quotas each year for countries that needed them.[16] Back in their respective cities, ACIM chapter leaders rallied the troops by using its newsletter the *Dispatch*, the Italian-language press, and Italian radio programs to call upon Italian Americans to pressure their lawmakers to publicly endorse the bill.[17]

Representing ACIM, Marchisio provided testimony before Congress in support of refugee relief legislation. Marchisio's testimony reflected ACIM's strategy to put American Cold War objectives front and center. Although Marchisio did make it clear that Italian Americans remained highly critical of the National Origins System, he did not try to reopen a contentious debate about the social and moral philosophies embedded in the nation's immigration laws. Instead, Marchisio's appeal was decidedly pragmatic and rooted in political expediency. Reminiscent of earlier appeals made by members of the OSIA, he argued that refugee relief would reinforce the United States' existing foreign aid programs and strategic goals in Europe. In Marchisio's telling, the Marshall Plan, NATO, and the Mutual Security Administration were merely "shots of morphine which lessen the patient's suffering but [will] not cure the malady" if the United States failed to address Europe's continuing "overpopulation" issues. Echoing both the view of the State Department and the Christian Democrats' message overseas, Marchisio argued it was no coincidence that Italy had both the greatest overpopulation crisis and largest communist party in Western Europe. He further asserted that "as the recognized leader of the free world," and a nation with a strong economy that can absorb additional manpower, the United States must take the lead in welcoming refugees. If it did not, American leadership would ring hollow and it would perhaps put an undue strain on the NATO partnership.[18]

Domestic debates surrounding the Refugee Relief Act coincided with national elections in Italy in which the Italian Communist Party again posed a viable threat to the Christian Democratic Party's dominance. Italian American elites once again endorsed a Letters to Italy Campaign that year. The campaign had far less popular support than the previous one, but the elections in Italy were not as threatening this time around either. What seemed more important to the Italian American leaders urging participation was that Italian Americans take the opportunity to link Italy's elections with the shortcomings of American immigration and refugee policies.[19] *Il Progresso* urged readers to reach out to their Italian loved ones and to support refugee relief at home. One article stated that if the emergency bill passed, it would reduce the number of "idle hands and hungry stomachs" in Italy that fall prey to communist influence and "give the Italian people a ray of hope" to resist communist propaganda.[20] ACIM leaders also instructed letter writers to promise Italians that at that very moment Americans were "laboring to help ease the Italian problem of overpopulation through emergency legislation."[21] In short, ACIM used the elections in Italy as just another leverage point to lobby for Congress to pass the Refugee Relief Act.

A nationally orchestrated ACIM lobbying campaign rounded out Italian American efforts to support refugee relief legislation. ACIM national officers sent directives to chapters to urge their members and other Italian Americans in their communities to send telegrams and letters to their local congressmen supporting refugee relief bills. Over one hundred thousand letters, telegrams, and other messages from ACIM members in support of refugee legislation reached lawmakers that year.[22] Moreover, if the records from ACIM's Detroit branch are indicative of the organization's national strategy, ACIM recruited other Italian American organizations, businesses, and unions, as well as Catholic organizations, to join in the campaign. In

May 1953, Detroit-based groups and businesses such as the Esperia Club (an Italian American women's social club), the Piemontese Club and the Piemontese Ladies Social Club, Our Lady of Peace Guild, the Allegrina Construction Corporation, the National Custom Tailors' Association, the Cement Contractors Association, the Italian American Lawyers Club of Michigan, the Friends of Saints Peter and Paul Missionaries, and others joined in ACIM's lobbying campaign.[23]

The efforts of congressional liberals, White House lobbying, and public support from religious and ethnic organizations resulted in the Refugee Relief Act's (RRA) passage in August 1953. The terms of the RRA in many ways signaled a significant accomplishment for liberal nationalists. Arguments that asserted the need to further open immigration opportunities after the passage of the McCarran-Walter Act had been acknowledged in the act's widening of the gates by allowing for the entry of more than two hundred thousand immigrants above accepted annual quotas over a three-year period. That accomplishment helped to legitimize liberals' critique of the McCarran-Walter Act as excessively restrictive, even if only slightly. Liberals also secured special legislation for refugees—whom the McCarran-Walter Act had completely overlooked—again signaling a deficiency in current immigration policies. However, the law reflected significant conservative influence as well. The bill was ultimately passed because its proponents largely framed the program as a measure to address Cold War concerns, not as a means to liberalize American immigration laws (even if they ultimately thought the legislation was a step in that direction). As evidenced from Marchisio's testimony, immigration liberals tended to use anticommunist rhetoric and Cold War concerns abroad to advocate to conservatives for its passage. For that reason, and because of the structural control that conservatives wielded in Congress, the final product reflected considerable conservative influence.[24]

The final version of the legislation allowed for 209,000 refugees, escapees, expellees, and a small number of relatives of American citizens to enter the country outside of regular quota allotments by the end of 1956. This number was far smaller than liberals had hoped for, but it did reflect an internationalist victory in that unlike the Displaced Persons Act of 1948, immigrants would not be mortgaged against future quotas for their countries and they would enter fully outside of the quota system. Suggesting the success of the transnational "communist of the stomach" narrative, the RRA allocated sixty thousand visas to Italy, fifty-five thousand to Germany and Austria, forty-seven thousand to eastern European countries, seventeen thousand to Greece, seventeen thousand to the Netherlands, and thirteen thousand distributed to other countries (including those in Asia and the Middle East). The law defined a refugee as "any person in a country or area which is neither Communist or Communist-dominated, who because of persecution, fear of persecution, natural calamity or military operations is out of his usual place of abode and unable to return thereto, who has not been firmly resettled and who is in urgent need of assistance for the essentials of life or for transportation."[25] A similar description followed for escapees who fled from communist-dominated areas of Europe and for expellees who were ethnic Germans forced to leave eastern European, communist-dominated areas. The RRA further recognized the "overpopulation" threat in Italy and Greece by allocating fifteen thousand Italian visas and two thousand Greek visas (out of the sixty thousand and seventeen thousand totals respectively) to relatives of American citizens who did not necessarily qualify as refugees.[26]

Conservative influence was also apparent in aspects of the law designed to protect national security. Fearing the potential for both political and economic subversion that refugees might bring to the country, security requirements in the RRA went far beyond anything faced by traditional immigrants who entered under the quota system. The bill authorized extensive background checks and medical exams for immigrants so that American agents abroad would have multiple and varied opportunities to weed out unsuitable immigrants and future citizens. It even gave American consulates discretionary power to deny applications for the mere suspicion of subversive political activity by the applicant. The law also required that an immigrant document a two-year period of residency in their exit country so that American consulate agents could get a sense of the migrant's recent political and economic activities.[27] Critics of the program later argued that this provision of the law was especially limiting because refugees, who by definition had recently left their homes, who had moved from one DP camp to another, and who did not have a permanent place of residence, often did not have a two-year residency in one area. Moreover, it was especially difficult for escapees and expellees to obtain background documentation and cooperation in security checks from hostile communist governments that they fled from in the first place. Those combined requirements either disqualified or created excessively long waiting periods for many applicants, which may have been what restrictionists had intended all along.[28]

Another impediment or security measure (depending on which side of the debate one favored) was the law's requirement that immigrants obtain employment and housing assurances before their visa was approved.[29] Immigrants had to secure an American sponsor (or more than one) who could guarantee that a newcomer had housing lined up, a job waiting for them, and a citizen's pledge to provide financial support for the immigrant so as to safeguard against the newcomer becoming a public charge. These stipulations, first implemented in the 1948 Displaced Persons Act, went far beyond any provisions in regular immigration laws to regulate the character or origins of immigrants. Sponsors often found the process of complying with such requirements burdensome and sometimes prohibitory. To guarantee housing for an immigrant, sponsors had to disclose sensitive information such as the amount of money they made each year, the value of their real and liquid property, the number of dependents for whom they were responsible, and the disclosure of other assets. For job assurances, employers had to agree to employ the immigrant at competitive wages, guarantee the immigrant worker's admission to a local union when applicable, and their businesses' operations had to be reviewed by the Departments of Labor and State. As a result of what many commentators at the time referred to as cumbersome and invasive requirements, it was sometimes difficult for agencies aiding refugees to find sponsors willing to undergo the investigations that came along with assisting a migrant.

Despite the challenges inherent in carrying out the RRA, ACIM considered its passage an important opportunity. It provided openings that were sorely needed for Italians who desired to immigrate to the country and for Italian Americans who wanted to support their relatives' ambitions. Its passage also lent legitimacy to Italian American calls for large-scale Italian immigration to the United States as a means of relieving population pressures in Italy. If Italians did indeed take advantage of the sixty thousand opportunities now provided to them, ACIM's leadership believed that it would demonstrate the need to open additional immigration slots for Italians.[30] It even legitimized ACIM itself. The organization was instrumental in galvanizing support for the program from Italian Americans all over the country. Alternatively, the Refugee Relief Program provided ACIM with the opportunity to more effectively carry out its mission to help Italian immigrants resettle in the United States and to challenge the foundations of the National Origins System.

## Maximizing Benefits for Refugees and Relatives

ACIM had formed to help Italians immigrate to the United States, but national origins quotas drastically constrained its scope of operations. Both migrants and sponsors turned to ACIM for help, but more often than not, ACIM could only inform petitioners of the uphill challenges they faced.[31] With growing backlogs for immigrant visas, the most ACIM could do was to urge supplicants to mobilize on behalf of immigration reform themselves. But with the introduction of the Refugee Relief Program (RRP) in 1953, and the ensuing availability of sixty thousand immigrant visas over the next three years, the terrain changed dramatically for ACIM, Italian immigrants, and Italian Americans alike.

If all sixty thousand Italian visas were to be utilized, as ACIM planned, its first course of action had to be the education of Italian Americans about the terms of the law and how they could take advantage of it for their family members. In pamphlets, articles in ACIM's newsletter, radio programs, and the Italian-language press, ACIM and other immigrant aid societies explained the terms of the act in plain language (in both English and Italian) to Italian American audiences.[32] One ACIM brochure, "The Refugee and You," broke down the law and explained the process of sponsoring a refugee in simple and concise language its readers could easily understand. ACIM sent out more than ten thousand brochures of this kind for distribution to members, potential sponsors, Catholic churches, and other Italian American organizations.[33] ACIM's national leaders, Juvenal Marchisio and Caesar Donanzan, also broke down information about the legislation in their communications to officers in all of ACIM's chapters throughout the country. Chapter officers in turn educated local ACIM members and other Italian Americans about the program. In addition, Marchisio and Donanzan toured ACIM chapters for two months in the fall of 1954 to make sure chapter leaders knew how to facilitate Italian American action on the RRA in their communities. While visiting member cities, Marchisio and Donanzan appeared on Italian-language radio programs and gave interviews in local Italian-language papers, explaining the RRA and ACIM's ability to assist immigrants and sponsors.[34]

One key aspect of the RRA that many Americans were unaware of was that it provided for the immigration of relatives of American citizens as well as refugees. In the case of Italy, forty-five thousand visas were allocated for refugees and fifteen thousand were reserved for relatives of American citizens.[35] With thousands of Italians facing upward of a five-year wait for a visa, this provision of the law provided the opening that many Italian American families had long awaited. But for many working- and middle-class Americans, who did not closely follow the news of the law's passage or the debates surrounding it, this information might have been obscured by the fact that the legislation was labeled a "refugee relief" measure. ACIM therefore worked to educate the Italian American public about this provision of the law and provided details about the circumstances under which their family members abroad might take advantage of the program.[36]

ACIM also promoted the RRP by publicizing stories of refugee arrivals and family reunification. One such feature recounted the arrival of the Rotondo family, who received the program's ten thousandth refugee visa. Elisa Rotondo and her two young daughters arrived in New York City on the SS *Independence* in January 1955. They were met by Elisa's husband, Giovanni, and her brother, Anthony, who traveled from Detroit where they were both already settled (along with Elisa's father) to receive their family and help them complete their journey. Like so many other migrant families, the Rotondos chose to construct transnational households and practiced strategies of chain migration with the hope of advancing their family's economic and social position. Their story was a familiar one—and one in which many Italian Americans could envision their own relatives taking part. So too was the narrative that Giovanni, the hardworking male head of household who had long sacrificed to set up the conditions favorable for his family's eventual resettlement, could now be reunited with his wife and children, and all would be well. Moreover, the Rotondos hailed from Cassino—where the Allies and Germans fought for many months, inflicting severe damage to homes and the countryside. The Rotondos thus conformed to the public's image of a "deserving" refugee family who had suffered through no fault of their own but were instead the victims of circumstances and war. The Rotondos, and stories like theirs, presented an idealized picture of the refugee immigrant family for consumption in both Italian American communities and wider audiences. Their tale was meant to inspire and call for others to take on the labor-intensive but immensely rewarding task of assisting other immigrants—refugees and relatives alike—in sharing in the Rotondos' experience.[37]

The Rotondos could claim both refugee and relative status. But many applicants either did not qualify as a refugee or would have had a very difficult time securing the documentation to prove it. Yet there was clearly a need for Italian immigration as refugee relief applications poured in and backlogs for regular immigration visas continued to grow. So ACIM officers, who understood the frustrations of Italian Americans who had often been trying for many years to bring their relatives to the country, began in early 1953 to encourage "regular" migrants to try to qualify as refugees and take advantage of the opportunity now presented to them. After all, as

FIGURE 3. "10,000th Visa," *Dispatch*, February 1955, box D, American Committee on Italian Migration–National Office, New York City Records, Center for Migration Studies.

the Rotondos' case illustrated, the categories of refugees and relatives were not mutually exclusive for many Italian applicants. With forty-five thousand visas allocated to refugees and only fifteen thousand reserved for relatives, ACIM officials calculated this strategy was the best way to maximize benefits for Italians in general.[38]

To increase their chances of success, ACIM officers attempted to manipulate or perhaps broaden the definition of *refugee*. Under the RRA, one qualified as a refugee as the result of displacement due to military operations, natural calamities, and persecution or fear of persecution. Displaced peoples or refugees from ceded Italian territory such as Venezia-Giulia and Trieste therefore found it relatively easy to qualify for refugee status. They were considered refugees as the result of military operations, and since they fled Yugoslavian-controlled territory in the 1950s, they also claimed persecution or fear of persecution from the communist regime in power. The case of refugees from natural calamities was also relatively clear-cut. Italians who were displaced by disastrous floods in the Po Valley and in Catanzaro in 1953 were generally approved under this category. But there was some room to maneuver in other circumstances, particularly when one attempted to claim refugee status resulting from a military operation. Southern Italians residing in towns that were bombed, invaded, or occupied during World War II and who could show that their homes, businesses, or property had been damaged or destroyed beyond repair were generally granted visas. Italians who had previously lived and worked in Italy's colonies or Italian-occupied territory and who were forced to return to Italy after lands were ceded also had relative success in proving their refugee status.[39]

But ACIM made bold attempts to expand the boundaries of who might qualify as a refugee. Since there seemed to be a little latitude in defining who qualified as a refugee from military operations, ACIM agents encouraged all applicants who had ever lived in an Italian colony to claim displacement. For example, ACIM members preparing applications argued that a family who had lived in Eritrea for several years, then returned to Italy well before the onset of World War II, was displaced by military operations. In most of these cases, either because of clever preparation on ACIM's part or indifference by American immigration officials, ACIM's pursuit was successful.[40] ACIM officials also tried to broaden the boundaries of refugee status even further by attempting to establish approval for peoples they seemed to consider economic refugees. In cases where the applicant was from a poor region of Italy, usually in the South where underdevelopment, unemployment, and overpopulation were endemic, ACIM would make an argument that refugee status be granted to applicants.[41] Some of these petitioners were in search of a stable livelihood and were frequently short-term migrants within and outside of Italy and were, ACIM claimed, "out of usual place of abode and unable to return thereto," as the law stipulated.[42] Cases where this argument was made were almost always cases of relatives of American citizens who were trying to qualify as a refugee to increase their chance of obtaining a visa they had long sought by other means. However, ACIM's efforts in this regard largely failed. There was simply too little justification for distinguishing "economic" refugees from regular migrants. Moreover Congress, the State Department, and Immigration and Naturalization Services (INS) believed it important to maintain a sharp distinction between political refugees and economic migrants as a matter of policy.[43] Blurring the lines would be a dangerous precedent to set. So despite ACIM's best efforts to finesse the law, significant numbers of Italians could not easily qualify as "bona fide" refugees.[44]

So ACIM pursued another tactic. Just months after the law's passage, Italian Americans began to press lawmakers to amend the RRA by reallocating the distribution of refugee and relative visas. ACIM and its partner organizations made the case that to ensure that the sixty thousand visas made available to Italians were actually utilized, the quotas for refugees and relatives should be inverted, with forty-five thousand visas available for relatives of American citizens and fifteen thousand reserved for refugees. They argued that such a change was still in keeping with the spirit of the law because overpopulation was, and always had been, the key issue in Italy. It mattered less if refugees or economic migrants left the country, only that it was critical that they left. They once again presented the narrative that having a safety valve on Italy's population pressures was what gave democracy in Italy, and indeed in Europe, a fighting chance.[45]

The combination of Italian American lobbying and continuing concerns for Italian stability did sway Congress and the RRA was amended to reflect ACIM's recommendations in August 1954.[46] With such a drastic redistribution of visas for Italy, the politically palatable fiction that the law addressed an "emergency" refugee crisis was maintained, but for all intents and purposes, the amendment was a powerful indication of the shortcomings of the National Origins System. The restructuring of the program was therefore a significant achievement for proponents of Italian immigration. It demonstrated congressional acknowledgment of the need for more Italian immigration, refugee or otherwise, and legitimated the position of Italian Americans that Italian quotas under the McCarran-Walter Act were too low. It also reinforced the lobby's strategy to use refugee relief legislation as a means of circumventing quota restrictions in order to achieve practical gains for Italian immigrants and their Italian American counterparts. Encouraged by the win, ACIM leaders wasted no time and began to campaign for extensions to the program and even additional special legislation for Italian immigrants well before the RRA was set to expire in 1956.

Whether it was the case of a refugee or a relative, ACIM also helped maximize the benefits of the RRA for Italian immigrants and their families by working to streamline the application process. The terms of the legislation, the process of qualifying as a refugee, and interactions with government agencies in the United States and Italy were complicated and even confusing to many would-be immigrants and sponsors, ACIM feared perhaps prohibitively so. Simplifying the process was one of the most important services ACIM offered its constituents. The first step in serving as intermediary between applicants, sponsors, and government agencies in Italy and the United States was to become certified as an official Voluntary Agency (VOLAG) sanctioned to work with refugees. After World War II when both national governments and international organizations were confronted with the modern era's greatest refugee crisis to date, states and NGOs alike looked for ways to systemize that process. In the United States, the State Department began to sanction a number of private organizations with authorization to work on behalf of refugee migration and resettlement. In 1953 when the RRP began, there were only about a dozen VOLAGs including the National Catholic Welfare Conference, Lutheran Family Services, and the Hebrew Immigrant Aid Society.[47] While the NCWC had already begun assisting Italians, it was charged with the enormous task of helping to resettle Catholics from all over the world, thus ACIM aimed to become the primary agency to provide assistance for Italians.

The process of sponsoring a refugee took many months, in some cases over a year, to complete. On the American side, it involved coordination with

State Department officials, staff in consular offices, and interactions with American sponsors. In Italy, ACIM worked with the government agency created specifically to process refugee relief cases, the Comitato Italiano Pro Profughi Stati Uniti (Italian Committee for United States Refugees, CIPSU), as well as provincial and local governments. Applications usually originated with the applicant personally or with an American relative who sought to sponsor a family member. But migrants and sponsors alike often found the program requirements, application materials, and process of se-curing necessary documentation overly cumbersome or beyond their capa-bilities. Navigating technical language, managing multiple deadlines, and interfacing with culturally, and sometimes literally, foreign bureaucracies were overwhelming hurdles for the men and women for whom the program was designed. ACIM intervened on their behalf. It simplified state docu-ments by sending out its own plainly worded questionnaires that sponsor and applicants could answer in either English or Italian for ACIM personnel to translate and transfer back to official applications. ACIM also managed the long application process. The agency reminded sponsors and applicants of deadlines, alerted them to problems such as incomplete applications or missing documentation in support of their application, and kept up corre-spondence with government agencies about the status of cases. In short, ACIM was the familiar and skillful mediating agency upon which sponsors and applicants could rely to complete and expedite a process that they may have been unable or reluctant to take on themselves.[48]

ACIM was inundated with thousands of requests for help. Reflecting the level of demand from the community, a few prominent Italian Americans not directly involved in ACIM organized the American Resettlement Council for Italian Refugees (ARCIR) about a year after the RRP began in order to sup-plement ACIM's efforts.[49] ARCIR's objectives were similar to those of ACIM. It promised to find sponsors for refugees, to process applications, and to as-sist refugees in the resettlement process. The only major distinction between the two organizations was that ARCIR focused exclusively on aiding Italian refugees without familial connections in the United States whereas ACIM assisted all Italian migrants.[50] At its height, ARCIR helped to process a little under two thousand applications involving over eight thousand persons.[51] It also compiled a list of the number of refugees in various occupations so that the candidates could be matched with appropriate sponsors. Each job title was followed by a description to ensure that a machinist in Italy performed the same skills as a machinist in the United States.[52] Although there was plenty of work to share, ARCIR's activities were short-lived. Within only months of its inception, it dissolved and turned its cases over to ACIM to complete.[53] ARCIR operated on sizeable donations from prominent founding members and large business interests, but ACIM already had the monetary and institutional support of many Italian Americans in the United States.[54] Moreover, it seems ARCIR's staff were less adept in dealing with the hefty bureaucratic requirements of the program than those working for ACIM.

One reason ACIM functioned more successfully than ARCIR owed to its relationship with agencies in the Italian government. Under ACIM's agreement with the CIPSU, the agency provided ACIM with a list of refugees and their necessary documentation including case histories, birth certificates, marriage certificates, and proof of refugee status. The CIPSU also helped supply applicants with other documents that were not always necessary but often helped their case. For example, education and employment records attested to the applicant's skill sets, technical abilities, or professional qualifications. When possible, applicants also provided proof of church membership, political party affiliation, and union membership in an attempt to demonstrate that they did not harbor any leftist leanings. Once applications were completed and all supporting paperwork was obtained, the CIPSU reviewed cases once more, verified the authenticity of applicants' documents, certified the applicant as a state-recognized refugee, and sent all materials to ACIM to process on the immigrant's behalf.[55]

The application process continued as American consulates in Italy scrutinized applications that ACIM had prepared with the help of the CIPSU. Much in the same fashion as their Italian counterparts, American consular agents reviewed applications and interviewed migrants to assess claimants' suitability as immigrants and to verify their refugee status. American officials also administered medical screenings—which of course were meant to protect the public welfare but were also traditionally used to deny visas to applicants thought likely "to become a public charge" because of ill health.[56] Applicants' criminal records were also carefully examined by American personnel. Those found to be guilty of petty crimes or morally questionable acts like adultery, bigamy, and abortion were sometimes disqualified from the program.[57]

Applicants' political histories received the most scrutiny. The passage of the RRA took place during a period of heightened anticommunist fervor in the United States. Well-known are notorious figures like Joseph McCarthy, who helped to turn anticommunist concerns into hysteria. But McCarthy was not alone. Other figures in both public and private sectors similarly advanced practices that promoted suspicion of newcomers and demanded conformity of beliefs and behavior in the interest of national security.[58] Those charged with guarding the country's gates were particularly sensitive to the demands the public placed upon them in such an atmosphere. Its not surprising that existing case records indicate that Italian refugees' political backgrounds were a main point of concern for immigration officials. A leadership role or other forms of active participation in communist, socialist, or fascist organizations almost always automatically disqualified a visa-seeker. However, mere membership in one of those parties, even if assumed under duress, as many Italians who had lived during the fascist-era claimed, or even a loose affiliation with a broadly defined leftist group could also be problematic. Conservatives argued that such associations reflected a sympathy for totalitarian regimes that, at best, suggested the applicant was unfit for democratic citizenship in the United States; at worst, it could be evidence of an intent to actively subvert the political and social order of the nation. Records indicate that ACIM members advised migrants on ways to demonstrate that their membership in a "subversive" political party, union, or other organization was compulsory, necessary to maintain one's livelihood, or that their participation in such a group was minimal. ACIM also helped applicants try to appeal a denial, but in most cases the State Department's word was final.[59]

The final step in securing a refugee relief visa was to obtain sponsorship for a migrant. Fearing the economic and social impact of refugees and displaced persons on the nation, lawmakers put check-stops in place to buttress against the potentially negative economic and social impact refugees might have on the nation. Liberals viewed these requirements as purposeful attempts to thwart or stall the successful entry of immigrants under the Displaced Persons Act and the RRA. Since both pieces of legislation primarily benefited southern and eastern Europeans, liberals also cited those provisions as yet another indication that a particular cohort of Americans continued to view certain ethnic groups as less fit for citizenship in the United States.[60]

American sponsors had to take responsibility for immigrants in the related areas of employment, housing, and welfare. First, an American sponsor had to ensure that immigrants would have jobs in place once they arrived. If the sponsor owned a business, he or she could personally guarantee the job. However, more commonly, the sponsor asked his or her boss, union organizer, or a small-business owner to guarantee a position for the applicant. The Department of Labor investigated each pledged job assurance to certify that both the position and company were authentic. It also made sure the refugee would not displace an American worker and that once the refugee arrived, he or she would receive competitive compensation so as not to drive down American wages. Some employment contracts even required that the newcomer join an appropriate trade union after a set period of time. American sponsors also had to guarantee that the immigrant had secured a place to live. In most cases, sponsors provided temporary housing in their own homes to immigrants or they arranged separate housing at a reasonable rate for the applicant and his or her family. Finally, sponsors had to guarantee that they would take responsibility in the event that the immigrant become a public charge. To demonstrate their financial ability to assist in an immigrant in this regard, sponsors had to disclose a list of dependents, their annual income, and the value of their bank accounts, real estate, and other assets for State Department review.[61] This almost unprecedented level of scrutiny is perhaps the greatest demonstration of the extent of anxiety Americans felt about the entry of refugees into the country.

Even though many Italian Americans were sympathetic to Italian refugees and wanted to see Italians take advantage of the program, it was sometimes difficult to find individuals or organizations willing to take on the legal and moral responsibilities of sponsoring a complete stranger.[62] So ACIM and its network of partner organizations exerted a great deal of effort to help connect refugees with sponsors willing to fulfill all three of these obligations. In cases where a family member or friend was able to be called upon, sponsors were found relatively easily. But even in cases where support networks existed, a sponsor might not have the resources to guarantee all three requirements. In those cases, ACIM helped fill in the blanks. Each ACIM case file contained a dossier on the prospective immigrant and his or her family that included information about each individual's education level, occupational skills, language capabilities, and other information. ACIM used that information to help immigrants secure jobs by reaching

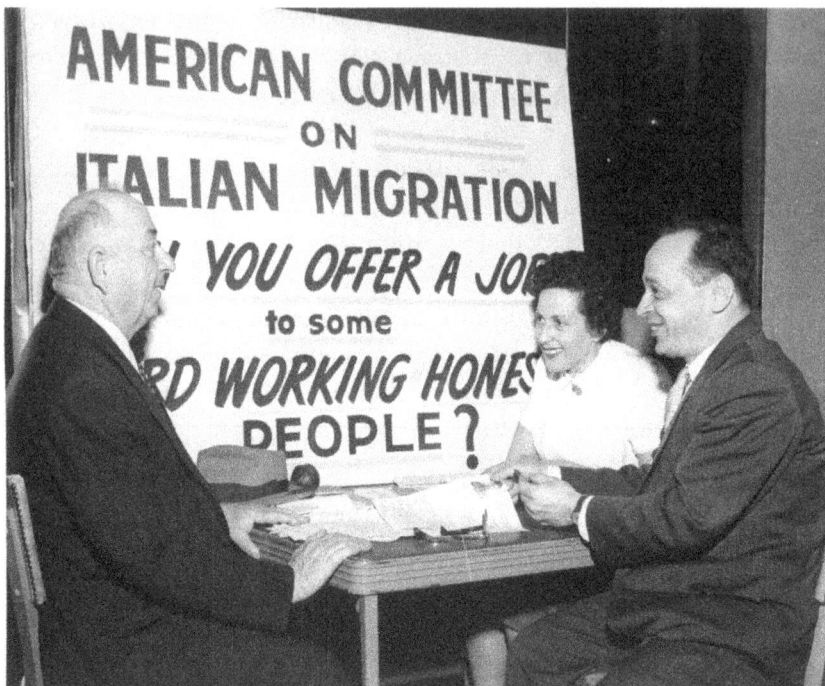

FIGURE 4. ACIM members (*right*) recruit sponsor (*left*) for refugees. Box D, American Committee on Italian Migration–National Office, New York City Records, Center for Migration Studies.

out to Italian American contacts in local businesses, labor unions, churches, social groups, ethnic organizations, and charities to find an appropriate job. Labor unions with Italian American leaders and large numbers of Italian American members were particularly active in assisting ACIM in this manner. The International Ladies' Garment Workers' Union, the United Shoemakers Union, and the Italian American Labor Council regularly provided notices of jobs to ACIM.[63] But ACIM members operated in less formal ways as well. ACIM members regularly canvassed their friends and acquaintances from other Italian American groups to which they belonged for information about employment opportunities for refugees. Likewise, ACIM members and Italian American priests who worked with ACIM often used connections in their churches to find jobs for refugees.[64] The same networks were also employed when either temporary or long-term housing assurances were needed. ACIM was sometimes able to negotiate free or reduced-rate short-term housing for newcomers through local contacts. In other cases, ACIM and the Italian Welfare League, another Italian American immigrant-aid organization, used donations and member fees to subsidize rents or provide housing loans for new immigrants.[65]

ACIM's assistance in locating sponsors was one of the most important duties it could take on in the case of refugees who had no contacts or networks to draw upon in the United States. In some ways, these were the cases that most typified the spirit of the law and were in fact the most in need because they were often without the material support and personal support systems that other immigrants had. They were also the most likely families to be living in DP camps in Italy because they did not have relatives or friends that were able to assist them in their homelands either. So ACIM spent a considerable amount of time and energy in connecting refugees with Italian American sponsors.[66]

One way ACIM connected refugees with Italian American sponsors was through its newsletter. In 1955, the *Dispatch* featured several refugee profiles in every issue. Leading with the headline "You Can Sponsor One of These Cases," ACIM detailed the situation of individuals and families who needed sponsorship. The featured cases represented typical circumstances that led to displacement, unemployment, homelessness, and political upheaval. For example, the *Dispatch* reported of Natale R., a fifty-one-year-old native of Caserta who was married with two daughters, nine and twelve years old. Natale's family had previously lived and worked in the French colony of Tunisia but faced repatriation when the French colonial government left. The family was now displaced from their home and living in an Italian refugee camp. The story reported that they were very "depressed" in the camp because they were without a home of their own and because of their idle existence without work, despite the fact that Italian authorities who interviewed the family had recommended them as "honest and hard-working." The profile also reported that Natale spoke Italian, French, and Arabic and had experience farming and cultivating vineyards.[67]

Common accounts included stories of Italians who had lost their homes, businesses, and farmlands to bombings and other events in the war.[68] Stories of victims displaced by environmental disasters, like the floods that struck Salerno and Catanzaro in 1953, were also common.[69] Other notable, but not uncommon, profiles included stories of communist escapees. "Arturo B.," a forty-seven-year-old accountant, had settled in Romania where he had been working for a bank until he was fired for his anticommunist political activity. He and his sister Berta, a dressmaker, escaped and returned to their native Italy. However, the two found bleak conditions upon their return and became homeless and jobless with only the DP camps to assist them. In the Chieti camp, Arturo reportedly learned painting, varnishing, and other construction trades that he was willing to perform in the United States, although he hoped to find work as an accountant. Italian officials described him as a "big, strong, healthy man, with a good presence, and has suffered a great deal for his democratic principles."[70] Likewise, the Giurin family fled Yugoslavia for Italy where they were also forced to take refuge in a camp in Italy. The *Dispatch* reminded readers, "This could have been you but for the happy circumstances that brought you or your parents into this land of opportunity and security." The story went on to emphasize Pietro Giurin's role as the admirable family patriarch in his resistance to "those who would enslave his mind" despite the peril and suffering it has caused him and his family. His only hope now was to find freedom and security in a new life in the United States.[71]

These descriptions were included to prompt an emotional connection with Italian American readers. One might feel sympathy toward a refugee who hailed from the same region as your family. Or perhaps the immigrants' personal attributes or experiences would generate sympathy and compel one to take action. In other cases, ACIM hoped that a reader would notice an immigrant's work experiences or skill sets and offer the refugee a job assurance. Moreover, many appeals called upon Italian Americans' sense of patriotism, particularly as Cold War crusaders, to help "democratic" peoples maintain their ideals and way of life.

Along with featuring refugee cases in the *Dispatch*, ACIM's national officers encouraged local chapter members to find sponsors for unknown refugees within their communities. National leaders advised branches to establish subcommittees devoted to obtaining unnamed assurances for refugees. The committees were to canvass local businesses, unions, Italian American societies, and churches to find jobs and housing for refugees. In what they called the "Adopt a Family Program," ACIM's national leaders suggested that an individual parish or ethnic organization might collectively sponsor a refugee family by having one member provide a job assurance, another supply a housing assurance, and the third pledge against the applicant becoming a public charge. ACIM leaders also appealed to Italian American Catholic sensibilities in imploring members of their community to remember their "fellow Italians and fellow brothers and sisters in Christ" in sponsoring a refugee.[72] Responding to these appeals, ACIM's national chapter in New York City placed thirty refugee families, its Buffalo, Chicago, and St. Louis chapters provided sponsors for sixty to seventy families each, and ACIM's Cleveland, Detroit, and Boston chapters reported smaller but significant success rates in refugee placement by mid-1955.[73]

Another way ACIM shaped immigration patterns and provided aid to immigrants under the RRA was in encouraging family migrations. ACIM representatives constantly counseled refugee relief applicants not to apply as an individual but rather to bring their entire families to the United States despite financial concerns and practical difficulties that may have constrained them from wanting to do so.[74] This advice of course stemmed from the practical constraints inherent in American immigration laws. If one migrated individually, backlogs for visas from countries like Italy might prevent a timely reunion with those who tried to follow. Therefore, ACIM helped Italian immigrants find competitive wages, affordable housing, and donated household materials to encourage family immigration and resettlement in spite of a family's relatively poor economic situation.[75] But practicalities were not the only reason for ACIM's advice. The importance of the family as a political, economic, moral, and spiritual unit was of course in line with Catholic social thought. Although Italian Americans generally subordinated Catholic ideas about family migration to the rhetoric of Cold War liberalism for the time being, religious ideals were nonetheless a powerful motivator.

Promoting family migrations also accomplished one of ACIM's broader goals in shaping the public image of Italian Americans during the Cold War. In the 1950s and 1960s, the nuclear family carried with it connotations that reflected particularly powerful cultural values in the United States. All over the country, Americans venerated the nuclear family as the primary social and economic bulwark against communism. Family-centric households reinforced Western and capitalistic gender roles that idealized male providers and female consumers in the postwar period. Moreover, historians have characterized the home as a psychologically protective space in an increasingly insecure world that Americans took both individual and collective solace in during the early Cold War.[76] By encouraging family migrations, ACIM encouraged Italian immigrants to conform to this form of social organization and to adopt these cultural values. ACIM hoped that in encouraging family migrations (and all of the economic and social dynamics that followed), some of the anxieties held by immigration restrictionists and cultural conservatives might be allayed. The same rationale would form the basis for their resettlement assistance programs.

There were, of course, not a small number of Americans who remained skeptical about letting large numbers of Italian immigrants enter the country. Those concerns were evident in battles over the passage of the RRA and in the ways Italian Americans responded to its passage. Like other liberals, Italian Americans hoped that the side-door entry of Italian immigrants and other groups largely restricted from entering the United States under National Origins System quotas would implicitly demonstrate the folly of selecting for newcomers primarily on the basis of racial and ethnic criteria. But social anxieties about new immigrants were so significant that Italian Americans in ACIM and other ethnic advocacy groups pushed intense cultural assimilation projects on newcomers. For them, it was vitally important that new immigrants project a public image that would be politically and socially acceptable to older-stock Americans. Italian American elites saw those measures as part of their immigration reform strategy. But their assimilationist program also reflected Italian Americans' own group identity. At midcentury, many Italian Americans seemed intent on holding onto the practical and social gains they had made as a group. If Italian Americans viewed themselves as members of the American mainstream, on par with older-stock whites, newcomers should also have access to that position—and, just as importantly, they should not derail it either.

## Resettlement Assistance and "A New Standard of Living"

In March 1959, ACIM published an article in its newsletter entitled "A New Standard of Living." The piece featured two Italian families, the Tuiachs and the Giurins, who had immigrated to the United States under the 1953 Refugee Relief Act (RRA). The article and accompanying photographs show the two displaced families, who had previously been languishing in refugee camps, now enjoying "a well-furnished home with all the modern equipment and appliances owned by the average American family." The story even drew special attention to four-year-old Fabbio Tuiach as the proud owner of a brand-new camera.[1] In 1958, a Chicago-based paper similarly chronicled Armedo Vasari's voyage from Trieste to the United States under the RRA. He and his wife, both former displaced persons, had resettled in a Chicago suburb where Armedo worked a manufacturing job and earned a wage that afforded his wife the luxury to stay at home and raise their twenty-month-old daughter. The article featured a photo of Armedo in his home garage working on the nineteen-foot cabin cruiser he had recently purchased. The

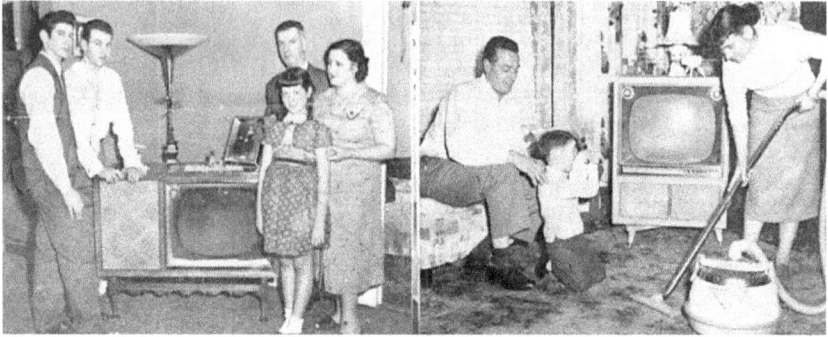

FIGURE 5. "A New Standard of Living," ACIM *Dispatch*, March 1959, box D, American Committee on Italian Migration–National Office, New York City Records, Center for Migration Studies.

article noted Vasari's efforts to learn English at night school and further asserted, "Talk to Armedo and you're immediately impressed by his love for America, by his knowledge of this country, his insights into the many opportunities here and his desire to become a United States citizen."[2]

Accounts such as these celebrated the rapid economic and cultural assimilation of the "new" Italian immigrant family. In the years after World War II, ACIM and its partner organizations were determined to craft an image of Italian immigrants that they believed better reflected their ethnic group's inclusionary position in the nation in the postwar period. Whether accurate or not, the stereotypical turn-of-the-century Italian immigrant embodied characteristics that many Americans considered problematic or even threatening to the nation. Most late nineteenth- and early twentieth-century Italian migrants were male sojourners whose presence in the United States challenged the accepted paradigm of immigrant assimilation through their transitory status, shipments of remittances back home, and the maintenance of transnational households that disrupted domestic norms and gender roles in the United States.[3] Many Italian Americans now seized the opportunity to remake that image, first by providing order and rationality to the migration process in the place of what once was a chaotic and unorganized experience and then by reshaping the image of the "typical" Italian immigrant. Therefore, in the postwar period, Italian American immigrant aid organizations worked to promote the immigration of family units who intended to permanently resettle in the United States. It was also for this reason that, under Italian American tutelage, new immigrants were encouraged to adopt American patterns of household consumption and thereby prove the Italian immigrant's ability to become desirable members of the nation.[4]

If many Italian Americans still believed themselves or their fellow ethnics to be subjects of discriminatory attitudes in the United States, the passage of refugee relief legislation now added the additional stigma associated with being a refugee to the group's image. The term *refugee* then (as it still does today) carried with it connotations of economic loss and impoverishment.[5] The conservative political climate of the postwar period and concerns about the impact that Europe's most destitute classes might have on the United States' economy induced lawmakers to include strict provisions in both the Displaced Persons Act and the RRA to insulate Americans from the potential economic and social threats refugees seemingly posed.[6] Italian American organizations thus made a calculated effort to combat the stigmas associated with the label by attempting to prove to the American public that Italians who immigrated under the RRA were, in fact, valuable producers and consumers who added to America's economic growth in the postwar period.[7]

In less than five years since their arrival, the Tuiachs, Giurins, Vasaris, and thousands of other Italian families had indeed made the transition from refugees to middle-class Americans. That was no more apparent than in the featured immigrants' household consumption patterns. These families did not appear to be destitute refugees who burdened American taxpayers. Nor were they migrant men without women, squirreling away their wages to send back home or to finance the migrations of others, who characterized earlier waves of Italian immigration in the United States.[8] They were families, firmly resettled in the United States, embracing postwar family and gender norms that were respected and valued in postwar America. Those families were becoming American producers and consumers, fueling economic growth and symbolizing the material abundance that an American way of life offered. They bought modern appliances for their American homes, fashionable clothing to wear to work and school, and automobiles for travel in their suburban neighborhoods. Perhaps more than any other characteristic, it was homeownership in middle- and working-class suburbs that was the most striking indication of the new social position of these Italian immigrants and their Italian American kin. In the context of American

Cold War culture in the 1950s, when Americans put a renewed emphasis on the importance of the nuclear family as a political unit and personal fulfillment through family-centered household consumption, homeownership was a marker of economic success and a badge of Americanism.[9] Moreover, residence in ethnically heterogeneous but racially exclusionary suburbs was a powerful and visible marker of both whiteness and social inclusion for Italians and other "new" ethnic groups in the postwar period who were no longer confined to ethnic enclaves or ghettos but were instead well integrated into mainstream American society.[10]

Although the Tuiachs, Giurins, and Vasaris deserve the lion's share of the credit for their acculturation to life in the United States, they did not make the transition to their new lives alone. ACIM and other Italian American organizations concerned with immigrant aid and immigration reform were enormously involved in shaping the immigration and resettlement experience for postwar immigrants. Almost no aspect of the immigrant's transition was overlooked. From helping immigrants and sponsors understand, navigate, and utilize American immigration laws, to facilitating the rapid social and cultural assimilation of newcomers, ACIM, the Italian Welfare League, labor unions, Catholic organizations, and other groups influenced the immigration and resettlement experience of new arrivals in a variety of ways. These organizations helped immigrants, particularly refugees, maintain family migrations, secure low-cost travel, navigate entry into the country and reach their final destinations, obtain affordable housing, find respectable employment, and integrate into their new communities.

The intended result of these efforts was to demonstrate that Italian immigrants deserved greater immigration opportunities. Moving away from arguments stressing Italian emigration needs during Italy's struggle to maintain economic and political stability during the Cold War, these narratives demonstrated that both Italian Americans and new Italian immigrants conformed to the economic, social, and cultural norms valued by the American mainstream at midcentury. One of the most commonly invoked justifications for immigration restriction, and one that was still considered legitimate in the postwar period, was that national groups who were culturally dissimilar to Americans would have a more difficult time assimilating to life in America than groups with more similar cultural and social traditions.[11] In helping Italian immigrants smoothly resettle and, furthermore, in publicizing success stories, Italian Americans were attempting to show that Italians were easily integrated and proper, even desirable, candidates for immigration and naturalization opportunities. The chairman of ACIM's Cleveland chapter once remarked, "The best and most eloquent argument for liberal immigration is the immigrant himself. The way he adapts or fails to adapt to the mores of the community, the way in which he behaves and assimilates into the American way of life, conditions the response of the community toward immigration in general."[12] In short, Italian American immigrant advocacy organizations believed that if they could demonstrate that Italian peoples made for desirable immigrants and, ultimately, citizens, few older-stock Americans would continue to support closing the gates to them.

But herein resettlement programs, and the logic behind them, reveal an element of postwar immigration reform campaigns that historians have yet to fully explore. In focusing on projecting a certain image of the new face of Italian immigration in the postwar period, Italian Americans did not take up the cause of all immigrants, nor did they advocate for broad changes to the nation's immigration codes on the basis of equity or fairness for all peoples. Their actions may have chipped away at the effectiveness of the McCarran-Walter Act, but that is where their efforts ended. Their programs did not challenge the notion that there were "desirable" and "undesirable" immigrants—or even the idea that immigrants could be judged as a group based on their national origins or ethnicity. They merely sought to advance the position of Italians within the already established hierarchies of racial and ethnic desirability that existed in American society by altering the formula or criteria for those judgments. The key difference would be that now social or behavioral demonstrations would replace biological or scientific considerations when Americans evaluated whom to welcome. Although Chinese and Japanese American immigrant advocacy groups also employed similar strategies to achieve upward mobility and immigration reform with some success in this period, their successes were similarly reliant upon establishing a racialized "model minority" or decidedly "not Black" group identity for their ethnic constituencies.[13] The strategies employed by all of these groups underscore a recognition that immigrant groups who could lay claims to the economic, social, and cultural trapping of whiteness would be more successfully included into the boundaries of the American mainstream. Consequently, it is important to recognize the conservative or even reactionary elements of the Italian American immigration reform campaigns evident here that coexisted alongside of liberal rhetoric that asserted the need for racial and ethnic equality in American immigration laws. Italian American resettlement initiatives thus demonstrate, at best, the limitations of white ethnic liberals. However, they might even suggest the largely rhetorical and shallow elements of white ethnic immigration reform campaigns.

## Family Migrations and Orderly Entries

New immigrants were encouraged to adopt lifestyles that reflected postwar values prioritizing domesticity, traditional gender roles, and conspicuous displays of consumption—all of which carried great meaning to Americans during the height of the Cold War. These projects undoubtedly began with the family. All over the country, Americans embraced the nuclear family as the primary bulwark against communism in the years after World War II as Americans came to view the home as a protective space in an increasingly insecure world. In those constructions, normative family life reinforced gender roles that idealized male providers and female consumers within a family household economy.[14] By encouraging family migrations, ACIM encouraged Italian immigrants to conform to this form of social organization and to adopt these cultural values. This began at the earliest stages of the immigration process. ACIM officials who worked with both immigrants and sponsors to complete immigration applications did all that they could to encourage family migrations. Such advice was born out of the logistics of immigration laws and the long waitlists Italian immigrants faced to call for their family members at some point in the future, but it was also the product of Italian American concerns to remake public perceptions of Italian immigrants.

Italian American immigrant aid organizations also tried to create a migration experience that was ordered, rational, and efficient in order to project the most functional image of Italian immigration possible. ACIM's handling of refugee relief applications surely reflected that impulse, as did the way ACIM and partner organizations helped cash-strapped immigrants, especially refugees, secure the necessary funds for their travel to the United States. While ACIM and the NCWC prepared an immigrant's visa application, they also put applicants who commanded little financial or social resources in touch with nongovernmental organizations such as the Intergovernmental Committee for European Migration (ICEM) or the International Social Services (ISS) to secure an interest-free travel loan to finance their journeys.[15] The ISS originated in the wake of World War I and provided financial assistance to international migrants since 1924. ICEM was created in 1951 with substantial financial and institutional support from the United States for the sole purpose of facilitating the international migration of "surplus" populations in Europe to receiving countries around the world.[16] Although the American public would have been loath to directly subsidize immigrant travel to the United States, American financial and logistical support for ICEM travel loans was framed as part of the nation's Cold War mission; by providing relief for population pressures overseas, western European democracies were preserved. In helping immigrants take advantage of these international and (indirect) state resources, ACIM and the NCWC were attempting to create a more modern, rational, and ordered migration experience for new immigrants. They also understood that low-interest, long-term, and often flexible loans issued by charitable NGOs would help newcomers migrate and resettle in the United States without being saddled with massive debt as they began their new lives.

Italian American organizations further continued to guide and structure the migration process once immigrants reached American gates. In the 1950s, most Italian immigrants continued to arrive by ship, primarily at New York City and other ports on the East Coast. The arrival and disembarkation process could be confusing to the immigrant and could appear chaotic and problematic to American observers—as it did at the turn of the century. Italian American organizations made a concerted effort to minimize those problems. When new immigrants arrived, either alone or as a part of a family unit, they had to collect all their belongings, navigate Customs and Border Security, deal with agents of the state, and continue on their journey amid chaos, confusion, and foreign surroundings. ACIM and its partner organization the Italian Welfare League (IWL) quickly identified this experience as one area where they could substantially assist newcomers. The IWL had been operating out of New York City since 1920 and had focused on providing monetary and material assistance to needy Italian immigrant families in the interwar period. It continued those functions in the postwar period, but responding to the resumption of large-scale Italian immigration to the country after World War II and the requests of ACIM to assist with immigrant arrivals, the IWL increasingly focused much of its energy on providing services to aid in the immigration process itself.

A common case began when an immigrant that ACIM had assisted was due to arrive in the United States. ACIM would alert the IWL of the pending arrival so that IWL volunteers could be physically present at the immigrant's point of entry. The dossiers ACIM sent to the IWL often included letters from relatives and photographs of the migrants to help IWL volunteers identify those who needed assistance. In other cases, Italian American family members wrote directly to IWL asking for assistance when they could not be there to receive their relatives themselves.[17] The IWL's services were especially important when immigrants had no family or friends either locally in New York City or in the country at all (in the case of a number of refugees). Then the IWL Port and Dock Committee, composed of over a dozen Italian American women who regularly volunteered on a daily or weekly basis, greeted and assisted arriving immigrants at docks and airports. An arriving ship was typically greeted by one to five women, depending on the expected number of arrivals and the availability of volunteers.[18] These bilingual greeters, who wore patches on their arms to identify themselves as aid workers, helped newcomers complete customs forms, locate luggage, and reach their final destinations by accompanying individuals and families to buses, trains, hotels, and homes. In some cases, the IWL or ACIM made additional loans to arriving families who did not have enough money for further travel or temporary lodging expenses.[19] Finally, committee members followed up with newcomers by sending letters and postcards to the immigrants' expected destinations to make sure they had arrived, to verify that their journeys had been smooth, to follow up on lost luggage claims, and to ask for suggestions on how to further improve their assistance. In follow-up letters, IWL volunteers also reminded newcomers that they could continue to take advantage of IWL's other resettlement services, such as social and legal aid.[20]

The IWL's Port and Dock Committee was a great asset to many Italians arriving under the RRA. When family members lived too far from New York City to meet their relatives, it was a great comfort to be greeted by a friendly face and receive helpful advice. Other migrants, particularly refugees, relied on Italian American organizations for assistance because they did not have existing support networks in the United States and often had less social and material advantages than other migrants. For them, the IWL's help upon arrival in interpreting forms, filling out paperwork, and reaching their final destinations was invaluable.[21] All told, from November 1954 to December 1956, the Port and Dock Committee met 170 ships docking in New York City and assisted over two thousand families—an average of seven ships and eighty-four cases a month during the peak arrival months of refugee migrations.[22]

Another important function of the IWL was to offer pro bono or sometimes low-cost legal counsel for Italian immigrants in New York and New Jersey. The IWL and other immigrant aid organizations recognized that legal representation was often necessary to ensure the immigrant's ability to remain in the United States or to secure the entry of family members. The IWL handled a range of cases but the vast majority in the postwar period were ones involving a migrant's unauthorized entry into the country and subsequent attempts to adjust one's immigration status to legal permanent resident alien. The spike in illegal entry cases seen by the IWL in these years suggest the lengths to which some Italians were willing to go to in order to migrate to the United States when they were barred from doing so by regular means. In the 1950s alone, IWL lawyers represented over five hundred Italians in status adjustment or deportation cases.[23] Indeed, Italian American organizations were willing to aid in these instances and made it a priority to help normalize an Italian immigrant's status and thus mitigate against further negative opinions directed toward Italians should the public begin to widely perceive the group as "illegal" immigrants.

## *"I Sarti Italiani Hanno Invaso L'America"*
## *[Italian Tailors Have Invaded America]*

Collectively, Italian American efforts to provide immigrants assistance with travel and in negotiating orderly entries into the country were aimed at creating a rational and efficient migration experience for postwar Italian immigrants. But these efforts were just the beginning of Italian American efforts to project a public image of a new kind of immigrant. It was also vitally important that newcomers secure gainful employment. It was not long ago that a considerable number of Americans judged Italian immigrants, as a group, to be intellectually inferior to earlier waves of immigrants, prone to criminality, and inclined to become recipients of charity. These views were institutionalized in the Dillingham Commission's 1911 report and, in part, served as the foundations for the restrictions placed on southern and eastern European immigration in the National Origins System.[24] Although racial determinism of this fashion was falling out of favor in academic and policy circles by the 1950s, such attitudes were not entirely eradicated, especially among the general population. Moreover, the refugee label attached to many postwar Italian immigrants added another layer of stigmatization by requiring those who arrived under refugee programs to obtain job and housing assurances (as well as guarantees that they not become a public charge) because the assumption was they would have difficulty doing so. Those clauses reflected public anxiety about the social and economic impact that refugees might have on the nation and perhaps even reflected concerns about the cultural characteristics of national or ethnic groups that stood to gain entry to the country via the RRA as well. To combat all these concerns, ACIM made job placement for new arrivals a priority.

In many cases, job placement was accomplished when individual Italian Americans sponsored family members, friends, people from their hometowns, or even complete strangers. Italian Americans used professional connections, union membership, and personal networks to find jobs for immigrants. In some cases, the sponsor was a business owner who personally assured the direct employment of the applicant. However, ACIM and other organizations quickly understood that in many cases individual sponsors were unable to help place an immigrant. Lack of employment could hold up applications or squash them entirely. Moreover, ACIM and its partners, particularly labor unions dominated by Italian American members, wanted to ensure not only that immigrants had jobs but that they secured *good* jobs. For many southern Italians with rural agricultural or working-class backgrounds and little formal education, skilled work in the United States offered the most viable route to relatively high wages and upward social mobility. ACIM recognized those constraints and thus spent considerable energy creating large-scale occupational programs to help place newcomers on paths that would facilitate their successful resettlement and perhaps even upward mobility in the United States.

The largest and most successful of these programs focused on securing jobs for Italian tailors. The American garment industry was in flux in the years after World War II. The industry, one of the first to go through industrialization and the deskilling that went along with it, had long relied upon cheap immigrant labor. In the late nineteenth and early twentieth centuries, it was largely Italian and Eastern European Jewish men and women who filled that niche. But those groups' immigration streams decreased considerably with the implementation of the National Origins Act, the onset of the Great Depression, and the outbreak of World War II. Furthermore, the American garment industry, like other industries that produced consumable goods, faced both manpower and material shortages during World War II as resources were diverted for war production. When the war ended, manufacturing of consumer goods resumed in full force, but the custom garment industry had difficulty rebounding. The war had afforded American workers, especially the white ethnic men and women who had been in the garment trades before the war, opportunities for upward mobility. The result was significant manpower shortages. Throughout the 1940s and 1950s, the US Department of Labor listed both "Tailor I" (highly skilled) and "Tailor II" (semiskilled) as needed professions in the country. These circumstances created some opportunities for African Americans and Chinese Americans to enter into the trade, but employers and unions alike slowed that movement.[25]

While (white) tailors and other garment workers were in short supply in the United States, they were abundant in Italy. Garment production in Italy only became highly industrialized in the postwar period as the field modernized as part of Italian reconstruction. But in the decade or so after the war, the majority of Italian tailors still operated in small and customized shops and were therefore trained in an artisanal fashion that was largely absent but nonetheless desired by high-end manufacturers in the United States. The strain on the Italian economy after the war also freed large numbers of skilled workers from related industries to migrate to the United States or elsewhere where they were willing to retrain.[26]

Seizing upon the situation, ACIM and the NCWC began to construct large-scale programs to place Italian tailors into positions in the United States in 1954 and 1955 as the volume of refugee relief applications picked up. A unionized skilled tailor in the United States earned about eighty dollars per week in 1955. That figure was roughly equivalent to the national average income of eighty-four dollars per week and would ensure the Italian immigrant and his or her family a decent standard of living.[27] To implement such a program, ACIM leaders cultivated relationships with other relief organizations who could coordinate the logistics and press the need for such programs, business leaders willing to sponsor immigrant tailors en masse, and labor leaders who would help ensure positive treatment, fair compensation, and placement for newcomers. Of the last group, Luigi Antonini, who held leadership positions in both the Italian American Labor Council (IALC) and the International Ladies' Garment Workers' Union (ILGWU), was a critical partner.[28] For their part, several of the corporations that ended up sponsoring refugees had connections to ACIM or to other Italian American organizations. By the 1950s, Italian Americans had moved up to leadership positions in the field and thus were able to do something to help facilitate Italian migration. Their motivations must be taken into consideration. It was not business interests alone that prompted American companies to sponsor Italian tailors. The process of sponsoring a foreign worker could take up to two years from beginning to end. And while labor shortages for tailors, shoemakers, and other professions account for companies' willingness to wait for extended periods of time for new sources of labor, a sentimental connection contributed in convincing some sponsors to undergo the long and arduous process of sponsoring Italian tailors.

The first "Tailors Project" to manifest itself was a partnership between ACIM, War Relief Services (WRS, a division of the NCWC), and the Hickey-Freeman Company. The clothing company based in Rochester, New York, had produced handmade and customized men's suits since the late nineteenth century. Like other companies of its kind, Hickey-Freeman's production of consumable goods dropped dramatically during the war years, but demand for its products grew equally as quickly when the war ended. From 1946 to 1948, Hickey-Freeman reported a more than 30 percent increase in production and had opened six new satellite facilities to supplement production at the main plant in Rochester.[29] Despite these impressive indicators of growth, Hickey-Freeman executives believed their success was limited not by demand but by a constant shortage of skilled tailors. In an attempt to fill their manpower needs, Hickey-Freeman implemented a training program in 1945 for nearly three hundred returning American soldiers.[30] However, with abundant opportunities elsewhere, very few veterans finished the program or remained in the trade for long. The former New York state commissioner of labor, Edward Corsi, called attention to the issue commenting, "If the shortage of skilled workers in the garment industry continues, in ten years it will be hard to find tailors in the United States who can produce a custom-made or fit a ready-made suit. Clothing manufacturers in Rochester are not only having difficulty recruiting trained workers but cannot even find apprentices to train despite the industry's high wages and excellent working conditions."[31]

In 1947, WRS worked out an agreement to bring a number of skilled custom tailors from Italy to work at Hickey-Freeman. When ACIM took over some of WRS's functions years later, it joined in the endeavor.[32] Most of Hickey-Freeman's workforce had historically hailed from Italy. Chain migration patterns mostly attracted southern Italians from Sicily, Campania, Abruzzo, and Calabria to Rochester for work in the garment trade and other manufacturing jobs in the early twentieth century.[33] By midcentury, Italian Americans had experienced significant upward mobility in Rochester, and Italian Americans occupied managerial and executive positions within the company. Paul Brescia was one such executive and played a key role in Hickey-Freeman's partnership with WRS and ACIM. Although there are no existing records explaining Brescia's motivations or the extent of his involvement in orchestrating the partnership, it is reasonable to conclude that he identified with the Italian American community and was aware of Italian migration needs after the war.[34]

The first installment of Italian tailors came in 1948 when the US Immigration and Naturalization Service granted Hickey-Freeman and War Relief Service's request to sponsor one hundred skilled tailors from Italy.[35] After 1948, Hickey-Freeman continued to sponsor tailors on a case by case basis until the RRA afforded the company greater opportunities to bring in more tailors. From 1952 to 1956, Hickey-Freeman used a combination of first preference sponsorship under the Immigration and Nationality Act and quotas granted under the RRA to bring approximately one thousand Italian tailors to Rochester. Because of the sheer number of immigration opportunities it provided, most tailors came under the RRA. Some of the tailors were recruited by WRS and ACIM, who forwarded qualified applicants to Hickey-Freeman for sponsorship. Others were directly recruited by Hickey-Freeman officials who performed informal scouting trips in Italy. In both cases, Hickey-Freeman executives preferred to sponsor tailors who either had family connections in Rochester or those without any family at all in the United States to help ensure their retention at the company. This stipulation limited WRS's and ACIM's placement of some tailors but ultimately worked out in the favor of refugees without family ties (who were generally those most difficult cases to find assurances for) in the United States.[36] Once at Hickey-Freeman, immigrant tailors were given standard industry wages under union contracts (eighty dollars a week) and were required to join their local union within a month of employment. The latter was a provision required by the Department of Labor in approving refugee employment to ensure that foreign workers would not drive down American wages or displace American workers.[37] That arrangement was quite satisfactory to Italian American immigrant aid organizations who worked to ensure that newcomers joined their local union so that they were able to secure a relatively high standard of living and would successfully settle in the United States.

In 1961, Hickey-Freeman conducted a special analysis of their workforce and found that of their 1,600 employees, 1,029 were foreign-born specialty tailors and seamstresses. Of those roughly 1,000 immigrant workers, 200 had immigrated and began working for the company before 1947, and the remaining 829 came after 1947 with the help of WRS and ACIM. Of the 829, 744 immigrated under the RRA, and the remaining 85 came under the first preference category of regular immigration quotas as skilled workers needed in the United States.[38]

WRS regularly reviewed Hickey-Freeman's sponsorship to ensure the Italian tailors were fairly treated. In 1954, several tailors complained to WRS that Hickey-Freeman was not living up to the terms of its deal. Those tailors left the company because they believed that they would receive a one-hundred-dollar-a-week salary and a newly furnished apartment upon their arrival. Those expectations were based on rumor and speculation. Most tailors received closer to eighty dollars a week, the standard union rate for male custom tailors, and Hickey-Freeman was certainly under no obligation to guarantee housing or other material aid for refugees. The company often helped ACIM to locate affordable housing in the area as a courtesy. WRS forwarded the tailors' complaints to the Italian Consulate in Buffalo to investigate the claim, but the consulate representative did not find any misconduct at Hickey-Freeman. By most accounts, Italian tailors were generally

FIGURE 6. Italian tailors, Hickey-Freeman Company, Rochester, New York (n.d.). Personal collection of the author.

satisfied with their working conditions and wages (which were governed by union terms). The investigator concluded that the disgruntled tailors most likely wanted to justify leaving their sponsored jobs to either move closer to family elsewhere or for another job opportunity. On the whole, however, the immigration programs sponsored by Hickey-Freeman and WRS were hailed as a great success by just about all parties involved.[39]

By 1956, several factors prompted a decline in the number of requests for Italian tailors and seamstresses from Hickey-Freeman. Firstly, the company anticipated the arrival of tailors and seamstresses whose cases were still being processed under the RRA throughout 1956 and 1957. But, Hickey-Freeman also decided that when the RRA expired in 1956, it would begin to deal directly with the Giunta Cattolica per L'Emigrazione, the official Catholic immigration agency in Italy, rather than continue its relationship with WRS and ACIM. The advantage of dealing with that agency over WRS and

ACIM was that the Giunta Cattolica per L'Emigrazione had direct connections with agencies (namely, the Intergovernmental Committee for European Migration and the International Catholic Men's Committee) that had the resources and infrastructure to make transportation loans to migrants, whereas WRS and ACIM did not.[40] Additionally, American companies' willingness to sponsor Italian tailors slowed in the late 1950s as conditions in the garment industry in both the United States and Italy changed. From 1945 to 1965, the fashion industry in Italy experienced drastic changes. Its growth was probably one of the most successful industrial recoveries of Italian reconstruction. In 1945 the ready-made clothing industry was virtually nonexistent in the country, but by the turn of the decade, American aid, participation in the newly formed European Common Market, and the growth of consumer culture in Italy all contributed to the dramatic growth of Italian textile production.[41] By the 1960s, as part of the Italian "economic miracle," modernized garment factories had replaced most small and customized shops in the country and their goods were successful and competitive on international markets. As a result of these changes in Italy, and indeed in world markets, the supply of Italian immigrant tailors in the United States decreased. Southern Italian tailors who had supplied American labor markets since the end of the war were now more likely to internally migrate to northern industrial centers than to migrate abroad.[42] Hickey-Freeman still attempted to recruit Italian tailors from 1960 to 1965 but not at the same rate. In 1961, only twenty-one Italian tailors were placed at the company. In part, this low number reflected limitations under the McCarran-Walter Act and the dramatic oversubscription of the Italian quota. But, in 1962 when Congress enacted legislation permitting first preference beneficiaries to enter the country outside of quota limitations, Hickey-Freeman was still only able to recruit forty-eight Italian tailors.[43]

During the peak years of the RRA, programs to sponsor Italian tailors brought enormous opportunities to Italian immigrants. Along with Hickey-Freeman, other Rochester-based garment companies—including Bond Stores, Fashion Park, the Michael-Stern Company, and Timely Clothes —brought Italian tailors to Rochester under first preference provisions and under the RRA. Unlike in the case of Hickey-Freeman, who initiated the immigration of Italian tailors with the help of WRS and ACIM, a local Italian American attorney, Francis D'Amanda, usually solicited the sponsorship of those companies on behalf of Italian immigrants he represented.[44] D'Amanda had a long history of involvement with Italian relief organizations and was briefly affiliated with the short-lived American Resettlement Council for Italian Refugees.[45] The result was that thousands of Italian tailors, seamstresses, and their family members were able to immigrate to Rochester in just a few years. Several of these immigrants became supervisors, section foremen, custom tailors, and seamstresses. As such, they were quickly able to achieve middle-class status in Rochester. The mass migration and success of these Rochester-based programs was noted by Italians and Italian Americans alike. As word spread of the migrations, Italian Americans all over New York State appealed to ACIM for help in getting their relatives sponsored by Hickey-Freeman. When these Italian Americans wrote ACIM, they often already had knowledge of the details of the programs— including pay rates, housing conditions, and transportation fees.[46]

The clothing industry in Rochester was just one of the many areas where ACIM placed refugee tailors. Italian American organizations also sponsored Italian tailors in a program intended to place them at various companies in New York City.[47] Although by midcentury New York City was losing ground as a manufacturing center to other cities in the United States, in 1950 it was still a major hub of manufacturing, and Italian immigrants and their children were still the largest represented ethnic group in the industry.[48] Moreover, thousands of refugee tailors were placed in clothing manufacturing companies on a case-by-case basis or in smaller limited-scale programs— for example, the Atlantic City Clothing Company provided assurances for twelve Italian tailors in 1956.[49] After the RRP ended, clothing companies in the United States continued to contact ACIM to offer to sponsor Italian tailors.[50]

ACIM's Chicago branch, the largest ACIM chapter after the national office in New York City, was also very successful in instituting occupation-based programs for aiding Italian refugee tailors as well. The Oxxford Clothing Company was one Chicago-based company that worked with ACIM to sponsor Italian tailors. Like Hickey-Freeman, Oxxford hired a small number of Italian tailors in the late 1940s and early 1950s, was satisfied with their work, and then came to ACIM for assistance in locating and sponsoring more tailors.[51] ACIM's New York and Chicago branches worked together with Antonini (and the ILGWU), the Italian embassy in Washington, DC, and the Federsarti (the Italian tailors union in Rome) to meet Oxxford's needs.[52] Italian Americans in Chicago involved with ACIM also recommended their friends and relatives.[53] As a result of those efforts, twenty-five families, fifty-six people in total, arrived on ACIM-chartered flights in 1956 and 1957 to fill positions at Oxxford.[54] ACIM continued to help dozens more Italian tailors and their families immigrate and work at Oxxford Clothing Company through 1965 as first preference immigrants.[55]

ACIM also helped create a similar program at the Hart Schaffner & Marx clothing company, which sponsored forty-nine Italian families (filling sixty positions) in Chicago under the RRA. Again, the Italian tailors worked out well, and in 1956 the company asked ACIM–Chicago to help it find and hire 150 more qualified tailors from Italy.[56] Surviving ACIM records for the forty-nine Italian families who initially went to work for Hart Schaffner & Marx allow us to better understand who ACIM placed in occupational programs and the nature of their migration. Five families were living in refugee camps in Rome at the time of their immigration and were considered displaced persons or refugees originally hailing from Italian-Yugoslavian border regions, Romania, or Greece. One family was displaced from its former colonial residence in Libya and had been temporarily living in Taranto, Sicily, before relocating to Chicago. Only one family was of northern Italian origin. The remaining forty-two families emigrated from provinces in central and southern Italy.[57]

Records from the Hart Schaffner & Marx project also shed light on family composition and resettlement patterns for migrants entering the country under the RRA. Nine of the immigrating families destined for Hart Schaffner & Marx had family in Chicago that helped assist in their family's resettlement. That left forty other families who did not have any ties to the Chicago area, demonstrating again that ACIM used large-scale occupational programs of this kind to try to give migrants without established support networks an advantage as they entered the country. Fifteen families immigrated as husband and wife units, ten of those with children. When children accompanied their parents, their ages ranged from two to twenty, with the majority traveling as teenagers. ACIM members helped spouses and older children find local employment along with the primary migrant. But eight men and twenty-seven women (most in their twenties and thirties) emigrated without spouses.[58]

The large proportion of women as the primary migrant in this sample is particularly interesting (and also reflected in a snapshot of the Oxxford Clothing Company cases). The women were either single or married, but five of the twenty-seven women who traveled without spouses brought one to three children with them, which would suggest at least some of the women intended to reconstruct their families at some point in the future in the United States.[59] While it was common in earlier periods for one wage earner to migrate first, establish conditions for family migration, and then send for the remaining family members, it was almost always a male head of household that preceded women and children. Scholars have observed the reverse by midcentury. One of the truly liberal aspects of the McCarran-Walter Act was the enaction of gender-neutral immigration policies.[60] From 1952 forward, female migrants, who had previously been dependent on a male head of household as a primary sponsor, could now call for their spouses and children to join them in their own right. This change created opportunities for migrant families with female heads of household who could claim American citizenship through their own birth or through a derivative claim, for families with relatives in the United States to sponsor migrants through a female line, and for skilled female workers. The relatively high pay earned by female tailors afforded them a new degree of authority within their households—either in the United States or in a transnational context. The result was that, through a combination of changes in American immigration laws and global labor markets, for the first time in the history of Italian immigration to the United States, significant numbers of Italian women were responsible for securing their family's economic livelihood, managing transnational finances, establishing homes abroad, and negotiating interactions with foreign states.[61]

Data taken from one of ACIM–Chicago's monthly reports for the Tailors Project also show how material aid was provided to migrants entering through ACIM-orchestrated occupational programs. During one single month in 1956, ACIM's Chicago chapter helped to resettle twenty-one people, including four families and six single migrants. Resettlement aid began on the day of the refugee arrivals, when ACIM members secured lodging for newcomers at a local YMCA. The next day, various members of the chapter helped each family get settled in prearranged homes or apartments. One family of three—a husband, wife, and child—were picked up by friends who were temporarily hosting the family. Within two weeks Father Luigi Donanzan of St. Michael's Church (and ACIM) found the family permanent residence in a furnished apartment near his parish. Likewise, two single men were taken to furnished rooms for rent close to St. Michael's Church. Two of the single women were taken in by an Italian American member of ACIM's Ladies Auxiliary Division. The Giachin family, a married couple, was taken in by an Italian immigrant family ACIM had helped resettled just a few months previously and who now wanted to reciprocate the favor. Within a few days, the other families were settled in a similar manner. The Vinnonas and Colonnas, both young couples, were taken to furnished apartments or rooms within days of their arrival. Priests at St. Francis Cabrini's Church had found an affordable furnished apartment for the Fonda couple and their child. The list of permanent addresses for each family accompanying the report indicates that all of the families resettled in Italian neighborhoods, many of them very close to Catholic parishes.[62]

But resettlement assistance went beyond merely securing migrants' housing. ACIM and the Italian Welfare League also issued loans to help recently arrived families pay rent during their first months in Chicago. In the aforementioned cases, ACIM paid YMCA bills for newcomers and made loans based on each family's needs. Each of the tailoring families that arrived in March 1956 received loans ranging from $10 to $375. The loans were most often earmarked for rent, utilities, and other household necessities. There was no fixed period to pay back the loans. Nor did ACIM expect to collect on every loan. As long as member donations kept the organization financially afloat, ACIM's collection was relaxed, thus allowing newcomers time to get on their feet.[63] Italian Americans also donated towels, linens, appliances, furniture, and other household goods to the Italian Welfare League, which it distributed to the tailors and their families. The process was not without complications. While many Italian Americans were generous in providing temporary or affordable housing, and in donating household necessities, there were of course limitations to generosity. In some cases, self-interest outweighed donations to fellow ethnics for Italian American apartment owners. In the case of the Traversa family, who arrived with a cohort of refugee tailors in March 1956, three apartments were promised to the family and were then lost to higher bidders before ACIM could make a down payment on the family's behalf. As a result, the family of five was forced to live at the YMCA much longer than many other families.[64]

ACIM made a conscious effort to publicize news of refugee arrivals and their smooth resettlement in Chicago. Articles and pictures of the arriving families appeared in several Chicago-area papers or the ethnic press during the years that the Refugee Relief Act was in place. Both the Chicago *Sun-Times* and the *New World* chronicled the arrival of the tailors and their families throughout 1955 and 1956. The *Dispatch* billed the program "a great success."[65] The publicity these programs received was significant. Within Italian American communities, such coverage helped Italian Americans learn about opportunities for their relatives; it also legitimized ACIM's standing as a successful ethnic advocacy group. More significantly, however, success narratives demonstrated that the RRA was being utilized by hardworking, "worthy" Italian immigrants who desperately sought entry to the United States and, once they arrived, filled key positions in the American labor market, thereby becoming contributing members of American society and helping to fuel the nation's economic growth.

Along with tailors, ACIM also orchestrated large-scale programs to bring Italian shoemakers to the United States under the RRA. Like tailors, custom shoemakers were, for a brief period, in short supply in the United States yet abundant in Italy where, again, artisanal training was still a dominant form of production. In New York City, ACIM worked with the F. DeNovellis Custom Shoe Company in 1955 and 1956 to bring twenty-seven Italian shoemakers and their families to the country. If the first installment worked out, DeNovellis pledged to sponsor twenty more before the RRA expired. Although ACIM solicited the relationship with the DeNovellis company, the president of the corporation and other executives were either Italian-born or second-generation Italian Americans who were sympathetic to the plight of Italian refugees. Workers were guaranteed eighty dollars a week and, like refugee tailors, were required to promptly join their local unions. The shoemakers hired were all male, and all but two came with their wives and children. Nearly 60 percent of the cohort was from Sicily, and most of the remaining cases originated from other regions of southern Italy.[66] In Chicago, ACIM paired with the Florsheim Shoe Company in a similar project to sponsor upward of one hundred custom and orthopedic shoemakers in 1955 and 1956. The wages and terms of employment were similar to the DeNovellis offer. Also like the DeNovellis tailors, all were male and of southern Italian origin. About half came with families, the others as single migrants, at least initially. Approximately half had relatives in Chicago who provided them with housing and ACIM found accommodations for the rest.[67]

In both programs, ACIM again worked with the CIPSU in Rome, the Giunta Cattolica per L'Emigrazione, and Italian American contacts (including ethnic businessmen and ethnic labor leaders) to locate and place refugee shoemakers in New York and Chicago.[68] As was the case with the tailor programs, ACIM's shoemakers projects gained instant notoriety in Italian and Italian American circles. Within months of its inception, Italian nationals were writing Florsheim directly for sponsorship.[69] The same went for tailors. After 1955, ACIM saw a drastic increase in applicants who claimed to be trained and experienced tailors and seamstresses. More and more immigration appeals included training certificates, resumes, letters of references from tailors, and pictures to verify a visa seeker's qualifications as a tailor. In some cases, people were so desperate to immigrate that they sent forged documents. Italians immigrated as tailors so often that from 1957 to 1960 it was standard INS policy to investigate every case of first preference Italian tailor immigration to ensure that the migrant was actually qualified as such and that he or she was actually working as a tailor after his or her arrival. The INS even tightened the definition of a tailor in 1961 to try to limit fraud and to obtain the most qualified immigrants possible.[70]

ACIM was able to create and maintain programs to help tailors and shoemakers immigrate because international market conditions worked in their favor. But immigrant-aid advocates also crafted programs that did not necessarily fill a specific occupational need in the United States. Some programs were put in place solely for the purpose of helping Italian immigrants take advantage of the RRA, to find gainful employment in the United States, and to achieve a relatively high standard of living after they had arrived. One such large-scale program that was initiated for the express purpose of helping Italian refugees provided immigrants with jobs at an Italian American–owned printing press in Connecticut. From 1953 to 1955 Charlton Press owner John Santangelo worked with ACIM to sponsor 209 cases (nearly one thousand people in total) under the RRA.[71] Santangelo had immigrated to the United States in 1923 from the small town of San Valentino in L'Abruzzo. In Santangelo's telling, he was impoverished and lacked a command of English. He worked odd jobs to save up enough money to begin his own entrepreneurial pursuits in the 1930s. More accurately, Santangelo made his

FIGURES 7A AND 7B. Documentation sent to ACIM by potential immigrants in support of their claims as "specialty tailors." Box E84, folder Maria Miciletto, and box E73, folder Maria Giacalone, ACIM–National (respectively).

living by printing and distributed bootlegged sheets of popular song lyrics for ten cents a copy (boasting the sale of seven million copies each month by 1933) before the American Society of Composers and Publishers took legal action and forced Santangelo to stop in a 1939 settlement. Santangelo nevertheless managed to parlay his profits into the establishment of Charlton Press in Derby, Connecticut. By 1950, Charlton was one of the largest letterpress printing plants in New England, with twenty satellite companies and forty-three regular publications. Sales peaked in 1954 at twelve million publications a month servicing seven hundred domestic and international distributors of song lyrics, comics, puzzle books, and magazines.[72]

Although Santangelo made his life and his fortune in the United States, Italy was never far from his consciousness. Santangelo was one of the largest single contributors to American Relief for Italy and to Boys' Town of Italy after the war. Santangelo also printed Italian-language anticommunist comics and other materials for the Vatican group Catholic Action to distribute to Italian voters in the lead up to the country's national elections in 1948. In 1955, Santangelo donated $5,000 to benefit ACIM's general operations, and in 1957 he followed up with a $10,000 donation to benefit various Italian institutions, including churches, parochial schools, religious orders, and civic organizations in his hometown and in other Italian cities.[73] Santangelo's charity toward Italy was not the only evidence of his continued connection to his homeland and the Italian people. Twice annually, totaling four months out of each year, Santangelo and his family returned to his hometown and other vacation destinations in Italy. During his time abroad, Santangelo witnessed the plight of southern Italians and decided to sponsor refugee migrations to the United States. In 1955, Santangelo promised assurances to migrating Italians he met all over the country, especially in his home region of Abruzzo, and subsequently forwarded those requests to ACIM. ACIM also initiated the placement of refugees at Santangelo's press. Because Santangelo accepted immigrants without significant skill sets or a command of English, often with large families, and those without any resources to their name, ACIM used Santangelo's sponsorship to place its most difficult refugee cases.[74] Santangelo's level of charity was unmatched by any other Italian American employer who provided job assurances to refugees in ACIM's records. Most simply did not have the means to employ hundreds or even tens of new employees. Sentiment was there, but on a much smaller scale. A typical ACIM case file reveals sponsors who drew upon connections at their own workplaces, unions, churches, social groups, and personal networks to help, at most, a handful of strangers find stable and well-paying jobs.[75]

The last of the large-scale job placement programs undertaken by ACIM on behalf of Italian immigrants in this period was the York County Farm Project. The project was hatched in 1954 by ACIM, Catholic Relief Services (CRS), the National Catholic Rural Conference (NCRC), and an Italian government agency, L'Istituto Nazionale di Credito per il Lavoro All'estero (the National Credit Institute for Workers Abroad).[76] The idea was to re-settle overpopulated people without land and employment in Italy to under-developed lands in the American South. Coordinators reasoned that the project served both foreign and domestic purposes. Italian refugees who had neither homes nor jobs would receive both, and moreover, people who currently did not own land and material property would have the opportu-nity to one day buy the land they worked and potentially achieve economic mobility otherwise unavailable to them. In the United States, immigrants would help bring industry and business to an underdeveloped and rural re-gion. They would also fill labor shortages in niche agricultural industries. The intention was to transport and resettle seventy-five southern Italian families to small parcels of land (three thousand acres in total) along the Broad River in the Piedmont region of York County, South Carolina.[77] The area was chosen for its similarity of climate to southern Italy, the availability of large tracts of cheap land, and for the proximity of local markets for sell-ing produce. After years of tobacco and cotton cultivation, considerable soil depletion had taken place in the area. However, southern Italian farmers had experience with fruit and vine cultivation in the rocky and sometimes unproductive soils of their native regions. The plan was therefore to pro-mote fig and grape cultivation by Italian refugee families from Italy with experience with rocky or infertile soils and who did not have relatives in the United States (so that they would be willing to relocate to rural South Carolina).[78]

The project was by far the most elaborate of all of ACIM's occupational programs to help refugees migrate. Planning and fundraising took more than a year. Lands had to be selected and purchased, and planners incorpo-rated the project and established a foundation in its name in order to raise start-up funds from the Italian American charitable donations and through the sale of stock to a broader audience. Organizers estimated they would need $350,000 to place the first twenty-five families with land, houses, barns, farm supplies, and other start-up equipment in an initial settlement wave and that an additional $300,000 would have to be raised to resettle the remaining fifty families. It was believed that the initial twenty-five farming families could gross $60,000 in the first year of operations and $100,000 in subsequent years. During that time, the remaining fifty families would immigrate and complete the project. Collective returns within the first ten years would be used to offset initial investments and still provide profits for the individual farming families.[79]

Almost all of the project planners' expectations proved unrealistic. Costs were underestimated and profits overestimated. Local businessmen interested in stimulating growth in the region made a number of large donations. Italian American individuals and fraternal organizations (such as the OSIA) "adopted a family" with $5,000 contributions. Catholic parishes with Italian American populations likewise raised substantial funds. But despite their efforts, promoters were nowhere near their target goal of $350,000 by the spring of 1955.[80] Although the project was billed as something more, it actually resembled a complicated sharecropping system. As a result, while ethnic and Catholic networks were able to stir up support for the project, it never gained much headway among a broader audience of investors. The final blow came when promised funds from L'Istituto Nazionale di Credito per il Lavoro All'estero failed to materialize. In the 1950s, the Italian government gave substantial contributions to similar resettlement projects directed by the Intergovernmental Committee for European Migration to relocate Italian farmers to Brazil, Chile, Venezuela, Argentina, Uruguay, and Paraguay. Unlike the United States, governments of those receiving nations actively solicited Italian immigrants in the postwar period and thus committed their own financial and logistical resources to support resettlement programs. Faced with limited resources, Italian officials decided to place their funds elsewhere.[81]

The York County Farm Project never truly materialized in full. Planners decided to go ahead with the project on a much smaller scale in the summer of 1955 when they purchased two thousand acres of land and began the resettlement of a handful of families on forty-acre plots equipped with three-bedroom homes valued at about $5,500 (all included running water, wells, baths, refrigerators, and wood-burning stoves) and farming supplies. The families that were resettled were all refugees—displaced from the transfer of northeastern lands to Yugoslavia or the floods in the Po River Valley. Each of the resettled families had no personal connections to anyone in the United States and had extremely large families. Two of the families had twelve and eight children a piece. Those atypical families would have had a great deal of trouble relocating in more expensive metropolitan areas. The families that did resettle in York County enjoyed a decent standard of living, especially compared to the conditions they left behind in Italy. They had their own land, houses, and amenities and found new opportunities for growth. They received English instruction from Father Shean of NCWC so that they might more fully integrate into the regional economy and to allow older children to venture into factory work in nearby towns. Combined household salaries earned at least two York County families enough surplus income to purchase a family vehicle.[82]

But even though the York County resettlement project ultimately fell short of its goals and had a limited impact on broader patterns of Italian immigration, it is noteworthy. It reflected religiously based ideas that migration (Italian or otherwise) was about more than geopolitical interests or the concerns of ethnic constituencies. The York County Farm Project proposed to bring "people without land to land without people" and in that spirit reflected the philosophies articulated in Pope Pius XII's 1952 message, *Exsul Familia*.[83] In that call to action, the pope endorsed the equitable distribution of the world's resources to all of God's children and, as a corollary, advocated the right of man to migrate in order to gain access to those resources (and thus support his family).[84] In that spirit, York County boosters saw the program as the manifestation of a religious mission that promoted equitable distribution of land and resources as well as the preservation of the family.[85] It also serves as an example of the alternative structure that refugee resettlement initiatives may have taken if Catholic voices had wielded more influence among Italian American immigration reform organizations in the postwar period. Since the Progressive Era, both secular reformers and Catholic lay organizations had put stock in the transformative, even assimilative, power of farm life on immigrant communities. These groups had long looked to rural resettlement programs as a means to promote upward social mobility, cultural assimilation, and humanitarian assistance.[86] More so than other occupational programs pursued by Italian American organizations in

FIGURES 8A AND 8B. York County Farm Project Brochure, 1955, box E35, American Committee on Italian Migration–National Office, New York City Records, Center for Migration Studies.

the postwar period, the York County resettlement project reflected the continuing influence of those traditions but also reminds us that those voices, more often than not, lost out to alternative visions within the immigration reform lobby.

## Creating Consumer-Citizens

Although the York County Farm Project represents something of an outlier among these projects, large-scale occupational programs sponsored by

ACIM and other aid agencies generally sought to place Italian immigrants in specialized jobs in the United States that provided immigrants, who often had few resources to their name and little formal education, with a path to upward mobility and middle-class status in the United States. The hope was that older-stock Americans would recognize the achievements of postwar Italian immigrants—even refugees who battled stigmas associated with their ethnicity and their refugee status—so that their successes would encourage changes to American immigration policies and solidify Italian Americans' own social standing. Intervention did not, however, stop there. Certainly, decent incomes would help newcomers achieve a high standard of living, but immigrant-aid groups consciously fostered the creation of "proper" homes and well-assimilated Americans in a variety of other ways as well.

Italian American and Catholic immigrant aid organizations supplied new immigrants with material donations of furniture, household materials, groceries, and clothing to help new arrivals get on their feet. ACIM and the IWL also made loans to immigrant families so they could purchase their own household goods within the first months of their arrival.[87] These donations demonstrated the material abundance available in the United States, exposed immigrants to American material culture, and encouraged newcomers to adopt consumption patterns that had become intertwined with American political and cultural identities in the postwar period.[88]

Italian American women were particularly instrumental in encouraging immigrants to adopt American standards of consumption. The IWL was primarily staffed by Italian American women who prioritized providing immigrants with resettlement assistance in the 1950s.[89] The National Conference of Catholic Women (NCCW), a subsidiary group of the NCWC, also played a large role in immigrant resettlement.[90] Finally, it was the Women's Division of each ACIM chapter that collected new and used household materials, furniture, clothing, and other materials, which they regularly distributed to immigrant families.[91] ACIM volunteers, again mostly women, also engaged in activities such as helping immigrants get their gas and electricity turned on, teaching newcomers how to properly use modern appliances that were donated, educating immigrants on installment buying, and advising them on how to make sensible purchases.[92]

Italian immigrants were generally receptive to Italian American efforts in this regard. Dozens of interviews collected from Chicago's postwar Italian immigrant community reflect the importance that newcomers assigned to their material success in the United States.[93] A quest for greater material comforts began in the immigrant's homeland. In Italy, the decision to immigrate to the United States almost always reflected the family's desire for better diets, homes, consumer goods, and opportunities for upward mobility. Although most Americans may not have perceived them as such, Italians at midcentury were rapidly becoming modern mass consumers whose behavior and lifestyles increasingly mirrored American standards of living.[94] Once in the United States, material abundance was an indication of one's success to both Italian immigrants and their Italian American counterparts. Sam Ori, who immigrated to the United States with his family at the age of twelve in 1946, remembered his family's struggle to "keep up with the Joneses."[95] Ori noted how his family felt pressure to always want more and have more, even though they lived in a predominantly Italian neighborhood. Even in ethnic neighborhoods, material acquisitiveness was a central element in defining "the American way" in the postwar period.

Italian American volunteers, especially women, also provided social aid to newcomers with the end goal of encouraging the social and political integration of Italian immigrants. Female volunteers in ACIM and the IWL visited immigrant homes where they helped teach Italian women English so they could better secure jobs and navigate American marketplaces. This service was especially important in the postwar period as fewer immigrants settled in Italian neighborhoods where one could get by with little knowledge of English. Aid workers likewise provided childcare for mothers so that they could attend English-language or citizenship classes. Volunteers from ACIM, the NCWC, and the NCCW also brought immigrant women to their local churches so that they could socialize with and learn from Italian American women in those communities.[96] The NCCW and ACIM both reasoned that if immigrants became regular members of local churches, they would socially assimilate more quickly and gain language skills and the moral education necessary for American citizenship.[97] Juvenal Marchisio believed such efforts would make newcomers "feel not alone but socially integrated and part of the community, and not strangers in an alien land."[98]

If newcomers could be shown to assimilate quickly and smoothly to American lifestyles and embrace American institutions, these organizations hoped they would buttress Italian American claims for social equality and immigration reform. So ACIM, the NCWC, and the NCCW promoted rapid nationalization for new immigrants as well. Those groups believed integration into the community around oneself was an important part of individual and community growth and benefited all the parties involved. They encouraged new immigrants to learn English, attend citizenship classes, and integrate into secular and religious communities around them. The next step was political participation. When possible, immigrant aid workers also helped aliens register with the proper authorities, sign up for naturalization classes, fill out citizenship papers, and witness naturalizations. Female volunteers were also active in encouraging new citizens to express their civic commitment to their new nation by encouraging and assisting new citizens in voting. Organization members also invited recent immigrants to discussion groups where they could be educated in political topics of interest to them—such as immigration reform and how to contact your congressional representatives.[99]

The records of ACIM–Detroit's branch for resettling refugees are particularly well-documented and illustrate the various ways Italian Americans tried to promote successful resettlement and rapid assimilation for new immigrants. One example is the aid that was given to the Veggian family, who seemed to face particular challenges on their path to success in the United States.[100] Giovanni and Concetta Veggian and their three children were from Rovigno, a northeastern Italian city that was ceded to Yugoslavia after the war. The Veggians, like thousands of other families in the region, subsequently fled their homes to claim Italian citizenship and often live in Italian refugee camps rather than stay in Yugoslavia under a communist government. The Veggians were granted immigration visas under the RRA and arrived in the United States in December 1956, but they arrived to a country where they had no personal support system to aid them. ACIM, in partnership with the NCWC and other international agencies, were instrumental in providing welfare assistance in these refugee cases. When the Veggian family arrived in Detroit, they were greeted by an ACIM member who extended the organization's services to them. The Veggians were in great need of ACIM assistance, because of their lack of a support network and because of the family's medical difficulties. Giovanni was fifty-one years old and had a history of tuberculosis. His age and condition made it difficult for him to find employment. An ACIM member with a relative in an administrative position at a local General Motors plant helped secure Giovanni a job as a janitor there. Concetta was blind in one eye and had severe arthritis. Dr. Nicola Gigante, an ACIM officer and private caregiver, provided medical care free of charge to both Concetta and Giovanni. However, even with treatment, Concetta's conditions were severe enough to keep her from securing domestic work, one of the only occupational options available to her because of her lack of linguistic and vocational skills. Therefore, ACIM also helped the Veggians' eldest son find part-time work to add to the family's income. Because of the severe economic difficulties the family faced, ACIM loaned the family over six hundred dollars during their first four months in the United States for rent, groceries, coal, gas, and appliance rentals. ACIM also secured a reduced rate on the apartment rental from the Italian American owner. Moreover, ACIM members donated a substantial amount of household goods to the family. The long list of materials received by the Veggians—including new and used mattresses, bedding, rugs, towels, a dining room set, dishes, glasses, pots and pans, a couch, two chairs, two small tables, a radio, and a sewing machine—indicate the vast amount of resources ACIM was willing to dedicate to an individual refugee family.[101]

ACIM provided social and legal assistance to the Veggians as well. ACIM members regularly visited the family and helped them write letters, make medical appointments, and apply for social security benefits. The Veggians also wanted to be reunited with their grandson, whom they took care of in Italy but who could not immigrate with them because of legalities. One of the Veggian daughters gave birth to a son in 1950. They alleged the child was the product of a rape by a Yugoslavian soldier and therefore had no parents to care for him after his mother's tuberculosis-related death in 1952. The Veggians then assumed primary care for their grandson. However, because of their grandson's illegitimate birth and the Veggians' failure to legally adopt the child, he was not granted a visa with the rest of the family and was placed in an orphanage in Genoa when refugee visas were issued to the Veggians. ACIM helped the Veggians with their grandson's immigration case. After exhausting regular channels of appeal, ACIM secured sponsorship of a private relief bill for their grandson's immigration from Michigan senator, Patrick McNamara.[102]

With ACIM's help, the Veggians overcame a number of difficulties and ultimately fared well in the United States, as did many other Italian immigrants. But ACIM was concerned that new immigrants embrace the "American way" and that their success was projected to American observers as well. ACIM went to great lengths to publicize that narrative and project an image of the Italian immigrant's fitness to American audiences. In 1956 officials in ACIM's National branch asked each chapter for information and photographs detailing refugee success stories that publicity directors could include in press releases. The request included instructions to photograph "clean-cut and presentable" immigrants in their new jobs, enjoying their new houses, learning to use American household gadgets, or engaged in English-language classes or other educational activities. ACIM's press officer also sought images that suggested newcomers' political assimilation as well, in asking for pictures of immigrants "looking on with amazement at historic buildings or other American places of interest" or attending patriotic events such as flag ceremonies.[103] Certainly the Tuiach, Giurin, and Vasari stories illustrate those efforts. So did others. For months, Chicago-based newspapers chronicled the arrival and integration of ACIM's refugee tailor and shoemaker families in their new workplaces, homes, and neighborhoods at ACIM's behest.[104] Likewise, in 1962 the *Chicago Tribune Magazine* ran a three-part series, "From Italy to Chicago: The Dramatic Success Story of our Italian-Americans," similarly noting the smooth transition from immigrant to "American" Italians had made.[105]

It was just as important to minimize bad press as it was to highlight immigrant integration. ACIM members conscientiously downplayed accounts where immigrants had more difficulty adjusting to life in the United States. The case of the Merola family, handled by ACIM's Detroit chapter, illustrates this point. Giuseppe Merola, his wife, Angelina, and their three children immigrated under the RRA in 1956. They moved to Detroit to join Giuseppe's oldest daughter from a previous marriage who had married an American soldier, Roy Jenkins, and immigrated under the War Brides Act a few years earlier. For reasons that are obscured by available records, relations between the Jenkins and Merola families broke down quickly. Despite pledges of support and housing assurances, Roy evicted his wife's family within three months of their arrival. At that point, ACIM representatives stepped in to aid the Merolas and anxiously noted in their files the need to keep the police and local media away from the family's turmoil. ACIM's Detroit chapter provided the family with free housing for six months, a temporary job for Giuseppe, and tuition-free schooling for the children at Sta. Maria's parochial school. They also supplied the family with donations of furniture, household goods, groceries, clothing, and medical care to help the Merolas get settled. Yet despite providing what ACIM caseworkers characterized as "assistance beyond their obligation," the Merolas were unable, or unwilling, to conform to ACIM's expectations. Giuseppe failed to provide for his family, and the family could not afford proper housing and other consumer goods. With a great deal of disappointment, ACIM workers ended their involvement with the Merolas by helping the family apply for public housing in the Detroit suburb of Hamtramck.[106]

The Merolas' story was not one that ACIM would publicly recount. More often than not, as the chairman of ACIM's Cleveland Chapter, Angelo Gagliardo, bragged in 1961, ACIM officials would claim that not a single immigrant they had assisted had become a public charge.[107] All of these examples suggest that ACIM considered immigrant success stories a vehicle for changing American perceptions about the desirability of Italian immigrants. When asked about recent Italian immigrants in a 1959 interview, Juvenal Marchisio highlighted newcomers' achievements and cultural assimilation to argue that more comprehensive immigration reform was now warranted. Speaking of recent Italian arrivals, he stated, "Most of them assimilated fantastically quickly. They are all employed and many have achieved a living standard not only equal to but sometimes superior to that of the average American in the community in which they settled. A great number already own automobiles, have purchased new homes, own television sets, washing machines and all other equipment which is common in the average American home."[108] Marchisio concluded that the Italian immigrant has now "earned the respect and admiration of all intelligent and understanding Americans" and that "whatever prejudice exists in the remote areas of the United States are based on ignorance of the true character of the average Italian."[109]

Certainly, Italian immigrants were not the only refugee group to be cast in such a light. There were intense public relations campaigns to help convince the American people to open the gates to Hungarian and Cuban refugees in 1956 and 1959, respectively, on the basis of those groups' ability to assimilate to American lifestyles as well. But there were several key differences between those campaigns and those showcasing the achievements of Italian refugees. Hungarian and Cuban public relations campaigns were almost entirely orchestrated by officials in the State Department and other government agencies who wanted to ensure public support for American foreign policy initiatives abroad and in using refugee entries as a weapon in the nation's Cold War arsenal. They were top-down in their structure. It was the Eisenhower administration, the Advertising Council, and large private corporations that orchestrated, funded, and executed such campaigns. There was no significant Hungarian American or Cuban American lobby with a stake in the game or a voice in the conversation (although that would change for Cuban Americans in later years).[110] But Italian Americans had motivation to get involved in public relations campaigns. They had for some time. In many respects, publicity surrounding refugee resettlement was not all that different in its origins than wartime loyalty displays or the Letters to Italy Campaign. Furthermore, Italian American resettlement programs did not originate in Washington, DC, but emerged out of ACIM offices, union halls, and churches. And in many ways, Italian Americans were among the first political actors to understand that public perceptions of refugees would be critical to keeping gates cracked open for their kin and countrymen.[111]

The fact that Italian Americans almost exclusively shaped the nature of refugee resettlement campaigns is telling in another way. In choosing to focus on resettlement initiatives in the manner that they did, a good number of Italian American immigration reformers largely accepted the premise that the success of recently arrived Italian immigrants did not just reflect individual achievements. Instead, the ability of the national or ethnic group as a whole to immigrate, adjust, and thrive as Americans was at stake. In working to ensure that new immigrants assimilated, and were thus considered a "desirable" or "fit" ethnic group by other Americans, Italian Americans were not challenging long-standing cultural assumptions about the role of race and ethnicity in American society. They were not challenging inclusionary and exclusionary aspects of American life and laws. They were only claiming that Italian ethnics—whether they be newcomers or American-born self-identifying ethnics—should be considered full members of the white, middle-class cultural mainstream. As a corollary to that logic, they believed the public would recognize that there no longer remained any legitimate rationale for restricting Italian immigration.

While Italian Americans were attempting to demonstrate the illegitimacy of the National Origins System and arguing the need for general immigration reform, their forms of resettlement assistance and assimilation programs suggest they were doing so in a fundamentally conservative way. It would therefore be a misunderstanding to merely characterize these actions as demonstrations of the boundaries of postwar liberalism. Rather, these efforts reveal a degree of political and cultural conservativism that Italian Americans, and perhaps other ethnic groups, largely embraced as they sought to redefine "whom shall we welcome" into the national fold in the years after World War II.

## The Corsi Affair

While Italian American ethnic advocacy groups ultimately helped tens of thousands of Italians immigrate to the United States under the Refugee Relief Program (RRP), many of those journeys almost did not take place. The hotly contested debates about the place of refugees and other immigrants in America did not end when the Refugee Relief Act was signed into law. In fact, liberals and conservatives continued to vie for control over the shape and the impact of the RRP throughout its duration. Italian immigrants, and their Italian American advocates, were at the center of many of those conflicts. Not even a year into the program, Italian Americans lobbied for, and secured, an amendment authorizing major reallocations of visas earmarked for Italian refugees to be transferred to relatives of American citizens (in other words, regular economic migrants).[1] The amendment was a major victory for Italian Americans and other immigration liberals who primarily saw the RRA as a tool to work around strict quota restrictions for southern and eastern European immigrations and to delegitimize the McCarran-Walter

Act in the process. The National Origins System's most ardent defenders, who only reluctantly approved the RRP from the very beginning, were incensed by what they considered to be such bold-faced actions to undermine the nation's regulatory regime and were equally determined to try to check liberals' ambitions to expand the program's reach. Those forces came to blows in 1955 when the nature of the program was once again called into question. Italian immigrants and Italian Americans took center stage in the public controversy that ensued.

The RRA allocated over two hundred thousand emergency visas for refugees and regular immigrants with relatives in the United States to immigrate outside of regular quota restrictions from 1953 to 1956. However, nearly a year after its implementation, only about twelve thousand refugee visas had actually been granted and almost forty-two thousand applicants continued to await long processing delays.[2] With the program set to expire at the end of 1956, its most passionate supporters, particularly members of religious and ethnic organizations, were especially outraged and widely criticized the program for failing to carry out the duties assigned to it. Surveying the situation at the end of 1954, liberals charged restrictionists administering the program, especially the program's director, R. W. Scott McLeod, with intentionally gutting the program from within and demanded action. Facing intense pressure from critics who demanded that the RRA be more than just a symbolic gesture to placate domestic and international audiences, the Eisenhower administration decided to recruit Edward Corsi to ostensibly reform the flawed, if not completely failing, program.[3] Corsi, a career administrator in the Republican Party, was an Italian immigrant who had long advocated for liberal immigration reforms and also enjoyed connections to Italian, Greek, and Jewish American organizations that were at the forefront of the charges that the program was being deliberately mishandled.

Corsi assumed a new position specially created by the Eisenhower administration to address problems associated with the administration of the RRA on January 1, 1955. But Corsi's tenure in office was short-lived. After only three months, Corsi was forced to step down from his post as special assistant to the State Department for refugee and migration problems. Opponents of the RRP, most notably the leading House immigration restrictionist, Francis Walter, could not abide Corsi's challenges to conservative control of the program. Walter and other defenders of the program countered liberal attacks with their own narrative, arguing that a lengthy vetting process was necessary to screen refugees and thus defend national security interests. Conservatives in Congress only agreed to the program because they conceded that refugee relief efforts were needed to address geopolitical concerns in Europe stemming from population pressures in places like Italy. But they still believed it was critical to select for the "right" type of immigrant and to guard against the entry of the "wrong" sort. This mentality was reflected in the increasingly rigorous background checks, security screenings, and liberal deportation policies that had become pro forma under their watch by the time that the RRA was constructed. Conservatives viewed the maintenance of unity as a vital component in winning the Cold War and saw political and even cultural divisions as potential opportunities for communists to exploit (which was, not unrelatedly, a similar critique offered regarding contemporary civil rights protests). Therefore, when the RRA opened immigration opportunities for tens of thousands of immigrants from diverse origins and countries with histories of authoritarian rule, many Americans believed there was cause for concern.[4] In short, it was too easy for the "wrong" type of immigrant to slip in under through the RRP.

When Corsi and the interests he represented challenged restrictionists' grip on the program, Walter and his allies in the State Department led a public assault on Corsi that included, among other critiques, fabrications that Corsi harbored communist sympathies. Those charges led to the demand that Corsi be dismissed from his post. Not wanting to make an enemy out of Walter and reflecting its ambivalence toward actually liberalizing the nation's immigration policies, the Eisenhower administration hardly came to Corsi's aid. For his part though, Corsi refused to step down quietly. In fact, Corsi counterattacked and in doing so questioned the nature and intent of the RRP, thus renewing the question of "whom we shall welcome." As a result, in the spring of 1955 the Corsi Affair focused national attention on an issue far greater than just a flawed immigration system. In the halls of Congress and in American media outlets, Americans debated not only immigration policies but also issues of identity formation and social membership. The Corsi Affair ultimately called into question the boundaries of racial and cultural inclusion for Italian Americans and a host of other "new" immigrant groups in the United States at midcentury.

*Reforming the Refugee Relief Program*

The roots of the Corsi Affair were located in the perennial debates that took place between liberals and restrictionists in the postwar period. Despite the critiques of liberal internationalists who proposed more open and flexible immigration and refugee policies as both a means to more effectively wage the Cold War in Europe (and elsewhere) and to undo the distinctly undemocratic, un-American, and racist values embodied in the National Origins System, the nation's postwar immigration and refugee policies continued to largely reflect conservative impulses. When the National Origins System was reaffirmed in 1952, liberals invested their hopes for immigration reform into the RRA, viewing it as both a mechanism to demonstrate the shortcomings of the National Origins System and an opportunity to create "side-door" channels for immigrant groups largely barred from coming to the United States through traditional quotas.

But once again conservatives, who wielded key positions in Congress, limited the impact of the RRA in the interest of protecting national security and preserving the cultural composition of the nation. Liberals had proposed legislation that would allow for over four hundred thousand refugee quotas over the next three years; restrictionists cut that number in half in the final bill. As they had in the case of the Displaced Persons Act, restrictionists were also successful in including provisions that required applicants to obtain housing and employment assurances to guarantee that they would not become public charges. Those requirements reflected public anxieties about the economic status and even the moral character of refugees. Restrictionists also fought for, and secured, extensive background checks and security screenings in an attempt to guard against the entry of political and cultural "subversives." They saw restrictive immigration policies, rigorous background screenings, and liberal deportation policies as mechanisms to guard against the infiltration of the nation and corruption of the population by political subversives (namely, communists and fascists). It was the same line of reasoning that compelled many conservatives to continue to support the maintenance of national origins quotas and other more subtle mechanisms of ethnic selection. In their minds, the maintenance of political and cultural homogeneity was a vital component of presenting a united front against communist advances.[5]

The final piece of the strategy was to lobby for the appointment Scott McLeod, a well-known immigration restrictionist and ally of conservatives in Congress, to head the RRP.[6] McLeod, a politically well-connected former member of the FBI, began his service in the Eisenhower administration as the department administrator of the Bureau of Security and Consular Affairs. In that role, he almost immediately earned the reputation of "hatchet man" for McCarthy and like-minded conservatives who sought to "clean up" the State Department after years of perceived mismanagement by the Truman administration. McLeod certainly understood his primary role to be ensuring "security" in the State Department and the nation more broadly by intensifying the nature and scope of investigations into departmental personnel. McLeod's responsibilities shifted slightly after his first year in office when a number of respected diplomats and some of his own security officers suggested that his leadership was destroying department morale, provoking anxiety among employees, and creating a general atmosphere of "fear and intimidation."[7] However, McLeod regained authority when the RRA was passed. The law's conservative architects specified that McLeod's office was to be put in charge of administering the program. McLeod's congressional allies were confident that he would bring that same obsession with security with him in his administration of the RRP. They were correct. From the start, McLeod instructed his staff in both the State Department and the Bureau of Security and Consular Affairs to meticulously scrutinize each application by conducting extensive background checks and personal investigations of refugees and their families in order to protect the nation from individuals he considered to be political and cultural subversives.[8] The end result was, as liberals would argue, a purposely slow-moving and overly burdensome program administered to impede rather than facilitate refugee immigration.

In conservatives' minds, McLeod's restrictive administration of the RRP would result in the preservation of the nation's cultural homogeneity. Administrative discretion has historically been one of the key methods governments have achieved what some scholars have referred to as "ethnic selection by subterfuge."[9] With the exception of ethnic Germans (who would not fully utilize their quota allocations), the beneficiaries of the RRA were primarily southern and eastern European immigrant groups whose entry into the United States restrictionists continued to severely limit by the McCarran-Walter Act. Realizing the implications of McLeod's administration of the program by the end of 1954, the Order Sons of Italy in America and other ethnic organizations argued that McLeod and others in charge of the program had no desire to see Italians, Greeks, Jews, and other "undesirable" groups gain access to national membership and predicted his leadership would render the program ineffectual when the program expired in 1956.[10]

McLeod's most vocal critic, congressman Emanuel Celler, launched a public assault on McLeod's administration of the program in August 1954. Citing the entry of only 2,200 refugees to date, Celler called for McLeod's ousting. His chief allegation was that McLeod's "ridiculous attitude" toward immigrants resulted in the "insist[ence] that his agents prowl around countries from whence come the D.P.s and question all and sundry concerning the character, habits, and associations of the applicant."[11] In December of that year, he called the RRP "an obstacle race of reports and investigations by a McLeod bureaucracy run riot in a mystic maze of enforcement" and characterized McLeod's administration as "insane, arbitrary, and savage."[12] Celler further asserted that the program needed to be headed by someone who was "not a mere cop" but who "appreciates the sensitive and merciful character of his position."[13] A number of prominent religious and ethnic groups who comprised the most important of the Voluntary Agencies approved to assist refugee admission and resettlement shared Celler's critique of McLeod and his criticism of the shortcomings of the Refugee Relief Act itself. They also contributed to public attacks on the program throughout 1954.[14]

With less than a vigorous record on immigration reform, Eisenhower was vulnerable to liberals' charges and was particularly open to criticism for his administration's appointment of McLeod as the program's director.[15] Although most historians note that Eisenhower genuinely supported the RRP in order to strengthen his administration's foreign policy goals in Cold War Europe, several question the depths of the administration's commitment to immigration reform more broadly.[16] In one scholar's estimation, the passage of refugee relief legislation "partially fulfilled the president's vague but repeated campaign promises to revise the [McCarran-Walter Act], without, however, the task of winning comprehensive immigration reform."[17] From this point of view, calling for refugee relief was a relatively easy way for Eisenhower to elicit favor from proponents of immigration reform, particularly influential ethnic and religious groups, but it would be flawed to interpret this action as evidence of Eisenhower's commitment to more liberal reforms in matters of immigration. Thus, Eisenhower's appointment of Scott McLeod may not have been solely a matter of avoiding conflict with restrictionists in Congress, as some scholars argue, but may suggest Eisenhower's own more limited views on liberalizing immigration and perhaps reflect his much more shallow commitment to advancing campaigns for greater equality in the United States more generally.[18]

The distinction between Eisenhower's support for the RRA and his ambivalence regarding broader immigration reform initiatives is critical for understanding his administration's decision to solicit Edward Corsi's participation in the program at the end of 1954. In many ways, there was no better choice. Corsi was a career appointee in the Republican Party having previously served as the commissioner of immigration at Ellis Island under Hoover, the director of Emergency Home Relief and then deputy commissioner of Public Welfare for New York City under the LaGuardia administration, and then headed New York State's Department of Labor under Governor Dewey.[19] He was an immigrant himself and maintained a relatively progressive record on immigration throughout his public life.[20] While serving as commissioner of immigration, he authored *In the Shadow of Liberty*, a book detailing the immigrant experience at Ellis Island and offering a pluralist vision for the incorporation of immigrants in the nation.[21] He intensified his advocacy for immigration reform at the end of World War II when he became an executive board member of the National Committee on Immigration Policy and advised a congressional subcommittee investigating American Immigration and Naturalization policy in 1948.[22] Corsi was intensely critical of Congress's decision to uphold the National Origins System in 1952 and supported the passage of the RRA but believed that the United States had an obligation to do far more for Europe's displaced peoples than it had done to date.[23]

Finally, and perhaps most significantly, Corsi enjoyed close ties to Italian American, Jewish American, and Greek American communities in New York. Corsi had a long history of leadership in New York's Italian American community. He had been a long-time member of the Order Sons of Italy in America, was a founding member and an officer on the Committee for a Just Peace with Italy, and was active in Italian American campaigns to assist in the reconstruction of southern Italy after the war.[24] In 1948, Corsi took a lead role in the Letters to Italy Campaign.[25] As New York's labor commissioner he worked closely with the Italian American Labor Council and also took part in diplomatic trips to Rome where he met with high-level Italian officials, including Premier Alcide De Gasperi and Minister of Foreign Affairs Carlo Sforza, to discuss issues related to Italian reconstruction and emigration needs.[26] Finally, Corsi helped found the American Resettlement Council for Italian Refugees, the short-lived voluntary agency that assisted in the resettlement of Italian refugees in the United States.[27] But Corsi worked closely with other American ethnic groups as well. In 1953 Corsi acted with B'nai B'rith, an international Jewish service organization and antidefamation group in the United States, to author a piece for their Freedom Pamphlets series entitled "Paths to the New World: American Immigration Yesterday, Today, and Tomorrow." In this publication, Corsi outlined the evolution of American immigration laws, argued against the historical intolerance of the nation toward immigrants, and critiqued both the National Origins System and the McCarran-Walter Act.[28] Corsi also had close relationships with Greek American community leaders, including ethnic power broker Spyros Skouras, the president of 20th Century Fox.

Corsi's sway with Italian Americans and other ethnic groups was noted as an asset in State Department discussions regarding his appointment.[29] But it soon became clear that Corsi's participation in the program was hardly ideal. Some problems stemmed from Corsi's strong personality, rogue style, and sense of self-importance. But the foremost issue was that it was unclear whether the administration actually wanted Corsi to take substantive action to reform the RRP or if it merely sought a public face that could restore legitimacy to the program and placate critics.

Corsi certainly thought he had been brought in to make changes and behaved accordingly. According to Corsi, he had been approached in December 1954 by Maxwell Rabb, President Eisenhower's advisor on minority problems, to work for the State Department to identify and address problems associated with the RRP. Corsi later recounted that while he welcomed the opportunity to reform the RRP, he told Rabb he had serious reservations about working with, or more precisely working under, Scott McLeod. Corsi had said of McLeod, "In the part of the country where I come from, [his] name was a name used to frighten babies."[30] Corsi claimed to have made it clear to Rabb in December that he would only accept the position if he had "adequate powers" to make necessary changes to the program and so long as he was not answerable to McLeod.[31] Following that meeting, Corsi received a telegram from the secretary of state, John Foster Dulles, that hardly clarified matters. The message stated that Corsi would act as a consultant who would report directly to Dulles but cautioned that the RRA "is administered by Scott McLeod and before we can make any final arrangements it would be necessary for you and him to have a meeting of the minds on that program."[32] Corsi did meet with McLeod and officially accepted the position on January 1, 1955. Yet, three days after Corsi began work, he received an official appointment from the secretary of state as the assistant administrator to the Refugee Relief Program. In other words, he would be Scott McLeod's assistant. Corsi threatened to quit, as this was the very job he specifically did not want. Several days later, Corsi's job title was officially amended to "special assistant to the secretary for refugee and immigration problems" and Dulles reaffirmed that Corsi would report directly to him.[33] Even so, Corsi's role in the department remained unclear. Confusion over Corsi's position, what authority he held, whom he reported to, or even his purpose in office all seem to suggest the Eisenhower administration's ambivalent commitment to making substantive reforms in the program. As the Corsi Affair unfolded in the spring of 1955, Corsi, and many Americans who supported him, came to believe that the administration was not truly committed to changing how the RRA was administered or to making broader reforms in national immigration policy. Rather, Corsi came to view his appointment as superficial, referring to it in one interview as a "smokescreen" or in another instance as "window dressing" made to appease critics and to seek favor from Italian, Jewish, and Greek American voters with whom he held sway.[34]

Corsi's official assignment was perhaps indicative of the administration's superficial intentions. The only specific task that Corsi seems to have been charged with was that he tour displaced persons camps, American consulates, and other Foreign Service agencies in Europe to investigate potential problems that emerged from the program's operations abroad.[35] By pointing Corsi toward faceless bureaucrats overseas and "inefficient" European officials, the administration was able to gain political points with Corsi's supporters while ignoring charges that McLeod's directives on how to

FIGURE 9. President Eisenhower and Edward Corsi, 1956. AP image.

process and evaluate applicants were the real source of impediments to the program.

Corsi was scheduled to depart for his European tour on January 24, but he was not content to sit idly by. Just days after taking office, Corsi met with representatives from several Voluntary Agencies that assisted in refugee resettlement. He heard their chief complaints and suggestions for the program's improvement. With speed and efficiency rarely associated with government bureaucrats, Corsi took action. Agency representatives commonly complained that each state had different definitions and requirements for immigrant housing and job assurances. Before he left for Europe, Corsi was able to streamline the process by getting the Department of Labor to agree to create uniform codes for assurances. Voluntary Agencies also pointed out that it could be difficult to convince individuals or companies to provide a job assurance for an immigrant when it could take upward of one year for the individual to arrive. To remedy the issue, they wanted their organizations to be able to guarantee an immigrant's general employment prospects and then help place the migrant in a specific position after he or she arrived. Corsi consulted with State Department legal advisors to push for a more liberal interpretation of the law which would allow VOLAGs rather than individuals to sponsor refugees.[36] Although an agreement had not been reached by the time he left for Europe, Corsi later commented, "Feeling grew among the voluntary agencies that for the first time there was a willingness to interpret the law in such a way that its purposes could be achieved."[37]

While Corsi's actions prompted hope in some circles, they produced anxiety in others. McLeod cautioned Corsi about the need to go slow with the program because neither public opinion nor Congress were in favor of admitting large numbers of immigrants to the country. According to Corsi, McLeod cautioned him, "Don't get excited about this program. We must go slowly. . . . Six out of seven people don't want any other foreigners in."[38] By the time Corsi departed for Europe, McLeod and restrictionists in Congress had concluded that Corsi must be reined in. Before Corsi left for his trip, McLeod warned him, "Everybody on the Hill thinks you are terrible liberal," and encouraged him to "not go overboard on this business."[39] To ensure that Corsi "not go overboard," McLeod sent two of his own staffers along with Corsi to Europe to monitor and manage his activities.

The official purpose of Corsi's trip was to discuss visa procedures and investigate the workings of the RRP with foreign governments and American Foreign Service agents so that he could make recommendations on how to improve operations. However, soon after his arrival, Corsi became disillusioned with the mission. In his mind, the tour was nothing more than a facade. He complained that twenty days was not enough time to effectively understand the workings of the RRP in DP camps, American consulates, and foreign agencies in ten different cities. Moreover, Corsi objected to the fact that he was largely confined to meeting with US consular officials and rarely met with representatives of foreign governments who actually ran DP camps, set policies, and supplied documents for applicants. So, in an attempt to make his visit more effective, Corsi took matters into his own hands. Corsi personally tried to arrange a meeting with the West German minister of refugees. Roy Wade, one of McLeod's staffers, found out, canceled the meeting, and reprimanded Corsi for exceeding his authority.[40] However,

Corsi repeatedly ignored censure and made several attempts to interact with foreign officials more directly.

Corsi was more successful in generating connections in Italy. Corsi's Italian ancestry and his connections to Italian American communities at home made him a welcome guest in Rome, and because Italian officials reached out to Corsi, State Department staffers were less effective in limiting his interactions.[41] In informal meetings, Corsi claimed to have persuaded the Italian government to reorganize immigration bureaus on the provincial level, which would allow potential immigrants to obtain necessary documents at a single center on a single visit (instead of securing various documents from one government agency or another).[42] Moreover, since one of Corsi's overall problems with the program was the lack of coordination between foreign governments, domestic officials, and potential sponsors, he also asked the Italian government to compile an occupational index of the refugees in the twenty-seven Italian camps in the country. This measure would allow refugees to be more quickly and more accurately matched with American employers. Wade was quick to criticize the proposal. He argued that the qualifications for a tailor, for example, might mean one thing to the Italian government's Labor Department and another to the US Labor Department.[43]

McLeod's staff frequently complained that Corsi overstepped his authority in sidestepping protocol for arranging meetings and in his general demeanor. In Athens, Corsi audaciously suggested to Greek officials that the government begin a public works program that mirrored New Deal programs in the United States, stating that such an undertaking would get refugees, who had been languishing in DP camps for years, working again and improve morale. On the American end, he advocated doubling the number of consular officials to handle the increased number of Greek visa applications. Wade disapproved of Corsi's suggestions, arguing that they would be unable to hire qualified personnel in that short a time, that the Greek government would be unable to handle such caseloads, and that such an act would destroy the morale of those already working on Greek cases.[44]

Another point of controversy arose between Corsi and McLeod's staff over media relations. Corsi was dissatisfied with the publicity, or lack thereof, associated with his trip. If the idea was to publicize the continuing need for refugee relief both at home and abroad, official coverage fell short of this goal.[45] Corsi argued that one of the easiest ways to stimulate the program was to mount a massive publicity campaign to remind Americans of the urgent need for refugee relief in Europe. But Corsi believed that McLeod's staff seemed to be purposely limiting press coverage of the tour. Wade later admitted that he did indeed have express instructions from McLeod to keep Corsi from making a "publicity spree" out of the trip.[46] But any obstruction from McLeod's staff did not warrant Corsi's response. To counteract what he judged to be the department's inaction, Corsi took matters into his own hands. In Athens, Corsi personally called several Greek American contacts, including Spyros Skouras, to arrange additional interviews in Greece. These independently arranged interviews were not approved by the State Department and, indeed, were highly inappropriate. Some political insiders speculated that Corsi was not just promoting the RRP but using this coverage of his tour as an opportunity to pander to New York's Greek American community in anticipation of a future political bid there. Corsi made matters worse by failing to use an official government interpreter for those interviews; instead he asked his chauffer to interpret. McLeod's staff in Europe reprimanded Corsi and cautioned him that it was inappropriate to use an unofficial representative to make public statements on behalf of a State Department official.[47]

The next incident occurred in Geneva, where Wade again reprimanded Corsi, this time for revealing "highly inappropriate" information to the Intergovernmental Committee for European Migration.[48] And lastly, in Rome, after Wade gave Corsi repeated reminders about proper protocol in responding to questions during press conferences, Corsi continued to ignore the department's instructions. As far as Corsi was concerned, only Dulles could direct him on proper protocol. Furthermore, Corsi continued to seek out additional press coverage. Corsi and Wade fought for days over the issue of calling a press conference on their second stop in Italy. Wade was the only one with the authority to call an official press conference, and since he repeatedly refused Corsi's requests, Corsi ended up arranging coverage on his own through personal contacts in the Italian press. When Wade found out, he allowed Corsi to release only a preapproved written statement. However, Corsi continued to find work-arounds to the gag order. Correspondents for *Il Progresso Italo-Americano* accompanied Corsi in Rome and on his visit to DP camps in Naples. Wade complained that Corsi allowed these reporters access to too much information and on several occasions Wade ultimately removed them.[49]

Corsi did indeed overstep his authority and behave inappropriately in Europe. What is interesting, however, is that Corsi was not officially censured or ultimately dismissed for any specific misconduct during his tour. Corsi's critics were less concerned about potential security concerns posed by Corsi's behavior than his attitude about the program itself. It was Corsi's proactive efforts to achieve substantive changes in the administration of the RRP, and his efforts to reinvigorate public support for refugee migration, that ultimately prompted restrictionists to mount an attack when Corsi returned home.

After his trip, Corsi began to compile data from his European tour, started making recommendations for reforming the administration of the program, and began an intense campaign to reinvigorate public support for refugee relief. In the weeks after his return, Corsi made numerous speeches and statements about the need to liberalize refugee and general immigration policy in the United States. He spoke to immigrant-aid organizations, such as the Immigration and Refugee Services of America and at the National Committee on Citizenship and Immigration, on the conditions of refugee centers and the cumbersome requirements that private and governmental agencies in Europe had to process in order for a refugee to emigrate. He asked these agencies to continue to pressure the government to liberalize the administration of the RRA.[50]

Corsi also began announcing elaborate and unrealistic plans to relieve the plight of European refugees. One scheme promised American subsidies for the transportation of tens of thousands of Italian and Greek refugees to the United States. Both nations suffered from a shortage of passenger shipping vessels, which slowed refugee emigration. Yet, this plan is correctly labeled a "scheme" because Corsi came up with this idea, announced it, and promoted it without so much as discussing it with others in his office and without having the resources to finance it. He defended the plan by arguing that the publicity generated by the idea would help renew interest in the program and in the plight of refugees. Another publicity project envisioned by Corsi, the Amalgamated Clothing Workers Union, and the Clothing Contractors of Greater New York proposed an elaborate public celebration along the Hudson River on the Fourth of July to welcome two hundred recently arrived Italian refugee tailors.[51]

Corsi undertook far more practical reforms as well. One of the key problems Corsi identified was a lack of coordination between foreign governments, officials in Washington, and prospective American employers. In the last few months of 1954, prospective employers of immigrants had been slowing their sponsorship of individuals. Recent experience had taught American companies that there would be an uncharacteristically long waiting period under the RRA and, in the end, the immigrant may not even come at all. Corsi hoped to reverse this trend by having the State Department and foreign governments work together to compile a census of the number and kind of skilled workers in other countries and to distribute this information to industries looking for workers. As a former labor commissioner, Corsi was uniquely positioned to reach out to labor leaders and employer representatives to find out about job availability for refugees in New York State. He began working with Italian American chapters of the Amalgamated Clothing Workers, the International Ladies' Garment Workers' Union, and the United Shoe Workers Union. Corsi and Luigi Antonini, a leader in both the Italian American Labor Council and the International Ladies' Garment Workers' Union, worked to find employment and housing sponsorship for up to five thousand Italian women to fill positions in American garment industries. Antonini had suggested this endeavor a year ago but had failed to receive support from McLeod's office.[52] Corsi also prompted Italian and Greek ethnic business leaders to organize committees among their respective ethnic communities to promote the issuance of assurances.[53]

Corsi's official report for Secretary Dulles, filed in March 1955, advocated a more liberal and sympathetic interpretation of the RRA overall, a reaffirmation of the emergency nature of the program, and specific reforms for administration of the program in Europe. He argued that at the time the law was passed, it was purposely worded in order to make a truly effective RRP all but impossible. Each potential immigrant had the formidable tasks of finding residency and employment sponsorship before their arrival, had to pass rigorous residency and security tests, and underwent investigations to determine any past communist or fascist affiliations or sympathies. If the administration actually wanted to see results, they would need substantial liberalizations to the program. He suggested that administrative machinery in the State Department needed to be tightened to eliminate excessive security checks, red tape, and bureaucratic controls, which he credited with causing the basic failure of the act in the last year and a half. Corsi recommended other reforms as well, including an overhaul of the European end of the operation. Corsi found dysfunctional refugee camps and consular agencies in European countries, particularly in West Germany and Italy. He criticized leaders who lacked initiative and energy. He lamented the lack of authority, the inability to deal with emergencies, a failure of teamwork, and a loss of morale in camps and consulates. To deal with these problems, Corsi recommended an audit of a number of sample cases to determine the existence of delays, inefficiencies, or failures by leaders and staff. He suggested that consular services be divided into those that handled regular immigration requests and those that handled refugee applications to make the process more efficient. He also advocated for new leadership in Europe and suggested that new posts be created for each country. These new positions would have the ability to centralize operations of camps, consulates, and foreign governments. Finally, he asked the president and the secretary of state to publicly reaffirm the emergency character of the program in order to expedite results and to republicize the program's needs and goals.[54]

### Ousting and Counterattack

Just as Corsi issued his formal report, opposition to his efforts reached new heights. McLeod had always resented Corsi's presence and any efforts he made to speed the issuing of refugee visas. Likewise, one of the RRA's primary architects, Congressman Francis Walter, took a personal interest in Corsi's appointment and spearheaded the campaign to push him out of office. Walter, a member of the House Un-American Activities Committee, launched a vigorous campaign in March 1955 assaulting Corsi's character and challenging his fitness for office. Walter made it clear that he considered Corsi unfit to hold any position related to immigration since he had been an outspoken critic of the nation's immigration policies. But Walter did not stop there. Despite Corsi's considerable anticommunist credentials, including his leadership in the Letters to Italy Campaign, Walter charged that Corsi had formerly belonged to "Communist-front organizations" and had told "untruths" about his history.[55] The basis for the accusations lay in Corsi's purported membership in the American Committee for Protection of Foreign-Born and the Lawyers Guild Association in the 1930s. By the

1950s both of those progressive organizations had been dubiously characterized by conservatives as "communist-front" organizations.[56]

Notwithstanding the absurdity of Walter's claims, his tactics had their intended effect with a public steeped in the political culture of the McCarthy
era. There was considerable debate in the State Department over what to
do about Corsi. Following Walter's attacks, Roderic O'Connor, John Foster
Dulles's special assistant, noted that Corsi's "connection with the program
has won us some ease from criticism and he has brought to the program a
considerable degree of drive and more liberal attitude which it has lacked
in the past."[57] O'Connor further advised the Secretary of State that "there
are definite political advantages in continuing to have Corsi with the Department in some role. These minority groups, and particularly the Italian
group, exert a great influence, particularly with elections coming on. For
all of them the matter of immigration is vitally important."[58] Yet despite the
points in his favor, Walter's weight in Washington and the stigmas associated with harboring "communist sympathizers" were formidable hurdles
for the administration to overcome. Corsi's behavior certainly did not help
either. Even Corsi's defender, O'Connor, cautioned Dulles that McLeod
ultimately considered Corsi "an uncontrollable man who has done more
harm than good."[59]

After some deliberation, Dulles met with Corsi on April 8. Corsi had
expected he and Dulles would review the official report he had made recommending reforms to the RRP. He was shocked to discover that Dulles had
called him in to ask him to step down from office. Officially, the administration took the position that Corsi's appointment had always been a temporary one—that Corsi had been assigned the task of surveying the RRP
to make recommendations on how to improve the program—and that the
task was now completed.[60] There is little indication in the records to show
that was the case. Privately, Dulles had made it clear to Corsi that in light
of Walter's accusations and his continued opposition to Corsi's participation
in the program, Congress would not grant Corsi the final security clearance
he needed to remain at his post.[61] Corsi reported that although Dulles told
him "some Congressmen [are] quite skillful in using the frailest evidence to
smear people's reputations" and that, personally, he did not believe there was
anything in Corsi's history "that would in the slightest degree impeach [his]
loyalty," the administration was ultimately unwilling to make an enemy of

Walter over the issue. Dulles reminded Corsi that the administration must "maintain friendly relations with Congress in order to obtain the appropriations and legislation necessary for the Act."[62]

Corsi, however, refused to fade away quietly. On April 12, the *New York Times* published a front-page open letter from Corsi to the secretary of state in which he attacked the administration for dismissing him and charged the administration with giving up on the RRP. In his counterattack, Corsi argued that any immigration program was doomed to failure and would continue to be "until [Dulles] and the Administration are willing to rescue it from the grips of an intolerant minority both in Congress and within the department itself which believes that in this world there are superior and inferior races."[63] Thus, Corsi put the Eisenhower administration on the defensive about both its refugee and immigration policies and expanded the nature of the debate by suggesting that matters of racial and ethnic fitness were involved as well. In his opinion, it was deep-seated racial and ethnic prejudices that were at the heart of both his ousting and systemic restrictions against the entry of "undesirable" immigrants to the country.

In the State Department's response to Corsi's charges, Dulles and the administration tried to shift the parameters of the debate back to Corsi personally. Although the administration had originally defended Corsi and claimed that he was merely being let go because his task had been completed, in the wake of Corsi's accusations department officials now argued that Corsi's performance in office had been unacceptable. Dulles countered that Corsi had attempted to usurp administrative responsibilities of the law that properly belonged to Scott McLeod. Critics in the State Department further pointed out Corsi's impulsive and unpredictable behavior on his European tour. They also cited Corsi's public appearances back home in which he gave speeches offering what they called false hopes and committing the government to "fantastic schemes which just couldn't be done under the law."[64]

But despite the administration's legitimate criticism of Corsi's job performance, Corsi, his supporters, and the media continued to present his dismissal as part of a larger battle over American immigration policies.[65] For them, the circumstances of Corsi's dismissal embodied a broader public debate about the nature of the nation's immigration policies and which immigrant groups were welcomed into the nation by the American people. Corsi and his supporters were convinced that Walter was purposefully working to undermine the intentions of the RRA and to maintain restrictions against certain "undesirable" foreign groups. Corsi charged, "[Walter] is not fighting me. He is fighting what I represent. He is fighting my liberal interpretation of the law and my contempt for the way the law has been administered in the past."[66] Corsi further alleged the primary reason he was pushed out was Walter's desire to keep the immigration of Italians, Greeks, and other beneficiaries of the law restricted. Corsi repeatedly reminded the public of Walter's record engineering racially and ethnically discriminatory immigration laws. Moreover, Walter's own remarks seemed to corroborate Corsi's charges. When asked by a reporter about Corsi's allegations, Walter was said to have contemptuously replied, "I'm not afraid of dagoes."[67] Some newspaper accounts of Walter's affront also noted that while he besmirched Corsi's ethnic origins, Walter traced his own ancestry to the oldest of Americans, including one ancestor who was a surveyor for William Penn.[68] Taken together, Corsi's forced ousting and Walter's slur against Italian Americans were powerful indications to many Americans that ethnic and racial prejudices were, in fact, central to debates about both the RRA and the nation's immigration policies more broadly.

Although Walter disputed the context and even the veracity of the statements attributed to him, many Americans believed he could, and did, characterize Corsi and his supporters in such a manner. Italian Americans and other Ellis Island immigrant groups were especially affected by Walter's alleged remarks because they believed they lived in a society where a number of people still thought of Italians as "dagoes." Although Italian Americans and other new ethnic groups could increasingly claim membership in the American mainstream by midcentury, Walter's attitude toward Italian Americans, combined with the government's tacit approval of restrictions that largely blocked widespread immigration from southern and eastern Europe, seemed to indicate that they had yet to achieve full equality with older-stock Americans. Francis Walter and his ilk periodically reminded Italian Americans of their precarious hold on full membership in the nation. Italian Americans keenly observed that in the 1951 hearings when the McCarran-Walter Act was being debated, Senator Pat McCarran expressed anxiety about the potential presence of "militant communists, Sicilian bandits, and other criminals" in the country.[69] In this way, the Corsi Affair confirmed to many interested observers that those ideas were still alive and well in some circles.

Italian American organizations were quick to come to Corsi's defense, denounce Congressman Walter, and support Corsi's allegations that racial and ethnic prejudices toward certain immigrant groups were the real issues at hand. The OSIA was outraged by Corsi's dismissal and Walter's role in the affair. The group's antidefamation committee focused on the Corsi case at their annual meeting in 1955 and concluded that "significant harm has been done not only to Edward Corsi and to the minority group of which he is a member, but also to the many other minority groups in America; that in many sections of America hate-mongers and bigots can still obtain an audience; and that deep seated prejudices based upon national background, religion, and race still control the thinking of many misguided but responsible Americans."[70] The OSIA lobbied President Eisenhower to reinstate Corsi and urged the president to follow through on the reforms Corsi had begun.[71] George Spatuzza, supreme venerable of the OSIA, likewise wrote Eisenhower imploring him to protect the RRP and fully lend the administration's support to the movement to abolish the National Origins System.[72] Members of the OSIA–Michigan Chapter warned the president that "bungling" the RRP would provide fodder for communists in Italy.[73] The OSIA then sent its report to other ethnic organizations, to the *New York Times* and other major papers, and to congressional representatives in districts with large Italian American populations. OSIA members threatened their representatives that the Corsi Affair would have a direct effect on their future political decisions.[74]

Countless other Italian American organizations responded in a similar fashion. Italian American fraternal organizations such as the Columbian League, the Knights of Columbus, and others wrote Corsi, their representative officials, and President Eisenhower protesting the recent turn of events.[75] The Columbian League of New York claimed that they had only campaigned for Eisenhower in the past because he promised to amend the McCarran-Walter Act. Since that goal now seemed more and more elusive, the league threatened to turn the 1.4 million Italian American votes in their state against Eisenhower if Corsi was not reinstated and if the administration did not take immigration reform efforts seriously.[76] Ad hoc groups also emerged in direct response to Corsi's dismissal. Most often these types of organizations were dominated by Italian American businessmen, professionals, and politicians who defended Corsi's work on behalf of Italian immigrants and other refugees.[77] And although it was probably a futile endeavor because of Walter's entrenched position in Congress, others began to organize foreign-born coalitions to work against Walter's congressional re-election in Pennsylvania.[78] One individual, Joseph Martorana, even telegrammed President Eisenhower personally, imploring him, "Won't you please stop this Italian hater now?"[79]

*Il Progresso Italo-Americano* responded to Corsi's dismissal and Walter's attacks in a front-page open letter to the congressman. The letter, claiming to represent the sentiments of the paper's editors and hundreds of thousands of readers, reprinted Walter's slur and condemned him. The letter associated Walter's remarks with the now discredited racial theories embodied in the National Origins System and the immigration act bearing Walter's name. The message called for a wholesale revision of the National Origins System, protested Corsi's unfair dismissal, and reminded the public that Italian Americans and other ethnic groups were mobilized in support of Corsi and the immigration reform movement.[80]

Although Italian American groups and individuals were among Corsi's most active supporters, others came to his aid as well. Civil rights advocate A. Philip Randolph noted the link between the Corsi Affair, unjust immigration policies in the country, and racial inequality. Randolph wrote the president, pointing out that the administration was allowing "bigots" in the country to sabotage both school desegregation initiatives and the country's immigration and refugee laws.[81] Groups like the Jewish Anti-Defamation League, the Polish American Congress, and the Citizens Committee for Revision of the McCarran-Walter Act also used the Corsi Affair to reaffirm the importance of the goal of overall immigration reform.[82] The nine largest social service agencies in the country, that assisted 90 percent of the immigration cases processed under the 1948 Displaced Persons Act and the 1953 Refugee Relief Act, also voiced their support for Corsi. These groups—including the National Catholic Welfare Conference, the National Council of the Churches of Christ in the United States, the Hebrew Immigrant Aid Society, and the Lutheran Refugee Services—met with the secretary of state in the wake of Corsi's dismissal with the hope of convincing him to reinstate Corsi and to press the administration to adopt Corsi's proposed reforms.[83] Finally, congressional liberals also offered support for Corsi and outrage over his dismissal.[84]

Corsi and his allies kept the Corsi Affair front-page news in major American newspapers, foreign-language presses, *TIME Magazine*, and on national television shows like *Face the Nation* for weeks.[85] In these outlets, Corsi's camp transformed his dismissal into a national debate about the nature of American immigration and refugee policies. One editorial in the *New York Herald Tribune* argued that Corsi's ousting was a sign that the current administration was not "earnestly or seriously concerned with facing up to refugee problems and remedying the defects of the 1952 Immigration Act."[86] On *Face the Nation*, Corsi told the American public point blank, "I don't think there is the slightest desire on the part of anybody in the State Department to liberalize the McCarran-Walter Act."[87] The charges were effective. Responding to significant public outrage, Congress called for formal hearings in April 1955. The official focus of the two week-long hearings was to investigate whether the RRP was being sabotaged from within by Scott McLeod and other officials who favored immigration restriction. However, that investigation often bled into related topics, including a broader discussion about the nature of the nation's general immigration policies and the underlying causes behind Corsi's dismissal. Immigration liberals were hopeful that these hearings would achieve reforms within the RRP and highlight the racial and ethnic intolerance that they believed undergirded the nation's unduly restrictive immigration policies.

Testimony began with McLeod, who was called upon to explain the general workings of the program and to account for its slow operation to date. McLeod spent the bulk of his testimony describing the many start-up activities his office engaged in to get the RRP off the ground. He argued that his office had to hire and train personnel in the United States and Europe, establish procedures for administering the act and working with foreign governments, and standardize internal operating procedures. In McLeod's view, those tasks naturally slowed the program's operations in the first year.[88] But while McLeod's explanations were certainly valid for justifying some of the delay in processing refugees, his testimony was not entirely convincing. The program had been fully operational for more than a year, but only 24,810 visas had been issued, while 170,523 applications were in the pipeline awaiting action.[89] Moreover, McLeod's office had also processed and refused 5,128 applications in that time.[90] The numbers suggested that the program was operating at an unnecessarily slow pace and that it had an astoundingly high rejection rate of nearly 20 percent.

Corsi had argued that McLeod's own hostility to the RRP was reflected in these numbers. He charged McLeod with personally instructing staff to proceed slowly and to perform extensive background checks on applicants in an attempt to limit the program's effectiveness. When confronted by the committee with those charges, McLeod hardly disputed them. In fact, he took pride in the restrictive nature of the program. McLeod said he was "glad about it." McLeod further added that when it came to matters of national security, he made it a point to "do my utmost to see that no subversives enter the United States, Communists, Fascists, or anything else."[91]

Although McLeod justified many of the start-up delays associated with any new program, portions of McLeod's testimony also seemed to corroborate Corsi's charges. However, on the following day, when Corsi was called to testify, he squandered much of the momentum that had been generated the previous day. Corsi did manage to repeat the now familiar allegation that McLeod was personally hostile to the program and had counseled Corsi and others in the State Department to move slowly in issuing visas. His most damning charges characterized McLeod and his top personnel as "police-trained" and said the "administration of the act is wholly dominated by the psychology of security" so that "refugees are invested to death."[92] But for the most part, Corsi focused on personal grievances about the way he had been treated rather than offering substantial critiques about the administration of the RRP. Only toward the end of his testimony, after many prompts by the examining congressmen and an emotional outburst on his part over the senators' apparent lack of sympathy for his situation, did Corsi testify about the actual workings of the program. Even then, Corsi continued to report about his personal experiences and had to be steered back on topic by committee members. By the end of the day, Corsi only levied one additional critique of the program: that it was being poorly administered in consular offices and refugee camps abroad, causing European governments to lose confidence in the program.[93]

On the third day of the hearing, Francis Walter took the stand. His contempt for both the Refugee Relief Program and Corsi was palpable. Walter began his testimony with a jab at the law itself, calling it "a phony refugee relief bill" (referring to its allowances for the entry of relatives of American citizens), and described, at length, its contentious passage by a divided Congress.[94] By characterizing the RRP as phony, Walter cast aspersions on both liberals, including Corsi, and immigrants themselves as somehow manipulating the American people into opening gates that were properly kept closed by playing on sympathy for refugees. Both he and McLeod (in previous testimony) were especially concerned that the RRA provided for the immigration of traditional migrants as well as refugees.[95] Both men cast regular economic immigrants—most of who emigrated from Italy and Greece—as somehow "sneaking in" under the guise of refugee relief. Walter drew a distinction between German refugees "who came from behind the Iron Curtain" and who represented, in his mind, "refugees in every sense of the word" and immigrants who he believed unfairly benefitted from the program.[96] He suggested that the American people's unwillingness to allow anyone other than "bona fide" refugees into the United States was responsible, at least in part, for the slow progress of the program. Thus, Walter defended McLeod's office for carefully reviewing housing and job assurances provided for immigrants so that the American people would not have to face the undue burden of providing for the welfare of new immigrants down the road. He likewise praised McLeod's security checks for keeping communists, criminals, and other "undesirables" out of the country.[97]

Both McLeod and Walter wanted to keep American gates tightly guarded to protect the nation's economic health and national security. But Walter, who arguably harbored stronger nativist sentiments than McLeod, even levied attacks on refugees and displaced persons, whom he sometimes characterized as more deserving immigrants. In offering explanations for why the RRP was moving slowly, Walter also argued that the American people felt less sympathy for refugees now than they did in previous years. In part, this change in attitude was a result of the improving economic situation in Europe. But Walter also blamed the actions of refugees themselves. He recounted that many immigrants who came to the country under the Displaced Persons Act had pledged to work as needed agricultural workers once they arrived in the United States.[98] But, more often than not, he claimed, "within a few weeks they are off to an overly populated area, where people live who speak the same language."[99] According to Walter, the American people had become "disillusioned" by DPs and refugees who had manipulated them in the past.[100] Of course, careful selection for the "right" type of immigrant could prevent such problems. Walter noted that he personally sponsored ten DPs and that "they are all doing well, and they are all Americans, and not hyphenated either."[101] Therefore, Walter's justifications to limit refugee relief also contained implicit and explicit criticisms of cultural pluralism.

Walter was no less forthcoming in his contempt for Corsi personally and Corsi's attempts to liberalize American immigration policies. Walter freely admitted that he had urged Dulles to dismiss Corsi because of his views on immigration. Walter charged Corsi with "contumacy, disdain, and contempt" for the nation's immigration laws and argued that such a person had no place administering those policies. Particularly galling to Walter was Corsi's testimony in 1952 before President Truman's Commission on Immigration, where Corsi spoke out against the National Origins System. Corsi had said that the act was "based on archaic concepts" and must be "junked entirely." Walter was likewise offended by Corsi's comparison of the National Origins System with "the same type of pathological mentality that brought the German people to destruction."[102]

These testimonies reveal that conflicting views about race and inclusion in the United States were just below the surface of debates regarding the nation's immigration and refugee policies. Certainly both Corsi's and Walter's public comments and testimonies made that clear. So did other remarks that came out of the hearings. On Corsi's first day of testimony, he frequently became agitated and was reported to have shouted at senators when he felt aggrieved.[103] He then began his second day of testimony with a sarcastic pledge "to try to keep [his] Anglo-Saxon temper under control."[104] Similarly noteworthy was the testimony of Gerald K. Smith on the final day of the hearings. Smith was a professional nativist, the founder of the America First Party, and the chairman of the National Committee to Defend the McCarran-Walter Act. Smith's very presence at the proceedings was telling. Smith was an outspoken and notorious anti-Semite, a Holocaust denier, and a white supremacist who commanded attention from the far right.[105] He appeared before the committee to argue that the RRA was nothing more than a Jewish-orchestrated tactic to destroy the McCarran-Walter Act and to "breakdown the Anglo-Saxon traditions of the country."[106] Smith further equated what he saw as the detrimental results of the RRP with racial integration and open immigration policies. This type of accusation was typical of Smith, who linked Jews with the infiltration and proliferation of communism in the United States and who also charged American Jews with manipulating African American "pawns" to achieve the demise of Anglo-American institutions.[107] Smith's testimony prompted Louis Marhoefer, a consultant to the Senate investigating committee, to remark that Smith's words reflected "the great grassroots sentiment of our people" toward immigration.[108] He went on further to remark that that sentiment was properly hostile toward refugees for "fear we're going to get another Einstein."[109] In the postwar period, Einstein had supported Wallace's progressive party, favored socialist ideas, and criticized the culture of anticommunist conformity in the United States. He also supported civil rights reforms and a pro-Israel foreign policy.[110] Marhoefer's reference thus suggested fears that refugees were racially, ethnically, and culturally foreign and that they were more likely to harbor politically threatening ideas as well.

### The Fate of the Refugee Relief Program

If such commentary revealed the true nature of the controversy, the Senate's official conclusions did not. In the end, the investigating committee determined that individuals may have been responsible for some of the program's failings and that there was certainly a conflict of authority between McLeod and Corsi. The committee did not, however, find fault with McLeod's administration of the program. Ultimately, it was the restrictionary nature of the RRA rather than McLeod's management that kept refugee immigration slow-moving.[111] But even though the committee's findings were anticlimactic, the Corsi Affair continued to resonate with the American people. The entire controversy managed to shift public opinion toward greater support for the RRP and perhaps, in the long term, swayed some in recognizing the problems generated by the National Origins System itself. In his sweeping study of the formation of American immigration policies, Aristide Zolberg notes that in 1955 and 1956 a critical shift had taken place where defenders of racial restriction increasingly found themselves on the defensive. He notes that Walter began to face heavy criticism nationally and in his own constituency and that "immigration reform had become a nonpartisan national issue, with a consensus that McCarran-Walter required revision."[112] What historians have overlooked, however, is how the Corsi Affair played no small part in highlighting to Americans the problematic role that racial prejudices continued to play in creating and administering the nation's immigration policies, to say nothing for the selection of new Americans.

Such a shift was reflected in the April 17 *New York Times* cover story, "Corsi Firing Reopens Immigration Debates." The article outlined the discriminatory clauses of the RRA and suggested thousands of applicants had been unfairly barred from entry under McLeod's watch because of racial restrictions. Furthermore, the article linked the program's failures with the racially based restrictions in the McCarran-Walter Act. The piece concluded with a condemnation of restrictionists in Congress and the State Department, warning the public that the small minority alone feared "the mongrelizing influence" immigration had on "the American bloodstream."[113] Likewise, immigrant advocacy organizations continued to capitalize on the publicity the Corsi Affair provided to step up their arguments for liberalizing both the RRP and the nation's general immigration laws. Finally, Senator Lehman and Congressman Celler, long-time proponents of immigration reform, also proposed legislation to reform the RRP and to remove Scott McLeod as the program's administrator. Reform bills proposed striking the most restrictive aspects of the current program and included several of the suggestions Corsi had made in his report to Dulles months earlier to liberalize the program.[114]

The Corsi Affair also put pressure on the Eisenhower administration to win back the support of the ethnic Americans and other liberal internationalists who had supported Corsi's position throughout the controversy.[115] One *New York Times* columnist speculated that Corsi's ousting cost the Republican Party the loyalty of hundreds of thousands of Italian Americans and other naturalized voters in New York State with relatives desiring to immigrate. The president had only narrowly won New York State in 1952 and did so with the support of that critical ethnic voting bloc.[116] Several officials in the administration were worried about the "political hot water" the administration would face in the next election.[117] So on the heels of the Corsi hearings, Eisenhower ended his virtual silence on the controversy. In a special press conference in May, Eisenhower called on Congress to take action to speed the admission of refugee immigration to the United States and to thereby reaffirm the nation's "great tradition of sanctuary."[118] He endorsed ten amendments to the RRA, which drew substantially upon the recommendations Corsi had made to Dulles in his March report.[119] The administration also decided it could not keep McLeod in charge of the program. An April 1955 memo from Maxwell Rabb to Roderic O'Connor, the special assistant to the secretary of state, reflected these sentiments. According to Rabb, "the Administration could salvage a good deal from this unfortunate Corsi affair. You can help persuade the groups concerned with immigration and minority relations that the Administration was not repudiating Corsi's liberal attitude if you would appoint an appropriate man to his spot or an equivalent spot."[120] So in May 1955, State Department officials weighed several candidates for the position—all of the proposed replacements were either Catholic or Jewish and most had long-time associations with immigrant advocacy organizations.[121] By early June, the administration had settled on Pierce Gerety, a Roman Catholic and long-time immigrant-aid advocate, as deputy administrator of the Refugee Relief Program.[122] Although McLeod remained the nominal head of the program so that the administration could save face and preserve its political alliances, Gerety had complete operational authority.[123] Thereafter, Gerety pursued "a more evenhanded administration" of the program and advocated "more sensitivity to ethnic politics" in affairs of immigration.[124]

Ultimately, the overall success of the program when it was set to end in 1956 owed a great deal to the publicity garnered from the Corsi Affair and from the public outrage produced by the controversy. For the first year and a half of the program's operation, less than 25,000 refugee visas had been issued; however, nearly all of the 214,000 available visas had been issued by the end of the program in 1956.[125] The Corsi Affair put pressure on the program's administrators to cut down on the red tape that Corsi and other liberals had complained about from the start, and several of Corsi's recommendations for internal reform were put into effect. One of the most significant of those changes was new allowances that permitted refugee resettlement agencies to make employment and housing assurances for refugees. Moreover, Congress continued to closely monitor the program and the administration's commitment to it in the following years.[126] Finally, Congress continued to debate amendments and even extensions to the program until 1957—providing opportunities for Italian Americans and other interest groups to exploit as they sought further liberalizations to the nation's immigration policies. But, if the Corsi Affair ultimately helped to usher in benefits for immigrant advocates, it also reminded Italian Americans of the upward battle their fellow ethnics (and they themselves) continued to face.

## From Refugee Relief to Family Reunification

Even in the face of opposition, as evidenced by the controversies demonstrated in the Corsi Affair, Italian American immigration reform advocates viewed the Refugee Relief Program as one of the most significant achievements advancing their cause in the postwar period. It was a major piece of legislation that challenged the National Origins System and, albeit somewhat incompletely, the racial assumptions behind it. Its passage also reflected, at least in part, the political influence that Italian Americans and other white ethnics wielded at midcentury. In practical terms, the Refugee Relief Act facilitated the entry, that in many cases had been long-awaited, of sixty thousand Italian immigrants to the United States. Many of those immigrants were bona fide refugees, but the vast majority could be more properly categorized as traditional economic migrants who were able to take advantage of side-door entry opportunities to the United States. As a result, Italian immigrants (and their Italian American relatives) garnered the most benefits of any one national group from the emergency program from 1953 to 1956.

These facts encouraged Italian American activists to continue to advocate for refugee relief legislation in the years following the end of the Refugee Relief Program. ACIM once again led the charge, lobbying first for reallocations and extensions to the program before it ended in 1956 and then for new refugee relief bills specific to Italians by the end of the decade. ACIM's leaders and members hoped their plans would, once again, facilitate Italian immigration via the side-door and further delegitimize the National Origins System in the process. Reflecting the dual impulses of their reform efforts, Italian Americans pursued a strategy here that primarily benefitted their own ethnic group specifically yet advanced at least a piecemeal attack on the National Origins System that might lead to broader immigration reform measures in the process.

In pursuing additional refugee visas for their compatriots, Italian Americans continued to argue that the problems associated with displaced persons and general overpopulation issues remained a threat to the economic and political stability of a democratic Italy. By appropriating Cold War concerns and employing anticommunist rhetoric, Italian Americans swayed even conservatives to crack open the gates to refugees and regular migrants and were also able to wield critiques against the McCarran-Walter Act in a strategic way. Refugee relief legislation suggested that the nation's current immigration laws were not adequately structured to handle real-world migration needs, contemporary refugee crises, or even the demands of constituent groups in America. Moreover, their position allowed Italian Americans to wield such critiques without having to expel the political capital that a direct assault on the McCarran-Walter Act would require. But there was a critical flaw in that strategy—namely, its shelf life. The argument that American immigration could save Italian democracy was tenuous even at its height in 1953 and garnered limited results when it was employed again in 1956 and 1957. Throughout the 1950s, the political, economic, military, and cultural links between Italy and the United States had only deepened, so much so that by the middle of the decade it was extremely unlikely that Italy might pivot toward a Soviet orbit. The somewhat dubious claims that the fate of Italian democracy lay in the hands of American gatekeepers became all but impossible for Italian Americans to sustain by the end of the decade, and their legislative efforts largely failed. An ultimately unconvincing push to provide refugee relief for Italian nationals migrating out of Tunisia in 1959 marked the last time Italian Americans made the language of anticommunism the lynchpin of their immigration reform campaigns.

By the end of the decade there was an observable shift in Italian American immigration reform campaigns. In the late 1950s and early 1960s immigration liberals, including Italian Americans, began to more forcefully advance the idea that family reunification principles provided a more moral, humanitarian, and democratic basis for which to govern immigration to the United States. Italian Americans, and other immigration liberals, had long argued that the racial, ethnic, and religious hierarchies fostered by, or at least legitimized in, the National Origins System were the central problem at hand. However, in the conservative political and social climate of the immediate postwar period, it seemed more politically expedient to emphasize the practical limitations that the National Origins System placed on American foreign policy initiatives than to mount a full-fledged liberal assault against the nation's discriminatory immigration system. Other immigration reform groups arguably took a similar position.[1] Those critiques of the National Origins System were also not uncommonly overshadowed by Italian American preoccupations with demonstrating their group's fitness for immigration and citizenship opportunities. But by the late 1950s, those tactics yielded less fruit than they had in previous years, and Italian American immigration reform advocates appeared more willing to embrace a more direct attack on the core principles behind the National Origins System.

Progressive shifts in American political culture by the end of the decade provided Italian Americans with another avenue to achieve immigration reform as the rhetoric of anticommunism failed them. One significant change came as African American activists increasingly called upon all three branches of the federal government to ensure that all citizens enjoyed the basic political, civil, and human rights to which they were entitled. Their activism ultimately challenged the American people to more critically examine their own complicity in accepting the shortcomings of democracy, and even Christianity, in virtually all aspects of American life and law. Not unrelatedly, American politics were also affected by an increasingly influential discourse on human rights that largely emerged in the international arena. The UN Charter on Human Rights, war crimes trials, decolonization struggles, atomic energy control debates, and, most significantly in terms of immigration, international concerns regarding displaced persons and refugees all compelled Americans to think more deeply about the moral foundations of certain domestic and foreign policies in the decade or so after World War II. American and Soviet rivalries for ideological legitimacy and moral authority helped to heighten awareness of human rights issues (and their violations) by American lawmakers and the public.[2]

Gradually, Italian Americans and other immigration reform advocates capitalized on these changes in America's political and social landscapes to offer a more pronounced critique of what they considered to be the racial and cultural discrimination codified in the National Origins System. But Italian Americans were motivated by a variety of forces in their turn toward a more liberal campaign for immigration reform, and those motivations need to be better understood to gain a clearer picture of both the Italian American immigration reform movement and the broader liberal reform movement. Scholars have characterized white ethnic immigration reformers as inspired by or drawing from the civil rights movement.[3] However, there may have been something more opportunistic for many Italian Americans in the way they waged their immigration reform campaigns in the 1960s.

## The Beginning of the End: Campaigns to Extend Refugee Relief, 1956 to 1960

The RRA was more beneficial to Italians than any other national group. Between 1953 and 1956, sixty thousand nonquota immigration visas were added to the approximately five thousand national origins visas allocated to Italians. The legislation helped relieve the massive backlog of immigration requests that had been coming from Italy since the end of the war. ACIM was instrumental in promoting use of the RRA for that purpose. As early as 1955 it was clear that the Italians would use all the refugee relief visas made available to them and that their quota was becoming significantly oversubscribed—by almost twenty-five thousand requests.[4]

As Italians were exhausting their share of refugee relief visas, State Department officials projected that some eighteen thousand visas allocated to Germany and Austria under the RRA would go unused. ACIM leaders began jockeying as early as 1955 for the reallocation of those unused visas for Italian and Greek immigrants.[5] Echoing their original position, activists argued that as Mediterranean countries and gateways to Western Europe, both Italy and Greece were strategically important sites where communism must continue to be contained. Advocates also reminded Americans that each country had only narrowly defeated communist encroachments with American assistance in the recent past and that both nations continued to face the challenges of "overpopulation." Finally, ACIM once again argued that by relieving population pressures in Italy and Greece via more open immigration, the United States could reduce the costly foreign aid packages currently provided to the anticommunist governments of both countries.[6]

Immigration liberals in Congress favored extensions to the RRP as a means to wage the Cold War and to liberalize immigration policies at home and generally supported ACIM's proposals.[7] As early as 1955, Senator John F. Kennedy was calling for additional Italian and Greek allotments (emergency or otherwise) so that Italy and Greece could "remain stable healthy members of the free world."[8] The major obstacle to any liberalizations in this regard continued to be Congressman Walter and other restrictionists who maintained control of key structural positions in both the House and Senate. As chairman of the House Subcommittee on the Judiciary, Walter kept most bills that would increase immigration stalled within the committee. There were a few exceptions. One notable one was a bill he proposed to provide refugee relief for a little over one hundred Basque sheepherding families in 1956 (H.R. 6888). Walter championed the obscure cause in response to Nevada ranchers who faced labor shortages in the wool industry and who had turned to Walter as their benefactor after Pat McCarran's death in 1954. With Walter blocking any other legislation, congressional liberals strategically tacked on amendments for the reallocation of unused refugee relief visas to the Sheepherders' Bill in 1956.[9]

Following its now familiar organizing strategy, ACIM did what it could to rally community support for the amendment. Marchisio directed the campaign within ACIM's internal network by instructing chapter leaders to initiate local letter-writing campaigns to their congressional representatives on behalf of proposed reallocation bills. ACIM also publicized the organization's legislative goals and appeals for support in its newsletter, the Italian-language press, and Italian-language radio programs. At the grassroots level, ACIM members, who were members of other Italian American organizations, unions, and religious lay groups, would spread the campaign through their extended networks.[10]

Despite ACIM members' vigorous campaigning for reallocation measures in the summer of 1956, the proposed legislation failed to pass in the 84th Congress. The bill squeezed through the Senate but was killed in the House. The *New York Herald Tribune* reported that Congressman Walter "refused to accept a major provision providing for redistribution of unused quotas from Western Europe among nations with small quota allowances," indicating that concerns about the national origins of the population continued to be the key issue at hand.[11] Also working against the bill's passage was that fact that the RRA still had months left before it expired at the end of the year, causing many lawmakers to feel only a limited sense of urgency to amend or extend the program.[12]

ACIM continued its efforts nevertheless. Because it was not a direct challenge to the McCarran-Walter Act, Italian Americans still considered refugee relief legislation the most viable option for extending immigration opportunities to Italians. ACIM continued to press the issue in 1957, calling upon lawmakers to take action on "pipeline" and family reunification cases. Pipeline cases were in some sense, a rebranding of the previous year's campaign. Individuals in the "pipeline" included applicants who had already been screened, processed, and approved by American officials but who did not obtain visas because the slots available to their country had already been filled. At the start of 1957, there were 24,841 Italian and 11,290 Greek pipeline cases. ACIM campaigners made the argument that it was only fair that people who had invested their time and hope in refugee migration, rather than place their names on the waiting list for regular immigration, be afforded the opportunity to immigrate that they had reasonably expected. If these cases were not allowed to proceed, applicants would have wasted up to three years and considerable effort on the process and would be placed at the end of regular immigration visa requests only to have to start their applications all over again. Moreover, because many of these cases were considered displaced persons, and therefore created special burdens for the Italian and Greek states, ACIM argued they were deserving of special consideration.[13]

But ACIM pursued another tactic as well. It also sought an extension of the RRA in 1957 based on the reunion of refugee families. Some Italians who had immigrated under the RRA chose to migrate alone and then send for their families after they got resettled in the United States. ACIM almost always urged refugees with families not to migrate alone because when their family members did follow they would have to wait for a regular immigration visa—which could be upward of ten years in Italian cases.[14] But many immigrants believed their circumstances could not justify their entire family's migration. Such was the case for Pasquale Mallimo, who decided that bringing his wife and seven young children with him when he immigrated under the RRA in 1956 would minimize his chances of achieving economic success in the United States.[15] By 1957, over eighteen thousand spouses and children of Italians who had entered the country under the RRA were now attempting to follow their loved ones but faced extremely long waiting periods because of the oversubscribed Italian quota.[16]

ACIM and other Italian American groups argued that keeping those eighteen thousand individuals separated from the breadwinner that preceded them violated the spirit of the RRA and contributed to Italian hardships. An ACIM spokesman asserted that ignoring the situation jeopardized American "leadership of the free world" and "supplied the fuel that oils the propaganda machine of the communists" abroad. ACIM leaders even used anticommunist rhetoric to indict restrictionists in their opposition to continuing assistance for refugees. One ACIM press release chided Congressman Walter that try as he might, even he "cannot pretend to find communists among these women and children" and thereby justifiably oppose their entry into the country.[17]

ACIM received support on the issues of pipeline cases and family reunification appeals from Congressman Kenneth Keating and Senator John F. Kennedy, both of whom met with Marchisio to discuss legislation they wished to propose on behalf of the Italian refugees in question.[18] Congressman Keating's bill corresponded so closely with the Italian American goals that ACIM called it "an ACIM bill."[19] Trying to control and limit the possible outcomes of such legislation, Congressman Walter also proposed a refugee relief bill but limited his support only to family reunification cases.[20] Once again, ACIM coordinated Italian American lobbying activity for the Keating and Kennedy bills in 1957. More than one hundred ACIM chapters embarked on an intense letter-writing campaign to their lawmakers in support of their legislation.[21] ACIM members also reached out to other Italian American organizations to support the cause, and ACIM leaders appeared on Italian-language radio programs to urge Italian Americans to take action.[22] Italian American activists even issued a call to action in support of those bills in an open statement the organization printed in the *New York Times*.[23] Finally, Marchisio offered testimony in congressional hearings on behalf of the proposed legislation in 1957. Marchisio again emphasized anticommunist arguments to try to sway lawmakers, arguing that the separation of refugee families only contributed to "the communists' constant barrage of criticism of the restrictions in American immigration laws."[24]

Congress did pass the legislation. In many ways the new immigration law, Public Law 85-316 (cosponsored by Walter and Kennedy), reflected Italian American political influence and could be considered a real achievement for ethnic activists. ACIM leaders certainly believed so, calling the legislation "the Italian Immigration Act of 1957" in the *Dispatch*.[25] But while Italian Americans certainly had much to celebrate, the results were slightly more mixed than ACIM leaders publicly acknowledged. Firstly, the Special Immigration Act of 1957 (as it was later called) sanctioned the reallocation of the eighteen thousand unused German and Austrian visas from the RRA to Italians, Greeks, and others with oversubscribed quotas. But with approximately twenty-five thousand Italian and eleven thousand Greek pipeline cases still active in 1957, the demands of all petitioners could not possibly be met.[26] Nor did the legislation guarantee that families separated by the RRA would be given preference and thus be reunited with family members who had preceded them. But the 1957 legislation did address Italian American arguments about negative consequences caused by the separation of families in that it also granted nonquota entrance to all first, second, and third preference visa petitioners (in other words, immediate family members of Americans or naturalized immigrants) who had registered for a visa before July 1, 1953. That aspect of the law benefitted Italians more than any other nationality. About twenty-seven thousand Italians fell under this category and would now be able to gain immediate entry as nonquota immigrants (who would not be mortgaged against their country's future quota numbers). Italians were keen to take advantage of these openings. In only the first month after the act's passage, more than one thousand immigration visas were issued to Italians.[27] So the 1957 legislation allowed the immediate immigration of those Italians who had been waiting the longest for immigration visas and thereby moved the refugee and regular immigration visa requests from 1953 to 1956 to the top of the list for the Italian quota.[28]

Both provisions of the new law reflected an acknowledgment by lawmakers that the national origins quotas often caused undue hardships for separated families (at least for European immigrants) while they waited years, in some cases, for an immigration visa. The second part of the legislation also recognized that the Italian quota was heavily oversubscribed, and in making an allowance for increasing Italian immigration, even on an ad hoc basis, it suggested that perhaps Italians did not deserve such a low annual quota. Thus, this provision offered a limited critique of the National Origins System, reflecting growing sympathy for white ethnic arguments for immigration reform or, at the very least, acknowledging the political power of white ethnic voters. Even though the law benefitted Italians more than any other group, Senator Kennedy still wrote to ACIM after its passage to reassure Italian Americans that his work on their behalf was not over.[29]

But ACIM leaders were somewhat slow to recognize important shifts taking place. ACIM initially credited the law's passage to lawmakers' recognition of the need to intervene in Italy's overpopulation crisis via refugee relief.[30] The veracity of that assumption is highly unlikely, however. By the mid-1950s, the political and economic recovery of Western Europe was well underway. Indeed, 1957 was hailed as the year of Italy's so-called economic miracle. By the time of the law's passage, the country's industrial and agricultural output increased dramatically, and its international trade soared. Furthermore, social and political stability accompanied economic growth. Italians regularly elected governments led by the Christian Democrats, and the Italian Communist Party's strength receded slightly. Finally, Italy's membership in NATO and the European Economic Community in the mid-1950s only strengthened American perceptions that Italy was indeed a stable democratic partner in Europe.[31] Beyond the improving conditions in Italy, the Cold War had become a truly global conflict by the mid-1950s, with Western Europe becoming one of the less pressing points of concern. It was far more likely that members of Congress with large "Ellis Island" constituencies—even secure lawmakers like Francis Walter—felt the need to placate Italian American voters who prioritized homeland politics, Italian immigration rights, and their own social equality in the United States in their decisions at the polls.[32]

The passage of the 1957 Immigration Act might have suggested Italian Americans would garner more success if they began to emphasize the undemocratic and inhumane aspects of the nation's immigration policies by focusing on family reunification goals and abandoned their dedication to working for special legislation for Italy based largely on anticommunist arguments. After the law's passage, the Jewish American Congress noted how both the Civil Rights Act of 1957 and this special immigration legislation reflected a recognition of some of the nation's racist and undemocratic policies and suggested the need for further reforms in that manner.[33] ACIM's leadership was undoubtedly influenced by these political shifts and soon began to emphasize the hardships of separated families as well. However, they were not yet ready to completely abandon a strategy that had worked well for them over the past decade. In 1959 and 1960, ACIM devoted a great deal of resources and energy to spearhead what turned out to be its last, and ultimately unsuccessful, push for refugee relief legislation for Italian immigrants. This last-ditch effort focused on a very specific group of migrants: Italian "refugees" from Tunisia.

Italians had been migrating to Tunisia since the mid-nineteenth century, when Italian unification and the economic policies that followed pushed many southern Italians outward in search of greater economic opportunities.[34] This trend was part of the turn of the century Italian diaspora, and Tunisia was only one of many locales where both Italian migrant workers and permanent settlers found opportunities for upward mobility.[35] Under French colonial rule, Italian migrants benefitted from policies that welcomed Italian migrants in Tunisia as residents and laborers. As a result, approximately one hundred thousand Italians called Tunisia home at the onset of World War II. Although the Italian population was increasingly born in Tunisia, scholars argue that most ethnic Italians in the colony continued to identify as Italian. On the whole, migrants and their families largely retained their Italian citizenship and resisted French initiatives that encouraged them to naturalize. Moreover, until the outbreak of World War II, they overwhelmingly lived in homogenous ethnic quarters of Tunisian cities where they frequented Italian schools, churches, hospitals, and social organizations.[36]

World War II and the decolonization movements that followed complicated life for Italians in Tunisia. As part of the wave of postwar nationalist movements, Tunisia gained independence in 1956 and a nationalist government formed under the presidency of Habib Bourguiba. Like other new regimes in the region, the government sought to reassert its own peoples' interests. As a result, the Bourguiba government tied citizenship to one's

Arabic heritage and adopted nationalization policies closely modeled on Nasser's policies in Egypt, which sought to expel foreign influences from the nation. In 1959, the government announced a policy of Tunisification that drastically curtailed property rights and employment opportunities for foreigners.[37] Under these circumstances, most of the sixty-seven thousand Italian and ten thousand French nationals still living in Tunisia were abruptly compelled to leave their homes.[38] Although some would emigrate elsewhere, most were forced to migrate to the nation where they held citizenship.

The migration of these tens of thousands of "Italian Tunisians" presented several challenges for the Italian state. Although Italy had made remarkable economic gains since the end of the war, there was still widespread unemployment or underemployment in the late 1950s, particularly in the South. The vast majority of Italians in Tunisia hailed from southern Italy and were likely to return there for lack of a better alternative.[39] But many areas in the South remained underdeveloped, had higher levels of unemployment or underemployment compared to the North, and continued to experience housing shortages. The return of tens of thousands of individuals would only exacerbate those problems, as the DC government estimated that no more than 15 percent of Italian migrants from Tunisia could expect to be absorbed by the Italian economy in 1960.[40] Even the concept of "return" in this context was problematic. Almost forty thousand of those Italians leaving Tunisia were second or third generation Tunisian-born Italians, many of whom had never set foot in Italy. The vast majority of these migrants were not returning to familial homes and personal support networks. Moreover, most Italians still living in Tunisia in the late 1950s were unskilled laborers who were hit hard by nationalization policies. The new laws contributed to their high levels of unemployment and decreased property values after independence, which meant the migrating population brought little social or financial capital with it.[41] The combination of these factors led Italian officials to believe that many of these migrants would need state assistance and would seek temporary shelter in refugee camps. In 1960, Italy still housed almost forty thousand refugees and existing camps were already filled to capacity.[42] New camps in Bari, Naples, and Puglia were thus earmarked for incoming Italian Tunisian migrants in 1959.[43]

Given the concerns coming out of Italy, the previous success of refugee relief initiatives in the United States, and the overall goals of ACIM and its partner organizations, ACIM leaders decided to take up a campaign on behalf of Italian "refugees" from Tunisia in 1959. But the campaign faced formidable challenges right from the start. First and foremost, it was highly questionable whether Italians fleeing from Tunisia actually fit American definitions of refugees, escapees, or expellees and were thus eligible for American aid. They certainly did not qualify as escapees or expellees and their qualifications for refugee status may not have been any more convincing. Italians in Tunisia were the equivalent of legal permanent resident aliens of the state, not citizens. Moreover, their Italian citizenship was not in question, nor was their legal right to migrate to Italy threatened.

But ACIM pushed American lawmakers to recognize migrants as refugees by making the case that although Italians fleeing Tunisia were not stateless persons in the technical sense of the term, they were in fact "persons forced to leave their place of usual abode" and they did not have prospects of firm resettlement elsewhere because Italy's economy would not be able to support them.[44] But one had to be more than just stateless to qualify for American assistance. To date, Americans had recognized refugees as those groups or individuals who had been persecuted, or feared the prospect of persecution, on the grounds of race, religion, or political opinion. It helped if the government persecuting such persons was communist; that was not the case in Tunisia.[45] ACIM's leaders therefore made the argument that the Tunisian government had adopted policies that had discriminated against, and indeed had persecuted, all non-Arabs on the basis of their race and religion. The sticking point in the case of Italians in Tunisia was that the potential refugees in question were not legal citizens of Tunisia and could not claim the same rights as citizens from the government. As a result, ACIM leaders lobbied American lawmakers to widen the accepted definition of *refugee* to include persons who faced persecution on the basis of their nationality as well. The argument was legally dubious and politically problematic, implying that foreign nationals held some claim to citizenship rights in the states in which they were living.[46]

To strengthen this somewhat far-fetched proposition, ACIM activists pointed out that Americans had recently opened their doors to ten thousand Dutch nationals who were compelled to leave the newly independent state of Indonesia under Sukarno's nationalist government.[47] There was, however, a key difference in these two cases. The Sukarno government's anti-Western posturing was considered far more threatening than Arab nationalism by American anticommunists who saw the geopolitical center of the Cold War in Asia as American military involvement mounted in Korea, Vietnam, and elsewhere in the region. Under such circumstances, even staunch immigration restrictionists could be swayed by anticommunist logic to adopt a more liberal position toward such "refugees." Indeed, Francis Walter cosponsored the refugee relief legislation that Congress passed on behalf of the Dutch in 1958. In the context of the Cold War, "refugees" from places like Hungary, Cuba, and Indonesia simply mattered more to Americans than Italians in Tunisia.[48]

There were other challenges as well, not least of which was the relative obscurity of the cause itself. While the Italian government was certainly concerned about the impact of the migrants on Italy, and was perhaps even more focused on carving out a position for itself in the Mediterranean as a bridge between the West and newly emerging Arab states, most Americans were either unaware of or, at best, unconcerned about the delicate issues at play in the region.[49] Indeed, the plight of Italian refugees from Tunisia was relatively unknown within many Italian American communities. Unless one had a relative affected by the situation in Tunisia or Italy, few Italian Americans were informed about the issue. ACIM's leadership even had to devote the early months of their campaign to educating Italian Americans about the issue and attempt to drum up support for the migrants within their own community.

To publicize the plight of Italian Tunisians, Juvenal Marchisio traveled to Italy and Tunisia in February 1960 to survey and report on refugee living conditions.[50] Upon Marchisio's return, ACIM published his reports in the *Dispatch*, where Marchisio informed ACIM members on the state of six refugee camps in Bari, Naples, and Puglia, where Italian refugees from Tunisia had already begun to arrive. According to his reports, the six camps were already at capacity, and while there was new construction underway for about one thousand more refugees, there were still fifty thousand or so Italians who still intended to emigrate from Tunisia. In each camp, he observed hundreds of families, regardless of their size, sheltered in single nine-by-twelve-foot rooms without running water or indoor plumbing.[51] Even the most basic supplies, such as food, clothing, and shoes, were in short supply in the camps. Marchisio also noted the lack of social services, such as vocational training or medical care, offered by either the government or private organizations at the camps. In ACIM articles, Marchisio argued to fellow ACIM members that camp environments were a humanitarian tragedy and, more importantly, that the conditions were dangerous because they created a general "inertia" and "lack of the will to work" among refugees. He suggested that these conditions might lead some camp dwellers to despair and to become permanent burdens to the state.[52] In portraying the camps in this light, ACIM leaders were making the now familiar case that such a situation created conditions where the Italian Communist Party could prey on desperate camp residents and might ultimately, in the long term, destabilize liberal democratic rule and free-market capitalism in Italy. However, this scenario seemed increasingly unlikely in 1960 to both Italian Americans and a more general audience.

*Dispatch* coverage of the Tunisian crisis also included an account of Marchisio's time in Tunisia, where he painted a picture of some fifty thousand struggling Italian nationals desperately clinging to the few assets they had left. By the time of Marchisio's visit, the Tunisian government's refusal to grant work permits to foreigners had led to long periods of unemployment for most Italians, which in turn led to the loss of businesses and residential property. As a result, almost all Italian nationals had moved into slum areas in Tunis as a last stop before emigrating elsewhere.[53] In the *Dispatch*, Marchisio lamented the "physical and moral misery [that] is beyond description" in Tunis and warned his largely Catholic audience at home that "de-Christianization" was taking place among Italian Tunisians.[54] He pointed out that economic decline among Italian Tunisian churchgoers and new state policies that he considered hostile to Christianity led to the closure of the six Catholic churches that catered to Italians in the city.[55] Herein, Marchisio attempted to incite action from religious members of ACIM, and he and other ACIM leaders tried to create a sense of affinity between Americans, who identified with a Judeo-Christian heritage, and Catholic refugees who suffered at the hands of a regime hostile to Christians.

ACIM leaders also used the *Dispatch* to print personal appeals from Italians in Tunisia for help and to recount stories of the few individuals who made it to the United States and who were now thriving.[56] They likewise sent out their standard calls to chapters to appeal to their congressperson to take action on the issue.[57] But despite several months of trying to rouse the rank and file to take action, ACIM members and other Italian American organizations that had previously supported ACIM campaigns for refugee relief failed to turn out on this issue. Only one ACIM chapter held a benefit on behalf of Italians leaving Tunisia.[58] The Italian American Labor Council sent a formal resolution to Congress denouncing racial discrimination against workers and historic residents in Tunisia, but it was the only organization in ACIM's extended network to take any kind of action on the issue.[59] For the most part, only officers in ACIM's national office and a small number of Italian Americans with relatives affected by the migration wave showed any significant interest in the campaign. The masses' lack of support for the issue is telling in many ways. It demonstrated the degree to which ACIM leaders had placed their faith in pursuing refugee relief legislation as an expedient way of attacking the National Origins System and accruing special immigration opportunities specifically for Italian immigrants. It also signaled the last breath of that strategy as the geopolitics of both Italy and the Cold War shifted and as family reunification legislation began to seem like a more viable alternative.

If ACIM leaders had difficulty convincing the rank and file of the importance of this issue, it had an even greater problem getting a broader audience to care. Leading American newspapers failed to pick up the story. Moreover, American lawmakers were notably unresponsive to ACIM appeals. ACIM held its first annual symposium in Washington, DC, in May 1959. It passed a resolution at the conference calling for Congress to pass refugee relief legislation for fifteen thousand Italians fleeing Tunisia.[60] Two hundred delegates met with President Eisenhower and Senators Keating, Pastore, and Symington to press the issue. However, it quickly became apparent that their goal was wildly unrealistic. ACIM's usual allies in Congress would only go as far as to support legislation for five thousand refugee visas—and even those bills were considered long shots by all the parties involved.[61]

Recognizing their weak position, ACIM leaders then endeavored to link their cause with World Refugee Year, declared by the United Nations in July 1959 to take place the following year. The campaign, undertaken by noncommunist members of the United Nations and NGOs concerned with migration, was an attempt to raise awareness and stimulate action on behalf of displaced persons and refugees all over the world.[62] When independent bills for Italian refugee relief failed, ACIM called on lawmakers to add Italian refugees from Tunisia into legislation passed in response to World Refugee Year.[63] But on the whole, World Refugee Year campaigns yielded only hollow gestures from the United States. Once again reflecting restrictionists' hold on immigration legislation and the White House's ambivalence on the subject, Congress paid lip service to the movement by passing legislation that allowed a meager five thousand refugees from all over the world to immigrate to the country on parole status over the next two years. Such an insignificant response from lawmakers indicated a general indifference to admitting refugees on purely humanitarian grounds.[64]

One is also struck by racial anxieties that worked against Italians in Tunisia and must be noted in the context of how Italian Americans understood the treatment of Italians in American immigration laws. If Italian Americans were still considered provisional whites or less desirable whites in some circles, identification with Italians from Tunisia surely would not help their case. Americans certainly characterized Tunisians as nonwhite, culturally foreign, and undesirable immigrants. Furthermore, nearly half of Italians fleeing Tunisia in 1960 were second or third generation Tunisian-born, raising fears about Italian and Tunisian intermarriage and cultural assimilation among those migrants. Leaders of the Italian Tunisian relief effort clearly felt the need to address such concerns. ACIM leaders selected one appeal from an Italian migrant to be widely circulated among Italian American organizations and a cohort of sympathetic lawmakers.[65] The letter chosen for distribution focused overwhelmingly on racial and cultural issues to justify why Italians in Tunisia warranted American help. In his appeal, the letter's author, Giuseppe Messina, exclaimed, "I hope to God that perhaps you will be able to help me in my human and urgent need, to enable me to go to a civilized country where racial hatred does not exist" and thus painted a picture of Italians as a persecuted minority who, because of their race and religion, suffered at the hands of a barbaric state.[66] Throughout the letter, Messina's whiteness, Christian identity, and European heritage were set off against the Arabic "race," an Islamic government, and an "uncivilized" society that callously chased Italians out because of their otherness. Marchisio found it particularly distressing that the people who "contributed heavily to the country's economy" and "built the roads, the houses, and developed trade in the stores and shops they operated" were now being forced to leave.[67] In this use of imperialist apologia, Juvenal Marchisio used the racialized discourse of settler colonialism to distinguish the merits of Italian migrants from ethnic Tunisians. In press releases and appeals to lawmakers, Marchisio noted the "industry, sobriety, and will to work" of Italians in Tunisia who, according to him, had transformed "arid desert lands into garden oases" and stood as a testament to the migrants' (racialized) ability to now make similar cultural and economic contributions to the United States.[68]

However, in their quest to assuage doubts about the desirability of Italian refugees from Tunisia, Italian American campaigners may have hurt their cause. Extending refugee relief to the former white settler colonizers of now independent states had to be weighed against the international politics of the Cold War as the United States attempted to pull developing nations like Tunisia into its orbit.[69] Marchisio and other Italian American leaders were certainly aware of such concerns. The fact that they were willing to emphasize the colonial heritage of Italians in Tunisia suggests the degree to which they believed the whiteness of this particular group was called into question. For these many reasons, the campaign for Italian Tunisian refugee relief was ACIM's biggest failure and ultimately helped convince Italian American leaders to abandon calls for refugee relief as their primary reform strategy.[70] However, the fact that they even attempted to work such a campaign is revealing. It suggested both the depths of the group's commitment to pursuing refugee relief as a reform strategy and the organization's narrow focus on securing legislation to benefit Italians specifically—even when better alternatives existed.

### Transitioning toward Family Reunification, 1958–1961

Even though Italian Americans continued to pursue emergency refugee relief for Italians, the passage of Public Law 85-316 in 1957, the family reunification principles it contained, and the tangible results of its enactment had a major impact on many Italian Americans and ushered in a turning point in the immigration reform strategies they pursued.[71] In 1958, ACIM and the IWL devoted much of their efforts to the task of helping Italians take advantage of the new legislation. Both organizations educated the public about the law, helped process applications, reopened old or dormant cases, and provided resettlement assistance for new immigrants.[72] By October 1958, about twenty thousand Italians had immigrated (and about five thousand more were soon expected) under what ACIM was now calling the Family Reunion Act of 1957.[73] Although the campaign for Italian Tunisian relief offers a notable exception, the Family Reunion Act had galvanized Italian Americans to launch an aggressive campaign for further family reunification legislation beginning in 1958.

With almost sixty-five thousand Italians waiting for immigration visas (the largest backlog for any single country at the time) and a projected waiting period upward of ten years in some cases, adopting arguments that advanced family reunification made a great deal of sense for Italian American activists—so much so that one marvels that reformers did not embrace such a tactic as their primary strategy earlier.[74] In the past, refugee relief bills had provided Italians with immigration opportunities over and above their annual quota of about five thousand or so visas they were eligible for under the National Origins System, but certainly any family reunification legislation had the potential to do the same. Indeed, the failure of Italian American organizations to accentuate family reunification claims before the end of the decade suggests the extent to which Italian Americans believed that anticommunist approaches to immigration reform would yield the most beneficial results possible for Italians in the conservative atmosphere of the immediate postwar period. But with the successes of family reunification laws in 1957, the changing politics of the Cold War at home and abroad, and a slightly more progressive political climate in the country, Italian American activists were beginning to rethink the strategies they pursued.

Following the 1957 Immigration Act, ACIM and other Italian American organizations more frequently began to speak about the need to open immigration opportunities for Italians in a somewhat new light. ACIM began to pay special attention to the plight of fourth preference immigrants (siblings and unmarried children of US citizens), whose chance for gaining entry was nothing but a "farce" according to the organization in 1958.[75] Newspaper articles, other publicity materials, and appeals to lawmakers all began to emphasize, in a heretofore unseen manner, the emotional and economic hardships of families who were separated by what they considered the country's overly restrictive immigration laws. They certainly had plenty of material with which to work. Since its inception, ACIM had been flooded with requests of all kinds from both Italians and Italian Americans asking for help in their mission to be reunited with their family members.[76] Although all types of relationships were strained by physical separations, Italian American campaign materials tended to focus on showcasing the plight of adult children who had been separated from their parents and other family members in the United States because they had reached the age of maturity (twenty-one years) before they were able to secure an immigration visa. It was not uncommon for a head of household or some other combination of family members, particularly those with limited resources who immigrated under the RRA, to come to the United States with the intention of sending for a child or children later on only to find that they had aged out of eligibility in the meantime.[77] A typical appeal publicized by ACIM included a letter from "L.C." of Brooklyn, who joined her husband and daughter in the United States "with a heavy heart" because she was forced to immigrate without her two oldest daughters. Another "L.C.," this time in Detroit, lamented her separation from her only daughter still living in Catanzaro and asked, "Why are we permitted to file applications for our loved ones only to discover that it is useless?" She continued, "I keep telling her [L.C.'s daughter] to hope and pray that some day we will be together again. I suffer loneliness and a longing to see her. Is there any hope?"[78]

By publicizing these emotional stories, ACIM's leaders were attempting to illustrate the unjust and inhumane aspects of the National Origins System that Italian Americans credited as the source of such torturous experiences. To evoke sympathy among the wider public, ACIM was strategic in the way that it portrayed family separations. In reality, most Italians waiting for immigration visas were in fact brothers or sisters of American citizens, not children. While it was possible to argue that the separation of brothers and sisters created undue burdens on families, those were not the most emotionally acute cases and surely many Americans were anxiously aware that new chain migration streams would be created through a new head of household receiving an immigration visa, so ACIM deliberately focused on a more poignant and less threatening narrative of the separation of children and parents.[79]

In these campaigns, Italian Americans were taking more direct aim at the McCarran-Walter Act than they ever had since its passage. In that regard, their attacks mirrored the actions of other liberals who were also increasingly advocating for more equitable ways of selecting for immigrants, such as occupational and familial preferences. But in other respects, these arguments were still quite narrow and ultimately self-serving. With the largest backlog of requests for fourth preference visas of any nation by far, Italians would be the primary beneficiaries of any special legislation to address the problem. Moreover, ACIM and other Italian American organizations rarely made any mention of other immigrant groups facing similar hardships. Occasionally, ACIM reminded the public and lawmakers that Greek quotas were also oversubscribed, but certainly the hardships faced by non-European immigrants were almost entirely missing from their appeals. In 1958 and 1959, ACIM did not press lawmakers to consider sweeping changes to the quota system; instead they focused on securing special legislation for Italian families waiting for fourth preference visas. Throughout 1958, lawmakers sponsored, with some regularity, dead-end bills that sought to increase the Italian quota alone to fifty thousand visas annually.[80] These early campaigns for family reunification legislation critiqued the national origins quotas that created huge backlogs for Italians but fell short of arguing that such laws were unfair and undemocratic in their treatment of various racial, ethnic, and religious groups.

The end goal of these early campaigns advocating for the principle of family reunification was to secure additional special legislation for the non-quota entry of fourth preference Italian immigrants. Attacks against the National Origins System remained largely indirect, limited, or rhetorical in 1958 and 1959. Italian American organizations put their time and resources into lobbying for legislation that would allow for the special entry of currently oversubscribed fourth preference quotas (from Italy and Greece) rather than discussing the foundations of those oversubscriptions found in the National Origins System.[81] Once again, this strategy might reflect the political efficacy of such reforms; it might also suggest, again, that Italian Americans were, on the whole, less concerned with liberalizing immigration and ensuring democratic equality for all immigrants than with securing preferential status for their own ethnic group so that they might obtain the same opportunities that older-stock whites already enjoyed. In the spring of 1959, when ACIM organized its first annual symposium to be held in Washington, DC, where ACIM leaders held an audience with President Eisenhower and leading lawmakers, ACIM passed two major resolutions: one calling for refugee relief for Italians fleeing Tunisia and the other calling for special legislation for fourth preference cases.[82] ACIM again fell short of levying a direct attack against the National Origins System itself. After meeting with ACIM representatives, Senators Keating and Pastore, along with Senator Kennedy (who was not present), made no mention of offering broad immigration reform bills but did all promise to make special fourth preference legislation a priority that year—a provision that would benefit Italians more than any other group.[83]

Several lawmakers proposed special fourth preference legislation bills in 1959 that seemed to have more traction than previous attempts. The leading bills were sponsored by Senator Keating, Senator Kennedy, and Congressman Walter—in Walter's case, in an effort to once again mitigate the effects of the more liberal bills. Italian American organizations strongly favored Senator Keating's bill, which proposed granting nonquota immigration visas to all fourth preference cases registered by the end of 1959. Under Keating's proposal, about eighty-three thousand visas would be granted, and with the most fourth preference cases by far, Italy would receive more than sixty thousand of those visas.[84] Although the bill was unlikely to pass, ACIM tirelessly campaigned on its behalf throughout the spring and summer of 1959. ACIM chapters lobbied dozens of lawmakers and engaged in a prolonged negotiation with Congressman Walter in an unlikely attempt to sway him in supporting the measure.[85] Walter, of course, considered the proposal entirely unreasonable, citing the detrimental economic impact more than eighty thousand new workers (plus the tens of thousands of close family members who would join them) would have on the American economy. He and other defenders of the National Origins System also considered the proposal a direct attack on the nation's quota laws (which it was) that would, in effect, negate their very purpose (which it would). However, it was clear that something needed to be done to appease the Italian American lobby and other immigration liberals, so Walter, in his usual style, proposed a much more limited reform bill. Walter's bill allowed for the nonquota entry of only fourth preference cases registered by the end of 1952. Only seventeen hundred Italian cases fell under that category.[86] Despite Walter's resistance, Italian Americans and other immigration liberals were able to coax out amendments to Walter's bill that included moving the cutoff for fourth preference cases to the end of 1953—bringing Italy's benefits up to about thirty-three thousand visas.[87] It was a significant achievement for the lobby and demonstrated not only its influence but the increasing willingness of Congress to support some degree of immigration reform. Walter's amended bill, which was signed into law in September 1959 (Public Law 86-363), provided special nonquota status to some fourth preference cases and close relatives of refugees still not in the United States. It also made slight amendments to the McCarran-Walter Act by expanding eligibility for second, third, and fourth preference visas.[88] ACIM hailed the legislation as "a step in the right direction" and took steps to help Italian Americans, recent immigrants, and Italians waiting for visas navigate the technical aspects of the new law.[89]

The Italian American lobby's experience with the 1959 fourth preference campaign proved to be a critical turning point. By that time, it was becoming clear to almost all participants that appeals for refugee relief (for Italy at least) no longer commanded lawmakers' concerns in ways that they had at earlier moments in the Cold War. At the same time, the passage of legislation in 1957 and 1959 suggested that members of Congress, even immigration restrictionists, were increasingly open to arguments that emphasized how family-based migrations provided a humane and economically sound way to gradually open the nation's gates to more immigrants. Indicative of that trend, Congress also quietly extended nonquota eligibility for spouses and minor children of first preference immigrants at the end of 1959.[90] In doing so, lawmakers sanctioned the reunification of first preference immigrant families and freed up visas for second and third preference immigrants to join their family members in the United States.

The ethnic lobby's pivot toward family reunification campaigns came just as congressional liberals were becoming more active in their support for broader immigration reform legislation and embracing a defense of family reunification policies as morally and politically legitimate. Over the course of the decade, there was slow-moving but growing support for more progressive political and social reforms among liberals in immigration and other arenas. Senator Lehman had first introduced an ultimately doomed but ambitious regulatory schema based on family reunification principles and occupational preferences as early as 1953.[91] By the end of the 1950s though, a small but growing number of lawmakers began to join him in seriously pursuing family reunification policies. There were several reasons for that shift. Firstly, the principle of family reunification was already built in to the nation's existing immigration policies in the practice of granting nonquota immigration visas to very close relatives of citizens and recent immigrants.

Since the concept was already accepted as a legitimate foundation for governing migration, reformers could begin to challenge the National Origins System by expanding or altering existing laws regarding family migration—first by decreasing the potency of the national origins quotas and then by eliminating them entirely. Secondly, liberals could argue the principles of family reunification offered a more humane and democratic way to govern migration. In theory, if not always in practice, there were no racial, ethnic, or religious biases that existed under its matrix, and thus liberals could proclaim to the nation, and the world, that democracy in America would once again find fuller expression in such reforms. And although it would take time to win them over, conservatives could ultimately find elements of family reunification that they would be willing to accept. After all, they tended to view the family as an entity that helped to preserve traditional morality and heteronormative economic and social structures. They also took solace in the expectation that, based on recent migration patterns and current population demographics, family reunification policies would not radically alter the racial or cultural composition of the nation.[92]

The result was that even though conservatives still opposed overall immigration reform, liberals began to at least propose family reunification–based reform legislation by the late 1950s. A bill offered by Senator Kennedy in 1959 was case in point. Although it never made it out of committee, Kennedy's proposal went beyond creating special nonquota opportunities for families separated by backlogged national quotas and became a model for future reform bills.[93] His bill proposed entirely replacing the National Origins System with "a formula based upon the blood relationship between citizens and resident aliens already here and those who seek admittance."[94] In a press release announcing the bill, Kennedy remarked on his motivations stating:

> In these days when we Americans desperately need a clear idea of our national goals and a real conception of what our society represents, it is especially important that we re-examine our immigration policies. Our basic legislation was developed under the illusion that we were a nation of separate nationalities and that our greatness required a continuation of a policy under which each nationality was compartmentalized. Such a law divides rather than unifies us. It is discriminatory against friendly nations. It is too inflexible to meet demonstrable needs. Perhaps most important, it is based upon an unnatural fear that we cannot assimilate people with different customs and different habits.[95]

Herein Kennedy articulated one of the more powerful statements in support of a pluralistic conception of the nation and color-blind citizenship of the decade. As such, the grievances immigration liberals had long held against the National Origins System were beginning to find expression in policy proposals.

Immigration liberals' arguments for family reunification got even more traction the next year as Kennedy geared up for his White House bid. In the Senate, Kennedy had clearly demonstrated his belief that liberalizing immigration was in the nation's best interest on both domestic and international levels. His leadership in this regard was particularly important as Senator Lehman, who had long championed immigration reform, retired in 1957. Kennedy was active outside of Congress as well. In 1958, he chronicled the many contributions immigrants had made to the nation throughout its history and made a case for immigration reform when he authored "A Nation of Immigrants" for the Anti-Defamation League of B'nai B'rith.[96] In that text, Kennedy offered broad appeals for reform, such as the (thereafter often quoted) statement "Immigration policy should be generous; it should be fair; it should be flexible. With such a policy we can turn to the world, and to our own past, with clean hands and a clear conscience."[97]

In what was projected to be a very close election, Kennedy needed to draw upon the support of white ethnic voters. So even while he downplayed his ethnic and religious identifications in other circles, Kennedy traded on his Catholicism and his image as a self-identifying Irish American to attract support from "Ellis-Island Americans."[98] Kennedy's platform included an immigration plank that catered to both the civil rights movement and ethnic interests. He called for the adoption of family reunification policies as a more equitable and fitting replacement to the National Origins System and pledged to put the full support of the White House behind immigration reform if elected.[99]

Although immigration reform advocacy helped to get Kennedy elected, comprehensive liberalizations to immigration laws were slow-moving early in his term. Restrictionists still occupied key positions in the House and Senate. Francis Walter and James Eastland threatened to block any White House–backed legislation that attempted to dismantle the National Origins System. Knowing he still commanded the support of white ethnics and not wanting to alienate the more conservative members of his party during a tumultuous period of civil rights protests and international threats, Kennedy let immigration reform largely fall by the wayside in 1961 and 1962.[100] But in 1961, immigration liberals, especially Italian Americans who had begun to take notice of the shift in political culture and amended their tactics accordingly, did attempt limited expansions to family reunification legislation. Importantly, they did so in a way that blended their new commitment to broad reforms based on the principles of family reunification and the particular needs of Italian Americans and Italian immigrants.

ACIM and its partners campaigned to extend Public Law 86-363 (passed in 1959), which granted special nonquota status to fourth preference cases waiting for visas before the end of 1953. Italian American organizations lobbied that the law be extended to include petitioners registered by December 31, 1955. The proposal would benefit approximately sixty-five thousand Italians and was introduced by John Pastore (the first Italian American elected to the Senate), who made immigration reform a top priority.[101] Although they did ultimately advance the notion that family reunification policies provided a more fair and democratic way to regulate immigration than National Origins System quotas in their campaign, Italian Americans also made relatively conservative arguments. In an attempt to win over restrictionists, they argued that the economy was strong enough to absorb additional newcomers and that head of household breadwinners who would immigrate under new legislation were likely to support three dependents on average and would ultimately become consumers and "serve as stimulants to the economy."[102] Italian Americans also argued that the measure would not create cultural problems. In appeals to their congressional representatives, ACIM members argued, "Because of their close relationship to the American citizen petitioners (sons, daughters, brothers, and sisters) they are among the most easily assimilated into our society."[103] Congressman Walter predictably blocked the bill, but he did propose his own "liberalizations" in an attempt to placate ethnic interests and forestall more substantive changes to immigration policies.[104] Walter's bill, which passed as Public Law 87-885 in October 1962, extended nonquota status for fourth preference cases registered before March 31, 1954 — only three months past the previous cutoff date. About sixteen thousand Italians would be able to take advantage of the amendment, which was a far cry from Italian Americans' initial goal but another "step in the right direction" as far as the lobby was concerned.[105]

It took Italian Americans time and some degree of convincing to embrace broader measures for immigration reform based on family reunification arguments. Although they were perhaps proceeding in a limited, rather tenuous fashion, by the early 1960s Italian American immigration reform activists were beginning to prioritize campaigns that embraced family reunification as the guiding principle on which to base immigration laws. These campaigns were self-serving and cautious in their nature, but they also marked the Italian American lobby's movement toward a more direct critique of the National Origins System and ultimately closer to the position of liberals who increasingly saw the principle of family reunification as a viable replacement to national origins quotas that actually expressed a more democratic and equitable conception of national membership for a number of groups in America. However, for much of the postwar period, Italian Americans adopted strategies that did not directly challenge the rules that governed American immigration. Instead, they chose to whittle away at the National Origins System's effectiveness and legitimacy by securing the passage of special immigration legislation (usually for refugees, later for extended families) that benefitted Italian immigrants.

Such a strategy suggested two phenomena at work. In primarily focusing on finding ways to increase Italian immigration to the United States, Italian Americans activists seemed rather narrowly concerned with American perceptions and attitudes toward Italians (and Italian Americans by extension). This tactic calls into question the degree to which Italian Americans were actually committed to a broader liberal movement to abolish the National Origins System. Their efforts to continue to push for refugee relief for Italians at a time when those efforts seem misplaced are particularly striking. Yet, in another respect, Italian American strategies reflected political realities. In the conservative political climate of the immediate postwar period, immigration liberals were forced to adopt sideways attacks on the National Origins System when they realized they did not have the political capital or public support to repeal it.[106] Bearing that in mind, Italian American appeals for special immigration legislation (either via refugee relief or family reunification) can also be viewed as part of a broader movement where immigration liberals devised ways to highlight the shortcomings of the McCarran-Walter Act. That goal may have been a secondary concern to many Italian American activists, falling behind their related quests to increase Italian immigration and improve their own ethnic group's social standing, but it may still have been an important goal nonetheless.

But at the end of the day, the fact that Italian Americans focused for so long on securing special legislation that narrowly benefitted Italians and that they were relatively reluctant to press the point that they were fighting for racial, ethnic, and religious equality for all immigrant groups is significant. Italian Americans seemed to use Cold War liberalism to advance their cause but were hesitant to embrace a more expansive definition of liberalism until very late in the movement. Calls for the National Origins System's abolition were almost always in the background of Italian American efforts—even as other groups, including liberals in Congress and Jewish American organizations, increasingly made a critique of the National Origins System the center of their campaigns. The disconnect between these strands of the movement perhaps suggest that the immigration reform coalition in the postwar period was not quite as united in either its tactics or its ideology as it has been understood by some scholars. Moreover, in the case of Italian Americans, we better understand just how self-interested some members of this coalition behaved. Italian Americans may have well been content to secure benefits exclusively for their ethnic group; it was only when they saw diminishing returns on their campaigns that they brought their arguments more in line with those of other immigration liberals. In the grand scheme of things, Italian Americans began to emphasize their group's struggle as part of a larger problem that had to do with fairness for all individuals or groups under the law rather late in the game. These conclusions suggest the tenuous, fleeting, and imperfect nature of the coalition that emerged in the postwar period to dismantle the National Origins System. It also confirms, as Mae Ngai suggests, that coalition members espoused a version of liberalism rooted in the liberal nationalism of the Cold War period and the continuing Eurocentrism of American society.[107] It is therefore necessary to continue to qualify the ways in which immigration reformers framed their campaigns to abolish racial, ethnic, and religious inequality in American immigration and citizenship laws. The next chapter will continue that discussion by taking a critical look at the arguments that Italian Americans commonly employed when they put their organizations' full weight behind the broad crusade to abolish the National Origins System that went into full force in the 1960s.

# SEVEN

# The End of the National Origins System
# and the Limits of White Ethnic Liberalism

In October 1963, Rena C. Trevor, a Chicago-based community activist and advocate of both women's rights and racial equality, penned an editorial entitled "The Negro Has Rights Too" for *Fra Noi*, the city's Italian American Catholic monthly.[1] In it, the author lamented what she judged to be her ethnic and religious community's ambivalence toward the civil rights movement. She argued that "it would seem illogical that any Italian Americans, who have known the humiliation of being discriminated against would practice this same discrimination against any other group of human beings. Yet this paradox exists." Surveying the state of affairs, Trevor divided Italian Americans into different categories. She observed one group who remembered their "past humiliations" by "first-class Americans" but observed that now, "instead of extending a helping hand to those who are still struggling to make the journey, they scurry to build barricades around 'their plateau' and occupy their time with hurling rocks down on those who would also climb to their place in the sun." In another almost equally disappointing group, Trevor placed those individuals who recognized parallels between themselves and African Americans and "who pride themselves on their liberal attitudes toward the civil rights cause" but who only "pay lip service to their enlightened views until they are put to a personal test. Faced with housing integration and open occupancy laws, they begin to rationalize over just how many rights the Negro should have. 'We have our rights, too' they cry. 'If we allow the Negro to move into our neighborhoods, our property values will go down.' So when all is said and done, they are willing to strike a bargain—their belief in human values in exchange for a few thousand dollars equity in their homes." Lastly, Trevor observed another group of Italian American Catholics, sadly in the minority, who drew upon both religious doctrines and their own experiences to guide their stance on civil rights. In her opinion, those Italian Americans "culled from their experiences of discrimination a fiery determination to fight this type of injustice. Moved by compassion, they not only look for equality for themselves, but for all humans who are denied their rights by those bigots who think God has smiled only on them."[2]

Many of the same divisions that Trevor observed among Italian Americans on the issue of civil rights were also present as Italian Americans simultaneously pursued a cause much more near and dear to their hearts—the abolition of the National Origins System. As Trevor's analysis suggests, Italian Americans also took issue with the National Origins System for a variety of reasons. Some who were deeply committed to racial, ethnic, and religious equality in the United States (and around the world) saw the nation's immigration laws, first and foremost, as racist, undemocratic, un-Christian— in short, a violation of the nation's liberal ideals and fundamentally un-American. Others paid lip service to racial inequality in their immigration reforms campaigns but tended to prioritize practical gains for Italians, or sometimes European immigrant groups more broadly, over more racially expansive reforms. And there were still others, who were primarily concerned with advancing the position of Italian immigrants, and Italian Americans by extension, above all else. Each of those impulses have been present in Italian Americans' postwar immigration reform campaigns to varying degrees, at different points in time, or sometimes even overlapping with one another.

By the early 1960s, liberal critiques of the National Origins System reached their ascendency within Italian American circles. Many Italian

Americans had long professed both secular and religious forms of liberalism that challenged the nation's regulatory system, but by the turn of the decade their arguments took a more central position in Italian American immigration reform campaigns. Much of that shift came with the changing political climate of the era. Piecemeal attacks on national origins quotas that came in the form of refugee relief legislation and other special measures to create cracks in the gates or side-door channels were yielding diminishing results for Italian immigrants at the same time that liberals in Congress and elsewhere more forcefully advocated family reunification schemes as an alternative to the National Origins System. By the early 1960s, civil rights demonstrations contributed to growing public support for reforms to eliminate overt expressions of racism from American laws. This slow but significant shift in public opinion helped to create the opportunities for which liberal immigration reformers had long waited. At the same time, significant openings emerged from other arenas as well. Structural changes, such as the death of Francis Walter in 1963 and gains for liberals in Congress in 1964, seemed to signal that the moment for change had arrived.[3] Finally, the fact that backlogs for immigration visas at the turn of the decade came mostly from the relatives of US citizens who hailed from Europe (even if they were from southern and eastern Europe) rather than Asia helped to assuage anxieties about the racial and cultural effects that such a change in policy might have on the nation. Faced with new political realities, immigration conservatives were becoming at least slightly more open to some of the rhetoric of family reunification. The concept of family unity was already built into the nation's immigration laws, so moving in that direction was not an altogether farfetched proposition. Moreover, conservatives put great stock in "the family" as a force necessary for promoting social order, and many even saw familial support networks as assimilative agents. Liberal reformers built off those foundations.[4]

As these critical shifts became apparent in the early 1960s, liberals in Congress, with the backing of the Kennedy White House, introduced the Hart-Celler Bill in 1963. The legislation proposed phasing out the National Origins System over a five-year period and replacing it with a preference system that favored skilled workers who filled labor shortages in the United States and the reunification of families who had been separated by the forces of international migration. It took time to navigate structural impediments in Congress and to secure public support for its passage, but the tide had clearly turned by the time President Johnson took office and the bill ultimately passed and was signed into law in October 1965. Comprehensive legislative histories of the debates surrounding the Hart-Celler Act and its ultimate passage exist. None of these studies, however, adequately understand the ways in which Italian Americans (and a number of other ethnic groups) framed their support for reform legislation during this overwhelmingly liberal, but ultimately fleeting, moment in American history.[5]

The new law signaled a striking yet, according to some analyses, incomplete expression of American liberalism.[6] Its advocates, including key ethnic and religious organizations, argued that a system of family reunification was a more humane, democratic, and practical way of controlling immigration than were current regulations. Italian Americans were a vital part of the coalition that advanced that platform—tentatively at first but with increasing vigor by the early 1960s. Part of that shift was, of course, strategic. But secular and religious liberalism had long provided an ideological foundation for mobilizing Italian American advocates of immigration reform, as Trevor's analysis of her community's political inclinations suggests. A significant shift came as voices such as Trevor's were able to rise to the foreground by the turn of the decade as reformers increasingly believed liberal ideologies could finally yield policy results and as more and more Americans were genuinely drawn to the liberal political and social advances that seemed to be happening all around them.[7] Still, more attention should be paid to the nature of the liberal arguments that Italian Americans helped to advance in the 1960s and to what those expressions signified about national membership and identity for Italian Americans.

However, even as liberal ideas and policy reforms gained potency among Italian American activists, those more conservative impulses that Trevor commented on remained present, and even significant, in shaping the ways Italian Americans framed their objections to the National Origins System, crafted their proposals for alternative plans for regulating immigration, and thought about their group's place in the nation. Italian Americans and other liberal immigration reformers built on the ideology of cultural pluralism that had developed during the interwar period and World War II era to argue for the universal nature of immigrant "gifts" or "contributions" that helped to shape the United States' political, economic, and cultural development.[8]

Narratives posited that all immigrant or ethnic groups, regardless of their racial classification or national origins, ought to be afforded fair access to immigration opportunities because they all brought unique benefits to the nation. On its surface, this rhetoric would seem to reflect liberal ideals, and historians have generally viewed it in this manner. However, a closer examination of those arguments and their application also reveals conservative elements of immigration reform—particularly when it came to boundaries of racial inclusivity and exclusivity. Even at the height of Italian American liberal advocacy for immigration reform, there were significant constraints on their idea of liberalism.[9]

### *"An Unjust, Unscientific, Discriminatory Immigration Law"*

On December 15, 1963, over five thousand Italian Americans representing more than forty organizations gathered at a rally cosponsored by ACIM and the NCWC in Chicago's McCormick Square to protest the nation's immigration policies.[10] Speaking at the rally was local Italian American community leader and immigration reform advocate Daniel Corelli, who told his fellow ethnics that they were "victims of an unjust, unscientific, discriminatory immigration law" and implored the audience to "come out of the shroud of injustice and stereotype of which our immigrant ancestors and we have been the scapegoats."[11] Here Corelli echoed a major critique that had been levied by critics of the National Origins System since its inception in the 1920s. Opponents, particularly ethnic Americans, had long viewed it as a law that represented the most unfair and undemocratic aspects of American society. In fact, ACIM's charter document listed "the revision of our immigration laws so that they will be in harmony with American and democratic concepts of racial equality" as one of its primary goals.[12] But when ACIM was established in 1952 there was little public or legislative support for the type of liberalizations to American immigration laws that members of the organization supported. However, by 1963, significant changes had taken place that encouraged Daniel Corelli and other Italian Americans to campaign for immigration reform in more liberal terms.

This shift emerged in tandem with, and in large part out of, the civil rights movement and other campaigns for liberal political and social reforms that

FIGURE 10. Signs from ACIM's immigration rally in Chicago, December 1963. ACIM–Chicago Chapter Records, folder 62 Photographs and Newspaper Clippings, Italian American Newspaper Collection, Immigration History Research Center Archives, University of Minnesota.

had gained ground in that period. As African American civil rights reformers increased their activism for racial equality in the late 1950s and early 1960s, white ethnics similarly capitalized on the heightened scrutiny Americans paid to issues of political and social equality by advancing their own proposals to achieve ethnic equality.[13] Several Italian Americans observed such a change in the national mood as the civil rights movement gained ground. One member of the OSIA testifying before Congress on behalf of the Hart-Celler immigration reform bill in 1965 commented, "I think that we have gone way beyond the thinking that we had in 1952. . . . In 1965 we live in an era where there is a greater understanding among all the peoples of the earth today, not only in matters of politics but in matters of religion, in matters of race, in matters of nationality."[14] Similarly, Mario Biaggi of the Columbia Association also commented in 1965 that "there has been a social awakening in the American mind" since the passage of the McCarran-Walter Act.[15] Thus by the early 1960s, many Italian Americans increasingly felt comfortable framing their group's history of racial or ethnic marginalization as part of a larger narrative of race-based injustice that betrayed the meaning of democracy in America.

Italian American immigration reformers also adjusted their tactics as other liberals, particularly those in Congress, reframed their attack against the National Origins System. For perhaps the first time in decades, lawmakers had proposed a viable alternative to the National Origins System. Herbert Lehman, Emanuel Celler, John F. Kennedy, and others in Congress increasingly took on the issue of immigration reform in the late 1950s by advancing the idea of family reunification legislation as a replacement to the National Origins System and a way to make American immigration policies better reflect the nation's professed democratic beliefs in fairness and equality for all peoples.[16] John F. Kennedy's election seemed to offer hope in that direction as well, and in 1963 as the Kennedy administration gradually took a more progressive stand on issues of civil rights it also put its weight behind legislation to that effect. The Hart-Celler Act (strongly endorsed by the Kennedy administration) complemented the principles of the civil rights movement and addressed the grievances long articulated by ethnic and religious groups.[17] The bill called for the gradual elimination of national origins quotas over a five-year period, abolished the Asia-Pacific Triangle entirely, and advanced regulation based on color-blind criteria of occupational preferences and the philosophy of family reunification. Altogether, the major aspects of the bill reflected the ideological reforms immigration liberals had advanced in recent years and promised, in the words of Senator Edward Kennedy, "equality and fair play for the people of all nations."[18]

It was in this context that Italian American immigration reformers similarly began shifting away from campaigns that were content with amending or chipping away at the effectiveness of the McCarran-Walter Act while still leaving national quotas intact so long as Italian immigrants benefitted. There had always been Italian Americans that had critiqued the National Origins System by arguing it was undemocratic, unfair, and discriminatory to racial, ethnic, and religious minority groups in the United States. However, their voices did not come to the forefront until the 1960s. They correspondingly endorsed family reunification legislation, reasoning that it provided a more fair and equitable way of regulating immigration that did not give preferential treatment to any one racial or ethnic group over another. Even though there were clearly elements of political opportunism reflected in this shift, as Italian immigrants stood to gain considerably under this new system, this turn also reflected the ascendancy of liberal aspects of the Italian American immigration reform lobby.

Growing Italian American collaboration with other liberal immigration reform organizations was evidence of this shift. Italian American participation in such organizations was actually quite limited before the 1960s—so much so that in 1959 at ACIM's first annual symposium, Joseph DeSerto, ACIM's Chicago Chapter chairman, felt compelled to make a speech before two hundred delegates imploring members to consider more active cooperation with other immigrant advocacy groups.[19] When Italian American immigration reformers did reach beyond their ethnic organizations, they tended to stray no further than collaborating with Catholic groups. But in the 1960s, ACIM, the OSIA, the IWL, the Italian Catholic Federation, and other Italian American organizations increasingly participated in several interethnic and/or interfaith organizations dedicated to achieving immigration reform.[20] The largest and most influential of these organizations was the American Immigration and Citizenship Conference (AICC).[21] ACIM was one of thirty-one member organizations of the AICC's predecessor, the American Immigration Conference, established in 1954, which sought "a more humane, nondiscriminatory alternative to the existing national origins quota system," but that was about the extent of ACIM's participation in the organization.[22] Throughout the 1950s, ACIM occasionally sent a delegate to attend the organization's annual meetings, but for the most part, it merely endorsed the AICC's overarching goal of amending or abolishing the National Origins System.[23] But even that participation must be qualified by the fact that ACIM's time, money, and organizing efforts generally revolved around programs and initiatives that focused primarily on increasing immigration opportunities for Italians during the 1950s. The AICC had called for family reunification laws, a complete elimination of all national or racial quotas, and other major amendments to the McCarran-Walter Act by 1958, but it was not until about 1962 that ACIM priorities came closer in line with those of the AICC.[24] It was only by the mid-1960s that ACIM began to focus its efforts on pressuring lawmakers to support immigration laws in line with the nation's "humanitarian traditions" and "democratic professions" as the AICC had advised.[25]

As a result of this shift, Italian American immigration activists were among those who endorsed family reunification legislation in the 1960s. Some of their arguments were familiar. For example, Italian Americans were already comfortable with the language of Cold War liberalism. In their earlier campaigns to secure special legislation for Italian immigrants and in their more recent expressions of support for broad-based immigration reforms, activists highlighted the link between racial equality in the nation's immigration policies and American Cold War foreign policy concerns. As Congress debated the Hart-Celler Bill in 1964 and again in 1965, Juvenal Marchisio echoed President Kennedy's remarks when he reminded Congress that the country needed an immigration policy "that will permit us to look at the whole world with clean hands and a clear conscience." He added that the country's current laws reflected the "timid and isolationist attitude of the 1920s" and were "as out of date as a model 'T' Ford."[26] A decade earlier, such a statement might have been used to explain why the Italian Communist Party remained a potent force in Italy. But by 1964, Marchisio and other Italian Americans applied their arguments more broadly. They increasingly echoed other liberals or civil rights reformers who likewise argued that racist policies, laws, and accepted social practices were incompatible with American definitions of democracy and American efforts to cultivate political, military, and economic alliances around the world.[27]

But Marchisio went beyond expressions of Cold War liberalism in his 1964 and 1965 appeals. ACIM's leader spoke in a fashion that organization had generally shied away from in the previous decade when he rebuked American lawmakers for their general complacency with the National Origins System by arguing, "The conscience of a nation is not just a collection of the prejudices and attitudes of its citizens. The conscience of a nation is also the reservoir of its ideals and the mirror of its aspirations." Marchisio further challenged Congress to adopt reforms that "would help free us from the implication of superiority or inferiority of peoples" and create changes so that "our basic migration law may be more in harmony and conformity with our American principles of racial equality."[28] In another departure from what one might have expected a decade ago, Joseph Errigo (OSIA) also employed much more progressive rhetoric in his 1965 congressional testimony. Errigo told the committee, "We ask for justice for all people. We ask that all potential immigrants be granted equal opportunity to prove their qualifications to enter this country."[29] In an appeal to Senator Dirksen of Illinois to support the Hart-Celler Bill, George Spatuzza, the national leader of the OSIA, similarly proclaimed, "Our beloved country, the champion of democracy, should not and must not sanction discrimination."[30]

Testimony of this nature reflected the culmination of a turn in ACIM's tone and legislative priorities in recent years. At ACIM's Second Annual Symposium held in Rome in 1961, speakers (coming from secular and religious perspectives) emphasized the need for fairness and equality for all peoples. Father Caesar Donanzan reminded delegates that ACIM's work had always reflected "the ambition to help bring about in our country an immigration policy that reflects the heart of America, its professed principles of racial equality and a living showcase of democracy in action."[31] Delegates then adopted and sent to Congress a resolution emphasizing the nation's founding creed that "all men are created equal" regardless of their "race, color, religion, or national origin."[32] ACIM's next symposium, which took place in Washington, DC, in 1963, reflected the same sentiments. Donanzan's remarks that year lamented that the country's immigration laws were still "based on the theory that people born in one part of the globe are superior to those born in another part."[33] It was also that year in which delegates concentrated their efforts on pressing President Kennedy to put the administration's weight behind comprehensive immigration reform, which he sent to Congress the week following ACIM's symposium. One participant at the DC gathering, Salvatore Gambino, reflected on the broad context of what he and others in ACIM were engaged in, commenting, "We are not fighting only for immigration that is fair to the Italians; we are fighting for immigration that is fair to all racial groups and the quicker we broaden the base, the more our children who have been taught to be American of Italian extraction will join in the fight for equal justice and equal rights."[34] In his mind, the struggle for immigration reform had become a fight for social justice with implications far beyond the realm of immigration reform. For Gambino, Rena Trevor, and others, ACIM's mission carried great weight in the ongoing struggle to redefine racial and social boundaries in the nation and to perfect the meaning of democracy in America for future generations.

Participants increasingly saw themselves as fighting not only to enact new immigration laws but to redefine the criteria for full membership in the nation as well.

## *"Immigration Laws Compatible with Man's Dignity as a Child of God"*

Italian Americans gathered at the Chicago Immigration Rally in 1963 also heard Rev. Msgr. Joseph Fitzgerald from the NCWC applaud the audience for their efforts "to create immigration laws compatible with man's dignity as a child of God."[35] Fitzgerald denounced the National Origins System for codifying the idea "that a person's worth and value is determined by his place of birth" and argued that "this measure of a man's dignity is opposed to every religion that believed that God is our Father and we are His children" as well as "our national creed that all men are created equal." He suggested instead that the nation be led by religious ideas about man's natural or God-given "right to migrate."[36]

There was a strong Catholic presence at the Chicago rally in 1963. The rally was cosponsored by the NCWC and ACIM. Italian American Catholics—including priests, other church officials, and members of lay Catholic organizations and Catholic charities—played a significant role in helping to organize the rally and garner turnout. After weeks of publicizing the event in churches, religious groups, ethnic clubs, and other organizations, thousands of Chicago's Italian American Catholics gathered at one of seven local churches, where they were then shuttled on chartered buses to attend the gathering.[37] Church officials and other participants in religious organizations were among the speakers that day that stressed how a Catholic worldview regarding migration rights should be applied to American immigration laws. In short, Chicago's Italian American Catholic community was instrumental in ensuring the success of the rally and demonstrating to American lawmakers and the general public that they were a significant political force that demanded attention.

As the speaker indicated, and the rally's audience would suggest, many Italian Americans supported immigration reform initiatives, at least in part, because of their religious beliefs. Indeed, many Catholic beliefs were at odds with America's immigration laws and ultimately compelled many devout individuals to take action. Because of the elevated social position Catholics and Jews enjoyed since the nation embraced a tri-faith or Judeo-Christian identity during World War II and the Cold War, many Catholics were not shy about attacking policies on religious grounds during the postwar period.[38] A number of Italian American Catholics thus drew on Catholic philosophies and social thought to condemn the National Origins System and to work for its abolition on those grounds.[39] Since 1952, they had been influenced by the Catholic worldview articulated in *Exsul Familia*, which defended man's "right to migrate" and argued for moral limitations on the state's authority to restrict migration. In 1963, Pope John XXIII further elaborated on his predecessor's defense of man's right to migrate when he issued the encyclical *Pacem in Terris*. That treatise reinforced, among other things, the point that the state's right to govern man was limited by moral boundaries and added that states have a moral obligation to accept immigrants who have a reasonable hope of providing a better future for themselves and their families through migration. Like Pius XII before him, this pope also argued for man's membership in a human, universal family that transcended nations to support his argument.[40] Both documents thus reinforced and expanded existing Catholic worldviews about the family, the state, and migration. The result was that Italian American Catholics used these arguments to argue that the nation's immigration policies violated not only the nation's Judeo-Christian heritage but its liberal political foundations as well. In this sense, the religious critique of the nation's immigration policies reinforced arguments based on secular liberalism.

A Catholic worldview on migration influenced Italian American immigrant-aid advocates in many ways. In some cases, it could be an individual's primary motivation for becoming active in immigration reform activities. That may have been the case for one particularly devout Catholic woman active in ACIM, Carolyn (Sinelli) Burns.[41] Burns was an officer in ACIM's Detroit Chapter, a member and an officer of several other Italian American social or cultural groups, and a devout and active Catholic.[42] Her religious affiliations included membership and leadership roles in lay groups at her local church, in the St. Peter and Paul Missionary Society, the National Conference of Catholic Charities, and the Detroit Chapter of the National Council of Catholic Women (NCCW).[43] Burns wrote often, and at length, about how Catholic principles influenced her political and social activism.

First and foremost, she, and other Catholics, opposed the nation's immigration policies chiefly on religious grounds. Another NCCW member asserted that religious concerns directly motivated her group's political positions: "If she [the Catholic woman] supports a U.S. policy, it is because that policy is somehow rooted in the claims of the Mystical Body and the social thought of the Church. If she does not support it, it is because that policy is somehow at odds with it."[44] Burns often spoke and wrote about herself as a small "part of the Mystical Body," which made her and all other peoples a part of a Holy Family of mankind.[45] To her, nothing was more important than the love, charity, and connectivity that could be found among the constituent parts of that body. This view took the teachings of *Exsul Familia* to heart and Burns correspondingly denounced the immoral and unchristian restrictions on immigration that were in place in the United States under the National Origins System.

Burns and other socially active Catholic women also contemplated their roles as wives and mothers in promoting social change. Burns often spoke of, and personally demonstrated, how the housewife was not unimportant but was, in fact, a "woman of involvement" who had the power to shape her own family's attitudes and actions and who could remake the wider world through charity and activism.[46] The implication was that a woman's individual actions reverberated out to a much larger community. Thus, with a family-centered worldview of herself as a wife and mother, Burns considered her political activism in support of immigration reform to be not only justifiable but necessary. Finally, Burns believed deeply in notions of Christian charity and therefore sought to provide material, social, and spiritual support for others wherever possible.[47] To that end, Burns joined and helped to lead ethnic and religious organizations that worked to provide legal, material, and spiritual aid to immigrants (especially displaced peoples).

Catholic influences were present in aspects of the postwar immigrant-aid programs sponsored by ACIM, the IWL, and of course the NCWC. As seen in Burns's pursuits, the mission to provide economic or material assistance to help immigrants resettle in the United States reflected notions of Catholic charity, support for families, and social equity as much as it did anything else. The York County Resettlement Project, which brought "people without land to land without people," is an excellent example of the ideology of *Exsul Familia* brought to life. Finally, ACIM was founded for the express purpose of facilitating Italian immigration, which was such a pressing concern for tens of thousands of Italian Americans because of their desires to be reunited with their family members who sought entry into the United States. One recent analysis has even suggested that Italian American campaigns to secure special legislation for fourth preference immigrants (brothers, sisters, and adult married children of citizens) demonstrated that the definition of the family itself was significantly expanded by Italian Americans, who clearly conceptualized of the unit beyond the nuclear family dynamic.[48] But, on a policy level, it was not until the early 1960s that Italian American organizations demanded a regulatory system based on principles of family reunification or, relatedly, invoked religious doctrines that defended all peoples' God-given rights as appropriate guiding principles for regulating immigration in a fair and democratic nation.

The connection between Catholic theology and a family reunification model for regulating immigration is so natural that, again, it is striking that it took almost a decade for Italian Americans to make family reunification campaigns their primary strategy to achieve immigration reform. After all, Catholics viewed the family as the basic unit of society, and familial relationships helped determine men's and women's spiritual and material lives. The fact that reforms based on family ties did not make more headway among Italian Americans (who overwhelmingly identified as Catholic) sooner is a testament to the conservative political climate of the postwar period and the utility the lobby found in framing their campaigns in a Cold War context. In 1952, Marchisio used language from *Exsul Familia* on a television debate about immigration to urge Americans to pass refugee relief legislation and thus preserve a "lasting peace" in Europe. Invoking the pope's words, Marchisio argued, "Some nations are vastly overcrowded and their people hungry while others are practically unpopulated and have a surplus of the necessities of life," and went on to argue that if international stability was to be achieved, Americans must give "the surplus populations of the free world an opportunity to migrate."[49] Herein, Marchisio and others in the movement applied the idea of "man's right to migrate" to the context of Cold War geopolitics but ignored or downplayed how the doctrine might suggest the need for Americans to more critically examine the moral foundations on which their laws were based. The OSIA's Nicholas Petruzzelli also borrowed extensively from Catholic theology in the early 1950s to make a slightly more expansive argument that the United States unjustly guarded its own abundant natural resources at the expense of "Europe generally and Italy in particular" where resources were scarcer and labor overabundant. He subsequently argued that American immigration laws were "clearly immoral and unjust" and that the OSIA ought to "fight tooth and nail for the removal of what the Communists call the American 'GOLD CURTAIN,'" but even that rhetoric was still firmly rooted in Cold War liberalism.[50] Even Rev. Msgr. John O'Grady of the National Conference of Catholic Charities kept the Cold War foreign policy concerns at the center of his critique of the National Origins System when in 1952 he remarked, "Our immigration legislation and policies will be regarded more and more as a measure of our attitude toward other peoples."[51]

However, by the turn of the decade, Italian Americans spoke less about the Cold War and more about the ways in which Americans were part of a holy family that transcended nations. This shift was no more apparent than in ACIM's Second Symposium on Italian Migration in 1961. Held in Rome, gatherings took place in the Basilica of St. John and Paul, the Campidoglio, or the halls of the Vatican itself. The vast majority of the conference's speakers were members of the clergy and the clear focus was on issues of religion as they related to (Italian) migration. Topics ranged from "the right of man to migrate," to notions of Christian love and charity in immigrant aid, to the effects of poverty and the maldistribution of material resources around the world on migration.[52] That same year also witnessed a turning point in which Italian Americans increasingly reframed their campaigns for immigration reform in a religious context. Father Louis Donanzan of ACIM's Chicago Chapter called the nation's immigration policies "a moral problem," citing the inhumane separation of nearly 140,000 Italian peoples from their family members in the United States as the foundation for that critique.[53] In a speech before the Buffalo archdiocese the following year, Juvenal Marchisio drew upon aspects of *Exsul Familia* that he had not commonly invoked in the past to argue that God created all men and created bonds of affection between them as well. For him and other Catholics, this meant that "all men are members of the same human family" and that membership in that family "transcends national, political, geographic, and racial barriers." Correspondingly, he reasoned that it was the Catholic's duty to "appeal to the conscience of the nation" to "carry out God's command to share our bread with the hungry, our land with the oppressed, our opportunities with those in need, and our homes with the uprooted and tempest-tossed strangers." He then encouraged his audience to support family reunification–based immigration laws as a more effective and fair way for Americans to share their country's wealth and resources with all of God's people.[54] Although one must acknowledge the context and venue for this speech, one can hardly imagine Marchisio framing such an appeal for immigration reform in these terms a decade earlier. The emphasis on transcending racial barriers is particularly striking and demonstrates how Italian American immigration advocates increasingly embraced, or at least capitalized on, the progressive turn in American society.

In 1963, at ACIM's third national symposium in Washington, DC, Rev. Caesar Donanzan blended a Catholic critique of American immigration laws with the organization's position in support of secular liberalism. Donanzan railed against the National Origins System's preference for "natives of Anglo-Saxon nations" and its corresponding denial of "basic rights" to natives of "Latin and Slavic nations." As such, he lamented, "the National Origins System does not only not reflect the principles of equality and justice for all embodied in the Constitution, but it also does not mirror the eternal teachings of Christ regarding the brotherhood of men under the fatherhood of God." Donanzan continued, "Against these abuses and injustices, Pope Pius XII raised his voice in the postwar years and appealed to countries to recognize the right of migration" and added that Pope John XXIII echoed those sentiments just months ago. He concluded his remarks with a quote from *Pacem in Terris*: "The fact that one is a citizen of a particular state does not detract in any way from his membership of the human family as a whole nor from his citizenship in the world community."[55] Donanzan also made reference to "the mystical body of Christ," which he and other Catholics understood to represent the link between the individual and God and which also stood as a metaphor for the brotherly links between all men under God and reminded Christians of their social duty to offer charity to their fellow neighbors. Thus, Donanzan implored lawmakers in attendance at the event to recognize both the religious and liberal political traditions that he and others in ACIM believed should serve as a guide for immigration reform.[56]

Herein we see that in the later phase of the immigration reform movement, Italian Americans used Catholic social thought to contribute to the expansion of American liberalism on both religious and secular grounds. An ACIM editorial in 1962 echoed the Declaration of Independence to argue that migration is a "natural, inalienable right." But in the place of the familiar "all men are created equal" refrain, the author substituted "all men everywhere are bound together by a solidarity which transcends national, political, geographic and even racial barriers; all men have a right to the riches of this Earth, and all have the responsibility of making these riches available to all members of the human family."[57] That rhetoric clearly drew upon Catholic ideology to make a case for equal immigration opportunities for all peoples. Similarly, when Marchisio testified before Congress on the need to abolish the National Origins System in 1964 and again in 1965, he suggested that racial and ethnic quotas were out of step with the nation's religious beliefs as well as its political principles. On both occasions, Marchisio also argued that the United States should take the lead in adopting more humane policies that would "promote international migration from overpopulated countries to other areas of the world that are land rich and man poor."[58] The humanitarian and egalitarian principles behind "the right of man to migrate" were powerful arguments that helped convince lawmakers to establish immigration policies that were based on some notion of equity and fairness for all peoples.

One can only conclude that the civil rights movement and the increasingly liberal politics of the period encouraged Italian Americans to embrace a more expansive use of the Church's position on migration. After all, an international Catholic movement defending "individual human dignity" had already manifested itself and garnered results in Europe.[59] By the turn of the decade, it was American politics and culture that had substantially changed. Italian Americans subsequently became more comfortable expressing Catholic social thought and religious philosophies to defend political liberalism in their arguments for immigration reform. In many ways, these arguments mirrored the religious critique Martin Luther King Jr. and other civil rights activists articulated as they pressed Americans to recognize how Christian beliefs compelled liberal reform action when it came to matters of racial equality.[60] This understudied aspect of the liberal immigration reform movement deserves further attention. In invoking Catholic social philosophies, Italian American Catholics were responding to mainstream secular critiques of the National Origins System and were integral players contributing to the construction of a liberal discourse on matters of political democracy, social justice, and human rights that was emerging in domestic and international spheres in the 1960s.[61]


## *"A Worthy Reward for the Contribution of Immigrants"*

Even as speakers at the 1963 immigration rally in Chicago used the rhetoric of both secular and religious liberalism to make their case against the National Origins System, one must acknowledge the significant limitations found in their particular brand of liberalism. Daniel Corelli, who called the National Origins System "unjust, unscientific, and discriminatory," also asked his audience if the National Origins System was "a worthy reward for the contribution of immigrants to American culture and life."[62] Following the rally, ACIM's Chicago chapter passed a resolution on immigration to send to their state's congressional representatives and to President Johnson. The resolution characterized the rally as "the assembled loyal and patriotic American citizens . . . fully aware, and proud of the contribution made by those of Italian origin to the building and development, and to the culture, of this, their cherished country of adoption or birth." The resolution noted how Italian Americans "have instinctively given their sons, and spilled their blood, in every war fought by this country to defend and uphold the principles upon which it was founded" and how "not withstanding the foregoing Americans, of Italian descent, have suffered discrimination, degradation, and humiliation . . . under the existing iniquitous, unjust, and restrictive immigration law."[63] Rather than claim that all Americans, by virtue of their citizenship status alone, were entitled to equal treatment under the law, Italian Americans at the rally—and on many other occasions—qualified those claims with the rhetoric of "immigrant contributionism" demonstrated here.

The logic of immigrant "gifts" or "contributions" to the nation relied on a pluralistic construction of Americanism in which immigrant groups were understood to have, on the whole, assimilated to life in America but also allowed for the idea that those groups could also retain distinct racial, ethnic, religious, or cultural characteristics. Under this schema, there was an overarching unity and shared sense of identity among Americans, but society was also understood to be enriched by the diversity that still thrived within it.[64] From this worldview, a narrative followed that posited that all immigrant groups had helped to enrich the nation (economically, politically, and/or culturally) in some significant way and therefore ought to be acknowledged, or even rewarded, for the contributions they had bestowed upon the nation and its culture. Immigration liberals commonly employed this logic to justify their claims that various immigrant groups ought to be recognized for their contributions to the nation with greater immigration opportunities.

The immigrant gifts narrative first evolved in the interwar period, but academics, media elites, lawmakers, ethnic Americans, and others frequently invoked the rhetoric of immigrant gifts in the years after World War II when they talked about immigration reform.[65] John F. Kennedy's *A Nation of Immigrants* provides perhaps the most notable example of this trend. The text was originally commissioned by the Jewish antidefamation league B'nai B'rith in 1958 as part of the organization's "One Nation" pamphlet series and was posthumously published as a book in 1964. *A Nation of Immigrants* chronicled immigrant contributions by nationality group to American life from the colonial period to the present day and concluded with a discussion of the current need for immigration reform. In the text, Kennedy argued that the National Origins System unfairly discriminated against so many immigrant groups who had clearly proven themselves to be worthy of immigration and citizenship rights through their past deeds and actions.[66]

Historians have argued that the growing acceptance of pluralist constructions of society such as Kennedy's *A Nation of Immigrants* played a significant role in fostering greater political and social inclusivity in postwar America for all racial, ethnic, and religious groups and thus have understood it as an important component of American liberalism. But scholars have also rightly noted that postwar pluralism continued to be limited by issues of race. Thus, the rhetoric of immigrant contributionism reveals some important limitations of postwar liberalism—almost always hinging on continuing notions of racial exclusivity.[67]

Like most other practitioners of the immigrant gifts narrative, Kennedy acknowledged the contributions of immigrants of all races, religions, and national origins. Thus, it appears as though pluralist arguments were universally applied to all immigrants. But this rhetoric was not as inclusive as it seemed. Because the nation had historically guarded against the entry and naturalization of national groups considered to be nonwhite, the rhetoric of contributionism was, in effect, highly Eurocentric. Most often, its propo-nents were themselves self-identifying white ethnics and they told their own stories—the stories of the Irish, German, Norwegian, Italian, Polish, or other European immigrant group experiences in the United States. Joseph DeSerto (ACIM–Chicago) penned an open letter to Illinois senator Everett Dirksen (who opposed the passage of the Hart-Celler Bill) in the pages of the Catholic periodical *Fra Noi* in 1965 railing against the National Ori-gins System and the racial assumptions behind it. His message denied the existence of "a master race," refuted the notion "that the greatness of my country is due only to Anglo-Saxon Protestants," and reminded readers of the contributions of "Christopher Columbus, Amerigo Vespucci, Cabot, Einstein, Fermi, La Salle, Lafayette, Salomon, Mazzei, Dubinsky, Teller, Astor, Cudahy and Pupin."[68] But for all of DeSerto's condemnations against racial discrimination, his list of notable immigrants (many of whom hardly qualified as actual "immigrants") included only white figures and was typical of many protests of its kind. Moreover, he went on to endorse the passage of the Hart-Celler Act because its passage would finally "remove the stigma that people of Southeastern European ancestry were undesirables."[69] As this example suggests, accounts of nonwhite immigrants occupied a much smaller space in many immigrant gifts narratives—and when they did ap-pear, they smacked of tokenism. The end goal of such critiques was in fact the affirmation that the Ellis Island cohort occupied the same legal, social, and cultural spaces as older-stock whites in America.[70]

Historical boundaries of racial inclusion and exclusion in the United States hemmed in the scope of pluralist arguments and shaped the nature of their content as well. The argument most frequently employed by cham-pions of the immigrant gifts narrative in the postwar period was the notion that America's historic and present economic successes were achieved in no small part because of the innovations, labor, and ambitions of millions of immigrants. Contributionist narratives regularly chronicled the particular contributions of various immigrant groups to industries where they had a great impact. One need look no further than Frank Capra's famous *Why We Fight* film series (1942–1945) for evidence of this trend. In the final install-ment of the series, *War Comes to America*, Capra depicted what it meant to be

American—from Jamestown in 1607 to the present day (but notably omitting that pesky Civil War in his narrative). Immigrants and tropes associated with them figured prominently in the story—culminating with scenes of various immigrant groups literally and figuratively "building" the nation.[71] According to these types of accounts, Chinese railroad workers, German brewers, Mexican agricultural laborers, Norwegian dairy farmers, Italian ditchdiggers, and Bohemian meatpackers all featured in the nation's economic greatness. In the postwar period, liberals frequently argued that in order to continue to promote economic growth, Americans should widen the nation's gates to immigrants who functioned as producers of that wealth, as the previous examples would suggest, and also added arguments that those same immigrants and their children ultimately became American consumers as well. But while advocates of contributionism could include all immigrant groups, regardless of their race or marginalized economic position, into the role of producer, they had a much more difficult time incorporating nonwhite immigrant groups into the other critical element of their argument—as a consumer. By the early twentieth century the American way was in large part defined by conspicuous displays of consumption.[72] Therefore immigrants' and their children's ability to buy homes, dress like their older-stock American counterparts, enjoy healthy diets, and partake in other material and leisure goods implied that a degree of American acculturation had occurred for the country's most recent arrivals. But it has been well-argued that both American laws and customs actively discouraged the political, social, and even economic incorporation of many nonwhite immigrant groups into mainstream American consumer culture throughout much of the late nineteenth and early twentieth centuries.[73]

A critical look at the immigrant gifts narrative therefore demonstrates that its logic was predicated, at least on some level, on an immigrant group's demonstrated ability to "successfully" assimilate to life in the United States. This of course presented racial limitations to its application; assimilation was a much more attainable task for European immigrants than for others. It is true that Asian Americans also employed contributionist arguments and stressed their groups' assimilability in their parallel quests for social advancement and legal equality in the postwar period. But recent scholarship has adeptly shown that Asian Americans were largely able to achieve legal and social gains in the postwar period because they actively and effectively constructed a decidedly "not-black" group identity resulting in the creation of a third model-minority categorization for themselves by the mid-1960s.[74]

But there is an even deeper issue with the assimilationist foundations of contributionism. Its advocates argued that immigrant groups who had assimilated well to life in America (demonstrated through contributions to the nation) ought to be rewarded for their demonstrated successes with greater immigration and naturalization opportunities.[75] The keynote speaker at ACIM's 1963 symposium in Washington, DC, said as much when he argued, at the conclusion of his address entitled "Italian Contributions to American Culture," that the nation's current immigration law "offends against the gratitude of this nation."[76] But the entire concept that "worthy" or "good" immigrant groups be rewarded for so-called meritorious behavior with greater immigration rights was actually based on similar logic that undergirded the National Origins System. The major difference being that biological determinism was replaced with behavioral demonstrations of fitness. But the fact remained that this line of reasoning did not challenge the notion that some immigrant groups were thought to make better citizens than others—it merely sought to alter the criteria for determining whom to reward. It betrayed the liberal defense of a democratic citizen's equal rights in a republic or even the Catholic idea that the state can only restrict man's God-given right to migrate to protect the greater good. Therefore, Italian American protests based on secular and religious liberalism are limited, maybe even undermined, by the ways in which white ethnics in particular applied the rhetoric of immigrant contributionism to their crusade for immigration reform throughout the postwar period. The immigrant gifts narrative thus reveals that rather conservative elements of white ethnic politics, and white ethnic identity formation, remained present in the movement— even in 1965.

All of these elements of the immigrant gifts narrative were present in Marchisio's testimony before Congress in support of the Hart-Celler Bill in 1964 and again 1965. In his statement to Congress on both occasions, Marchisio posed the question "Why should the country welcome more Italian immigrants?" One reason, he offered, was the economic achievements Italian immigrants and their children had demonstrated over the years. He argued that Italian immigrants and their children had been instrumental in building up key sectors of the economy, including agriculture, the garment trades, construction, the restaurant industry, and defense work. According to Marchisio:

> No one can deny that Italians are frugal, sober, and industrious. The proof of it is found in the relief statistics of this country, which show that the Italian immigrant rare, if ever, becomes a burden on the receiving country. A conspicuous characteristic of the Italian is a provident disposition. Their ambition is to own their own home, no matter how modest it may be, to deposit the surplus of their earnings for the growing need of their families and to meet future exigencies, and to give to their children the opportunities of education that were denied to them in their own native land because of their economic condition.[77]

Herein, Marchisio made a case for the Italian immigrant's economic contributions and suggested that Italians were desirable immigrants because they also shared cultural values accepted by most Americans and were thus capable of assimilation. Marchisio continued to suggest the assimilable political nature of Italians by noting the group's high rate of naturalization and ethnic Italians' recent service in the American armed services during World War II. Marchisio concluded his argument with the statement, "The American people sympathize with and would support any effort to bring to this country these people who can do, as they have done in the past, so much in the upbuilding [*sic*] of America."[78] It was, of course, practically impossible for nonwhite immigrant or ethnic groups to make such claims. Asian immigrants were largely excluded from immigrating and barred from naturalizing for nearly a century because of their supposed cultural foreignness and presumed unassimilable nature. Although legally classified as white, Mexican immigrants were often discouraged from permanent resettlement in the United States (let alone naturalization) and not actively encouraged to assimilate or adopt American lifestyles. African Americans were so excluded from this narrative that they were not even included in the basic immigrant paradigm. Marchisio's testimony can therefore be read as an expression of Euro-American whiteness, even white privilege for expanded immigration and naturalization rights, not as an argument for universal immigrant rights.[79]

Another major limitation of contributionism, as it was used by Italian Americans and other white ethnic groups, was that it allowed a particular immigrant or ethnic group to talk about immigrant contributions in universal terms but in practice to focus almost exclusively on their own group's particular history or experiences in the United States. Italian Americans and other white ethnics could at once claim they were advocating for all immigrants, but by focusing on themselves, they were never forced to examine how their own group's past experiences or current concerns may differ from those of nonwhite immigrant or ethnic groups. In fact, during the course of Joseph Errigo's testimony before Congress in 1965, questioning by committee members revealed that he (and perhaps the OSIA, whom he represented) was unaware of the intricacies of the Asia-Pacific Triangle and how it functioned.[80]

When Daniel Corelli used the term *immigrants* in his speech at the Chicago rally in 1963, he did not really mean all immigrants; he meant Italian immigrants. Corelli's address pointed out that the National Origins System was based on "lies and half-truths about persons from southern Europe." It was littered with the names of notable Italian immigrants and their accomplishments. And Corelli spent a great deal of time dispelling popular prejudices or stereotypes assigned to Italian immigrants. The point of these efforts was Corelli's claim that Italian immigrants and their American-born descendants were victims who had suffered in silence for far too long. Corelli asked his audience, "Why should we twenty-five million Americans of Italian extraction sit muted and disgraced, second class citizens? . . . We must make out voice *heard* and *appreciated* and *respected*. We must keep ever before the minds of our country, of our President, and our congressmen and senators, yes of the world, this urgent plea for self-respect and honor."[81] Corelli was, in fact, appalled that some Americans continued to think of Italian Americans as less desirable than older-stock ethnic groups whose undisputed claims to whiteness allowed them the immigration and naturalization privileges of full or first-class citizens. ACIM's resolution following the rally certainly indicated Corelli's audience agreed. The resolution concluded with a plea for the abolition of the National Origins System in order to "permi[t], once more, the newcomers from the land of our ancestors, to enrich America" and to, "by removal of the present stigma, restore citizens of Italian origin to first class American citizenship."[82]

Corelli's highly racialized language and his call that the nation address specifically Italian American grievances hardly suggested that he and many

Italian Americans in attendance at the 1963 rally shared an ideological affinity with movements that advocated for universal political rights for all Americans. In fact, Corelli noted that despite the urgency of their cause, he believed there was practically no chance that the current session of Congress would take up the issue of immigration reform "because *another* bill for civil rights has now demanded the attention of the nation and of the world."[83] This rhetoric hardly reflected a commitment to democratic liberalism for all groups. Instead, it prioritized the concerns of white ethnics over other racial groups. Corelli's scathing words even suggested the emergence of the rhetoric of white ethnic grievance unfolding not as a backlash to the civil right movement but in tandem with it.[84]

A similar (but far more moderate) sentiment was present in Frank Annunzio's (D-IL) remarks before Congress in support of the Hart-Celler Bill in 1965. Ignoring the obvious examples of slavery or Jim Crow laws, Annunzio began by arguing that "to my mind, no more obnoxious, racist idea has ever been incorporated into the statute books of the United States [than the National Origins System]. The inevitable result is a system which practices the most vicious kind of discrimination" and "the clear implication is that the quality of a human being is dependent upon his place of birth." He illustrated that point by comparing the share of quotas allocated to Britons, Germans, and Scandinavians to those of Italians, Greeks, and Poles and concluded that "under the present law, Americans of southern and eastern European extraction are told that more of their kind are neither wanted or needed. Their contributions to this country's development and their just claims to equal treatment under the law are ignored." Although Annunzio's politics were relatively progressive, in typical pluralist fashion, Annunzio's account made no mention of any non-European groups. Moreover, like Corelli before him, he went beyond mere indifference to the struggles of other racial groups. Annunzio observed, "It seems strange to me that at a time when the Congress is taking vigorous action to insure that no American will be denied their full privilege of citizenship because of race, we still maintain an immigration policy which relegates millions of other Americans to second-class citizenship because of national origin."[85] The implication here, as elsewhere, was that on some level the nation's focus on civil rights seemed to compel action on immigration reform, lest Euro-American claims to full equality, or indeed privileges enjoyed by older-stock whites, get left by the wayside.

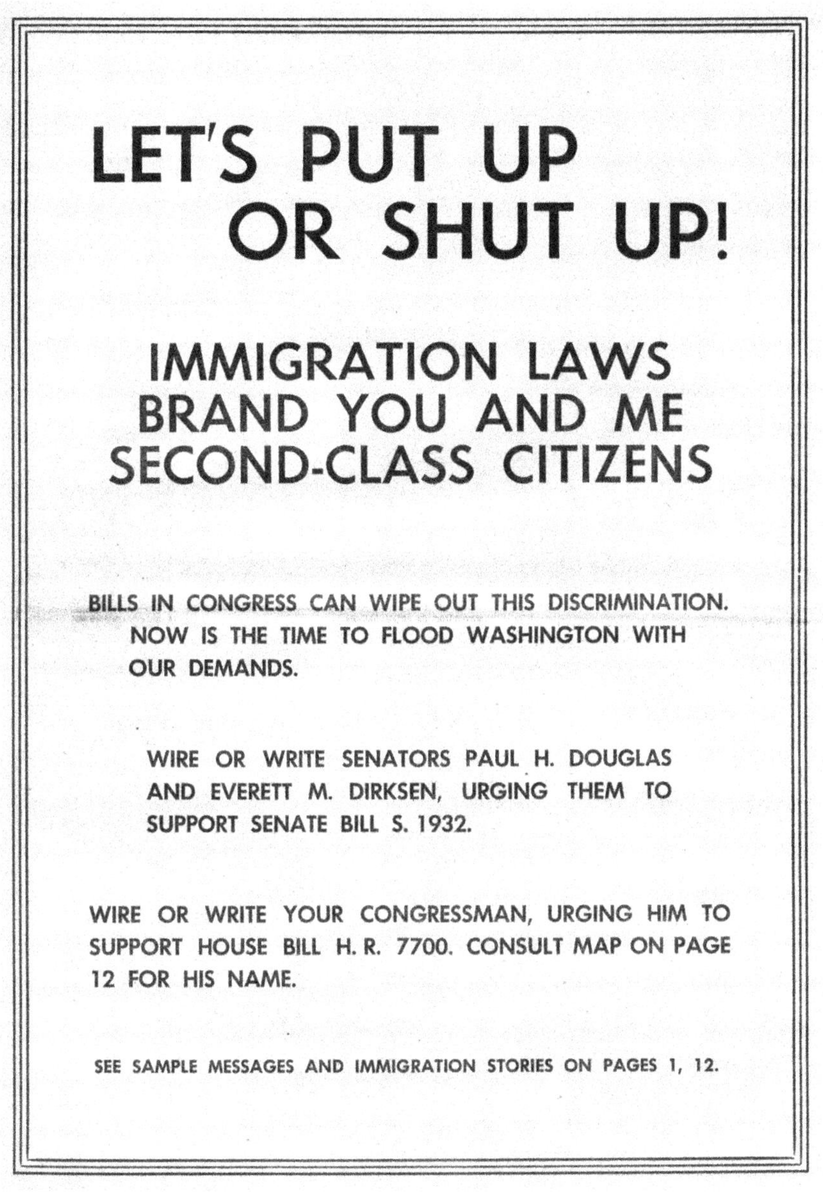

# LET'S PUT UP
## OR SHUT UP!

## IMMIGRATION LAWS
## BRAND YOU AND ME
## SECOND-CLASS CITIZENS

BILLS IN CONGRESS CAN WIPE OUT THIS DISCRIMINATION. NOW IS THE TIME TO FLOOD WASHINGTON WITH OUR DEMANDS.

WIRE OR WRITE SENATORS PAUL H. DOUGLAS AND EVERETT M. DIRKSEN, URGING THEM TO SUPPORT SENATE BILL S. 1932.

WIRE OR WRITE YOUR CONGRESSMAN, URGING HIM TO SUPPORT HOUSE BILL H. R. 7700. CONSULT MAP ON PAGE 12 FOR HIS NAME.

SEE SAMPLE MESSAGES AND IMMIGRATION STORIES ON PAGES 1, 12.

FIGURE 11. "Let's Put Up or Shut Up," February 1964, *Fra Noi*, a weekly periodical for Italian American Catholics in Chicago. Immigration History Research Center Archives, University of Minnesota.

Questions about the whiteness of southern and eastern European immigrant groups were hardly new concerns in the 1960s. Throughout the postwar period, Italian Americans used the language of contributionism to demonstrate their group's claims to full membership in the nation (which continued to be a highly racialized claim in the two decades after World War II) in their campaigns for immigration reform and on other occasions as well. Annual Columbus Day celebrations in particular offered Italian Americans a chance to advance those claims and are therefore worthy of some attention. The holiday provided Italian Americans with opportunities and public platforms to highlight or even reinterpret aspects of the Italian immigrant experience in the United States. They were also occasions on which Italian Americans reconstructed their group's place in the nation. Finally, Italian Americans linked the figure of Columbus with that of "the immigrant" and thus used the holiday to lay claim to immigration and citizenship rights that rivaled those asserted by America's oldest-stock immigrant groups. In 1958, one celebrant demonstrated the charged nature of those celebrations, remarking, "If we had [the McCarran-Walter] law in 1492, Columbus himself would have had a hard time landing."[86]

Immigrant gifts discourse was a standard part of Italian American celebrations of Columbus Day in the postwar period. The OSIA's John Guarino proclaimed in 1958, "To us, Columbus Day affords an opportunity to take inventory of the feats, not only of Columbus, but of all those good sons of Italy, who have brought in peace and war great contributions."[87] In peacetime the economic contributions of immigrants and their children were paramount. According to Frank Gigliotti (OSIA), Italians have helped to make the United States a great country, for "we have dug its ditches, mined its coal, forged her steel, planted many vallies [sic] with vineyards and olive trees."[88] Marchisio recalled Italian American sacrifices for the country's economic greatness when he asked a Columbus Day crowd in 1954, "How many graves [have] the sons of Columbus opened for themselves while opening subways and mines for the progress of America?"[89] Similarly in 1962, the OSIA's Joseph Errigo argued that "transplanted Europeans" had "gone into some field or endeavor for which they seemed especially qualified, and had done some outstanding thing to enrich the new nation."[90] Others focused on chronicling the specific contributions of notable Italian immigrants—including political leaders like Fiorello La Guardia, innovators like Enrico

Fermi, and cultural figures like Joe DiMaggio.[91] Speakers also used Columbus Day to showcase their group's wartime contributions. The day was used to commemorate how naturalized citizens and the children of immigrants steadfastly fought "for the preservation of democracy" against fascism in World War II and against communist forces in Italy and in the Korean War.[92] These and other deeds led Guarino to assert, "The land discovered by Columbus is an immigrant country, its greatness, its strength were made and are being made through the combined efforts of all us immigrants or sons of immigrants."[93]

But Italian Americans were often not content with merely demonstrating Italian immigrant contributions to the nation. Many Columbus Day celebrants often rewrote or reinterpreted popular narratives in American history in an attempt to convince a broader audience of full Italian American membership in the nation. Moreover, this revisionist history was closely linked to the immigration reform movement. For example, Italian Americans frequently reimagined Columbus as America's first immigrant in the years after World War II.[94] By conveniently ignoring the facts that Columbus never actually set foot on North America, that the United States did not exist as a nation in the late fifteenth century, and that Columbus never actually immigrated anywhere at all, Italian Americans attempted to rewrite American history with Italians playing a formative role in the nation-building narrative. In this schema, Italians were recast not as recent arrivals but as some of the very first Europeans who migrated to areas that would become the United States. In such an account, all other immigrants—including the English, French, Germans, and other older-stock groups—actually followed in Italian footsteps. These historical reconstructions led George Spatuzza, the leading figure in the Order Sons of Italy in America in the postwar period, to conclude, "Only the uninformed would regard the Italian people as Johnnys-come-lately."[95]

Columbus was only the first in a long list of Italians that Italian Americans cited as contributing to the development of the nation. The achievements of other Italian explorers—including Giovanni da Verrazzano, John Cabot (Giovanni Caboto), Amerigo Vespucci, the lesser-known Henri de Tonty—were frequently noted in Columbus Day celebrations as Italians who contributed to the development of the United States (despite the fact that, once again, none of these men were actually immigrants).[96] Although

Tonty was the most obscure of all these figures, he was the most prominently featured and creatively reimagined in Columbus Day speeches made
by Chicago-area OSIA leaders. George Spatuzza referred to Tonty, who
explored the Great Lakes region in the seventeenth century, as an American
"frontiersman" and "the true founder of Illinois." In Spatuzza's accounts,
Tonty helped established European settlements in the face of great adversity, he interacted with (and sometimes fought) "rebellious Indians," and
paved the way for "settlers, trade goods, and missionaries" into the area.[97]
By crafting Tonty into a character who so embodied characteristics central
to the national mythology of the frontier, Spatuzza claimed that Italians
shared quintessentially American experiences and values. Similarly, a 1961
song written by an Italian American composer to commemorate Columbus
called him "our greatest pioneer."[98] In this manner Columbus, Tonty, and
others joined a pantheon of revered American frontiersmen credited with
the development of the nation, including mythic American figures such as
Davy Crockett, Meriwether Lewis, and William Clark.

In his account of Tonty, Spatuzza inserted Italians into American colonial history, where they were generally absent otherwise. This was another
common strategy employed by Italian Americans on Columbus Day. Italian American celebrants similarly chronicled the roles Italians played in the
American Revolution and the American Civil War. In claiming "Italians
fought shoulder to shoulder with the founding fathers of this great republic
of ours," one speaker again wrote Italians into an era of American history
from which they were traditionally absent. By doing so, they claimed that
Italians had actually been in the United States as long as any other older-
stock immigrant groups. They also used these examples to demonstrate
ethnic Italians' commitment to defending America's democratic political
values.[99]

Italian Americans in the postwar period were also fond of arguing that
without Columbus's contributions, key events in the development of American democracy would not have taken place. Errigo claimed, "It is doubtful if
[democracy] could have been possible elsewhere had not America been discovered."[100] Marchisio remarked of Columbus, "His faith and courage called
America into being."[101] Year after year, Spatuzza claimed that without Columbus's discovery, the Pilgrims may not have landed at Plymouth Rock, and
thus the country's tradition of providing a liberal sanctuary for political and

religious dissidents would never have been established.[102] Similarly, when the OSIA's John Ottaviano Jr. testified before a House Subcommittee on Immigration and Nationality in May 1965, he remarked, "Every ship that comes to America got its chart from Columbus."[103] Or better yet, Spatuzza argued there would have been "no Boston Tea Party—no Lexington—no Concord—no Bunker Hill—no Declaration of Independence . . . —no United States" without Columbus.[104] Finally, according to Spatuzza, "Without Columbus's achievements, man's freedom would still be unknown, civilization would not have marched on as it has, and the world would still be today, in a large part, in the hands of ruthless rulers, to the detriment of mankind."[105] These words, spoken during the height of the Cold War, fantastically suggested that American leadership against authoritarian regimes could all be traced back to one Italian's contributions to the nation.

These reinterpretations of American history that put Italian peoples present, both physically and culturally, at the founding moments of the nation posited one of two arguments: Either Italians were in fact old-stock Americans (there were just fewer Italians than there were, for example, English immigrants until more recently) or Italians shared cultural similarities with older-stock groups. In either case, they helped establish Italian American claims to both whiteness and full membership in the nation. In their thinking, that privileged status included access to the same immigration and citizenship rights as older-stock whites. On Columbus Day Spatuzza once asked, "Who would deny the right of those of you of Italian heritage to take your place with the descendants of the Mayflower voyagers?"[106] Herein we see that the entire immigrant gifts narrative did not necessarily call into question antiquated claims that certain racial, ethnic, or national groups possessed inherent or demonstrable traits common to their group. Its advocates merely claimed that certain immigrant groups, like the Italians, have historically displayed proper or "good" traits for citizenship in America. Marchisio's congressional testimony called Italians "frugal, sober, and industrious" and cited the group's "provident disposition" and "ambition" to become homeowners. Italian American Columbus Day speakers likewise spoke about the positive characteristics possessed by all Italian immigrants. In particular, they focused on the Italian people's democratic nature flowing from the days of the ancient Roman Republic to the present (glossing over other periods of Italian history). They similarly pointed to Rome as the center of Christendom and the religious character of the Italian people. These particular subjects carried great meaning when one considers popular nativist charges that Catholics made for poor democratic citizens. But in framing the Italian immigrant experience in this light, Italian Americans did not use Columbus Day to advance appeals for universal immigrant equality, nor did they argue against antiquated arguments that posited certain immigrant groups displayed particular natural or learned traits. They merely asserted Italian access to the pantheon of "desirable" immigrant groups. In an open letter in which he reflected upon the success of recent Columbus Day festivities in Chicago and anticipated the upcoming immigration rally in 1963, Congressman Frank Annunzio (D-IL) tellingly proclaimed, we will "no longer tolerate being labeled as descendants of an inferior race in a shameful immigration law."[107]

The narrative of immigrant gifts or contributions that thrived throughout the postwar period, even well into the 1960s at the height of calls for complete political and social equality for all peoples, hardly represented a progressive expression of liberal ideas that all peoples, regardless of their race, ethnicity, religion, or even the recentness of their group's arrival to the country should be accorded fair and equitable immigration and citizenship opportunities. Perhaps we can excuse the limitations of its logic in 1952, but by 1963, or better yet 1965, its continued use by white liberals deserves closer scrutiny. Its inclusion alongside liberal arguments (both secular and religious) for immigration reform suggests the need to qualify the extent to which Italian Americans, and perhaps white ethnic groups more broadly, understood their campaigns to be part of a broader struggle for legal equality and social justice in the postwar period. Scholars have credited pluralist rhetoric with effectively demonstrating the assimilability or even whiteness of the Ellis Island cohort as a key factor in convincing conservatives to ultimately pass the Hart-Celler Bill in 1965. Those Eurocentric immigrant gifts narratives also helped to allay conservative fears about the changing racial and cultural composition of the population by reinforcing the notion that the country was primarily a nation of European immigrants and hinting that it would remain the case in the future as well.[108]

A wide range of ideological and social issues compelled Italian Americans to pursue broad-based reforms to the nation's immigration laws by the 1960s. Their participation in a liberal coalition advancing legislation that promoted equity, fairness, and morality in immigration and citizenship laws was based on individual and group beliefs in democratic and religious equality. However, there were significant limitations or tensions that existed for many Italian Americans even as they advanced "liberal" arguments for immigration reform. Their understandings or definitions of liberalism may have been quite different from other members of the immigration reform coalition. We are also confronted with competing interests and ideologies simultaneously finding expression within a single Italian American organization, or within a set of organizations, that composed that ethnic group's immigration reform lobby. The complexity revealed here highlights just one of the many difficulties presented in trying to understand a diverse liberal immigration reform coalition in the postwar period—particularly the role that white ethnic groups played in it. Even when socially active Italian Americans embraced liberal reforms, racial constructions continued to hem in their worldviews and legislative goals. Italian American immigration reform campaigns ultimately demonstrate that this group did contribute to a rising tide of progressive reforms in the United States at midcentury, but the conservative aspects of the movement also reveal its limitations, or perhaps even shallowness, for many white ethnic Americans

It is critically important to understand the nature of Italian American liberalism and how it fits into the broader narrative of the postwar immigration reform movement because it has consequences for how we characterize the movement overall. Some historians argue that Italian Americans and other white ethnics were either inspired by the civil rights movement or had long been engaged in their own sort of civil rights struggle and thus we should view immigration reform as part of a broad push for liberal equality that enjoyed a brief but enormously significant moment of success in the late 1950s and early 1960s.[109] They point out that like African Americans, Ellis Island immigrants and their children also claimed equal access to housing, higher education, social spaces, and employment opportunities in the postwar period.[110] Scholars also note that white ethnics similarly called upon older-stock Americans to recognize their groups' cultural contributions to the nation and thus their equal position as American citizens in this period.[111] But while the immigration reform movement (and the concerns of ethnic and religious organizations in moving it forward) deserves greater attention in narratives about postwar liberal reform movements, there are dangers in reading too much into these parallel movements. White ethnics encountered much less resistance in pushing for their social inclusion than African Americans experienced in their calls for political and social equality. In fact, many historians correctly point out that the political, economic, and social gains the Ellis Island cohort achieved at midcentury often came at the expense of, or explicit exclusion of, African Americans in social welfare programs, housing, employment, higher education, and social spaces.[112] Whether it was explicitly acknowledged, new immigrant or ethnic groups understood, on some level, that their whiteness helped to affirm their place in the American mainstream at midcentury.[113] The liberal ideological foundations shared between civil rights activists and immigration liberals were always stronger in theory than they were in practice. Most ethnic and religious organizations advocated for reform from a Eurocentric perspective, and certainly lawmakers had a Eurocentric bias when they debated and finally enacted major reform legislation in the 1960s.[114] For most Italian Americans, the commitment to racial equality appears shallow at best and their rhetoric seems, more often than not, employed for self-serving ends. Moreover, Italian Americans participated in broad-based (interracial, interethnic, and interfaith) immigration reform organizations only on a limited basis. On the whole, Italian American organizations generally pursued immigration reform legislation that would specifically help Italian immigrants first and only embraced broader liberal reform efforts when it was in their group's interest to do so. Even when Italian Americans argued that their actions were aimed at delegitimizing the National Origins System, their focus on demonstrating the assimilability of the Italian immigrant and the contributions that Italian peoples brought to the country hardly challenged established social hierarchies or racialized beliefs about a particular group's "fitness" for citizenship opportunities in America.

## The Deep Roots of White Ethnicity, 1965 and Beyond

On October 3, 1965, standing on Liberty Island with the Statue of Liberty in the backdrop, President Johnson signed the new Immigration and Nationality Act into law. The passage of the long-fought-for legislation abolished the National Origins System and, along with other pieces of landmark legislation, including the Civil Rights Act (1964) and the Voting Rights Act (1965), heralded a new promise of racial equality in the nation. While signing the bill, President Johnson remarked that the new law "corrects a cruel and enduring wrong in the conduct of the American Nation" and that never again would "the twin barriers of prejudice and privilege" cast a shadow on America's gates.[1] In framing the new law in this way, Johnson highlighted how postwar immigration reform efforts shared an ideological affinity with the civil rights movement and reflected many Americans' ongoing struggles to better ensure liberty and equality for all Americans.

But even while the Immigration and Nationality Act promised to foster a more democratic and socially inclusive society, Americans also understood the new law in much more conservative ways. More than anything else,

FIGURE 12. Signing of the Immigration Act, 1965. LBJ Library photo by Yoichi Okamoto.

Johnson's decision to sign the bill into law in front of the Statue of Liberty signaled the Ellis Island immigrant narrative as the now normative immigration experience in America.[2] The administration considered and then rejected the idea of a signing ceremony at Jamestown or Plymouth, with the White House Director of Public Information, Jack Rosenthal, noting both locations suggested "quite the wrong emphasis."[3] White House memos also revealed that if the Senate took longer than expected to the pass the bill, the administration wanted to delay signing the legislation until the "symbolic date" of October 12th, Columbus Day.[4] The message here was clear, the passage of the law was understood, more than anything else, as a nod to Ellis Island ethnics' past grievances, their efforts to achieve immigration reform, and a fulfillment of their quest for full political and social inclusion in the nation.

Johnson's positioning of the legislation in this manner was hardly surprising. That same narrative had been advanced throughout congressional debates on the bill for the past two years. Speaking before Congress in 1964, Attorney General Robert Kennedy emphasized how national origins quotas "implie[d] what we in the United States know from our own experience is false: that regardless of individual qualifications, a man or woman born in Italy, or Greece, or Poland, or Portugal, or Czechoslovakia, or the Ukraine, is not as good as someone born in Ireland, or England, or Germany, or Sweden."[5]

Kennedy, not surprisingly, failed to mention immigrants from China, Japan, Korea, or from any other country largely inhabited by nonwhites in his defense of the administration's immigration reform bill.[6] President Johnson similarly omitted references to Asian Americans and Asian immigrants as he spoke to the American people on that historic day on Liberty Island (even though such references were present in an earlier draft). Earlier versions of Johnson's speech also suggested a more direct link between immigration reform and the civil rights movement with phrases such as "We are moving to strike away the racial and ethnic boundaries that splinter the spirit of our society. For the ghettos that still separate us cannot be dissolved until we rid ourselves of laws that create ghettos in our minds."[7] In the end, though, President Johnson ultimately eschewed a more broadly antiracist message and chose to open his remarks with the claim that "this bill that we will sign today is not a revolutionary bill." In doing so he invoked a message that affirmed the inclusionary status of Americans of southern and eastern European stock and seemed to even suggest it was an almost natural progression for the position of those white ethnic groups by 1965.[8]

Moreover, Johnson, like other immigration liberals, either did not think the abolition of the National Origins System would fundamentally alter sources of new immigration or was purposefully downplaying the potentially more radical outcomes of the legislation for political purposes.[9] Reflecting enduring racial biases and Eurocentric views on immigration, Emanuel Celler, Robert Kennedy, Edward Kennedy, and other liberal immigration reform advocates incorrectly predicted that Asian, African, and other sources of nonwhite immigration would remain low under the new system. Senator Edward Kennedy even assured skeptics in the debates surrounding the legislation that "the ethnic mix of this country will not be upset" by new regulations and predicted that "the most populated and deprived nations of Africa and Asia" will not look to the United States for refuge.[10]

Immigration reform campaigns constructed by Italian Americans were hardly revolutionary either. The somewhat ambivalent or even contradictory positions held by liberal immigration reformers in Congress were common among Italian Americans who simultaneously called for racial, ethnic, and religious equality in American immigration laws as a principle, yet in practice, their reform efforts often reflected Eurocentrism and a socially (and racially) conservative vision of Americanism. Even though Italian Americans abstractly called for racial, ethnic, and religious equality in American immigration laws, their campaigns variously embraced displays of anticommunism, household mass consumption, and narratives of immigrant assimilation or contributionism largely to assert their own group's "fitness" for immigration and citizenship rights in the United States, as well as their particular group's cultural membership within the American mainstream. Each display was highly racialized and did not contest accepted political and social boundaries but rather reaffirmed them. In this formulation, Italian Americans were just as concerned with their group's political and social equality with older-stock whites as they were with their stated goal of liberalizing American immigration laws.

In examining both the white ethnic immigration reform movement in the postwar period and the conservatism that coexisted with liberalism within Italian American campaigns, we are better able to understand the nature of white ethnicity in the years that followed. The years after 1965 witnessed a series of "white ethnic revivals" characterized by a notable increase in white American-born individuals feeling, proclaiming, and behaving in ways that signified a new, renewed, or revised sense of ethnic identification in their individual private lives and, more importantly, on a group level in the public sphere in the late 1960s through the 1980s.[11]

The most comprehensive studies of white ethnic revivals examine, among other things, the roots of these movements.[12] Although there was an array of factors that contributed to public surges of white ethnicity from the late 1960s through the 1980s, one factor tends to stand out—the civil rights movement. In most views, white ethnic revivals were either inspired by or, alternatively, responded to the civil rights movement in formative ways. In one narrative, the civil rights movement is credited with providing white ethnics with an ideological foundation, political model, and language to draw upon to articulate their own constructions of group pride, political and social grievances, and redefinitions of their place in the nation.[13] In that account, the civil rights movement altered "the dominant discourse of national civic life" by introducing "a new and contagious idiom of group rights and group identity on the American scene."[14] The result was a sharp political and cultural shift away from a classical definition of individual liberties to thinking in terms of group rights.

But Italian Americans and other ethnic and religious groups were not merely inspired by the civil rights movement; they were mobilized at roughly the same moment in a parallel fashion to civil rights reformers to combat political and social problems in the nation associated with discrimination against racial, ethnic, and religious groups. Catholics and Jews mobilized in notable ways throughout the 1940s and 1950s in defense of their group rights to obtain equal access to housing, education, and social opportunities in America.[15] This study has shown that Italian Americans were already thinking in terms of, and acting in a defense of, their "group" rights as they challenged the nation's immigration policies and their own once-marginalized social position from the late 1940s through 1965. It may be more accurate to argue that members of ethnic and religious groups, along with civil rights activists, collectively ushered in a new discourse of group rights throughout the postwar period. These views suggest that constructions of white ethnicity and group identity formation began to evolve in fundamentally significant ways before 1965.

Alternatively, the civil rights movement can also be understood as a pivotal moment in the construction of white ethnic revivals because the political, social, and cultural changes it helped to produce prompted a political and social backlash among many white ethnics. As the argument goes, white ethnics began to embrace a revitalized and reconstructed sense of ethnicity to oppose the expansive results of the civil rights movement, which yielded the liberal promise of legal and social equality for all groups but also ushered in a new era of racial consciousness for minority groups as well as affirmative action programs to attempt to redress past injustices and structural barriers to racial equality. Following these events, some white ethnic Americans sought to distance and ultimately absolve themselves from traditional white privilege and the nation's history of racial discrimination by refashioning the narrative of the Ellis Island immigrant or ethnic experience in America. The result was that after 1965, many white ethnics increasingly identified as members of groups that had historically faced ethnic and/or religious discrimination by the dominant Anglo-American society but overcame the limitations associated with those experiences by hard work, perseverance, and individual ambition. White ethnics had pulled themselves up from their bootstraps, whereas African Americans and other minorities now sought "unfair" forms of public assistance to make it in America. The narrative they constructed of course ignores the complicity of white ethnics in more recent expressions of racism in the United States and the many privileges (and indeed social welfare benefits) historically conferred upon all white Americans.[16]

While a backlash to the civil rights movement is clear among Italian Americans and other white ethnic groups, there is also far more continuity in conservative expressions of group identity and the social politics it helped produce than scholars have previously identified. Members of the Italian American immigration reform lobby had already begun to move in a more racially and socially conservative direction when they embraced the rhetoric of immigrant or ethnic contributionism to argue that lawmakers reward Italians and other (mostly European) immigrant groups for their meritorious contributions to the nation and their successful assimilation to American cultural norms. Not recognizing elements of this shift before 1965 obscures the homegrown nature of white ethnic conservatism and makes the white ethnic turn toward political and social conservatism in the late 1960s, 1970s, and 1980s much more difficult to understand. If we think of white ethnics primarily as members of a liberal reform coalition that pushed for immigration reform on the grounds of racial, ethnic, and religious equality in the postwar period, how then can we explain so many white ethnics' identification with Richard Nixon's "silent majority" by 1968 or the rise of "Reagan Democrats" some years later?[17]

One scholar suggests that white ethnic elites were always more committed to the principles of postwar liberalism than were their working-class counterparts who actually felt the personal effects of calls for racial equality in sectors such as employment and housing and that the shift in white ethnic behavior circa 1965 was largely a class-based one.[18] But the narrative crafted by Italian American elites and the rank and file alike in the postwar period argued that southern and eastern European immigrants should be accorded more immigration rights (and therefore access to American citizenship) because they made good workers and consumers, because they rarely became public charges, and because they contributed to the cultural and economic advancement of the nation. That framing demonstrates a much more limited commitment to the notion that all individuals and groups were due certain political and social rights solely by virtue of their membership in the nation from a much earlier date. That narrative was prevalent in Italian American communities at midcentury and was easily reconciled with economic and social views that dominated discourse on the Right by the late 1960s.

These arguments indicate the need to reassess the origins of public expressions of white ethnicity in the late twentieth century and suggest the need to rethink the periodization of white ethnic revivalism. At the very least, it is clear that there were deeper roots to both the liberal and conservative elements of the post-1965 white ethnic revivals than have been previously acknowledged. A "renewed" feeling of ethnic belonging or identification, and public expressions in that regard (at least for Italian Americans), were well underway in the immediate postwar period. Italian Americans did not have to rediscover their ethnicity after 1965; it had been a central element of their individual and group identifications throughout the postwar period. Perhaps scholars have too narrowly focused on post-1965 expressions of white ethnic revivals because they have advanced a narrative where Italian Americans and other Ellis Island ethnics came to identify primarily not in ethnic terms but as "whites" throughout the course of the twentieth century.[19] Certainly factors such as drastically reduced immigration flows from Europe to the United States after 1924, the coming of age of the second, third, and fourth generations of Ellis Island immigrants, the homogenizing trends that took place in American society after World War II, and the nation's acceptance of a pluralist narrative (at least for whites) contributed to Euro-American assimilation. Herein, ethnic identifications that remained after "new" immigrants were incorporated into the racially exclusive mainstream are largely understood as symbolic or, at best, as most salient in peoples' private rather than public lives. However, even while Italian Americans increasingly identified as white (and incorporated whiteness into what it meant to be Italian American), ethnic identifications and concerns continued to be significant forces in hundreds of thousands of "ethnic" peoples' public and private lives in the postwar period.[20] White ethnics were privileged in that they were seldom viewed by others primarily in ethnic terms by the 1960s, but the absence of that external locus of identity did not then mean that one's ethnic identity became entirely meaningless to a significant number of individuals as they came to understand themselves and the world around them. If we undervalue the existence of, or the evolution of, Euro-American ethnicity in the period from 1924 to 1965, we run the risk of misunderstanding other political and social phenomena—the origins and nature of white ethnic revivals as only one example.[21]

Just as little attention is paid to white ethnic identification in the post-war period, scholars have also largely overlooked the significance of postwar European immigration to the United States and the impact it had on established ethnic communities.[22] Hundreds of thousands of European immigrants came to the United States in the late twentieth century and helped to revitalize ethnic communities and ethnic feelings or identification among individuals whose lives they touched. While the journeys and experiences of postwar Italian immigrants are not the main focus of this study, a close relationship existed between newcomers and Italian American individuals who sponsored immigrants by providing them with housing, jobs, resettlement assistance, and social connections. "Ethnics" and immigrants thus lived and worked in close proximity with newcomers and shared social spaces with them. While the decline of Euro-American ethnic enclaves in American cities after World War II certainly changed the nature of these interactions from earlier waves of migration, the connections established between these two groups were meaningful nonetheless and warrant further attention.[23] It has long been understood that new immigrants tend to provide sources of ethnic renewal within their particular communities. The changes to the nation's immigration policies in 1965 facilitated the entry of approximately three hundred thousand Italian immigrants alone in a little over a decade corresponding, not coincidentally, with the height of white ethnic revivals in the United States (1968 through the 1980s).[24] Rather than write off these immigrants as remnants of an earlier migration flow, there is a need to examine the impact that groups of European immigrants had on established ethnic communities in the United States in the late twentieth century.[25]

American immigration scholars often characterize 1965 as a breaking point in terms of immigration waves, laws and policies, and the changing identity of the nation. But those changes need not mask the many sources of continuity that drove political and social developments in immigration policy, ethnic identity formation, and racial politics in the United States. If immigration laws, in the words of one scholar, "literally determine who 'we' are" as a nation, the immigration reforms of 1965 and the campaigns that led to their enactment offer both a revolutionary and a conservative vision of that nation.[26]

1. "President Kennedy Sees ACIM Delegates," *Dispatch*, June–July 1963, box 2, folder 1963 ACIM Dispatch, Carolyn Sinelli Burns Papers, Bentley Historical Library, University of Michigan (hereafter Sinelli Burns Papers).

2. "Inclusion" and "exclusion" refer to both political and social membership. Michael Walzer, *Spheres of Justice* (New York: Basic Books, 1984), 31–63; Linda Bosniak, *The Citizen and the Alien: Dilemmas of Contemporary Membership* (Princeton, N.J.: Princeton University Press, 2006); and Hiroshi Motomura, *Americans in Waiting: The Lost Story of Immigration and Citizenship in the United States* (New York: Oxford University Press, 2006).

3. Meg Greenfield, "The Melting Pot of Francis E. Walter," *Reporter*, box 3, folder 1961 Immigration and Citizenship Conference, Sinelli Burns Papers; and John F. Kennedy, *A Nation of Immigrants* (New York: Popular Library, 1964).

4. Matthew Frye Jacobson, *Roots Too: White Ethnic Revival in Post-civil Rights America* (Cambridge, Mass.: Harvard University Press, 2008).

5. Reflections on John F. Kennedy, *Fra Noi*, Chicago, January 1964, Immigration History Research Center Archives, University of Minnesota. The paper's eulogizing of Kennedy admires how "he maintained a conscious pride of his ancestral land . . . and he could, like millions of his fellow-citizens of Italian descent, feel the joy of 'returning' to the soil which one has known either through personal youthful experience or through the tales and traditions handed down from grandfather, to father, to son." The same article also notes the Kennedy family's three-generation arc from immigrant to "wealth, position, success, and the maximum power permitted in a democratic society," overcoming the "hostility of the 'know-nothings' of each generation." These sentiments about Kennedy even find expression as a recurring theme in HBO's *The Sopranos*.

6. Gary Gerstle argues an Irish and German (American) Catholic power bloc had emerged by the 1930s/40s as both an ally and rival to ruling Protestants in the nation. Gary Gerstle, *American Crucible: Race and Nation in the*

*Twentieth Century* (Princeton, N.J.: Princeton University Press, 2001), 256; and Matthew Frye Jacobson, *Whiteness of a Different Color: European Immigrants and the Alchemy of Race* (Cambridge, Mass.: Harvard University Press, 1998).

7. Leonard Pasqualicchio, Remarks on Columbus Day, Arlington, Virginia, October 13, 1963, box 1, Leonard Pasqualicchio Papers, Immigration History Research Center Archives, University of Minnesota.

8. "Remarks to American Committee on Italian Migration," June 11, 1963, Speech Files, President's Office Files, Presidential Papers, Papers of John F. Kennedy, John F. Kennedy Presidential Library.

9. Wendy Wall, *Inventing the "American Way": The Politics of Consensus from the New Deal to the Civil Rights Movement* (New York: Oxford University Press, 2008).

10. For just a few examples, see Alan Kraut, *Silent Travelers: Germs, Genes and the Immigrant Menace* (Baltimore: Johns Hopkins University Press, 1995); Erika Lee, *At America's Gates: Chinese Immigration during the Exclusion Era, 1882–1943* (Chapel Hill: University of North Carolina Press, 2003); Daniel Kanstroom, *Deportation Nation: Outsiders in American History* (Cambridge, Mass.: Harvard University Press, 2007); Margot Canaday, *The Straight State: Sexuality and Citizenship in Twentieth-Century America* (Princeton, N.J.: Princeton University Press, 2009); Martha Gardner, *The Qualities of a Citizen: Women, Immigration, and Citizenship, 1870–1965* (Princeton, N.J.: Princeton University Press, 2009); and Hidetaka Hirota, *Expelling the Poor: Atlantic Seaboard States and the Nineteenth-Century Origins of American Immigration Policy* (New York: Oxford University Press, 2017).

11. Americans reconciled their views on race and immigration by promoting the idea that Western Hemisphere immigrants were not in fact immigrants at all but were "migrants" that could be used as temporary, exploitable, and transitory laborers. As such, they were generally not encouraged to assimilate or naturalize. The state also found ways to deny those immigrants, and even their American-born children, full membership. Rachel St. John, *Line in the Sand: A History of the Western U.S.–Mexico Border* (Princeton, N.J.: Princeton University Press, 2011); David Gutierrez, *Walls and Mirrors: Mexican Americans, Mexican Immigrants and the Politics of Ethnicity* (Berkeley: University of California Press, 1995), 13–116; Mae Ngai, *Impossible Subjects: Illegal Aliens and the Making of Modern America* (Princeton, N.J.: Princeton University Press, 2004), 1–90, 127–166; Cybelle Fox, *Three Worlds of Relief: Race, Immigration, and the American Welfare State from the Progressive Era to the New Deal* (Princeton, N.J.: Princeton University Press, 2012); and Cindy Hahamovitch, *No Man's Land: Jamaican Guest Workers in America and the Global History of Deportable Labor* (Princeton, N.J.: Princeton University Press, 2012).

12. Aristide Zolberg, *A Nation by Design: Immigration Policy in the Fashioning of America* (Cambridge, Mass.: Harvard University Press, 2006), 199–292; John Higham, *Strangers in the Land: Patterns of American Nativism 1860–1925*

(New York: Atheneum, 1963); Desmond King, *Making Americans: Immigration, Race, and the Origins of the Diverse Democracy* (Cambridge, Mass.: Harvard University Press, 2000); and Robert A. Divine, *American Immigration Policy, 1924–1952* (New Haven, Conn.: Yale University Press, 1957).

13. Zolberg, *Nation by Design*; Higham, *Strangers in the Land*; King, *Making Americans*; and Divine, *American Immigration Policy*. For works that challenge a Eurocentric view of the origins of immigration restriction in the 1920s, see Ngai, *Impossible Subjects*, 1–55; and Lee, *At America's Gates*.

14. Higham, *Strangers in the Land*; Jacobson, *Whiteness of a Different Color*, 39–90; King, *Making Americans*; and Matthew Pratt Guterl, *The Color of Race in America, 1900–1940* (Cambridge, Mass.: Harvard University Press, 2001), 14–67.

15. King, *Making Americans*, 218–25. Although Jewish Americans did organize against quotas and attempted to draw other ethnic organizations into the struggle, their efforts were largely unsuccessful. See Libby Garland, *After They Closed the Gates: Jewish Illegal Immigration to the United States, 1921–1965* (Chicago: University of Chicago Press, 2014), 148–76; and Katherine Benton-Cohen, *Inventing the Immigration Problem: The Dillingham Commission and Its Legacy* (Cambridge, Mass.: Harvard University Press, 2018), 72–103.

16. Diana Selig, *Americans All: The Cultural Gifts Movement* (Cambridge, Mass.: Harvard University Press, 2008).

17. Roger Daniels, *Guarding the Golden Door: American Immigration Policy and Immigrants since 1882* (New York: Hill and Wang, 2004), 118; Daniel J. Tichenor, *Dividing Lines: The Politics of Immigration Control in America* (Princeton, N.J.: Princeton University Press, 2002), 176–218; Zolberg, *Nation by Design*, 311–17; and Robert Fleegler, *Ellis Island Nation: Immigration Policy and American Identity in the Twentieth Century* (Philadelphia: University of Pennsylvania Press, 2013).

18. Ngai, *Impossible Subjects*, 227–64; Tichenor, *Dividing Lines*, 176–218; and Fleegler, *Ellis Island Nation*, 103–90.

19. David Reimers, *Still the Golden Door: The Third World Comes to America* (New York: Columbia University Press, 1985); Reed Ueda, *Postwar Immigrant America: A Social History* (Boston: Bedford/St. Martin's Press, 1994); Gabriel Chin and Rose Cuizon Villazor, eds., *The Immigration and Nationality Act of 1965: Legislating a New America* (New York: Cambridge University Press, 2015); and Zolberg, *A Nation by Design*, 311–81.

20. Tichenor, *Dividing Lines*, 176–218; Daniels, *Guarding the Golden Door*, 113–28; Carl Bon Tempo, *Americans at the Gate: The United States and Refugees during the Cold War* (Princeton, N.J.: Princeton University Press, 2008); and Donna Gabaccia, *Foreign Relations: American Immigration in a Global Perspective* (Princeton, N.J.: Princeton University Press, 2012), 122–49.

21. Here again liberal elites in the White House and Congress tend to take center stage. Daniels, *Guarding the Golden Door*, 113–28; Tichenor, *Dividing*

*Lines*, 176–218; Zolberg, *Nation by Design*, 311–36; Peter Schrag, *Not Fit for Our Society: Immigration and Nativism in America* (Berkeley: University of California Press, 2010), 160–61; Carolyn Wong, *Lobbying for Inclusion: Rights Politics and the Making of Immigration Policy* (Stanford, Calif.: Stanford University Press, 2006); Kunal Parker, *Making Foreigners: Immigration and Citizenship Law in America, 1600–2000* (New York: Cambridge University Press, 2015), 185–220; Julian Zelizer, *The Fierce Urgency of Now: Lyndon Johnson, Congress, and the Battle for the Great Society* (New York: Penguin Books, 2015), 165, 220–21; James Patterson, *Grand Expectations: The United States, 1945–1974* (New York: Oxford University Press, 1996), 353, 468, 473–74, 482; G. Calvin Mackenzie and Robert Weisbrot, *The Liberal Hour: Washington and the Politics of Change in the 1960s* (New York: Penguin Books, 2008), 180–81; Chin and Villazor, *Immigration and Nationality Act*, 4, 11–59; and Margaret Sands Orchowski, *The Law that Changed the Face of the Nation: The Immigration and Nationality Act of 1965* (New York: Rowman & Littlefield, 2015).

22. A new cohort of scholarship has started to focus on the concerns and actions of these groups. For some notable works, see Madeline Hsu, *The Good Immigrants: How the Yellow Peril Became the Model Minority* (Princeton, N.J.: Princeton University Press, 2015); Madeline Hsu and Ellen Wu, "Smoke and Mirrors: Conditional Inclusion, Model Minorities, and the Pre-1965 Dismantling of Asian Exclusion," *Journal of American Ethnic History* 34, no. 4 (Summer 2015); Maddalena Marinari, "Liberty, Restriction, and the Remaking of Italians and Eastern European Jews (1882–1965)" (PhD diss., University of Kansas, 2009); Grainne McEvoy, "Justice and Order: American Catholic Social Thought and the Immigration Question in the Restriction Era, 1917–1965" (PhD diss., Boston College, 2014); and Elizabeth Venditto, "Nation-Building and Catholic Assistance to Migrants in Italy's Transition from Land of Emigration to Immigration, 1861–1990," (PhD diss., University of Minnesota, 2014).

23. Ngai, *Impossible Subjects*, 228–29.

24. Gerstle, *American Crucible*; Wall, *Inventing the "American Way"*; Carol Anderson Horton, *Race and the Making of American Liberalism* (New York: Oxford University Press, 2005); Kevin M. Schultz, *Tri-Faith America: How Catholics and Jews Held Postwar America to Its Protestant Promise* (New York: Oxford University Press, 2011); and Samuel Moyn, *Christian Human Rights* (Philadelphia: University of Pennsylvania Press, 2015).

25. Ngai, *Impossible Subjects*, 228.

26. Schultz, *Tri-Faith America*, 8.

27. Ngai, *Impossible Subjects*, 228–29.

28. Ngai acknowledges the limitations of white ethnic liberalism (Ngai, *Impossible Subjects*, 227–30, 245–46). See also Fleegler, *Ellis Island Nation*, 161–90; and Horton, *Race and the Making of American Liberalism*.

29. Salvatore LaGumina, *From Steerage to Suburb: Long Island Italians* (New York: Center for Migration Studies, 1988); and Joel Perlmann, *Italians Then, Mexicans Now: Immigrant Origins and Second-Generation Progress, 1890 to 2000* (New York: Russell Sage Foundation, 2005).

30. Fleegler, *Ellis Island Nation*.

31. For the challenges of studying ethnic group identity and its meanings at any given historical moment, see Virginia Yans, "On 'Groupness,'" *Journal of American Ethnic History* 25, no. 4 (Summer 2006); and Kathleen Neils Conzen et al., "The Invention of Ethnicity: A Perspective from the U.S.A.," *Journal of American Ethnic History* 12, no. 1 (Fall 1992). For personal versus public group identity, see David Gerber, *Authors of Their Lives: The Personal Correspondence of British Immigrants to North America in the Nineteenth Century* (New York: New York University Press, 2006), 1–91.

32. One scholar describes this kind of liberalism as "revolutionary pluralism" in contrast to the consensus politics embraced by most white ethnics during the Cold War. John Enyeart, "Revolutionizing Cultural Pluralism: The Political Odyssey of Louis Adamic, 1932–1951," *Journal of American Ethnic History* 34, no. 3 (Spring 2015).

33. Penny Von Eschen, *Race against Empire: Black Americans and Anticolonialism, 1937–1957* (Ithaca, N.Y.: Cornell University Press, 1997). Leftist and feminist Progressives active in the New Deal were similarly forced toward more centrist positions. Landon Storrs, *The Second Red Scare and the Unmaking of the New Deal Left* (Princeton, N.J.: Princeton University Press, 2013).

34. Jacobson, *Roots Too*; and Jonathan Rieder, *Canarsie: The Jews and Italians of Brooklyn against Liberalism* (Cambridge, Mass.: Harvard University Press, 1985). For the liberal and conservative tensions that existed among Catholics in the postwar period, see Todd Scribner, *A Partisan Church: American Catholicism and the Rise of Neoconservative Catholics* (Washington, D.C.: Catholic University Press of America, 2015).

35. Ellen Wu, *The Color of Success: Asian Americans and the Origins of the Model Minority* (Princeton, N.J.: Princeton University Press, 2014); Madeline Hsu, *Good Immigrants*; and Hsu and Wu, "Smoke and Mirrors."

36. This point is also made in Maddalena Marinari, "Divided and Conquered: Immigration Reform Advocates and the Passage of the 1952 Immigration and Nationality Act," *Journal of American Ethnic History* 35, no. 3 (Spring 2016).

37. Selig, *Americans All*; Schultz, *Tri-Faith America*; Wall, *Inventing the "American Way"*; and Gerstle, *American Crucible*.

38. Ngai, *Impossible Subjects*, 227–30, 245–46; Fleegler, *Ellis Island Nation*, 161–90; and Horton, *Race and the Making of American Liberalism*. In Thomas Sugrue's sweeping study of the broad civil rights movement in the North, there is no mention of immigration reform or collaboration with white ethnics

on the subject. Thomas Sugrue, *Sweet Land of Liberty: The Forgotten Struggle for Civil Rights in the North* (New York: Random House, 2008).

39. For movement in that direction, see Marinari, "Divided and Conquered."

40. Ngai, *Impossible Subjects*, 240. Jewish American groups are examined in detail for the role they played in shaping postwar refugee policies in Gil Loescher and John Scanlan, *Calculated Kindness: Refugees and America's Half-Open Door, 1945–Present* (New York: Free Press, 1986), 1–48; Marinari, "Liberty, Restriction, and the Remaking of Italians"; and Garland, *After They Closed the Gates*, 177–212. For other white ethnic groups involved in attempts to shape postwar immigration policy, see Anna Jaroszynska-Kirchmann, *The Exile Mission: The Polish Political Diaspora and Polish Americans, 1939–1956* (Athens: Ohio University Press, 2004); and Rachel Rains Winslow, *The Best Possible Immigrants: International Adoption and the American Family* (Philadelphia: University of Pennsylvania Press, 2017), 34–69.

41. Frank Cavaioli, "Patterns of Italian Immigration to the United States," *Catholic Social Science Review* 13 (2008); Stefano Luconi, *From Paesani to White Ethnics: The Italian Experience in Philadelphia* (Albany: State University of New York Press, 2001); and Salvatore LaGumina, *New York at Mid-Century: The Impellitteri Years* (Westport, Conn.: Greenwood Press, 1992).

42. For Italian American and/or Catholic electoral and political strength, see Fleegler, *Ellis Island Nation*, 90, 147–48; and Zolberg, *Nation by Design*, 302. For the Italian American congressional caucus, see Betty Santangelo, *Lucky Corner: The Biography of Congressman Alfred E. Santangelo and the Rise of Italian Americans in Politics* (New York: Center for Migration Studies, 1999).

43. For the continuing significance of ethnic identifications, see Jordan Stanger-Ross, *Staying Italian: Urban Change and Ethnic Life in Postwar Toronto and Philadelphia* (Chicago: University of Chicago Press, 2009); and Richard Alba and Victor Nee, *Remaking the American Mainstream: Assimilation and Contemporary Immigration* (Cambridge, Mass.: Harvard University Press, 2005). For the argument that primary sources and thus scholarly analysis over-represent the cohesiveness and importance of ethnic group demarcations in individual lives, see Fredrick Cooper and Rogers Brubaker, "Identity," in *Colonialism in Question: Theory, Knowledge, History*, by Frederick Cooper (Berkeley: University of California Press, 2005), 85.

44. Bon Tempo, *Americans at the Gate*; Tichenor, *Dividing Lines*, 176–218; Zolberg, *Nation by Design*, 311–81; and Loescher and Scanlan, *Calculated Kindness*.

45. Ellen Percy Kraly, "U.S. Refugee Policies and Refugee Migration," in *Immigration and U.S. Foreign Policy*, ed. Robert W. Tucker, Charles B. Keely, and Linda Wrigley (Boulder, Co.: Westview Press, 1990). This number does not account for unauthorized entries, for ethnic Italians who held or claimed American citizenship, or for ethnic Italians who entered via other national

quotas. For unauthorized Italian emigration, see Sandro Rinauro, *Il cammino della Speranza, l'Emigrazione clandestine degli Italiani nel Secondo Dopoguerra* (Turin, Italy: Einaudi, 2009).

46. Mark Wyman, *Round-Trip to America: The Immigrants Return to Europe, 1880–1930* (Ithaca, N.Y.: Cornell University Press, 1993). Wyman concludes that between one-third and one-half of those immigrants may have been migratory laborers and thus were counted as immigrants more than once or, alternatively, they returned to Italy or emigrated elsewhere.

47. Michele Colucci, *Lavoro in movimento, l'emigrazione italiana in europa, 1945–1957* (Rome: Donzelli, 2008); Frederico Romero, *Emigrazione e integrazione europea 1945–1973* (Rome: Edizioni Lavoro, 1991); Patrizia Audenino and Maddalena Tirabassi, *Migrazioni Italiane, Storia e storie dall'Ancien regime a oggi* (Turin, Italy: Bruno Mondadri, 2008), 125–51; and Andreina De Clementi, *Il Prezzo della ricostruzione. L'emigrazione italiana nel secondo dopoguerra* (Rome: Laterza, 2010). Whether to consider these migrations a diaspora is a matter of debate. Rogers Brubaker, "The 'Diaspora' Diaspora," *Ethnic and Racial Studies* 28, no. 1 (January 2005); Donna Gabaccia, *Italy's Many Diasporas* (Seattle: University of Washington Press, 2000), 153–73; and Stefano Luconi, "Italian Migrations and Diasporic Approaches: Historical Phenomena and Scholarly Interpretations," in *The Cultures of Italian Migration: Diverse Trajectories and Discrete Perspectives*, ed. Graziella Parati and Anthony Julian Tamburri (Teaneck, N.J.: Fairleigh Dickinson University Press, 2011).

48. Hiroshi Motomura, *Immigration Outside of the Law* (New York: Oxford University Press, 2014), 235.

1. ITALIAN AMERICAN IDENTITY AND POLITICS: WORLD WAR II TO THE COLD WAR

1.. Salvatore LaGumina, "In Search of Heroes: Italian Americans in World War II," *Italian Americana* 20, no. 1 (Winter 2002); Stefano Luconi, "Contested Loyalties: World War II and Italian Americans' Ethnic Identity," *Italian Americana* 30, no. 2 (Summer 2012); and Lawrence DiStasi, "War within War: Italian Americans and the Military in World War II," in *Una Storia Segreta: The Secret History of Italian American Evacuation and Internment during World War II*, ed. Lawrence DiStasi (Berkeley, Calif.: Heyday Books, 2001).

2. Peter D'Agostino, "Craniums, Criminals, and the 'Cursed Race': Italian Anthropology in American Racial Thought, 1861–1924," *Comparative Studies in Society and History* 44, no. 2 (April 2002); Matthew Pratt Guterl, *The Color of Race in America, 1900–1940* (Cambridge, Mass.: Harvard University Press, 2001), 14–67; Matthew Frye Jacobson, *Whiteness of a Different Color: European Immigrants and the Alchemy of Race* (Cambridge, Mass.: Harvard University Press, 1998), 1–90; and Alan Kraut, *Silent Travelers: Germs, Genes and the Immigrant Menace* (Baltimore: Johns Hopkins University Press, 1995). For the role that gender played in stereotyping of Italian immigrants, see Jennifer Guglielmo, *Living the Revolution: Italian Women's Resistance and Radicalism in*

*New York City, 1880–1945* (Chapel Hill: University of North Carolina Press, 2010), 79–109; and Desmond King, *Making Americans: Immigration, Race, and the Origins of the Diverse Democracy* (Cambridge, Mass.: Harvard University Press, 2000), 218–25.

3. Elazar Barkan, *The Retreat of Scientific Racism* (New York: Cambridge University Press, 1992); Diana Selig, *Americans All: The Cultural Gifts Movement* (Cambridge, Mass.: Harvard University Press, 2008); and Jacobson, *Whiteness of a Different Color*, 91–138.

4. Thomas Guglielmo, *White on Arrival: Italians, Race, Color, and Power in Chicago, 1890–1945* (New York: Oxford University Press, 2003); Lizabeth Cohen, *Making a New Deal: Industrial Workers in Chicago, 1919–1939* (New York: Cambridge University Press, 1990); Cybelle Fox, *Three Worlds of Relief: Race, Immigration, and the American Welfare State from the Progressive Era to the New Deal* (Princeton, N.J.: Princeton University Press, 2012); and David Roediger, *Working toward Whiteness: How America's Immigrants Became White; The Strange Journey from Ellis Island to the Suburbs* (New York: Basic Books, 2005), 199–234.

5. Cohen, *Making a New Deal*, 53–158; Roediger, *Working toward Whiteness*, 157–98; Simone Cinotto, *The Italian American Table: Food, Family, and Community in New York City* (Chicago: University of Illinois Press, 2013); and Miriam Cohen, *Workshop to Office: Two Generations of Italian Women in New York City, 1900–1950* (Ithaca, N.Y.: Cornell University Press, 1993).

6. Barkan, *The Retreat of Scientific Racism*; and Carl Degler, *In Search of Human Nature: The Decline and Revival of Darwinism in American Social Thought* (New York: Oxford University Press, 1991). There are notable exceptions to this trend, including forced sterilizations in the United States after World War II. Susan Cahn, *Sexual Reckonings: Southern Girls in a Troubling Age* (Cambridge, Mass.: Harvard University Press, 2007), 156–180; and Alexandra Minna Stern, *Eugenic Nation: Faults and Frontiers of Better Breeding in America* (Berkeley: University of California Press, 2005).

7. Gary Gerstle, *American Crucible: Race and Nation in the Twentieth Century* (Princeton, N.J.: Princeton University Press, 2001); Wendy Wall, *Inventing the "American Way": The Politics of Consensus from the New Deal to the Civil Rights Movement* (New York: Oxford University Press, 2008); and Selig, *Americans All*.

8. This trend carried on during the Cold War. For interwar religious pluralism, see Selig, *Americans All*, 113–50. For World War II and postwar religious pluralism, see Wall, *Inventing the "American Way,"* 163–277; and Kevin M. Schultz, *Tri-Faith America: How Catholics and Jews Held Postwar America to Its Protestant Promise* (New York: Oxford University Press, 2011).

9. Robert L. Fleegler, "'Forget All Differences until the Forces of Freedom Are Triumphant': The World War II–Era Quest for Ethnic and Religious Tolerance," *Journal of American Ethnic History* 27, no. 2 (Winter 2008).

10. Gerstle, *American Crucible*, 264–65.

11. Jennifer Guglielmo and Salvatore Salerno, eds., *Are Italians White? How Race Is Made in America* (New York: Routledge, 2003).

12. The major exception to that trend were labor elites who checked fascist support from rank-and-file members. Rudy Vecoli, "The Making and Unmaking of the Italian American Working Class," in *The Lost World of Italian American Radicalism: Politics, Labor, and Culture*, ed. Philip Cannistraro and Gerald Meyer (Westport, Conn.: Praeger, 2003). See also international socialists in the United States and Italy, notably, Gaetano Salvemini and members of the Mazzini Society. John Patrick Diggins, *Mussolini and Fascism: The View from America* (Princeton, N.J.: Princeton University Press, 1972), 399–421.

13. Stefano Luconi, *La "diplomazia parallela." Il regime fascista e la mobilitazione politica degli italo-americani* (Milan: Angeli, 2000); Diggins, *Mussolini and Fascism*; Matteo Pretelli, *Il fascismo e gli Italiani all'estero* (Bologna: CLUEB, 2010); Philip V. Cannistraro, *Blackshirts in Little Italy: Italian Americans and Fascism, 1921–1929* (New York: Bordighera Press, 1999); and Gaetano Salvemini, *Italian Fascist Activities in the United States* (New York: Center for Migration Studies, 1977).

14. Luconi, *La "diplomazia parallela."*

15. Diggins, *Mussolini and Fascism*.

16. Ralph Arlotti, interview, 2005, unpublished oral histories, Post-WWII Italian American Oral Histories, Italian American Collection, Senator John Heinz History Center. Arlotti (b. 1927, Cosenza) immigrated to the United States in 1937. He was a US citizen, deriving citizenship from birth through his father's status, but spent formative years in Italy. When Arlotti turned eighteen in 1945, he volunteered for the US Navy but failed to serve because the war soon ended.

17. Luconi, *La "diplomazia parallela"*; Cannistraro, *Blackshirts in Little Italy*; Nadia Venturini, *Neri e Italiani ad Harlem: gli Anni Trenta e la Guerra d'Etiopia* (Rome: Edizioni Lavoro, 1990); T. Guglielmo, *White on Arrival*, 113–28, 172–76; and Stefano Luconi, *From Paesani to White Ethnics: The Italian Experience in Philadelphia* (Albany: State University of New York Press, 2001), 39–117.

18. Venturini, *Neri e Italiani ad Harlem*; Diggins, *Mussolini and Fascism*, 302–6; and T. Guglielmo, *White on Arrival*, 113–22. Jessica Harriet Lee contends that Italian American pro-Fascist displays did not ultimately hurt them politically because of the political power they wielded as a large voting bloc. Jessica Harriet Lee, "To the Seventh Generation: Italians and the Creation of an American Political Identity, 1921–1948" (PhD diss., Columbia University, 2016).

19. Luconi, *La "diplomazia parallela"*; and Diggins, *Mussolini and Fascism*. For more on the OSIA, see Ernest L. Biagi, *The Purple Aster: A History of the Order Sons of Italy in America* (New York: Veritas Press, 1961).

20. Philip A. Cannistraro and Elena Aga Rossi, "La Politica Etnica e il Dilemma dell' Antifascismo negli Stati Uniti: Il Caso di Generoso Pope," *Storia*

*Contemporanea* 17, no. 2 (1986); Stefano Luconi, "Generoso Pope and Italian American Voters in New York City," *Studi Emigrazione* 38, no. 142 (2001); and Diggins, *Mussolini and Fascism*, 84–95, 342–51, 400–4.

21. Roger Daniels, *Prisoners without Trial: Japanese Americans in World War II* (New York: Hill and Wang, 1993).

22. Mary Elizabeth Basile Chopas, *Searching for Subversives: The Story of Italian Internment in Wartime America* (Chapel Hill: University of North Carolina Press, 2017); Stephen Fox, *The Unknown Internment: An Oral History of the Relocation of Italian Americans during World War II* (Boston: Twayne Publishers, 1990); Guido Tintori, "New Discoveries, Old Prejudices: The Internment of Italian Americans during World War II," in *Una Storia Segreta: The Secret History of Italian American Evacuation and Internment during World War II*, ed. Lawrence DiStasi (Berkeley, Calif.: Heyday Books, 2001); and Guido Tintori, "Italiani Enemy Aliens. I Civili residenti negli Stati Uniti d'America durante la Seconda Guerra Mondiale," *Altreitalie* 28 (January–June 2004). Tintori argues that Italian American electoral influence was critical in dampening the government's scrutiny of Italian nationals.

23. Nancy Carnevale, "No Italian Spoken for the Duration of the War: Language, Italian American Identity and Cultural Pluralism in the World War II Years," *Journal of American Ethnic History* 22, no. 3 (Spring 2003).

24. Lawrence DiStasi, "War within War." For a more developed discussion about state and public scrutiny of a number of racial and ethnic groups' loyalty during the war, see James Sparrow, *Warfare State: World War II Americans and the Age of Big Government* (New York: Oxford University Press, 2011), 78–112.

25. Christopher Sterba, *Good Americans: Italian and Jewish Immigrants during the First World War* (New York: Oxford University Press, 2003). Peter Vellon makes the case for WWI as a seminal moment in Italian Americans' self-construction of group identity as whites. Peter Vellon, *A Great Conspiracy against Our Race: Italian Immigrant Newspapers and the Construction of Whiteness in the Early 20th Century* (New York: New York University Press, 2014).

26. Gerstle, *American Crucible*, 187–237; Wall, *Inventing the "American Way"*; Fleegler, "'Forget All Differences'"; and Schultz, *Tri-Faith America*, 1–67.

27. For a typical example of Italian Americans quickly and publicly attempting to change their group's image, see "Sons of Italy Statement," *Il Progresso Italo-Americano*, July 2, 1943; and Nancy Carnevale, *A New Language, a New World: Italian Immigrants in the United States, 1890–1945* (Urbana: University of Illinois Press, 2009), 158–78.

28. Other notable chapters operated in New York and Pittsburgh. Girolamo Valenti and George Quilici correspondence, box 3, folder 17, George Quilici Papers, Italian American Collection, Immigration History Research Center Archives, University of Minnesota (hereafter Quilici Papers); "The Italian

American Victory Council of Chicago," George Quilici to Franklin Roosevelt, October 12, 1942, box 3, folder 17, Quilici Papers; and Dominic Candeloro, *Chicago's Italians: Immigrants, Ethnics, Americans* (Chicago: Arcadia Publishing, 2003), 137–39.

29. George Quilici to Ugo Carusi, Assistant to the US Attorney General, September 16, 1943, box 3, folder 17, Quilici Papers; "Greater Chicago Italian American Day" Program, box 3, folder 18, Quilici Papers; and "Italian-Americans Reach Bond Goal on First Day," *Chicago Sun Times*, August 30, 1943.

30. George Quilici to Ugo Carusi, Assistant to the US Attorney General, September 16, 1943, box 3, folder 17, Quilici Papers.

31. "Statement of Judge George Quilici to the House Foreign Affairs Committee," June 12, 1946, box 3, folder 19, Quilici Papers.

32. "The Role of Italian Americans Today," *L'Unità del Popolo*, July 15, 1944.

33. "Italian American Victory Council of Chicago Declaration of Policy," box 3, folder 18, Quilici Papers.

34. "Italian American Victory Council of Chicago Declaration of Policy," box 3, folder 18, Quilici Papers.

35. George Quilici, "Speech at the Amalgamated Center, Chicago," June 6, 1951, box 3, folder 18, Quilici Papers.

36. Ellen Wu, *The Color of Success: Asian Americans and the Origins of the Model Minority* (Princeton, N.J.: Princeton University Press, 2014), 63–110. See also African American loyalty displays in Gerstle, *American Crucible*, 187–237.

37. For limitations of wartime pluralism, see Wall, *Inventing the "American Way*," 132–59; and Gerstle, *American Crucible*, 187–237. For limitations specific to Italian Americans, see Carnevale, *New Language, a New World*, 158–78.

38. "Chicago's Army of Italian Folk Out to Win War," *Chicago Tribune*, June 15, 1942.

39. George Quilici to Joseph Facci, Foreign Language Division, Office of War Information, September 16, 1943, box 3, folder 17, Quilici Papers; "Appeal Here to Italy to Quit War," *Herald American*, July 16, 1943; and "Italy! Quit War, Chicagoans Plea," July 20, 1943, *Herald American*.

40. George Quilici to War Control Board, October 28, 1943, box 3, folder 17, Quilici Papers; and George Quilici to Cordell Hull, February 19, 1944, box 3, folder 17, Quilici Papers.

41. American Relief for France and Greece received similar amounts in 1945 and 1946. "National War Fund to Open Its Last Drive This Month," *New York Times*, August 4, 1945, box 1, folder August 1945, Juvenal Marchisio Papers, Center for Migration Studies (hereafter Marchisio Papers); and "Taylor Urges Self Rule for Italian People," *New York Herald Tribune*, January 2, 1947, box 2, folder January 1947, Marchisio Papers.

42. "Analysis of Material Contributed to American Relief for Italy, Inc.,," box 6, folder Miscellaneous Documents, Marchisio Papers; Notes of Meeting with Juvenal Marchisio, re: American Relief for Italy Inc., March 6, 1946, box 3, folder 17, Quilici Papers; "American Relief for Italy, Inc," *L'Unita Del Popolo*, May 20, 1944; Meeting Minutes, October 18, 1946, box 1, folder General Membership: Minutes 1946–1948, Italian American Labor Council Collection, Tamiment Library, Robert F. Wagner Labor Archives, New York University (hereafter IALC Collection); box 4, American Committee of Italian War Relief of St. Paul Collection, Immigration History Research Center Archives, University of Minnesota. For accounts of the International Ladies Garment Workers Union's relief donations, see *Il Progresso Italo-Americano*, February 26, 1946, March 4, 1946, April 7, 1946, and April 28, 1946.

43. "Analysis of Material Contributed to American Relief for Italy, Inc," box 6, folder Miscellaneous Documents, Marchisio Papers; "Inventory of Collected Materials," box 4, folder 2, Order Sons of Italy in America–Pennsylvania Grand Lodge Collection, Immigration History Research Center Archives, University of Minnesota (hereafter OSIA–PA Grand Lodge Collection); and *American Relief for Italy News*, March 1945–July 1947.

44. *Il Progresso Italo-Americano*, January 1946–December 1946. Total amount found in August 13, 1946 issue.

45. "U.S. Doctors Sending Aid," *American Relief for Italy News*, April 1945, box 3, folder 18, Quilici Papers.

46. G. D. Procopio and Juvenal Marchisio correspondence, July–October 1949, Giuseppe D. Procopio Papers, Immigration History Research Center Archives, University of Minnesota (hereafter Procopio Papers); Procopio Bio, Procopio Papers; and "Calabria Nostra" Booklet, April 8, 1949, box 1, Procopio Papers. As another example, in 1946, Local 48 of the ILGWU sent $1,000 to Vasto, Abruzzo, the hometown of many of its members. Meeting Minutes, May 26, 1948, box 1, folder General Membership: Minutes 1946–1948, IALC Collection.

47. "Bronx Committee for the Aid of Italian Children," *Il Progresso Italo-Americano*, January 20, 1946.

48. The donations were collected from 1945 to 1955, and the building was dedicated in 1956. "Report of the Supreme Venerable," Order Sons of Italy in America Supreme Convention, Philadelphia, October 1955, box 1, folder 14, George Spatuzza Collection, Immigration History Research Center Archives, University of Minnesota (hereafter Spatuzza Collection).

49. "Order of the Sons of Italy in America, Dedication in the Boys' Town of Rome of the Building Donated by the Grand Lodge of the State of New York," box 6, Howard E. Molisani Papers, Immigration History Research Center Archives, University of Minnesota (hereafter Molisani Papers); "Boys Town of Italy Brochure," no. 4, 1978, box 6, Molisani Papers; "Fathers and Sons,"

*Attenzione*, December 1984, box 6, Molisani Papers; Boys' Towns of Italy Yearbooks, 1960–1965, box 2, Molisani Papers; and vol. 1 and 2, box 1, Boys' Town of Italy, Inc. Collection, Rare Books and Special Collections, New York Public Library.

50. Sara Fieldston, *Raising the World: Child Welfare in the American Century* (Cambridge, Mass.: Harvard University Press, 2015).

51. John Lamberton Harper, *America and the Reconstruction of Italy, 1945–1948* (New York: Cambridge University Press, 1986), 22–75; James Edward Miller, *The United States and Italy, 1940–1950: The Politics of Diplomacy and Stabilization* (Chapel Hill: University of North Carolina Press, 1986), 131–53; and Alessandro Brogi, *Confronting America: The Cold War between the United States and the Communists in France and Italy* (Chapel Hill: University of North Carolina Press, 2011).

52. Miller, *United States and Italy*, 131–45, 154–61.

53. Harper, *America and the Reconstruction of Italy*; Paul Ginsborg, *A History of Contemporary Italy: Society and Politics, 1943–1988* (New York: Palgrave, 2003), 72–185; Miller, *United States and Italy*; and Patrick McCarthy, *The Crisis of the Italian State: From the Origins of the Cold War to the Fall of Berlusconi* (London: Palgrave MacMillan, 1995), 40–60.

54. Harper, *America and the Reconstruction of Italy*; Miller, *United States and Italy*; and Frank Ninkovich, *The Wilsonian Century: U.S. Foreign Policy since 1900* (Chicago: University of Chicago Press, 1999).

55. Harper, *America and the Reconstruction of Italy*, 20–21.

56. Miller, *United States and Italy*, 176–84.

57. Saul Kelly, *Cold War in the Desert: Britain, the United States and the Italian Colonies, 1945–52* (New York: St. Martin's Press, 2000); and Miller, *United States and Italy*, 162–76, 193–205.

58. In 1954, Trieste was ultimately returned to Italy. Roberto Rabel, *Between East and West: Trieste, the United States, and the Cold War, 1941–1954* (Durham, N.C.: Duke University Press, 1988); and Diego De Castro, *La questione di Trieste: L'azione politica e diplomatica italiana dal 1943 al 1954* (Trieste, Italy: LINT, 1981).

59. Miller, *United States and Italy*, 193–249.

60. "Memorandum on a Fair and Just Peace with Italy," submitted to Secretary of State James Byrnes by the Committee for a Just Peace with Italy, Inc., June 1946, box 45, folder A Just Peace for Italy, Edward Corsi Papers, Rare Books and Special Collections, Syracuse University (hereafter Corsi Papers).

61. "A New Deal for Italy," *Il Progresso Italo-Americano*, March 7, 1948; "Resolution Approved for the Territorial Integrity of Italy," The Italian American Labor Council, May 10, 1945, box 8, Corsi Papers; "Memorandum on a Fair and Just Peace with Italy," submitted to Secretary of State James Byrnes by the Committee for a Just Peace with Italy, Inc., June 1946, box 45,

folder Just Peace for Italy, Corsi Papers; and The Committee for a Just Peace with Italy, Inc. Activities Summary, August 7, 1947, box 45, folder A Just Peace for Italy, Corsi Papers.

62. The committee also took out full-page ads in the *New York Times* on February 12, 1946, and the *Washington Post* on February 13, 1946, to publicize its platform. The Committee for a Just Peace with Italy, Inc. Activities Summary August 7, 1947, box 45, folder A Just Peace for Italy, Corsi Papers.

63. "Memorandum on a Fair and Just Peace with Italy," submitted to Secretary of State James Byrnes by the Committee for a Just Peace with Italy, Inc., June 1946, box 45, folder A Just Peace for Italy, Corsi Papers.

64. The case may be made that the OSIA especially retained some elements of what could be considered an imperial agenda throughout the 1950s. The organization continued to advocate for Italian trusteeship of former African colonies until 1955, well after other Italian American groups abandoned such arguments. "Report of the Supreme Venerable at the Supreme Convention," Order Sons of Italy in America, October 1949, box 1, folder 11, Spatuzza Collection. For more on Mussolini's formal and cultural colonial projects, see Mark Choate, *Emigrant Nation: The Making of Italy Abroad* (Cambridge, Mass.: Harvard University Press, 2008).

65. "Memorandum on a Fair and Just Peace with Italy," submitted to Secretary of State James Byrnes by the Committee for a Just Peace with Italy, Inc., June 1946, box 45, folder A Just Peace for Italy, Corsi Papers.

66. Letters from Senators to the committee, The Committee for a Just Peace with Italy, Inc. letter to members, March 6, 1947, and The Committee for a Just Peace with Italy April 7, 1947 Report, box 45, folder A Just Peace for Italy, Corsi Papers.

67. The Committee for a Just Peace with Italy, Inc. letter to members, March 6, 1947, box 45, folder A Just Peace for Italy, Corsi Papers.

68. The Committee for Religious Freedom in Italy letter to President Truman, February 25, 1947, box 45, folder A Just Peace for Italy, Corsi Papers.

69. Lobbying efforts included letter and telegram campaigns, dinners and formal meetings with senators, State Department officials, Italian cabinet members and the ambassador, and committee testimony before the Senate Foreign Relations Committee in April and May 1947. "The Committee for a Just Peace with Italy," n.d., box 45, folder A Just Peace for Italy, Corsi Papers; "Report for Period Ending April 7, 1947," box 45, folder A Just Peace for Italy, Corsi Papers; and Committee for a Just Peace with Italy and "Memorandum on a Fair and Just Peace with Italy," submitted to Secretary of State James Byrnes by the Committee for a Just Peace with Italy, Inc., June 1946, box 45, folder A Just Peace for Italy, Corsi Papers.

70. "The Committee for a Just Peace with Italy," n.d., box 45, folder A Just Peace for Italy, Corsi Papers.

71. Marina Maccari Clayton, "'Communists of the Stomach': Italian Migration and International Relations in the Cold War Era," *Studi Emigrazione* 41, no. 155 (2004). Alessandro Brogi likewise argues that American officials continued to view the French and Italian communist parties as "anomalies" rather than legitimate ideological and political foes well into the 1950s. Brogi, *Confronting America*, 156.

72. Walter LaFeber, *America, Russia, and the Cold War, 1945–2000*, 9th ed. (New York: McGraw-Hill, 2008); Michael Hogan, *The Marshall Plan: America, Britain, and the Reconstruction of Europe* (New York: Cambridge University Press, 1987); and Nicolaus Mills, *Winning the Peace: The Marshall Plan and America's Coming of Age as a Superpower* (Hoboken, N.J.: Wiley and Sons, 2008).

73. Wall, *Inventing the "American Way,"* 163–277; and "L. H. Pasqualicchio Statement on Behalf of the OSIA to U.S. House of Representatives, Foreign Affairs Committee, November 25, 1947," box 5, folder 18, Spatuzza Collection.

74. Miller, *United States and Italy*, 154–271; Robert A. Ventresca, *From Fascism to Democracy: Culture and Politics in the Italian Election of 1948* (Toronto: University of Toronto Press, 2004); and Ginsborg, *History of Contemporary Italy*, 72–120.

75. Miller, *United States and Italy*, 213–15; and Brogi, *Confronting America*.

76. The PSI split with hard-core socialists remaining in the PSI and democratic socialists forming the Italian Democratic Socialist Party (Partito Socialista Democratico Italiano, PSDI) in 1948. Many in the Italian trade union movement, however, viewed the PSDI as an American pawn. Ronald Filippelli, *American Labor and Postwar Italy, 1943–1953: A Study of Cold War Politics* (Stanford, Calif.: Stanford University Press, 1989).

77. Victoria de Grazia, *Irresistible Empire: America's Advance through 20th Century Europe* (Cambridge, Mass.: Harvard University Press, 2005), 336–75.

78. Ventresca, *From Fascism to Democracy*, 61–99; and Miller, *United States and Italy*, 154–271. Similar threats were made in 1953; see Brogi, *Confronting America*, 101–10, 133–56. For CIA funds to centrist parties in 1948, see Guido Formagioni, *La Democrazia cristiana e l'alleanza occidentale (1943–1953)* (Bologna: Il Mulino, 1998), 178.

79. Wendy Wall, "America's Best Propagandists: Italian Americans and the 1948 Letters to Italy Campaign," in *Cold War Constructions: The Political Culture of United States Imperialism, 1915–1960*, ed. Christian G. Appy (Amherst: University of Massachusetts Press, 2000); Stefano Luconi, "Anticommunism, Americanization, and Ethnic Identity: Italian Americans and the 1948 Letters to Italy Campaign," *Historian* 62, no. 2 (Winter 2000); and C. Edda Martinez and Edward Suchman, "Letters from America and the 1948 Elections in Italy," *Public Opinion Quarterly* 14, no. 1 (Spring 1950).

80. Ventresca, *From Fascism to Democracy*.

81. For the broader implications of public diplomacy more generally, see Justin Hart, *Empire of Ideas: The Origins of Public Diplomacy and the Transformation of U.S. Foreign Policy* (New York: Oxford University Press, 2013).

82. Generoso Pope and the San Gennaro Society in New York sponsored a parade through New York City's Little Italy with participants shouting "Viva L'Italia e Viva L'America!" "La Grandiosa Demonstrazione Popolare di Ieri del basso East Side Ispirata dalla campagna per l'invio di lettere e telegrammi ai cugiuni Italiani," *Il Progresso Italo-Americano*, April 11, 1948. For an example prayer vigil, see "Mass to Mark Election in Italy April 18," *Utica Observer Dispatch*, Utica, N.Y., March 29, 1948; and "2 Guest Priests to Lead Prayer Here as Italy Goes to Polls Next Sunday," *Utica Observer Dispatch*, April 11, 1948.

83. Wall, "America's Best Propagandists," 104–6.

84. "Uticans and Italy Vote," *Utica Observer Dispatch*, April 24, 1948.

85. "Uticans and Italy Vote."

86. Wall, "America's Best Propagandists," 91, 105.

87. Wall, 91, 105.

88. Eugene V. Alessandroni, "An Appeal to Our Italian Brothers," April 1948, box 5, folder 20, Spatuzza Collection.

89. Stephen Whitfield, *The Culture of the Cold War* (Baltimore: Johns Hopkins University Press, 1991), 77–100; and Jonathan Herzog, *The Spiritual-Industrial Complex: America's Religious Battle against Communism in the Early Cold War* (New York: Oxford University Press, 2011).

90. "To the People of Italy, From the People of America," *Messenger*, New York City, April 10, 1948.

91. Victor Anfuso, letter to Italy, March 28, 1948, Anfuso and Corsi Correspondence, box 12, folder 3, March 31, 1948, Corsi Papers. For similar language, see George Spatuzza, "Letter to Italy," box 1, folder 1, Spatuzza Collection.

92. Wall, "America's Best Propagandists," 101–4.

93. Account of letter, "Pleas to Italy Ask Vote against Reds," *New York Times*, April 4, 1948.

94. Wall, "America's Best Propagandists," 101.

95. Wall, 101.

96. Linda Reeder, *Widows in White: Migration and the Transformation of Rural Italian Women, Sicily, 1880–1920* (Toronto: University of Toronto Press, 2003); Mark Wyman, *Round-Trip to America: The Immigrants Return to Europe, 1880–1930* (Ithaca, N.Y.: Cornell University Press, 1993); Dino Cinel, *The National Integration of Italian Return Migration, 1870–1929* (Cambridge: Cambridge University Press, 1991); and Choate, *Emigrant Nation*. For transnational consumption patterns, see Cinotto, *Italian American Table*; and Kristin Hoganson, *Consumers' Imperium: The Global Production of American Domesticity, 1865–1920* (Chapel Hill: University of North Carolina Press, 2007).

97. Sonia Cancian, *Families, Lovers, and Their Letters: Italian Postwar Migration to Canada* (Winnipeg: University of Manitoba Press, 2010).

98. This figure is $8–10 million greater than the years preceding and following the elections. Ventresca, *From Fascism to Democracy*, 4–14, 240–41. For an Italian American organization that funneled remittances to Italy in the year or so before the 1948 election, see "Cooperative for American Remittances to Europe, Inc. Correspondence, 1947–1948," box 46, folder CARE, Corsi Papers.

99. For American tourism's impact on Cold War Europe, see Christopher Endy, *Cold War Holidays: American Tourism in France* (Chapel Hill: University of North Carolina Press, 2004).

100. George Spatuzza, "An Appeal to All Americans of Italian Origin," November 1947, box 1, folder 1, Spatuzza Collection. Appeal was circulated among Order Sons of Italy in America chapters and the press and was entered into the Congressional Record on November 20, 1947, by Charles Wayland Brooks.

101. Spatuzza, "An Appeal to All Americans of Italian Origin."

102. Wall, "America's Best Propagandists," 101.

103. "Italian Asks Help of U.S. Catholics," *New York Times*, March 22, 1948.

104. "The Italian Elections, the Time for Action," *Il Crociato*, Brooklyn, N.Y., March 13, 1948.

105. "Italian Elections, the Time for Action."

106. "To the People of Italy, From the People of America," *Messenger*, April 10, 1948; and Eugene V. Alessandroni, "An Appeal to Our Italian Brothers," April 1948, box 5, folder 20, Spatuzza Collection.

2. THE ITALIAN AMERICAN IMMIGRATION REFORM LOBBY

1. Daniel J. Tichenor, *Dividing Lines: The Politics of Immigration Control in America* (Princeton, N.J.: Princeton University Press, 2002), 182.

2. See Displaced Persons Act of 1948, Pub. L. No. 80-774, 62 Stat. 1009 (1948); and Internal Security Act of 1950, Pub. L. No. 81-831, 64 Stat. 987 (1950).

3. Marina Maccari Clayton, "'Communists of the Stomach': Italian Migration and International Relations in the Cold War Era," *Studi Emigrazione* 41, no. 155 (2004).

4. David Ekbladh, *The Great American Mission: Modernization and the Construction of an American World Order* (Princeton, N.J.: Princeton University Press, 2010); and Nick Cullather, *The Hungry World: America's Cold War Battle against Poverty in Asia* (Cambridge, Mass.: Harvard University Press, 2010).

5. "Proposes World-Wide Mass Immigration, Resettlement," *Order Sons of Italy in America News*, October 1949, Immigration History Research Center Archives, University of Minnesota (hereafter *OSIA News*). See also the OSIA resolution calling for American delegates to the United Nations to call for

international support for Italian emigration to stave off Italian communism. "Resolution," Grand Lodge of Massachusetts, 1950, box 1, folder Immigration and Naturalization Committee, Joseph Errigo Papers, Immigration History Research Center Archives, University of Minnesota (hereafter Errigo Papers).

6. The OSIA approved a resolution to advocate for the reallocation of unused quotas and the lobbying for "more liberal" immigration policies for Italians at their annual Supreme Convention in 1949. "More Liberal Immigration Laws," *OSIA News*, November 1949.

7. Nicholas Petruzzelli, "Three Point Program to Aid Italy," *OSIA News*, October 1949.

8. The other two of Petruzzelli's three points were: 1) Establish reciprocal trade agreements between the United States and Italy to ensure increased Italian consumption of American products and to put more purchasing power in Italian hands, and 2) encourage cultural exchanges between the United States and Italy via government programs exchanging students, artists, and traders. Nicholas Petruzzelli, "Three Point Program to Aid Italy," *OSIA News*, October 1949.

9. Nicholas Petruzzelli, "Contradictions in U.S. Policies Are Cited," *OSIA News*, March 1950.

10. Nicholas Petruzzelli, "Three Point Program to Aid Italy," *OSIA News*, October 1949; and "U.S. Immigration Policy as It Affects Italy," *OSIA News*, November 1947. For a similar point on the role of immigrant remittances in homeland economies, see "Italy's Dilemma, Government Must Export Some 1.2 Million People by 1952," *OSIA News*, March 1949.

11. Nicholas Petruzzelli, "Three Point Program to Aid Italy," *OSIA News*, October 1949; and "Proposal for the Order on Immigration Quotas," *OSIA News*, September 1950.

12. Nicholas Petruzzelli, "Proposal for the Order on Immigration Quotas," *OSIA News*, September 1950.

13. Gil Loescher and John Scanlan, *Calculated Kindness: Refugees and America's Half-Open Door, 1945–Present* (New York: Free Press, 1986).

14. "Report on Italy," 1951, box 23, folder 254, National Catholic Welfare Conference Addendum Collection, Center for Migration Studies (hereafter NCWC Addendum).

15. "Memorandum on Surplus Population in Italy," Intergovernmental Committee for European Migration, November 23, 1953, box 47, folder Corsi-Dulles Dispute Data, Edward Corsi Papers, Rare Books and Special Collections, Syracuse University; and Gerard Daniel Cohen, *In War's Wake: Europe's Displaced Persons in the Postwar Order* (New York: Oxford University Press, 2012), 100–25.

16. "Report on Italy," 1951, box 23, folder 254, NCWC Addendum; "Facts and Data on Overpopulation in Italy," *ACIM Dispatch*, February 1955, box D,

American Committee on Italian Migration–National Office, New York City Records, Center for Migration Studies (hereafter ACIM–National); Roberto G. Rabel, *Between East and West: Trieste, the United States, and the Cold War, 1941–1954* (Durham, N.C.: Duke University Press, 1988); and Bogdan C. Novak, *Trieste, 1941–1954: The Ethnic, Political, and Ideological Struggle* (Chicago: University of Chicago Press, 1970).

17. By 1948, over 73,000 Italians had left Libya, 47,500 Eritrea, 14,000 Somalia, and nearly 59,000 from Ethiopia. About 193,000 Italians remained in former Italian colonies in 1950 and would move in later years. "Report on Italy," 1951, box 23, folder 254, NCWC Addendum. Some Italian nationals had lived in colonies their whole lives and their "return" was largely in name only. For the "migrant nature" of Italian colonization in Africa, see Nicola LaBanca, *Oltremare: Storia dell'espansione colonial italiana* (Bologna: Il Mulino, 2002).

18. Patrick McCarthy, *The Crisis of the Italian State: From the Origins of the Cold War to the Fall of Berlusconi* (London: Palgrave MacMillan, 1995), 35–40; and Alessandro Brogi, *Confronting America: The Cold War between the United States and the Communists in France and Italy* (Chapel Hill: University of North Carolina Press, 2011).

19. Paul Ginsborg, *A History of Contemporary Italy: Society and Politics, 1943–1988* (New York: Palgrave, 2003), 121–209; and James Edward Miller, *The United States and Italy, 1940–1950: The Politics of Diplomacy and Stabilization* (Chapel Hill: University of North Carolina Press, 1986), 223.

20. Ginsborg, *History of Contemporary Italy*, 121–42; Alan B. Mountjoy, *The Mezzogiorno* (New York: Oxford University Press, 1973), 8–12, 19–26; Sydney Tarrow, *Peasant Communism in Southern Italy* (New Haven, Conn.: Yale University Press, 1967); and Russel King, *Land Reform: The Italian Experience* (London: Butterworth & Company, 1973). For the impact of American political concerns and influence on this process, see Emanuele Bernardi, *La riforma agraria in Italia e gli Stati Uniti. Guerra fredda, Piano Marshall e interventi per il Mezzogiorno negli anni del centrismo degasperiano* (Bologna: Il Mulino, 2006).

21. Sandro Rinauro, "Politica e geografia dell'emigrazione italiana negli anni della ricostruzione," in *L'Italia alla meta del XX secolo: Conflitto sociale, Resistenza, construzione di una democrazia*, ed. Luigi Ganapini (Milan: Guerini e Associati, 2005). Leftist parties also endorsed emigration but offered different solutions for how to achieve emigration and the support to give migrants. Sandro Rinauro, *Il cammino della Speranza, l'Emigrazione clandestine degli Italiani nel Secondo Dopoguerra* (Turin, Italy: Einaudi, 2009), 40–57.

22. Donna Gabaccia, *Italy's Many Diasporas* (Seattle: University of Washington Press, 2000), 154–58. Internal migrations were equally significant in these years as well. See Enrico Pugliese, *L'Italia tra migrazioni internazionali e migrazioni interne* (Bologna: Il Mulino, 2002); and Corrado Bonifazi, *L'Italia delle migrazioni* (Bologna: Il Mulino, 2013).

23. Michele Colucci, *Lavoro in movimento, l'emigrazione italiana in Europa, 1945–1957* (Rome, Donzelli, 2008); Elia Morandi, *Governare l'emigrazione: Lavoratori italiani verso la Germania nel secondo dopoguerra* (Turin, Italy: Rosenberg & Seller, 2011); and Rinauro, *Il cammino della Speranza*, 27–73. For the shortfalls in the government's efforts to resettle its citizens in these years, see Frederico Romero, *Emigrazione e integrazione europea 1945–1973* (Rome: Edizioni Lavoro, 1991), 34–66; and Gianfausto Rosoli, ed., *Un secolo di emigrazione italiana, 1876–1976* (Rome: Centro Studi Emigrazione, 1978).

24. Gabaccia, *Italy's Many Diasporas*, 153–60; Stefano Luconi, "Italy, Italian Americans, and the McCarran-Walter Act," in *New Italian Migrations to the United States*, vol. 1, *Politics and History since 1945*, ed. Laura Ruberto and Joseph Sciorra (Urbana: University of Illinois Press, 2017); and Lina Venturas, ed., *International "Migration Management" in the Early Cold War: The Intergovernmental Committee for European Migration* (Corinth, Greece: University of the Peloponnese, 2015).

25. For just a few works discussing bilateral agreements with countries in the Americas and Oceania, see Franca Iacovetta, "Ordering in Bulk: Canada's Postwar Immigration Policy and the Recruitment of Contract Workers from Italy," *Journal of American Ethnic History* 11, no. 1 (Fall 1991); Lucia Capuzzi, *La frontier immaginata, Profilo politico e sociale dell'immigrazione italiana in Argentina nel secondo dopoguerra* (Milan: FrancoAngeli, 2006); Fernando Devoto, *Storia degli italiani in Argentina* (Rome: Donzelli, 2006); and Fabiana Idini, "L'accordo di emigrazione assistita tra Italia e Australia (29 marzo 1951)," *Altreitalie* 45 (2012). For Europe, see Colucci, *Lavoro in movimento*; Morandi, *Governare l'emigrazione*; and Romero, *Emigrazione e integrazione europea*. For a detailed analysis of emigrant destinations, see Gianfasto Rosoli, "L'emigrazione italiana nel secondo dopoguerra," in *Emigrazione: memorie e realta*, ed. Casimira Grandi (Trento, Italy: Provincia Autonoma di Trento, 1990).

26. For ways that the DC government navigated American interests and adapted Marshall Plan funds to serve their own agenda, see Bruno Bottiglieri, *La politica economica dell'Italia centrista (1948–1958)* (Milan: Comunità, 1984); Carlo Spanoglo, *La stabilizzazione incompiuta. Il piano Marshall in Italia (1947–1952)* (Rome: Carocci, 2001); and Lucia Ducci, Stefano Luconi, and Matteo Pratelli, *Le relazioni tra Italia e Stati Uniti, Dal Risorgimento all consequenze dell'11 settembre* (Rome: Carocci, 2012), 105–21.

27. Loescher and Scanlan, *Calculated Kindness*; Roger Daniels, *Guarding the Golden Door: American Immigration Policy and Immigrants since 1882* (New York: Hill and Wang, 2004), 81–128; and Tichenor, *Dividing Lines*, 150–218.

28. Lizabeth Cohen, *A Consumer's Republic: The Politics of Mass Consumption in Postwar America* (New York: Alfred A. Knopf, 2003).

29. Tichenor, *Dividing Lines*, 178–81.

30. Mae Ngai, *Impossible Subjects: Illegal Aliens and the Making of Modern America* (Princeton, N.J.: Princeton University Press, 2004), 127–65.

31. Peter Gatrell, *The Making of the Modern Refugee* (New York: Oxford University Press, 2013).

32. Aristide Zolberg, *A Nation by Design: Immigration Policy in the Fashioning of America* (Cambridge, Mass.: Harvard University Press, 2006); Gerald Neuman, *Strangers to the Constitution: Immigrants, Borders, and Fundamental Law* (Princeton, N.J.: Princeton University Press, 1996); and Hidetaka Hirota, *Expelling the Poor: Atlantic Seaboard States and the Nineteenth-Century Origins of American Immigration Policy* (New York: Oxford University Press, 2017). For the historically gendered application of "likely to become a public charge" provisions, see Martha Gardner, *The Qualities of a Citizen: Women, Immigration, and Citizenship, 1870–1965* (Princeton, N.J.: Princeton University Press, 2009).

33. Zolberg, *Nation by Design*, 270–94; Tichenor, *Dividing Lines*, 150–67; Daniels, *Guarding the Golden Door*, 98–112; and Loescher and Scanlan, *Calculated Kindness*, 1–48.

34. Along with the 1943 repeal of the Chinese Exclusion Act, see also the token immigration quotas granted to Indian and Filipino immigrants (1946) as a nod to wartime alliances.

35. Tichenor, *Dividing Lines*, 177–83; and Carl Bon Tempo, *Americans at the Gate: The United States and Refugees during the Cold War* (Princeton, N.J.: Princeton University Press, 2008).

36. Tichenor, 177–83; and Bon Tempo, *Americans at the Gate*.

37. Mark Wyman, *DP: Europe's Displaced Persons, 1945–1951* (Ithaca, N.Y.: Cornell University Press, 1998); Ben Shepard, *The Long Road Home: The Aftermath of the Second World War* (New York: Anchor, 2012); and Loescher and Scanlan, *Calculated Kindness*, 1–48.

38. Tichenor, *Dividing Lines*, 182; and Loescher and Scanlan, *Calculated Kindness*, 1–48.

39. Loescher and Scanlan, *Calculated Kindness*, 1–24. Key Jewish organizations involved in the campaign included the American Council for Judaism, the American Jewish Committee, the Hebrew Immigrant Aid Society, and B'nai B'rith. These groups later aided and shared cause with the Italian American organizations in immigration reform campaigns of the 1950s and 1960s.

40. Tichenor, *Dividing Lines*, 182–86; and Loescher and Scanlan, *Calculated Kindness*, 1–24.

41. Tichenor, 182–86; and Loescher and Scanlan, 1–24.

42. DPs had to enter through western zones of Germany and Austria by December 22, 1945, which excluded many Jews who fled the Soviet Union, Poland, and other eastern European countries thereafter. Tichenor, 182–86; and Loescher and Scanlan, 1–24.

43. The 1950 extension to the Displaced Persons Act moved the eligibility date for applicants to January 1, 1949, and removed the agricultural preference category. However, visas continued to be mortgaged against future

immigration rather than allowed to enter outside of quota limitations. Zolberg, *Nation by Design*, 303–8.

44. Tichenor, *Dividing Lines*, 185–89; and Loescher and Scanlan, *Calculated Kindness*, 1–48.

45. Victor Anfuso, letter, July 21, 1947, re: HR 3568, box 1, folder 14 Italian Americans and Italian Communism, 1947–1948, Victor Anfuso Papers, Center for Migration Studies (hereafter Anfuso Papers).

46. The OSIA tried again in 1950 with a watered-down version of the 1947 bill sponsored by William Barrett (D-PA) and Louis Clemente (D-NY) for the special entry of thirty-seven thousand Italians (the number of visas calculated to be lost during WWII). Once again, the OSIA used anticommunist arguments to make their case for the legislation. See Luconi, "Italy, Italian Americans and the McCarran-Walter Act," 41.

47. Robert Tripp Ross, "Emergency Italian Immigration Act," *Congressional Record* (December 31, 1948), A 5593–95, box 36, folder Italy-Italian General, National Catholic Welfare Conference Collection, Center for Migration Studies (hereafter NCWC Collection).

48. Mussolini began restricting emigration abroad and redirecting it to Italian colonies in 1926. Monte. S Finkelstein, "The Johnson Act, Mussolini, and Fascist Emigration Policy: 1921–1930," *Journal of American Ethnic History* 8, no. 1 (Fall 1988). The United States restricted immigration via the National Origins System and liberal applications of the "likely to become a public charge" provision of American immigration law in the interwar period. Zolberg, *Nation by Design*, 199–292.

49. The actual number of unauthorized Italian entries is very difficult to ascertain—both because of the undocumented nature of the act and because of the relative lack of scholarship on this topic. There are, however, several hundred case files from the Italian Welfare League and statistics from the INS that support the claim that "thousands" entered in this fashion in this period. Box 134–68, 1950s Immigration Case Files, Italian Welfare League Records, Center for Migration Studies (hereafter IWL Records); and US Department of Labor and US Immigration and Naturalization Services, 1952–1960, *Annual Report of the Immigration and Naturalization Service*, 1952–1960 (Washington, D.C.: Government Printing Office, 1952–1960). Moreover, Rinauro's work documents that many more unauthorized individuals attempted to enter the United States (and elsewhere in the Americas) but were apprehended before they were able to do so. Rinauro, *Il cammino della Speranza*, 100–12. Jewish migrants similarly pursued unauthorized entry in this period. See Libby Garland, *After They Closed the Gates: Jewish Illegal Immigration to the United States, 1921–1965* (Chicago: University of Chicago Press, 2014).

50. General Records, Immigration Case Files, box 1–95, ACIM–National.

51. I sampled issues of *Il Progresso Italo-Americano* throughout 1948 and found that anywhere from one to three articles per week covered the arrival

of new immigrants. For further analysis of how Italian immigration affected Italian American communities in this period, see Elizabeth Zanoni, "'A Wife in Waiting': Women and the 1952 McCarran-Walter Act in *Il Progresso Italo-Americano* Advice Columns," and James S. Pasto, "Immigrants and Ethnics: Post–World War II Italian Immigration and Boston's North End (1945–2016)," in *New Italian Migrations to the United States*, vol. 1, *Politics and History since 1945*, eds. Laura Ruberto and Joseph Sciorra (Urbana: University of Illinois Press, 2017).

52. Other suggestions included increasing American consumption of Italian imports to stimulate the economy and new programs for cultural exchanges of students, artists, and traders to promote friendship, unity, and an exchange of ideas between the two countries. Nicholas Petruzzelli, "Three Point Program to Aid Italy," *OSIA News*, October 1949.

53. Robert Fleegler, *Ellis Island Nation: Immigration Policy and American Identity in the Twentieth Century* (Philadelphia: University of Pennsylvania Press, 2013); and Stefano Luconi, *From Peasani to White Ethnics: The Italian Experience in Philadelphia* (Albany: State University of New York Press, 2001).

54. For a brief period in the 1950s and 1960s there was even an informal congressional Italian American caucus. Betty Santangelo, *Lucky Corner: The Biography of Congressman Alfred E. Santangelo and the Rise of Italian Americans in Politics* (New York: Center for Migration Studies, 1999), 119, 141–44. Italian American political influence was even greater in certain local or regional areas with large Italian American populations. For example, the 1950 New York City mayoral election was a race between three Italian American candidates; Edward Corsi (R), Ferdinand Pecora (D), and Vincent Impellitteri (I). See Salvatore LaGumina, *New York at Mid-Century: The Impellitteri Years* (Westport, Conn.: Greenwood Press, 1992).

55. Tichenor, *Dividing Lines*, 188–97.

56. Penny Von Eschen, *Race against Empire: Black Americans and Anticolonialism, 1937–1957* (Ithaca, N.Y.: Cornell University Press, 1997); Mary Dudziak, *Cold War Civil Rights: Race and the Image of American Democracy* (Princeton, N.J.: Princeton University Press, 2000); and Thomas Borstelmann, *The Cold War and the Color Line: American Race Relations in the Global Arena* (Cambridge, Mass.: Harvard University Press, 2001).

57. Joining Celler later were other congressional liberals including Hubert Humphrey, Herbert Lehman, and Peter Rodino. Tichenor, *Dividing Lines*, 176–218; and Maddalena Marinari, "Divided and Conquered: Immigration Reform Advocates and the Passage of the 1952 Immigration and Nationality Act," *Journal of American Ethnic History* 35, no. 3 (Spring 2016).

58. While reformers proposed modifications to the National Origins System, their proposals did not dismantle the system, fearing this move would crush any hopes for their success. This was true even of the leading Italian American organizations at the time. See the OSIA Immigration and

Naturalization Committee's resolution on amendments to American immigration laws, 1950, box 1, folder Immigration and Naturalization, Errigo Papers; Tichenor, *Dividing Lines*, 193; and Fleegler, *Ellis Island Nation*, 114.

59. Tichenor, *Dividing Lines*, 188–97.

60. Tichenor, *Dividing Lines*, 188–97; and Fleegler, *Ellis Island Nation*, 114. The act also reflected conservative influences in provisions for the exclusion and deportation of individuals engaged in activities deemed politically subversive or a risk to national security. That aspect of the law built upon the 1950 Internal Security Act, which had implications for illegal aliens, legal permanent residents, and even naturalized citizens. Ngai, *Impossible Subjects*, 240; and Tichenor, *Dividing Lines*, 181–203.

61. Robert A. Divine, *American Immigration Policy, 1924–1952* (New Haven, Conn.: Yale University Press, 1957), 166–67.

62. Fleegler, *Ellis Island Nation*, 110–12.

63. *Congressional Record* (June 25, 1952), 8083.

64. Tichenor, *Dividing Lines*, 194–99.

65. *Joint Hearings before the Senate Subcommittees of the Committees on the Judiciary, S. 716, H.R. 2379, and H.R. 2816, Bills to Revise the Laws Relating to Immigration, Naturalization, and Nationality*, United States Congress, 82nd Cong., 1st Sess. (March 6–April 9, 1951); and Divine, *American Immigration Policy*, 172–73. Italian Americans did, however, view this bill as racially discriminatory, as evidenced by the coverage it received in the Italian-language press. See Luconi, "Italy, Italian Americans, and the McCarran-Walter Act," 44–48.

66. Marinari, "Divided and Conquered."

67. "A Brief History of the American Committee on Italian Migration," box 1, folder 1, American Committee on Italian Migration, Chicago Chapter, Immigration History Research Center Archives, University of Minnesota (hereafter ACIM–Chicago); and *Joint Hearings before the Senate Subcommittees of the Committees on the Judiciary, S. 716, H.R. 2379, and H.R. 2816, Bills to Revise the Laws Relating to Immigration, Naturalization, and Nationality*, United States Congress, 82nd Cong., 1st Sess., 754–57 (March 6–April 9, 1951) (statement of Juvenal Marchisio, Italo-American Immigration Committee) (hereafter Marchisio Testimony).

68. Maddalena Marinari, "In the Name of God . . . and in the Interest of Our Country: The Cold War, Foreign Policy, and Italian Americans' Mobilization against Immigration Restriction," in *New Italian Migrations to the United States*, vol. 1, *Politics and History since 1945*, ed. Laura Ruberto and Joseph Sciorra (Urbana: University of Illinois Press, 2017); and Todd Scribner, "Negotiating Priorities: The National Catholic Welfare Conference and United States Migration Policy in a Post–World War II World, 1948–1952," *American Catholic Studies* 121, no. 4 (2010).

69. ACIM Introductory Letter, April 1953, box A2 Chapter Correspondence, folder Chicago Chapter, ACIM–National; "ACIM Fact Sheet," box 2,

folder 1962 ACIM Miscellaneous, Carolyn Sinelli Burns Papers, Bentley Historical Library, University of Michigan; and "A Brief History of the American
Committee on Italian Migration," box 1, folder 1, ACIM–Chicago.

70. "Italo-Americans Forming National Group to Aid Motherland; Cardi-
nal Stritch Urges Emigration to U.S.," *Il Crociato*, Brooklyn, N.Y., October 20,
1951. The NCWC's subsidiary organizations, the NCRC and War Relief
Services, had been in Italy since 1944 and it established a formal department
on emigration in 1947.

71. Deborah Moore, *B'nai B'rith and the Challenge of Ethnic Leadership*
(Albany: State University of New York Press, 1981). One should also note the
long history of a confluence between Italian American ethnic organizations
and the group's Catholic identity/allegiances as a factor in those affiliations.
See Dierdre Moloney, *American Catholic Lay Groups and Transatlantic Social
Reform in the Progressive Era* (Chapel Hill: University of North Carolina Press,
2002), 37; and Robert Orsi, *The Madonna of 115th Street: Faith and Community
in Italian Harlem, 1880–1950* (New Haven, Conn.: Yale University Press,
1985), 51–52.

72. Marchisio served as a New York Domestic Court judge from 1937 to
1947. "Judge Juvenal Marchisio, The 'Man of the Hour,'" *National Chronicle*,
1965, box 7, folder 62, ACIM–Chicago; box E29, folder Biographies, ACIM–
National; and box 1, Boys' Town of Italy, Inc. Collection, Rare Books and
Special Collections, New York Public Library.

73. For more on the Scalabrini Fathers, see Peter D'Agostino, "The
Scalabrini Fathers, the Italian Emigrants Church, and Ethnic Nationalism in
America," *Religion and American Culture* 7, no. 1 (Winter 1997).

74. "Little People Storm Italy with Pleas to Beat Red Bloc," *Utica Observer
Dispatch*, March 16, 1948; "Beat Reds, 'Little People' Tell Italy," *Utica Daily
Press*, March 17, 1948; "Upstate Cities Adopt 'Utica Plan' to Defeat Commu-
nist Bloc in Italy," *Utica Daily Press*, March 22, 1948; "Mass to Mark Election
in Italy Apr. 18," *Utica Observer Dispatch*, March 29, 1948; "Uticans Send
14,0000 Letters to Italy Urging Defeat of Communists in Coming Election,"
*Utica Daily Press*, March 24, 1948; "League Wants More Letters Sent to Italy,"
*Utica Observer Dispatch*, April 2, 1948; "Republicans Back Letter Drive on
Italy," *Utica Daily Press*, April 2, 1948; "Many Groups Join Italian Letter Writ-
ing Campaign," *Utica Observer Dispatch*, March 24, 1948; "Italian Americans
Bombard Homeland with Anti-Red Pleas," *Utica Daily Press*, April 5, 1948; and
"The Italian Elections," *Messenger*, Utica, N.Y., April 17, 1948.

75. Box E29, folder Biographies, ACIM–National; Caesar Donanzan to
Father Natali, Holy Rosary Church, Lawrence, Mass., December 28, 1962,
box E84, folder Immigration Cases K–O, 1962, ACIM–National.

76. ACIM Introductory Letter, April 1953, box A2 Chapter Correspondence, folder Chicago Chapter, ACIM–National; and "ACIM Fact Sheet,"
box 2, folder 1962 ACIM Miscellaneous, Sinelli Burns Papers.

77. Dominic Candeloro, *Chicago's Italians: Immigrants, Ethnics, Americans* (Chicago: Arcadia Publishing, 2003).

78. Box 2–5, Sinelli Burns Papers.

79. 1952 Mailing Lists, box 1, folder ACIM 1952 Mailing Lists, Sinelli Burns Papers.

80. ACIM Introductory Letter, April 1953, box A2 Chapter Correspondence, folder Chicago Chapter, ACIM–National; and "Mrs. Impellitteri Urges Women to Act on Italian Migration," *ACIM Dispatch*, May 1952, box D, ACIM–National.

81. From 1952 to 1953, about 100 chapters existed; the number grew to 125 throughout the 1950s. Historical Sketch from ACIM Finding Guide, Center for Migration Studies; Invitation Letters, folder ACIM 1952 Mailing Lists, box 1, Sinelli Burns Papers; and Meeting Minutes, October 23, 1952, and Marchisio to Burns, September 18, 1952, box 1, folder ACIM 1952 Meetings and ACIM 1952 Miscellaneous, Sinelli Burns Papers.

82. For accounts from other cities, see "ACIM Chairman Touring US Cities on Migration Work," *ACIM Dispatch*, July 1952, box D, ACIM–National; and "Draft of Judge Marchisio Proposed Remarks on Cleveland's TV Panel," September 12, 1952, box E24, folder Marchisio Articles, ACIM–National.

83. Meeting Minutes, October 23, 1952, and Marchisio to Burns, September 18, 1952, box 1, folder ACIM 1952 Meetings and ACIM 1952 Miscellaneous, Sinelli Burns Papers.

84. "Report of the Supreme Venerable at the Supreme Convention, 1949, 1951, 1953, 1955," box 1, folder 11–14, George Spatuzza Collection, Immigration History Research Center Archives, University of Minnesota (hereafter Spatuzza Collection); and Supreme Convention Reports, 1955, 1957, 1959, 1963, 1965, box 1, folder 4, 5, 7, 8, 16, and box 2, folder 3, Order Sons of Italy in America, National Grand Lodge Collection, Immigration History Research Center Archives, University of Minnesota.

85. Ronald Filippelli, *American Labor and Postwar Italy, 1943–1953: A Study of Cold War Politics* (Stanford, Calif.: Stanford University Press, 1989); and Charles Zappia, "From Working-Class Radicalism to Cold War Anti-Communism: The Case of the Italian Locals of the International Ladies' Garment Workers' Union," in *The Lost World of Italian American Radicalism: Politics, Labor, and Culture*, ed. Philip Cannistraro and Gerald Meyer (Westport, Conn. Praeger, 2003). The only major exception to this trend was not a labor leader but Congressman Vito Marcantonio of Harlem (1936–1950), who maintained ethnic support while continuing to advance communist positions. Gerald Meyer, *Vito Marcantonio: Radical Politician, 1902–1954* (Albany: SUNY Press, 1989).

86. Box E22–24, folder Immigration Cases, ACIM–National; box E30–31, folder Immigration Cases and ILGWU, ACIM–National; box 45, folder ILGWU Luigi Antonini, ACIM–National; and box 1, Italian American Labor

Council Collection, Tamiment Library, Robert F. Wagner Labor Archives, New York University.

87. Constitution and By-Laws, box 33, IWL Records.

88. Family Case Accounts, box 15, IWL Records; box 64–76, folder Port and Dock Committee Reports 1952–1968, IWL Records; and box 64–76, folder Port and Dock Committee Reports 1952–1968, IWL Records.

89. 1952 Mailing Lists, box 1, folder ACIM 1952 Mailing Lists, Sinelli Burns Papers.

90. Meeting Minutes, October 23, 1952, box 1, folder ACIM 1952 Meetings, Sinelli Burns Papers; and Nicola Gigante Speech (October 27, 1952) and Horatio Tocco (ACIM) 1952 testimony offered to President's Commission on Immigration and Naturalization, box E16, folder President's Commission on Immigration and Naturalization, ACIM–National.

91. Nicola Gigante, Speech, October 7, 1952, box E16, folder President's Commission on Immigration and Naturalization, ACIM–National.

92. A notable exception may have been American Jews who generally believed that their interests were better served by using more expansive pan-racial, ethnic, and religious language; who did not necessarily identify with one particular country of origin; and who often held distinct priorities in immigration, refugee, and foreign aid goals. Loescher and Scanlan, *Calculated Kindness*.

93. Gary Gerstle, "The Protean Character of American Liberalism," *American Historical Review* 99, no. 4 (1994); Carol Anderson Horton, *Race and the Making of American Liberalism* (New York: Oxford University Press, 2005); Alan Brinkley, *The End of Reform: New Deal Liberalism in Recession and in War* (New York: Vintage Books, 1995), 8–11; and Alan Brinkley, "The New Deal and the Idea of the State," in *The Rise and Fall of the New Deal Order, 1930–1980*, ed. Steve Fraser and Gary Gerstle (Princeton, N.J.: Princeton University Press, 1989).

94. Gary Gerstle, *American Crucible: Race and Nation in the Twentieth Century* (Princeton, N.J.: Princeton University Press, 2001); Wendy Wall, *Inventing the "American Way": The Politics of Consensus from the New Deal to the Civil Rights Movement* (New York: Oxford University Press, 2008); Brinkley, *End of Reform*; and Horton, *Race and the Making of American Liberalism*, 121–65.

95. Wall, *Inventing the "American Way"*; Gerstle, *American Crucible*, 238; and Kevin M. Schultz, *Tri-Faith America: How Catholics and Jews Held Postwar America to Its Protestant Promise* (New York: Oxford University Press, 2011). Horton argues that liberals largely abandoned their quest for the state to ensure class-based rights in the postwar period and the implications of that were not apparent to working-class liberals until much later. Horton, *Race and the Making of American Liberalism*, 134–38.

96. *Joint Hearings before the Senate Subcommittees of the Committees on the Judiciary, S. 716, H.R. 2379, and H.R. 2816, Bills to Revise the Laws Relating to*

*Immigration, Naturalization, and Nationality, United States Congress*, 82nd Cong., 1st Sess., 761–62 (March 6–April 9, 1951) (statement of Henry Andreini, President of the American Chamber of Commerce for Trade with Italy, Inc.) (hereafter Andreini Testimony).

97. *Joint Hearings before the Senate Subcommittees of the Committees on the Judiciary, S. 716, H.R. 2379, and H.R. 2816, Bills to Revise the Laws Relating to Immigration, Naturalization, and Nationality, United States Congress*, 82nd Cong., 1st Sess., 333–34 (March 6–April 9, 1951) (statement of Amerigo D'Agostino, Legislative Representative of the Columbian Civic Club of New Jersey and the National Unico Clubs of America) (hereafter D'Agostino Testimony).

98. ACIM Introductory Letter, April 1953, box A2 Chapter Correspondence, folder Chicago Chapter, ACIM–National; and "ACIM Fact Sheet," box 2, folder 1962 ACIM Miscellaneous, Sinelli Burns Papers.

99. Scholars, of course, argue there were precursors or contributing ideologies to modern human rights ideology, including concepts from ancient Judaism, Stoicism, Enlightenment ideology and revolutions, and other subjects. The literature here is vast. For a comprehensive overview, I would recommend the bibliographic essay in Samuel Moyn's *Last Utopia*, in which Moyn argues that although the World War II era witnessed the birth of modern human rights, it was not until the 1970s that the ideology was truly harnessed as a movement. Samuel Moyn, *The Last Utopia: Human Rights in History* (Cambridge, Mass. Harvard University Press, 2010), 311–21.

100. As an example of the former, see Elizabeth Borgwardt, *A New Deal for the World: America's Vision for Human Rights* (Cambridge, Mass.: Harvard University Press, 2007). For the latter see, Samuel Moyn, *Christian Human Rights* (Philadelphia: University of Pennsylvania Press, 2015).

101. See, for example, Pope Leo XIII, *Rerum Novarum*, Encyclical Letter of Pope Leo XIII on the Conditions of Labor (1891), *Historical Catholic and Dominican Documents*, book 13, http://digitalcommons.providence.edu/catholic_documents/13. The encyclical critiques classically liberal governments and economies that the Church argued are both immoral and unworkable in practice. The treatise also argues against the focus on the individual as the basic social unit and argues instead for the continuing primacy of the family as the proper unit of social organization. John T. McGreevy, *Catholicism and American Freedom* (New York: W.W. Norton, 2003), 127–65.

102. Manifestations of that movement are reflected in the Irish Constitution (1937) and Pope Pius XII's Christmas Message (1942). Moyn, *Christian Human Rights*, 25–64.

103. Moyn also equates the postwar triumph of Christian Democracy in Europe with this trend. Moyn, 25–64.

104. *Rerum Novarum* was a particularly important precursor to the text. McGreevy, *Catholicism and American Freedom*, 127–65. On *Exsul Familia*,

see Rev. G. J. Dulland, "The Right to Migrate and the Teachings of Pope Pius XII," *Migration News* (November–December 1959).

105. Dulland, "Right to Migrate."

106. Pope Pius XII, *Exsul Familia*, August 1, 1952, in *The Church's Magna Charta for Migrants*, trans. and ed. by Reverend Giulivo Tessarolo (Staten Island, N.Y.: St. Charles Seminary, 1962); and Dulland, "Right to Migrate."

107. Pope Pius XII, *Exsul Familia*; and Dulland, "Right to Migrate."

108. Pope Pius XII; and Dulland. For more on the limits of the state's authority in service of the common good, the rights of families, and owner-ship of material property, see Pope Leo XIII, *Rerum Novarum*. This view of the state is also supported by other Christian (non-Catholic) theorists. See Moyn, *Christian Human Rights*, 125.

109. Pope Pius XII.

110. *Joint Hearings before the Senate Subcommittees of the Committees on the Judiciary, S. 716, H.R. 2379, and H.R. 2816, Bills to Revise the Laws Relating to Immigration, Naturalization, and Nationality, United States Congress*, 82nd Cong., 1st Sess., 758 (March 6–April 9, 1951) (statement of Daniel Santoro, the Ital-ian Historical Society of Staten Island).

111. Juvenal Marchisio, statement issued September 30, 1952. Reprinted in American Immigration Conference pamphlet "American Immigration Policy, Selected Statements," New York, May 1957, box 10, folder AICC Materials Sent to Members, Oct 1956–Oct 1957, American Immigration and Citizen-ship Conference Records, Social Welfare History Archive, University of Minnesota.

112. For a much more detailed discussion of the complicated positions adopted by American Catholics on immigration, see Grainne McEvoy, "Justice and Order: American Catholic Social Thought and the Immigration Question in the Restriction Era, 1917–1965" (PhD diss., Boston College, 2014).

113. Recognizing sweeping liberalizations were unlikely to pass, the NCWC endorsed the McCarran-Walter bill and focused on trying to mitigate some of its more restrictive elements related to racial and gender barriers that might disrupt family unity. Scribner, "Negotiating Priorities," 1–25.

114. For a definition and discussion of the markers of Cold War liberalism (and its relation to postwar immigration reforms), see Ngai, *Impossible Subjects*, 227–64. For some examples of Cold War liberalism, see Von Eschen, *Race against Empire*; Dudziak, *Cold War Civil Rights*; Thomas Borstelmann, *The Cold War and the Color Line: American Race Relations in the Global Arena* (Cambridge, Mass.: Harvard University Press, 2001); Christina Klein, *Cold War Oriental-ism: Asia in the Middlebrow Imagination, 1945–1961* (Berkeley: University of California Press, 2003); Wall, *Inventing the "American Way."*

115. "Italo-Americans Forming National Group to Aid Motherland; Cardi-nal Stritch Urges Emigration to U.S." *Il Crociato*, October 20, 1951.

116. Marchisio Testimony; Andreini Testimony; *Joint Hearings before the Senate Subcommittees of the Committees on the Judiciary, S. 716, H.R. 2379, and H.R. 2816, Bills to Revise the Laws Relating to Immigration, Naturalization, and Nationality, United States Congress,* 82nd Cong., 1st Sess., 511 (March 6– April 9, 1951) (statement of Leonard Pasqualicchio, National Deputy of the Order Sons of Italy in America, Washington, D.C.).

117. Horatio Tocco 1952 testimony offered to President's Commission on Immigration and Naturalization, box E16, folder President's Commission on Immigration and Naturalization, ACIM–National; and Andreini Testimony.

118. "Italian Election File," 1953, box E11, folder Italian Elections 1953, ACIM–National.

119. See Ngai, *Impossible Subjects,* 227–64. I would argue this is certainly the case for Greek Americans when looking at the campaigns for displaced persons legislation in the late 1940s and early 1950s. See Rachel Rains Winslow, *The Best Possible Immigrants: International Adoption and the American Family* (Philadelphia: University of Pennsylvania Press, 2017), 52–55. This claim is, however, complicated by the fact that both Japanese American and Chinese American groups seemed to have also rejected a wholesale fight for universal immigrant rights, despite the seeming vested interest they would have in the cause. In fact, the Japanese American Citizens League was vocal in its support for the McCarran-Walter Act because it chose political expediency, piecemeal reforms, and advancement for its own constituents' interests in American society over a more expansive agenda of racial equality. See Marinari, "Divided and Conquered"; Ellen Wu, *The Color of Success: Asian Americans and the Origins of the Model Minority* (Princeton, N.J.: Princeton University Press, 2014); Madeline Hsu, *The Good Immigrants: How the Yellow Peril Became the Model Minority* (Princeton, N.J.: Princeton University Press, 2015).

120. D'Agostino Testimony.

121. Marchisio Testimony; and *Joint Hearings before the Senate Subcommittees of the Committees on the Judiciary, S. 716, H.R. 2379, and H.R. 2816, Bills to Revise the Laws Relating to Immigration, Naturalization, and Nationality, United States Congress,* 82nd Cong., 1st Sess., 731 (March 6–April 9, 1951) (statement of Fortune R. Pope, Editor, *Il Progresso Italo-Americano* Newspaper, New York). For similar remarks, see also *Joint Hearings before the Senate Subcommittees of the Committees on the Judiciary, S. 716, H.R. 2379, and H.R. 2816, Bills to Revise the Laws Relating to Immigration, Naturalization, and Nationality, United States Congress,* 82nd Cong., 1st Sess., 728–31 (March 6–April 9, 1951) (statement of Peter W. Rodino Jr., Congressional Representative from the State of New Jersey).

122. Tichenor, *Dividing Lines,* 176–218; Bon Tempo, *Americans at the Gate,* 34–59; and Loescher and Scanlan, *Calculated Kindness,* 25–48.

3. REFUGEES AND RELATIVES: ITALIAN AMERICANS AND THE REFUGEE RELIEF ACT

1. Daniel J. Tichenor, *Dividing Lines: The Politics of Immigration Control in America* (Princeton, N.J.: Princeton University Press, 2002), 176–218; Carl Bon Tempo, *Americans at the Gate: The United States and Refugees during the Cold War* (Princeton, N.J.: Princeton University Press, 2008), 34–59; and Gil Loescher and John Scanlan, *Calculated Kindness: Refugees and America's Half-Open Door, 1945–Present* (New York: Free Press, 1986), 25–48.

2. Because of their close relationship to American citizens, most nonquota immigrants usually did not need or seek assistance from ACIM or similar organizations. Box E10, folder Immigration Case Files 1952–1953, American Committee on Italian Migration–National Office, New York City Records, Center for Migration Studies, New York (hereafter ACIM–National).

3. Box E10, folder Immigration Case Files 1952–1953, ACIM–National. The INS noted an increase in derivative citizenship claims since the end of the war. US Department of Justice, *Annual Report of the US Immigration and Naturalization Service 1953* (Washington, D.C.: Government Printing Office, 1953), 67–68.

4. Pub. L. No. 82-114, 1st Sess. (1951). Victor Anfuso began lobbying for this kind of legislation as early as a month after the 1948 elections. "Election in Italy," May 18, 1948, box 1, folder 14 Italian Immigration and Italian Communism, 1947–1948, Victor Anfuso Papers, Center for Migration Studies. The OSIA was also active in lobbying for the bill. L. H. Pasqualicchio, Chairman of the Committee on Immigration and Naturalization "Report to the Supreme Lodge Convention of 1951, Washington, D.C.," August 1951, box 1, folder 8, Order Sons of Italy in America Joseph Gorrasi Papers, Immigration History Research Center Archives, University of Minnesota.

5. Box E10, folder Immigration Case Files 1952–1953, ACIM–National; Immigration Case Files, box 134–68, 200–22, Immigration Case Files 1950s, Italian Welfare League Records, Center for Migration Studies, New York (hereafter IWL Records). For an example of restoring citizenship through special legislation, see Rocco Serritella Case File, box 4, folder 31, American Committee on Italian Migration, Chicago Chapter, Immigration History Research Center Archives, University of Minnesota (hereafter ACIM–Chicago).

6. Box E10, folder Immigration Case Files 1952–1953, ACIM–National.

7. Tichenor, *Dividing Lines*, 197–203. Tichenor argues that Eisenhower entered the presidential race in 1952 in part to defeat isolationists within the Republican Party and to ensure that internationalists steered foreign policy. He also argues that Eisenhower was heavily influenced by the findings of Truman's 1952 Commission on Immigration and Naturalization. For a more extended discussion of Eisenhower's position on immigration and refugee policies, see Chapter 5.

8. Tichenor, *Dividing Lines*, 197–203.

9. Statement of Reverend Monsignor Edward Swanstrom Executive Director of the NCWC to the President's Commission on Immigration, 1952, box E16, folder President's Commission on Immigration, ACIM–National.

10. US Department of Justice, *Annual Report of the US Immigration and Naturalization Service 1953* (Washington, D.C.: Government Printing Office, 1953).

11. Box E11, folder Legislative Background, 1952, ACIM–National.

12. For *Dispatch* articles advocating support for refugee relief, see Emanuel Celler, "Guest Editorial," ACIM *Dispatch*, June 1952; Victor Anfuso, "Guest Editorial," ACIM *Dispatch*, July 1952; and Herbert Lehman, "Guest Editorial," ACIM *Dispatch*, October 1952, box D, ACIM–National. For *Dispatch* articles that focused on Italy's population crisis and threats to democracy there, see ACIM *Dispatch*, August and September 1952; "The Effect of Aid," ACIM *Dispatch*, January 1953; "Jobless Italians Increase," ACIM *Dispatch*, February 1953, box D, ACIM–National.

13. The rest of the breakdown included 100,000 German expellees, 22,000 Greeks, 22,000 Dutch, 64,000 from West Germany and Austria, and 20,000 from all other NATO countries. ACIM also endorsed other alternative refugee legislation not adopted in 1952 and 1953. See box E4, folder Campaign for HR 7376 Celler Bill; folder Celler Bill HR 2076; folder Bill S 1917 Watkins Bill; and folder Bill HR 6827, S 2585 by Celler and Lehman, ACIM–National.

14. Box E1–95, folder Legislative Campaigns; and folder Annual Symposia, ACIM–National.

15. Marchisio Speech to President Eisenhower notes, March 18, 1953, box E16, folder President Eisenhower, ACIM–National.

16. "Celler, Swanstrom, Marchisio Discuss Emergency Migration Bill," ACIM *Dispatch*, March 1953; and "Eisenhower Discusses Migration with ACIM Leaders," ACIM *Dispatch*, April 1953, box D, ACIM–National.

17. Box E4, folder Re: Celler Bill HR 7376, ACIM–National.

18. *Sub-Committee No. 1, Committee on the Judiciary, Emergency Immigration Program Hearings, United States, House of Representatives*, 83rd Cong., 1st Sess., 182–96 (May 21–July 9, 1953) (statement of Juvenal Marchisio, American Committee on Italian Migration). See also Marchisio testimony before House Subcommittee, June 10, 1953, box E9, folder House Subcommittee Hearings, ACIM–National. Although the bulk of his testimony focused on refugee relief in a Cold War context, Marchisio did also include points about the benefits of general immigration to the United States and arguments in favor of Italian immigration in particular.

19. ACIM records contain a report of the 1953 Letters to Italy Campaign that indicates approximately thirty thousand messages were sent, along with several radio broadcasts and newspaper articles. See "Messages to Italy 1953,"

box E12, folder Letters to Italy Campaign 1953, ACIM–National; and Stefano Luconi, "I giornali italo-americani degli Stati Uniti e le elezione politiche italiane del 1953," *Archivo Storico Emigrazione Itlaiana* (May 2005).

20. "Americans of Italian Origin," *Il Progresso Italo-Americano*, May 25, 1953; "Drive Opened Here to Steer Italy's Vote," *Detroit News*, May 29, 1953; and Edward Corsi, "The Miracle of the New Italy," May 15, 1953, box E12, folder Letters to Italy Campaign 1953, ACIM–National.

21. Box E11, folder Italian Elections 1953, ACIM–National.

22. "Material to Congressional Leaders in through Public Support of H.R. 7376," box E4, folder Re: Celler Bill HR 7376, ACIM–National.

23. "1953 Detroit Chapter, American Committee on Italian Migration Administrative Expenditures," box 1, folder 1952–1957 ACIM Summary Reports, Carolyn Sinelli Burns Papers, Bentley Historical Library, University of Michigan (hereafter Sinelli Burns Papers).

24. Tichenor, *Dividing Lines*, 176–218; Bon Tempo, *Americans at the Gate*, 34–59; and Aristide Zolberg, *A Nation by Design: Immigration Policy in the Fashioning of America* (Cambridge, Mass.: Harvard University Press, 2006), 293–336.

25. Pub. L. No. 83-203 § 2a.

26. Pub. L. No. 83-203 § 4.

27. Pub. L. No. 83-203 § 11.

28. Tichenor, *Dividing Lines*, 176–218; Bon Tempo, *Americans at the Gate*, 34–59; and Zolberg, *Nation by Design*, 293–336.

29. Pub. L. No. 83-203 § 7a.

30. "Letter from Juvenal Marchisio to All Chapter Chairmen," March 15, 1954, box 1, folder 2, ACIM–Chicago.

31. Box E10, folder Immigration Case Files 1952–1953, ACIM–National.

32. A typical *Dispatch* article of this kind was "Procedures for Sponsoring Italian Refugees," *Dispatch*, June 1955, box D, ACIM–National. Many other articles of this type can be found through January 1953 to December 1955 of the *Dispatch*, box D, ACIM–National. For instructions in optimizing refugee relief appeals, see box E31, folder Immigration Cases "R," ACIM–National.

33. "Summary of ACIM Implementation of the Refugee Relief Act of 1953 with Regard to the Assurances Passed through ACIM-CIPSU and through National Catholic Relief Services," February 25, 1956, box 1, folder CIPSU, ACIM–National; and "The Refugee and You," box A9, folder Detroit Chapter Correspondence 1955, ACIM–National.

34. "Suggested Speech for Use by Local Chapter Chairmen," May 1955; "Suggested Speech to an Appeal to Benefit the American Committee for Italian Migration"; "Spot Announcement for TV and Radio"; and "Memorandum" from Joseph Jordan to all ACIM Chairmen re: Publicity Kit, May 1955, box 4, folder 28 Speeches and Releases, ACIM–Chicago.

35. Pub. L. No. 83-203 § 4.

36. "The Refugee and You," box A9, folder Detroit Chapter Correspondence 1955, ACIM–National; "Procedures for Sponsoring Italian Refugees," *Dispatch*, June 1955, box D, ACIM–National; and box E31, folder Immigration Cases "R," ACIM–National.

37. "10,000th Visa," *Dispatch*, February 1955, box D, ACIM–National.

38. Refugee Relief Cases, box F1–F5, ACIM–National.

39. Refugee Relief Cases, box F1–F5, ACIM–National.

40. Refugee Relief Cases, box F1–F5, ACIM–National.

41. 83 percent of the surviving refugee relief case files from ACIM–National in New York are of southern Italian origin. I am not including in my sample hundreds of ACIM cases that were refugee relief cases but were filed under regular annual immigration records and Refugee Relief cases where ACIM created an occupational-based program to bring large numbers of refugees to the country. Refugee Relief Cases, box F1–F5, ACIM–National.

42. Pub. L. No. 83-203 § 2.

43. Loescher and Scanlan, *Calculated Kindness*.

44. Refugee Relief Cases, box F1–F5, ACIM–National.

45. "Letter Juvenal Marchisio to All Chapter Chairmen," March 15, 1954, box 1, folder 2, ACIM–Chicago.

46. Pub. L. No. 83-751, 2nd Sess. Quotas for Greece and the Netherlands were similarly redistributed.

47. Elizabeth Winkler, "Voluntary Agencies and Government Policy," *International Migration Review* 15, no. 1 (Spring–Summer 1981); Robert G. Wright, "Voluntary Agencies and the Resettlement of Refugees," *International Migration Review* 15, no. 1 (Spring–Summer 1981); and Norman L. Zucker, "Refugee Resettlement in the United States: Policy and Problems," *Annals of the American Academy of Political and Social Science* 467 (May 1983).

48. Refugee Relief Cases, box F1–F5, ACIM–National.

49. ARCIR was started by Fortuno Pope, Amerigo D'Agostino, and Edward Corsi. "First Monthly Report," The American Resettlement Council for Italian Refugees, April 10, 1954, box E18, folder American Resettlement Council for Italian Refugees, ACIM–National.

50. The American Resettlement Council for Italian Refugees Information Packet, box E18, folder American Resettlement Council for Italian Refugees, ACIM–National; Constitution and By-Laws, The American Resettlement Council for Italian Refugees, box E18, folder American Resettlement Council for Italian Refugees, ACIM–National; and ARCIR records in box 36, Edward Corsi Papers, Rare Books and Special Collections, Syracuse University.

51. "Monthly Reports," The American Resettlement Council for Italian Refugees, June 10, 1954, July 30, 1954, and September 19, 1954, box E18, folder American Resettlement Council for Italian Refugees, ACIM–National.

Final data on ARCIR cases are reported on June 10, 1954, with a total of 1,861 applications involving over 8,000 persons, but records on July 30, 1954, report 280 assurances for 685 refugees and September 10, 1954, report 412 assurances for 1,045 refugees.

52. "Refugee List," The American Resettlement Council for Italian Refugees, June 22, 1954, box E18, folder American Resettlement Council for Italian Refugees, ACIM–National.

53. ARCIR's last known records are for September 1954.

54. For example, the Italian Manufacturers Association donated $50,000 for the first two years of operation. The American Resettlement Council for Italian Refugees Information Packet, box E18, folder American Resettlement Council for Italian Refugees, ACIM–National; and Constitution and By-Laws, The American Resettlement Council for Italian Refugees, box E18, folder American Resettlement Council for Italian Refugees, ACIM–National.

55. Juvenal Marchisio to Contessa Bianchi, June 10, 1955, box E29, folder CIPSU Background, ACIM–National; "Proposed Memorandum of Agreement," box E29, folder CIPSU Background, ACIM–National; CIPSU Rome branch to CIPSU Washington D.C. branch, November 1956, box F1, folder CIPSU, ACIM–National; and Juvenal Marchisio to Contessa Bianchi, June 10, 1955, box F1, folder CIPSU lists, Cases, Correspondences, and CIPSU, ACIM–National.

56. Alan Kraut, *Silent Travelers: Germs, Genes and the Immigrant Menace* (Baltimore: Johns Hopkins University Press, 1995).

57. Refugee Case Files, box F1–F5, ACIM–National. Case files (not exclusively pertaining to Italians who entered under the RRA) from the IWL also reflect this trend. Immigration Case Files, box 134–68, IWL Records. Charges of "moral turpitude" were highly gendered in their application, see Martha Gardner, *The Qualities of a Citizen: Women, Immigration, and Citizenship, 1870–1965* (Princeton, N.J.: Princeton University Press, 2009); and Margot Canaday, *The Straight State: Sexuality and Citizenship in Twentieth-Century America* (Princeton, N.J.: Princeton University Press, 2009), 19–54, 175–214.

58. Tichenor, *Dividing Lines*, 179; and Bon Tempo, *Americans at the Gate*, 34–59.

59. Refugee Case Files, box F1–F5, ACIM–National.

60. Bon Tempo, *Americans at the Gate*, 34–59.

61. Refugee Relief Cases, box F1–F5, ACIM–National; and "Letter from Juvenal Marchisio to All Chapter Chairmen," March 15, 1954, box 1, folder 2, ACIM–Chicago.

62. "Letter from Juvenal Marchisio to All Chapter Chairmen," March 15, 1954, box 1, folder 2, ACIM–Chicago.

63. ILGWU assistance in placing refugees and regular immigrants are the most numerous in ACIM's records. See Immigration Case Files, box E63, E64,

ACIM–National. For example cases, see box E64, folder Lucia Anteri, ACIM–National; box E64, folder Mario and Giovanna Cuilo, ACIM–National; box E72, folder ILGWU, ACIM–National; and box E74, folder Gaetano Conti and Francesca Messina, ACIM–National.

64. ACIM Letter to Italian Parishes, Re: Adopt a Family Program, July 12, 1956, box 1, folder 4, ACIM–Chicago.

65. Refugee Relief Cases, box F1–F5, ACIM–National.

66. Roughly one-third of ACIM's New York City Chapter's (its national branch where the most volume was handled) refugee relief case files have no noted relatives in the United States. Box F1–F5, ACIM–National.

67. "You Can Sponsor One of These Cases," *Dispatch*, March 1955, box D, ACIM–National. Four of the twenty-three cases featured included Italians who had lived in African colonies at some point.

68. "You Can Sponsor One of These Cases," *Dispatch*, March 1955, box D, ACIM–National. Four out of twenty-three cases featured were escapees/ Venezia-Giulia refugees.

69. "You Can Sponsor One of These Cases," *Dispatch*, March 1955, box D, ACIM–National. Ten of the twenty-three profiles featured in the *Dispatch* in 1955 were for flood victims.

70. "You Can Sponsor One of These Cases," *Dispatch*, March 1955, box D, ACIM–National.

71. "Refugee Camp Dwellers," *Dispatch*, October 1955, box D, ACIM–National.

72. Caesar Donanzan to ACIM officers, May 5, 1955, box 1, folder ACIM 1955 Miscellaneous, Sinelli Burns Papers; and ACIM Letter to Italian Parishes, re: Adopt a Family Program, July 12, 1956, box 1, folder 4, ACIM–Chicago.

73. By mid-1955, Buffalo had provided 68 assurances for unnamed refugees; Chicago, 61; St. Louis, 70; Cleveland, 25; Boston, 14; and Detroit, 4. Caesar Donanzan to ACIM Chapters, May–June 1955, box 1, folder ACIM 1955 Miscellaneous, Sinelli Burns Papers; and box A18, folder Chicago Chapter 1956 Correspondence, ACIM–National.

74. Refugee Case Files, box F1–F5, ACIM–National; and Refugee Case Files, box E30, E31, E39, E47, ACIM–National.

75. Caesar Donanzan to ACIM officers, December 1, 1955, box 1, folder Individual Refugee Cases Arrived in the US, ACIM–Chicago; and Refugee Case Files, box F1–F5, ACIM–National.

76. Elaine Tyler May, *Homeward Bound: American Families in the Cold War Era* (New York: Basic Books, 1988); and Lizabeth Cohen, *A Consumer's Republic: The Politics of Mass Consumption in Postwar America* (New York: Alfred A. Knopf, 2003).

4. RESETTLEMENT ASSISTANCE AND "A NEW STANDARD OF LIVING"

1. "A New Standard of Living," ACIM *Dispatch*, March 1959, box D, American Committee on Italian Migration–National Office, New York City Records, Center for Migration Studies (hereafter ACIM–National).

2. "Immigrant Vasari Extolls America," *Fra Noi*, Chicago, July 1961, Immigration History Research Center Archives, University of Minnesota.

3. For general trends in turn-of-the-century migration patterns, see John Bodnar, *The Transplanted: A History of Immigrants in Urban America* (Bloomington: Indiana University Press, 1985); and Mark Wyman, *Round-Trip to America: The Immigrants Return to Europe, 1880–1930* (Ithaca, N.Y.: Cornell University Press, 1993). For the gendered nature of turn-of-the-century Italian migration and its social and economic impact in the United States and Italy, see Linda Reeder, *Widows in White: Migration and the Transformation of Rural Italian Women, Sicily, 1880–1920*; and Samuel Baily, *Immigrants in the Land of Promise: Italians in Buenos Aires and New York City, 1870 to 1914* (Ithaca, N.Y.: Cornell University Press, 1999). For an excellent discussion of how single male immigrants threatened turn-of-the-century American cultural norms, see Nyan Shah, *Contagious Divides: Epidemics and Race in San Francisco's Chinatown* (Berkeley: University of California Press, 2001).

4. For the link between consumption and citizenship in the postwar period, see Lizabeth Cohen, *A Consumer's Republic: The Politics of Mass Consumption in Postwar America* (New York: Alfred A. Knopf, 2003); and Elaine Tyler May, *Homeward Bound: American Families in the Cold War Era* (New York: Basic Books, 1988). For the transnational context, see Victoria de Grazia, *Irresistible Empire: America's Advance through 20th Century Europe* (Cambridge, Mass.: Harvard University Press, 2005), 336–75.

5. Peter Gatrell, *The Making of the Modern Refugee* (New York: Oxford University Press, 2013), 1–13.

6. Carl Bon Tempo, *Americans at the Gate: The United States and Refugees during the Cold War* (Princeton, N.J.: Princeton University Press, 2008); and Gil Loescher and John Scanlan, *Calculated Kindness: Refugees and America's Half-Open Door, 1945–Present* (New York: Free Press, 1986).

7. Hungarian Refugees in 1957 encountered similar stigmas. See Bon Tempo, *Americans at the Gate*, 60–85.

8. Wyman estimates that upward of 50 percent of Italian immigrants from 1880 to 1930 were migratory workers (usually men) who returned to Italy after temporary migration to the United States. Wyman, *Round-Trip to America*; Baily, *Immigrants in the Land of Promise*; and Reeder, *Widows in White*.

9. May, *Homeward Bound*; and Cohen, *Consumer's Republic*.

10. For general trends on racial and ethnic inclusion/exclusion in postwar suburbs, see David Roediger, *Working toward Whiteness: How America's*

*Immigrants Became White; The Strange Journey from Ellis Island to the Suburbs* (New York: Basic Books, 2005); Cohen, *Consumer's Republic*; Thomas Sugrue, *The Origins of the Urban Crisis: Race and Inequality in Postwar Detroit* (Princeton, N.J.: Princeton University Press, 1996); and Kevin M. Schultz, *Tri-Faith America: How Catholics and Jews Held Postwar America to Its Protestant Promise* (New York: Oxford University Press, 2011). For Italian American suburbanization, see Richard Alba, *Italian Americans: Into the Twilight of Ethnicity* (Englewood Cliffs, N.J.: Prentice Hall, 1985); Salvatore LaGumina, *From Steerage to Suburb: Long Island Italians* (New York: Center for Migration Studies, 1988); and Richard Alba, "Social Assimilation among American Catholic National Origin Groups," *American Sociological Review* 41 (December 1976).

11. John Higham, *Strangers in the Land: Patterns of American Nativism, 1860–1925* (New York: Atheneum, 1963), 264–330; Daniel J. Tichenor, *Dividing Lines: The Politics of Immigration Control in America* (Princeton, N.J.: Princeton University Press, 2002), 176–218; Bon Tempo, *Americans at the Gate*, 34–85; and Robert Fleegler, *Ellis Island Nation: Immigration Policy and American Identity in the Twentieth Century* (Philadelphia: University of Pennsylvania Press, 2013), 103–90.

12. Angelo Gagliardo, Remarks at the Second Symposium on Italian Migration, ACIM, Rome, 1961, folder 58, American Committee on Italian Migration, Chicago Chapter, Immigration History Research Archives, University of Minnesota (hereafter ACIM–Chicago).

13. For Asian American efforts to remake their group identity and therefore affect economic, social, and political opportunities for Asian Americans, as well as influence American immigration policies, see Ellen Wu, *The Color of Success: Asian Americans and the Origins of the Model Minority* (Princeton, N.J.: Princeton University Press, 2014); and Madeline Hsu, *The Good Immigrants: How the Yellow Peril Became the Model Minority* (Princeton, N.J.: Princeton University Press, 2015).

14. May, *Homeward Bound*.

15. Box F1, folder re: Shoemakers Project, ACIM–National; Rev. Caesar Donanzan to Countess Bianchi, March 7, 1956, CIPSU, Rome, box F1, folder re: Shoemakers Project, ACIM–National; ACIM Report CIPSU Cases, April–May 1956, November 1956, box F1, folder PF1s Sent to Prospective Sponsors, ACIM–National; Caesar Donanzan to Marcella Bianchi di Lavagna, March 6, 1956, box F1, folder CIPSU Lists, ACIM–National; Marcella Bianchi di Lavagna to Caesar Donanzan, March 10, 1956, box F1, folder CIPSU, ACIM–National; CIPSU Cases, box E40, folder Immigration Cases "M," ACIM–National; and Arrival Lists, box F2, folder Carrier Arrival Notices, ACIM–National.

16. "Report of the First Session of the Provisional Intergovernmental Committee for the Movement of Migrants from Europe," Second Session,

February 9, 1952, box 1, vol. 1, Intergovernmental Committee for European Migration Collection, Center for Migration Studies (hereafter ICEM Collection). For ISS travel assistance (including adoptions), see International Social Services United States of America Branch Records, Social Welfare History Archive, University of Minnesota.

17. Box F2, folder Carrier Arrival Notices, ACIM–National. NCWC cases occasionally went to the IWL as well. Box E44, folder Notice of Arrivals, and folder Refugee Relief Program: Italian Immigration Lists, ACIM–National. The IWL also alerted Italian American and Italian travel agencies of the availability of the Port and Dock Committee's services. "Statistical Report for August 1961," Port and Dock Committee, box 66, Italian Welfare League Records, Center for Migration Studies (hereafter IWL Records).

18. There were about fifteen women who regularly volunteered (and several other less-frequent volunteers) for the Port and Dock Committee. Monthly Reports, Port and Dock Committee, October 1952–December 1965, box 64–71, IWL Records.

19. See December 31, 1956, Report and March 3, 1957, Report, box 1, folder 5–6, ACIM–Chicago; and Monthly Reports and Correspondence, Port and Dock Committee, October 1952–December 1965, box 64–71, IWL Records. The entire monthly records of the Port and Dock Committee span from 1952 to 1972, however I have only reviewed and analyzed 1952–1965 for the purposes of this project. Records from 1952 to 1954 are fragmentary.

20. Monthly Reports and Correspondence, Port and Dock Committee, November 1954–December 1956, box 76, IWL Records; and Walter Persegati to J. C. Viski, October 17, 1956, box 1, folder 5, ACIM–Chicago.

21. Monthly Reports and Correspondence, Port and Dock Committee, October 1952–December 1965, box 64–71, IWL Records.

22. Records are fragmentary before November 1954 and November and December 1955 are missing. The statistics for July 1956 may be incomplete because of confusion over the sinking of an Italian passenger liner, the *Andrea Doria*. I cut the sample off after December 1956 even though refugees were still arriving in 1957 because complete records for 1957 and 1958 are missing. Detailed accounts for the Port and Dock Committee resume in January 1959. The 2,024 cases totaled 3,832 people. Monthly Reports, Port and Dock Committee, November 1954–December 1956, box 64, IWL Records. The IWL continued to assist arriving immigrants until 1972, however the Port and Dock Committee's activities peaked during the 1950s when Italians were able to take advantage of special refugee relief legislation.

23. Of the 777 cases handled by the IWL in the 1950s, 506 were adjustment of status/deportation cases. IWL Immigration Cases Files exist for the 1940s through the 1960s, however I have only reviewed the 1950s cases as a sample. Immigration Case Files, box 134–68, 194–222, IWL Records.

24. Desmond King, *Making Americans: Immigration, Race, and the Origins of the Diverse Democracy* (Cambridge, Mass.: Harvard University Press, 2000), 58–81; Matthew Frye Jacobson, *Whiteness of a Different Color: European Immigrants and the Alchemy of Race* (Cambridge, Mass.: Harvard University Press, 1998), 39–90; and Katherine Benton-Cohen, *Inventing the Immigration Problem: The Dillingham Commission and Its Legacy* (Cambridge, Mass.: Harvard University Press, 2018).

25. For Eastern European Jewish garment workers and Italian garment workers in the United States, see Thomas Kessner, *The Golden Door: Italian and Jewish Immigrant Mobility in New York City, 1880–1915* (New York: Oxford University Press, 1977); Jennifer Guglielmo, *Living the Revolution: Italian Women's Resistance and Radicalism in New York City, 1880–1945* (Chapel Hill: University of North Carolina Press, 2010); and Miriam Cohen, *Workshop to Office: Two Generations of Italian Women in New York City, 1900–1950* (Ithaca, N.Y.: Cornell University Press, 1993). For twentieth-century changes in the industry, see Roger Waldinger, *Through the Eye of the Needle: Immigrants and Enterprise in New York's Garment Trades* (New York: New York University Press, 1986); Nancy L. Green, *Ready-to-Wear and Ready-to-Work: A Century of Industry and Immigrants in Paris and New York* (Durham, N.C.: Duke University Press, 1997); Margaret M. Chin, *Sewing Women: Immigrants and the New York City Garment Industry* (New York: Columbia University Press, 2005), 12–19; and Daniel Soyer, ed., *A Coat of Many Colors: Immigration, Globalization, and Reform in New York City's Garment Industry* (New York: Fordham University Press, 2005).

26. Nicola White, *Reconstructing Italian Fashion: America and the Development of the Italian Fashion Industry* (New York: Bloomsbury Press, 2000).

27. The national average income for all American families in 1955 was $4,418 a year or approximately $85 a week. US Census Bureau, "Money Income of Families—Median Income in Current and Constant (1997) Dollars, by Race and Type of Family: 1947 to 1997," in *Statistical Abstract of the United States: 1999* (Washington, D.C.: US Census Bureau), §31, 867–89.

28. Box 1–4, Italian American Labor Council Collection, Tamiment Library, Robert F. Wagner Labor Archives, New York University. For Antonini's influence in Italian reconstruction and democratization in the postwar period, his work on behalf of Italian American causes in the postwar United States, as well as his international influence as a labor leader, see Ronald Filippelli, *American Labor and Postwar Italy, 1943–1953: A Study of Cold War Politics* (Stanford, Calif.: Stanford University Press, 1989).

29. Hickey-Freeman supplemented normal production during the war by manufacturing officers' uniforms. G. Sheldon Brayer, *A Temple of Fine Tailoring: The Hickey-Freeman Story* (Rochester, N.Y.: Hickey-Freeman Company, Inc., 1999), 39–43.

30. Brayer, *Temple of Fine Tailoring*, 39–43.

31. Edward Corsi, "Let's Talk About Immigration," *Reporter*, June 2, 1955, box 9, Edward Corsi Papers, Rare Books and Special Collections, Syracuse University. Corsi was a former New York State commissioner of labor and former special assistant to the State Department for the Refugee Relief Act when writing the article. See also Brayer, *Temple of Fine Tailoring*, 40–41.

32. Edmund E. Cummings, Executive Assistant, WRS, New York City, to Msgr. John Maney, Chancellor of Bishop's Welfare and Emergency Relief Fund in Rochester, NY, April 19, 1955, box 1, folder Hickey-Freeman, War Relief Services (WRS), National Catholic Welfare Conference Collection, Center for Migration Studies (hereafter NCWC Collection); and E. E. Cummings to Robert McKeever, Pontificia Opera di Assistenza, Rome, December 10, 1964, box 1, folder Hickey-Freeman, box 1, NCWC Collection.

33. John W. Briggs, *An Italian Passage: Immigrants to Three American Cities, 1890–1930* (New Haven, Conn.: Yale University Press, 1978), 69–119; and Boris Mikolji, "Ethnic Groups in America: The Italians of Rochester," *Il Politico* 36, no. 4 (December 1971).

34. Bescia did give oral testimony in support of this conclusion, but transcripts of that exchange are not available. See Mikolji, "Ethnic Groups in America," 663.

35. Kenneth Keating assisted Hickey-Freeman and WRS in obtaining permission from INS for initial installments of Italian tailors. US Department of Justice, Immigration and Naturalization Service, to John R. Northrup, Hickey-Freeman Company, February 26, 1948, box 1, folder Hickey-Freeman, WRS, NCWC Collection; and Brayer, *Temple of Fine Tailoring*, 41.

36. Edmund E. Cummings, WRS, New York City, to Msgr. Andrew P. Landi, WRS, Rome, October 8, 1954, box 1, folder Hickey-Freeman, WRS, NCWC Collection.

37. Edmund E. Cummings, WRS, New York City, to Msgr. John Maney, Chancellor of Bishop's Welfare and Emergency Relief Fund in Rochester, NY, April 19, 1955, box 1, folder Hickey-Freeman, WRS, NCWC Collection.

38. Edmund E. Cummings, WRS, to Bruce Mohler, NCWC Bureau of Immigration, November 21, 1961, box 1, folder Hickey-Freeman, WRS, NCWC Collection.

39. Edmund E. Cummings, Executive Assistant, WRS, New York City, to Msgr. Andrew P. Landi, WRS, Rome, October 8, 1954, box 1, folder Hickey-Freeman, WRS, NCWC Collection.

40. Edmund E. Cummings, WRS, to Robert McKeever, Pontificia Opera di Assistenza, Rome, December 10, 1964, box 1, folder Hickey-Freeman, WRS, NCWC Collection; and E. E. Cummings, WRS, to James Norris, April 6, 1956, box 1, folder Hickey-Freeman, WRS, NCWC Collection.

41. White, *Reconstructing Italian Fashion*, 1–42; and de Grazia, *Irresistible Empire*, 336–457.

42. Memorandum for Record: File: Tailors, March 10, 1958, box 95 General Records, folder Tailors, NCWC Collection.

43. Immigrant workers continued to sustain Hickey-Freeman's workforce in subsequent decades. The source of the immigrants became increasingly diversified in the 1970s with tailors hailing from Italy, Greece, Lebanon, Turkey, Mexico, Poland, Yugoslavia, and Honduras. In 1977, fifty Hickey-Freeman recruits came from Turkey alone. Edmund E. Cummings, WRS, to Paul Brescia, Hickey-Freeman Company, May 11, 1959, box 1, folder Hickey-Freeman, WRS, NCWC Collection; Edmund E. Cummings, WRS, to Robert McKeever, Pontificia Opera di Assistenza, Rome, December 10, 1964, box 1, folder Hickey-Freeman, WRS, NCWC Collection; and Brayer, *Temple of Fine Tailoring*, 59–60.

44. Office Memo, WRS, Subject: Meeting with Mssrs. Rauber and Brescia, March 30, 1955, From E. E. Cummings, April 1, 1955, box 1, folder Hickey-Freeman, WRS, NCWC Collection; Judge Charles Lamiase to Caesar Donanzan, ACIM–National, box E23 General Records, Immigration Cases, folder April–June 1954, ACIM–National; and Rev. Caesar Donanzan to Judge Charles Lambiase, January 21, 1954, box E23 General Records, Immigration Cases, folder April–June 1954, ACIM–National.

45. "American Relief for Italy Member Profiles: Francis D'Amanda," *American Relief for Italy News*, New York City, January 1946; and American Resettlement Council for Italian Refugees Information Packet, box E18, folder American Resettlement Council for Italian Refugees, ACIM–National.

46. For example, Saraceno letter enclosed in Jack Danella, Chairman of ACIM–Utica Chapter, to Juvenal Marchisio, December 28, 1954, box E23 General Records, Immigration Cases, folder April–June 1954, ACIM–National; Angelo Di Nieri to Juvenal Marchisio, September 28, 1955, box E31 General Records, Immigration Cases, folder Immigration General Information, ACIM–National; and box E47, folder M–R Immigration Cases 1957, ACIM–National. See also Fourth Preference Immigration Visa Requests who note that they are tailors and would like to work at one of ACIM's partner companies, box E52, folder Fourth Preference English, ACIM–National.

47. There are countless examples of refugees processed by ACIM becoming tailors, seamstresses, cutters, pressers, and other garment workers in the New York City area. These cases were processed on an individual basis and were not part of a mass program. For example, box E22, folder Immigration Cases Jan.–March 1955, ACIM–National. Evidence supporting an occupation-based initiative for the city is noted in ACIM–National's archive, but the information is missing.

48. Approximately 33 percent of all manufacturing jobs in New York City at midcentury were garment industry jobs. Chin, *Sewing Women*; and Soyer, *Coat of Many Colors*.

49. For an example of a smaller program, the Atlantic City Clothing Company took twelve refugee tailors in 1956. Caroline Abate file, box E39 General Records, folder Immigration Cases "A" 1956, ACIM–National; and Randy and Demm Co. Inc. and Eagle Clothing Company, Brooklyn, box E39, folder Immigration Cases March 1954 and Immigration Cases "C" 1956, ACIM–National. For case-by-case placement for refugee tailors, see Immigration Case Files, box E30, E31, E39–41, E47, F2–5, ACIM–National.

50. Immigration Cases, box E63, E64, E72–74, ACIM–National.

51. Oxxford Clothes to ACIM Chicago, January 3, 1956, box E51, folder Oxxford Clothes, ACIM–National.

52. Box E51, folder Oxxford Clothes, ACIM–National; Luigi Antonini to ACIM–New York City, January 22–February 28, 1957, box E51, folder Oxxford Clothes, ACIM–National; and A. Minnucci, president of Federsarti, Rome, to ACIM–Chicago, July 29, 1958, box 1, folder 7–Correspondence 1958, ACIM–Chicago.

53. John Parochetti to Reverend Luigi Donanzan, June 1, 1959, box 1, folder 8–Correspondence 1959, ACIM–Chicago; and Leo Grandi to John Parochetti, June 8, 1959, box 1, folder 8–Correspondence 1959, ACIM–Chicago.

54. Box E51, folder Oxxford Clothes, ACIM–National; and "Passenger List MITWA #12337," and "List of Italian Refugees, Tailors and Dressmakers," box 1, folder 4–Correspondence 1956, ACIM–Chicago. The cases processed in 1957 were pipeline cases.

55. The IWL provided transportation loans for many of those cases. See A. Minnucci, president of Federsarti, to ACIM–Chicago, July 29, 1958, box 1, folder 7–Correspondence 1958, ACIM–Chicago; Angela Carlozzi, Italian Welfare League, to Vittorio Ranieri, ACIM–Chicago, December 15, 1958, box 1, folder 7–Correspondence 1958, ACIM–Chicago; and Oxxford manager, DiGiovanni, to Ernest Toben, Assistant Director, U.S. Dept. of Justice, INS, 1961, box 2, folder 11, ACIM–Chicago.

56. Again, demand for Italian tailors decreased by the end of the decade. Hart Schaffner & Marx, to ACIM–Chicago, n.d., box 1, folder 3 Correspondence 1955, ACIM–Chicago; F. DiGiovanni, Weinburg Corporation, to Ernest Toben, Assistant District Direct, U.S. Department of Justice, Immigration and Naturalization Service, September 8, 1961, box 1, folder 11 Correspondence 1961, ACIM–Chicago; Alex Aiello to ACIM/St. Michael's Church, September 5, 1961, box 1, folder 11 Correspondence 1961, ACIM–Chicago; Leo Grandi, ACIM–Chicago, to Alex Aiello, September 21, 1961, box 1, folder 11 Correspondence 1961, ACIM–Chicago; and Joseph De Serto to Tommaso Pasquale DiPierro, October 31, 1962, box 1, folder 12 Correspondence 1962, ACIM–Chicago.

57. "List of Italian Refugees, Tailors, and Dressmakers," box 1, folder 2, ACIM–Chicago.

58. Dates of birth are not available for five of the sixty migrants. "List of Italian Refugees, Tailors, and Dressmakers," box 1, folder 2, ACIM–Chicago; ACIM–Chicago to ACIM–National, January 30, 1956, box 1, folder 4 Correspondence 1956, ACIM–Chicago; and Angela Carlozzi, Italian Welfare League, NYC, to Vittorio Ranieri, ACIM–Chicago, December 15, 1958, box 1, folder 7 Correspondence 1958, ACIM–Chicago.

59. "List of Italian Refugees, Tailors, and Dressmakers," box 1, folder 2, ACIM–Chicago. For further evidence of individual migrants calling families later, see Vittorio Ranieri case, ACIM–Chicago, to David Maynard, American Consul General in Genova, September 26, 1958, box 1, folder 7 Correspondence 1958, ACIM–Chicago.

60. Aristide Zolberg, *A Nation by Design: Immigration Policy in the Fashioning of America* (Cambridge, Mass.: Harvard University Press, 2006), 312, 316; and Roger Daniels, *Guarding the Golden Door: American Immigration Policy and Immigrants since 1882* (New York: Hill and Wang, 2004), 342. For women's difficulties in securing skilled workers' visas still after 1952, see Martha Gardner, *The Qualities of a Citizen: Women, Immigration, and Citizenship, 1870–1965* (Princeton, N.J.: Princeton University Press, 2009), 212–19.

61. For an extended discussion of immigrant women in the postwar period, see Gardner, *Qualities of a Citizen*, 199–253; and Donna Gabaccia, *From the Other Side: Women, Gender, and Immigrant Life in the U.S., 1820–1990* (Bloomington: Indiana University Press, 1994). For more on the Italian case specifically, see Elizabeth Zanoni, "'A Wife in Waiting': Women and the 1952 McCarran-Walter Act in *Il Progresso Italo-Americano* Advice Columns," in *New Italian Migrations to the United States*, vol. 1, *Politics and History since 1945*, eds. Laura Ruberto and Joseph Sciorra (Urbana: University of Illinois Press, 2017); and Silvia Cassamagnaghi, *Operazione spose di guerra: Storie d'amore e di emigrazione* (Milan: Feltrinelli, 2014).

62. March 1956 Report, ACIM–Chicago Chapter, box A18 Chapters and Committees, folder Chicago Chapter 1956 Statistics and Refugee Information, ACIM–National.

63. March 1956 Report, ACIM–Chicago Chapter, box A18 Chapters and Committees, folder Chicago Chapter 1956 Statistics and Refugee Information, ACIM–National.

64. March 1956 Report, ACIM–Chicago Chapter, box A18 Chapters and Committees, folder Chicago Chapter 1956 Statistics and Refugee Information, ACIM–National.

65. "I Sarti Italiani Hanno Invaso L'America," *Oggi*, February 17, 1956. See also *New World*, Chicago, October 18, 1955, and October 21, 1955, and "Italian Families Start New Life in Chicago," *Chicago Sun-Times*, May 30, 1956, for additional coverage.

66. Of the two cases of men traveling alone, one was twenty-one years old and single. The other was fifty-six and his family status is unknown. Only one

migrant embarked from a refugee camp in Genoa. Box F1, folder re: Shoemakers Project, ACIM–National; and ACIM Report, CIPSU Cases, April–May 1956, New York City Shoemakers, box 1, folder CIPSU, ACIM–National.

67. Florsheim guaranteed one hundred assurances but ACIM–Chicago's records do no indicate how many actually immigrated. The terms were $75 a week for a 40-hour workweek and a requirement to join the local union. Florsheim Shoe Company to ACIM–Chicago, January 1956, box 1, folder 4 Correspondence 1956, ACIM–Chicago; Italian Consulate to ACIM–Chicago Chapter, November 8, 1955, box 1, folder 3 Correspondence 1955, ACIM–Chicago; ACIM–Chicago memo, March 7, 1956, box 1, folder 4 Correspondence 1956, ACIM–Chicago; and Walter Persegati, ACIM–Chicago, to Mr. S. F. Eagan, Florsheim Shoe Company, March 13, 1956, box 1, folder 4 Correspondence 1956, ACIM–Chicago.

68. Box F1, folder re: Shoemakers Project, ACIM–National; Rev. Caesar Donanzan to Countess Bianchi, CIPSU, Rome, March 7, 1956, box F1, folder re: Shoemakers Project, ACIM–National; ACIM Report, CIPSU Cases, April–May 1956, box F1, folder re: Shoemakers Project, ACIM–National; and November 1956, New York City Shoemakers, box F1, folder re: Shoemakers Project, ACIM–National.

69. Walter Persegati, ACIM–Chicago, to Nicolo Teriaca, Collesano, Italy, April 2, 1956, box 1, folder 4 Correspondence 1956, ACIM–Chicago.

70. For example cases of trying to qualify as a tailor, see box E55, folder ILGWU Cases, ACIM–National; and box E63, folder Immigration Cases A–C, D–L, ACIM–National. Requirements from the Department of Labor were raised from three years of minimum experience to five as a specialty tailor. Edmund E. Cummings, War Relief Services, to Paul Brescia, Hickey-Freeman Company, October 9, 1961, box 1, folder Hickey-Freeman, WRS, NCWC Collection.

71. Box E44, folder John Santangelo, ACIM–National; and *Dispatch*, April 1959, box D, ACIM–National.

72. "World's Largest Publisher of Song Magazines," *New England Printer and Lithographer*, November 1954, 50–56, box E51, folder John Santangelo, ACIM–National.

73. For a list of donations, see box E51, folder John Santangelo, ACIM–National; "Santangelo—Fabulous Immigrant," ACIM *Dispatch*, October 1955, box D, ACIM–National; and "Santangelo Gives $5000 to ACIM Despite Flood Losses," *Dispatch*, November 1955, box D, ACIM–National.

74. Box E44, folder John Santangelo, ACIM–National; and "World's Largest Publisher of Song Magazines," *New England Printer and Lithographer*, November 1954, 50–56, box E51, folder John Santangelo, ACIM–National.

75. Box F1–F5 Refugee Case Files, ACIM–National.

76. CRS and the NCRC were both subsidiaries of the NCWC. L'Istituto Nazionale di Credito per il Lavoro All'estero discussed donating up to

50 percent of the start-up capital for this project. This agency also provided finances for similar projects in Latin American countries.

77. Initial estimates were later scaled back from three thousand to two thousand acres of land.

78. "York County South Carolina Program for Raising Funds" and "Proposal: Resettlement Plan," box E35, folder South Carolina Project 1955, ACIM–National. For more on Catholic views of public good in promoting agricultural labor, see Rev. Richard Cushing, Archbishop of Boston, Address to ACIM, New York, NY, December 3, 1953, *Catholic Mind*, October 1954, 604–9.

79. With the exception of a few shared buildings and supplies, farms would be individual family enterprises. "York County South Carolina Program for Raising Funds," "The York County Farm Produce Company Investor's Pamphlet," and "Proposal: Resettlement Plan," box E35, folder South Carolina Project 1955, ACIM–National.

80. "York County South Carolina Program for Raising Funds" and "The York County Farm Produce Company," investor's pamphlet, box E35, folder South Carolina Project 1955, ACIM–National; and "New Farmers for Old Land," *Jubilee Magazine*, August 1957, 36–40, box 1, folder 1957 ACIM Miscellaneous, Carolyn Sinelli Burns Papers, Bentley Historical Library, University of Michigan (hereafter Sinelli Burns Papers).

81. "Memorandum Submitted by the Italian Delegation, Agricultural Development and Colonization," October 13, 1952, box 1, vol. 1, ICEM Collection; and "1952–1953b Report," Section on Projection, Analysis, and Problems, box 1, vol. 2, ICEM Collection.

82. "N.C.W.C. News Bulletin," July 18, 1955, box E36, folder Italy, ACIM–National; and "Farm Reclamation Project," *Il Crociato*, Brooklyn, N.Y., July 24, 1956, and "New Farmers for Old Land," *Jubilee Magazine*, August 1957, 36–40, box 1, folder 1957 ACIM Miscellaneous, Sinelli Burns Papers.

83. "The York County Farm Produce Company Investor's Pamphlet" and "Proposal: Resettlement Plan," box E35, folder South Carolina Project 1955, ACIM–National; and "New Farmers for Old Land," *Jubilee Magazine*, August 1957, 36–40, box 1, folder 1957 ACIM Miscellaneous, Sinelli Burns Papers.

84. Pope Pius XII, *Exsul Familia*, August 1, 1952, in *The Church's Magna Charta for Migrants*, trans. and ed. Reverend Giulivo Tessarolo (Staten Island, N.Y.: St. Charles Seminary, 1962).

85. A distant secondary goal of the project was to stimulate the development of Catholic communities in the American South. "New Farmers for Old Land," *Jubilee Magazine*, August 1957, 36–40, box 1, folder 1957 ACIM Miscellaneous, Sinelli Burns Papers; and Rev. Richard Cushing, Archbishop of Boston, Address to ACIM, New York, NY, December 3, 1953, *Catholic Mind*, October 1954, 604–9.

86. Rural resettlement or "distribution" programs were viewed as a solution to urban overcrowding by progressive reformers in the North and to labor shortage concerns by developers in South in the late nineteenth and early twentieth centuries. Benton-Cohen, *Inventing the Immigration Problem*, 72–103, 200–33; Deirdre Moloney, *American Catholic Lay Groups and Transatlantic Social Reform in the Progressive Era* (Chapel Hill: University of North Carolina Press, 2002), 69–115; and Cindy Hahamovitch, *The Fruits of Their Labor: Atlantic Coast Farmworkers and the Making of Migrant Poverty, 1870–1945* (Chapel Hill: University of North Carolina Press, 1997), 14–78.

87. For representative cases of resettlement assistance from ACIM and partner organizations, see Detroit Chapter Report 1952–1957, box A20 Chapters and Committees, folder Detroit Chapter, ACIM–National; and March 1956 Report, ACIM–Chicago Chapter, box A18 Chapters and Committees, folder Chicago Chapter 1956 Statistics and Refugee Information, ACIM–National.

88. Cohen, *Consumer's Republic*. These projects were transatlantic in nature. The Marshall Plan had already encouraged a shift in Italian consumption patterns and, correspondingly, an ideological shift about the nature of markets, the state, and citizenship. See Victoria de Grazia's work on the "consumer-citizen" in de Grazia, *Irresistible Empire*, 336–75.

89. Nicholas Falco, ed., *A Guide to the Archives: Records of the Italian Welfare League Inc.* (Staten Island, N.Y.: Center for Migration Studies, 1988).

90. "Suggested Recommendations for the Sub-committee on Immigration and Citizenship to the Detroit Area Conference of Catholic Women," box 4, folder "National Conference of Catholic Women, 1964," Sinelli Burns Papers.

91. Box E55, folder Immigrant Resettlement; box E65, folder Immigrant Resettlement; box E65, folder Immigration Resettlement; box E74, folder Immigration Resettlement and Resettlement Pending, ACIM–National. For a typical letter acknowledging household donations, see Louis Donanzan, ACIM–Chicago, to Saul Polk, June 2, 1956, box 1, folder 4, ACIM–Chicago.

92. ACIM Letter to Italian Parishes, Re: Adopt a Family Program, July 12, 1956, box 1, folder 4, ACIM–Chicago.

93. Italians in Chicago, Oral History Project Records, Immigration History Research Center Archives, University of Minnesota (hereafter Italians in Chicago). The collection includes interviews from 113 Chicago Italian Americans.

94. De Grazia, *Irresistible Empire*, 336–457.

95. Ori-56, Sam Ori, Italians in Chicago.

96. "American National Council of Catholic Women and Resettlement of Refugees," *International Catholic Migration Committee News*, January 1954, 3–4, box 18, folder 190, NCWC Collection; Committee on Immigration, National Conference of Catholic Women Yearbook, 1958, box 4, folder National Conference of Catholic Women, 1958, Sinelli Burns Papers; "Suggested Recommendations for the Sub-committee on Immigration and Citizenship to the

Detroit Area Conference of Catholic Women," box 4, folder National Conference of Catholic Women, 1964, Sinelli Burns Papers; Angelo Gagliardo, Chairman ACIM–Cleveland, Remarks at the Second Symposium on Italian Migration, ACIM, Rome, 1961, box 7, folder 58, ACIM–Chicago; and "Annual Report Form, Committee on Immigrant and Americanization," box 28, folder Immigration Follow Up, NCWC Collection.

97. "Detroit Chapter Report 1952–1957," box A20 Chapters and Committees, folder Detroit Chapter, ACIM–National; ACIM–National Office to Chicago Office, September 27, 1956, box 1, folder 5 1956, ACIM–Chicago; ACIM–Chicago Memo with captions of pictures of English Language Classes at St. Michael's School, 1956, box 1, folder 5, ACIM–Chicago; and ACIM to Italian Parishes, re: Adopt a Family Program, July 12, 1956, box 1, folder 4, ACIM–Chicago.

98. Juvenal Marchisio interview by IDAS, April 28, 1959, box E70, folder Biographies: General, ACIM–National.

99. "American National Council of Catholic Women and Resettlement of Refugees," *International Catholic Migration Committee News*, January 1954, 3–4, box 18, folder 190, NCWC Collection; Committee on Immigration, National Conference of Catholic Women Yearbook, 1958, box 4, folder National Conference of Catholic Women, 1958, Sinelli Burns Papers; "Suggested Recommendations for the Sub-committee on Immigration and Citizenship to the Detroit Area Conference of Catholic Women," box 4, folder National Conference of Catholic Women, 1964, Sinelli Burns Papers; Angelo Gagliardo, Chairman ACIM–Cleveland, Remarks at the Second Symposium on Italian Migration, ACIM, Rome, 1961, box 7, folder 58, ACIM–Chicago; and "Annual Report Form, Committee on Immigrant and Americanization," box 28, folder Immigration Follow Up, NCWC Collection.

100. There are five meticulously detailed cases of refugee resettlement assistance reported from the Detroit Chapter to ACIM's National Chapter from 1956 to 1957. I selected one case at random. Detroit Chapter Report 1952–1957, box A20 Chapters and Committees, folder Detroit Chapter, ACIM–National.

101. Detroit Chapter Report 1952–1957, box A20 Chapters and Committees, folder Detroit Chapter, ACIM–National.

102. Detroit Chapter Report 1952–1957, box A20 Chapters and Committees, folder Detroit Chapter, ACIM–National.

103. See, for example, cover image. ACIM–National to ACIM–Chicago, September 27, 1956, box 1, folder 5 1956, ACIM–Chicago; and ACIM–Chicago Memo with captions of pictures of English Language Classes at St. Michael's School, 1956, box 1, folder 5, ACIM–Chicago.

104. *Chicago Sun Times*, May 30, 1956, June 18, 1956, June 21, 1956, and *New World Chicago*, October 18, 1955, October 21, 1955.

105. "From Italy to Chicago: The Dramatic Success Story of Our Italian-Americans, Part 3," *Chicago Tribune Magazine*, August 19, 1962, box 5, folder 37, Maurice Marcello Papers, Immigration History Research Center Archives, University of Minnesota. Stories chronicled earlier waves of Italian immigrants and their American-born descendants as well as more recent arrivals.

106. Giuseppe Merola Report, Detroit Chapter Report 1952–1957, box A20 Chapters and Committees, folder Detroit Chapter, ACIM–National.

107. Angelo Gagliardo, Chairman ACIM–Cleveland, Remarks at the Second Symposium on Italian Migration, ACIM, Rome, 1961, Folder 58, ACIM–Chicago.

108. Juvenal Marchisio interview by IDAS, April 28, 1959, box E70, folder Biographies–General, ACIM–National.

109. Juvenal Marchisio interview by IDAS, April 28, 1959, box E70, folder Biographies–General, ACIM–National.

110. For public campaigns to "sell" Hungarian and Cuban refugees to the public, see Bon Tempo, *Americans at the Gate*, 75–81, 121–27. For Cuban American politics and the exile community, see Maria Cristina Garcia, *Havana USA: Cuban Exiles and Cuban Americans* (Berkeley: University of California Press, 1996).

111. The same could be said of the Jewish American lobby. Loescher and Scanlan, *Calculated Kindness*, 1–48.

5. THE CORSI AFFAIR

1. Pub. L. 83-751, 2nd Sess. Quotas for Greece and the Netherlands were reallocated reflecting "overpopulation" concerns in those countries as well.

2. The total number of all visas issued at the end of 1954 was slightly higher, seventeen thousand in total including nonrefugee relatives of US citizens. Carl Bon Tempo, *Americans at the Gate: The United States and Refugees during the Cold War* (Princeton, N.J.: Princeton University Press, 2008), 47.

3. Fitzgerald and Cook-Martin argue that "passing a law is performance intended for domestic and/or international audiences, but whether that performance is exclusively symbolic, or also aimed at changing material realities on the ground, depends on historical conditions." David Fitzgerald and David Cook-Martin, *Culling the Masses: The Democratic Origins of Racist Immigration Policies in the Americas* (Cambridge, Mass.: Harvard University Press, 2014), 35.

4. Daniel J. Tichenor, *Dividing Lines: The Politics of Immigration Control in America* (Princeton, N.J.: Princeton University Press, 2002), 176–218; Aristide Zolberg, *A Nation by Design: Immigration Policy in the Fashioning of America* (Cambridge, Mass.: Harvard University Press, 2006), 293–336; Roger Daniels, *Guarding the Golden Door: American Immigration Policy and Immigrants since 1882* (New York: Hill and Wang, 2004), 98–128; Bon Tempo, *Americans at the Gate*, 1–59; and Gil Loescher and John Scanlan, *Calculated Kindness: Refugees*

*and America's Half-Open Door, 1945–Present* (New York: Free Press, 1986), 1–48.

5. Tichenor, *Dividing Lines*, 176–218; Zolberg, *Nation by Design*, 293–336; Daniels, *Guarding the Golden Door*, 98–128; Bon Tempo, 1–59; and Loescher and Scanlan, *Calculated Kindness*, 1–48.

6. Barry Rubin, *Secrets of State: The State Department and the Struggle over U.S. Foreign Policy* (New York: Oxford University Press, 1985), 79–80. For a more generous reading of McLeod's appointment, see Morten Bach and Korcaighe Hale, "'What He Is Speaks So Loud That I Can't Hear What He's Saying': R.W. Scott McLeod and the Long Shadow of Joe McCarthy," *Historian* 72, no. 1 (Spring 2010).

7. Bach and Hale, "What He Is Speaks So Loud."

8. *Senate Committee on the Judiciary, Investigation on Administration of Refugee Relief Act: Hearings before a Subcommittee of the Committee on the Judiciary, United States Senate*, 84th Cong., 1st Sess., April 13–May 27, 1955, 1–33 (statement of Scott McLeod, Administrator, Bureau of Security, Consular Affairs and Personnel, Department of State) (hereafter McLeod, Senate Testimony).

9. Fitzgerald and Cook-Martin, *Culling the Masses*, 35, 105–9.

10. Order Sons of Italy, Committee on Immigration and Naturalization, Resolution, May 1954 re: Refugee Relief Program, box 1, folder Immigration and Naturalization Committee, Joseph Errigo Papers, Immigration History Research Center Archives, University of Minnesota (hereafter Errigo Papers); and "Protest Refugees Delay," *Order Sons of Italy in America News*, June 1954, Immigration History Research Center Archives, University of Minnesota.

11. "McLeod Criticized on Refugee Curbs: Celler Demands His Ouster as Director and Seeks to Liberalize '53 Act," *New York Times*, August 9, 1954.

12. "Celler Assails Refugee Relief," *New York Times*, December 14, 1954.

13. "Celler Assails Refugee Relief," *New York Times*, December 14, 1954; and Emanuel Celler Letter to the *Times*, "To Aid Refugee Entry," *New York Times*, February 28, 1955.

14. VOLAGs were particularly critical of the provision in the RRA that specified that sponsors must be individuals, not organizations, arguing that requirement made it more difficult to provide assurances for refugees and that it was done to purposely stall their entry. "Lutherans Score '53 Refugee Law," *New York Times*, February 3, 1954.

15. The administration frequently felt the need to publicly reassure the program's critics. For example, see "Refugee Prospect Cheers President," *New York Times*, March 25, 1954; and "Refugee Entry Upheld," *New York Times*, September 8, 1954.

16. Bon Tempo, *Americans at the Gate*, 36; and Tichenor, *Dividing Lines*, 176–201. Loescher and Scanlan note that Eisenhower was aware that the RRA might prove a political asset with Italian and Greek Americans. Loescher

and Scanlan, *Calculated Kindness*, 44–48. Zolberg notes Eisenhower's public criticism of the McCarran-Walter Act but argues that the administration did not place a high priority on the liberal effort to reform it. Zolberg, *Nation by Design*, 320; Theodore Buchanan Auker, "American Immigration Policy during the Eisenhower Administration" (master's thesis, Washington State University, 1973). For Eisenhower's appointment of McLeod, see Walter LaFeber, *The American Age: U.S. Foreign Policy at Home and Abroad* (New York: W. W. Norton, 1994), 539.

17. Bon Tempo, *Americans at the Gate*, 36.

18. For Eisenhower's views on racial and ethnic equality more broadly, see his ambivalent position on civil rights. Thomas Borstelmann, *The Cold War and the Color Line: American Race Relations in the Global Arena* (Cambridge, Mass.: Harvard University Press, 2001), 85–134.

19. Corsi fared better as a bureaucrat than a politician. He lost bids for New York City councilman in 1937, New York senator in 1938, and New York City mayor in 1950. Salvatore LaGumina, *New York at Mid-Century: The Impellitteri Years* (Westport, Conn.: Greenwood Press, 1992), 43–46. Interestingly, the 1950 mayoral race was a three-way race between three Italian-born candidates, indicating Italian American electoral influence in the city at midcentury. Corsi (Rep.) and Ferdinand Pecora (Dem.) lost to Vincent Impellitteri (Experience Party). See also, Roberta Thibault, ed., *Edward Corsi: Inventory of His Papers* (Syracuse, N.Y.: Syracuse University Library, 1969).

20. Corsi immigrated to the United States from Capistrano, Italy, in 1906 with his mother when he was ten years old. He hailed from an elite background and achieved upward mobility, receiving a Jesuit education at St. Francis Xavier College and a law degree from Fordham University in 1922. Early in his career, he clerked at Ellis Island and engaged in social work at a settlement house in Italian Harlem. Corsi's settlement house work brought him into contact with Congressman Fiorello LaGuardia and New York's Republican political machine. Like LaGuardia, Corsi represented the progressive wing of the party, which advocated for a more liberal immigration policy. Thibault, *Edward Corsi*; and LaGumina, *New York at Mid-Century*, 43–46.

21. Edward Corsi, *In the Shadow of Liberty* (New York: Arno Press, 1969). Later in life, Corsi said that he accepted the position as commissioner of immigration so that he could provide the most humane and compassionate administration of the nation's immigration policies as possible. Edward Corsi, "My Ninety Days in Washington," *Reporter*, May 5, 1955, 10–17, box 29, Edward Corsi Papers, Rare Books and Special Collections, Syracuse University (hereafter Corsi Papers).

22. For National Council on Postwar Immigration Policy, see box 50 Corsi Papers. For Congressional Testimony, see Edward Corsi, "Statement before the Subcommittee to Investigate Immigration and Naturalization of

the United States Senate Judiciary Committee," November 16, 1948, box 31, Corsi Papers.

23. Corsi, "My Ninety Days in Washington." For an example of a typical Corsi speech critiquing the nation's immigration policies, see Edward Corsi, Speech on Immigration Reform at the National Conference of Social Work, Buffalo, NY, May 23, 1946, box 31, Corsi Papers.

24. Box 9, 45, 52, Corsi Papers.

25. "Italy Needs Immediate Aid, Corsi Tells Young GOP," *Utica Observer Dispatch*, March 21, 1948.

26. For work with the Italian American Labor Council, see box 8, Corsi Papers. For activity under the Dewey administration, including the mission to Italy, see Corsi, "My Ninety Days in Washington"; and "De Gasperi Wants More Emigration," *New York Times*, September 12, 1948.

27. American Resettlement Council for Italian Refugee Records, box 36, Corsi Papers.

28. Edward Corsi, "Paths to the New World: American Immigration Yesterday, Today, and Tomorrow," box 11, folder 144, National Catholic Welfare Conference Addendum Collection, Center for Migration Studies (hereafter NCWC Addendum).

29. Dennis Flinn to John Hanes, memo, April 7, 1955, box 3, folder Corsi (Edward) (6), John Foster Dulles Papers, 1954–1959, Dwight D. Eisenhower Presidential Library (hereafter Dulles Papers).

30. Corsi, "My Ninety Days in Washington."

31. *Senate Committee on the Judiciary, Investigation on Administration of Refugee Relief Act: Hearings before a Subcommittee of the Committee on the Judiciary, United States Senate*, 84th Cong., 1st Sess., April 13–May 27, 1955, 37–39 (statement of Edward Corsi, former Special Assistant to the Secretary of State) (hereafter Corsi Senate Testimony); and Corsi, "My Ninety Days in Washington."

32. Telegram entered into Congressional Record, Corsi Senate Testimony, 37–39. See also State Department Press Release, No. 736, December 30, 1954, "Edward Corsi Appointed Special Assistant for Refugee and Migration Problems." Press release announced position and said, "Mr. Corsi will work with Scott McLeod, Administrator of the Refugee Relief Program, to carry out that program." Box 3, folder Corsi (Edward) (5), Dulles Papers.

33. Corsi Senate Testimony, 37–39. See also "Dulles Appoints Corsi to Unravel Snags in U.S. Refugee Program," *New York Times*, December 31, 1954, which says, "Mr. Corsi would work in conjunction with Scott McLeod" and that "Mr. Corsi would be responsible directly to Mr. Dulles. He will not take his orders from Mr. McLeod."

34. Edward Corsi interview, *Face the Nation*, CBS Television Network, April 17, 1955, box 3, folder Corsi (Edward) (5), Dulles Papers (hereafter Corsi interview); and "Corsi Ties His Ouster to Liberalism on Refugee Act," *New York Times*, April 10, 1955.

35. Corsi Senate Testimony, 37–41.

36. Corsi also tried to push for a more expansive definition of who would qualify as a refugee. *Senate Committee on the Judiciary, Investigation on Administration of Refugee Relief Act: Hearings before a Subcommittee of the Committee on the Judiciary, United States Senate*, 84th Cong., 1st Sess., April 13–May 27, 1955, 364 (statement of Herman Phlegler, Legal Advisor, Department of State); and Corsi, "My Ninety Days in Washington."

37. Corsi, "My Ninety Days in Washington."

38. Corsi Senate Testimony, 57.

39. Corsi Senate Testimony, 57.

40. Corsi, "My Ninety Days in Washington."

41. Corsi had also met high-ranking Italian officials on a previous trip he took to Italy in 1948 as New York State's commissioner of labor. Corsi likewise had personal and family connections that he exploited. Corsi Senate Testimony, 41–42, 207. "Corsi Conferisce Con le Autorita' Americane ed Italiane a Roma circa I Problemi dell'Emigrazione," box 3, Giuseppe D. Procopio Papers, Immigration History Research Center Archives, University of Minnesota.

42. Office Memo from Edward Corsi to the Secretary of State, John Foster Dulles, re: Refugee Relief Program, March 3, 1955, published in McLeod Senate Testimony, 146–49.

43. Corsi Senate Testimony, 211; and *Senate Committee on the Judiciary, Investigation on Administration of Refugee Relief Act: Hearings before a Subcommittee of the Committee on the Judiciary, United States Senate*, 84th Cong., 1st Sess., April 13–May 27, 1955, 335–36, 339–40 (statement of Roy L. Wade, Special Representative of the Administrator, Bureau of Security, Consular Affairs and Personnel, Department of State) (hereafter Wade Senate Testimony).

44. Wade Senate Testimony, 359; Telegram from Roy Wade to Scott McLeod, read during McLeod Senate Testimony, 184–85; and Corsi Senate Testimony, 214–16.

45. Corsi Senate Testimony, 41–42.

46. Wade Senate Testimony, 328.

47. Wade Senate Testimony, 328, 331–32, 347.

48. The records do not specify exactly what material Corsi supposedly disclosed. Wade Senate Testimony, 335, 346–47.

49. Wade Senate Testimony, 332–33, 348.

50. Box 71, folder 1 and 2, Immigration and Refugee Services of America Records, Immigration History Research Center Archives, University of Minnesota.

51. "State Dept's Side of the Corsi Case," *New York World Telegram and Sun*, April 13, 1955; "Tailor's from Italy: Corsi Sought Immigrants to Aid Clothing Industry," *New York Herald Tribune*, April 14, 1955; "Dulles and Staff Blamed by Corsi," *New York Times*, April 18, 1955; and Corsi interview.

52. "Tailors from Italy: Corsi Sought Immigrants to Aid Clothing Industry," *New York Herald Tribune*, April 14, 1955; and "Dulles and Staff Blamed by Corsi," *New York Times*, April 18, 1955.

53. Box 36, folder American Resettlement Council for Italian Refugees, Corsi Papers; and Corsi Senate Testimony, 216.

54. Office Memo from Edward Corsi to the Secretary of State, John Foster Dulles, re: Refugee Relief Program, March 3, 1955, published in McLeod Senate Testimony, 146–49; Corsi Senate Testimony, 194–95; and Edward Corsi to John Foster Dulles, reprinted in "Texts of Exchange Over Corsi Post," *New York Times*, April 12, 1955.

55. Edward Corsi, "Lets Talk about Immigration," *Reporter*, June 2, 1955.

56. Corsi Senate Testimony, 42–46, 48–49; "Corsi Denies Link to Left Wing Groups," *New York Times*, March 2, 1955; and "Walter Charges State Department By-Passed Senate on Corsi," *New York Times*, March 14, 1955. There is a vast literature dedicated to showing how politics and culture during the McCarthy era were used to discredit progressive organizations and New Deal programs. For a good overview, see Landon Storrs, *The Second Red Scare and the Unmaking of the New Deal Left* (Princeton, N.J.: Princeton University Press, 2013); and Ellen Schrecker, *Many Are the Crimes: McCarthyism in America* (Boston: Little, Brown, and Company, 1998).

57. Roderic O'Connor Memo to John Foster Dulles, Re: Refugee Relief Program, March 14, 1955, box 3, folder Corsi (Edward) (2), Dulles Papers.

58. Roderic O'Connor Memo to John Foster Dulles, Re: Refugee Relief Program, March 14, 1955, box 3, folder Corsi (Edward) (2), Dulles Papers.

59. Roderic O'Connor Memo to John Foster Dulles, Re: Refugee Relief Program, March 14, 1955, box 3, folder Corsi (Edward) (2), Dulles Papers.

60. As a conciliation, Dulles offered Corsi a new position in which he would survey possibilities for refugee migration in Latin America. "Corsi Is Dropped as Refugee Aid; Weighs New Post," *New York Times*, April 8, 1955.

61. Bach and Hale, "What He Is Speaks So Loud," 83–84.

62. Corsi, "My Ninety Days in Washington." For the Eisenhower administration's turbulent relationship with Congress during the height of the Red Scare see Jeff Broadwater, *Eisenhower and the Anti-Communist Crusade* (Chapel Hill: University of North Carolina Press, 1992).

63. "Texts of Exchange over Corsi Post," *New York Times*, April 12, 1955.

64. "State Dept's Side of the Corsi Case," *New York World-Telegram and Sun*, April 13, 1955; and "Tailors from Italy: Corsi Sought Immigrants to Aid Clothing Industry," *New York Herald Tribune*, April 14, 1955.

65. CBS News Radio Analysis of Affair, April 8, 1955, and Edward Morgan Broadcast, ABC, April 12, 1955, box 47, folder Research Data re: Corsi–Dulles Dispute, Corsi Papers; Corsi interview.

66. "Corsi Embittered by Dulles Ouster, Accuses Walter," *New York Times*,

April 9, 1955; and "Corsi Ties Ouster to His Liberalism on Refugee Act," *New York Times*, April 10, 1955.

67. "Walter in Corsi Rift," *Washington Star*, March 27, 1955; "Walter Charges State Department By-Passed Senate on Corsi," *New York Times*, March 14, 1955; and "I Am Not Afraid of Dagoes," *Dice il Congressman Walter*, in *Il Popolo*, Philadelphia, April 5, 1955. Walter disputed that he made such remarks in "Corsi Again Target of Walter Attack," *New York Times*, April 5, 1955.

68. "Walter in Corsi Rift, Hates to Go to Dulles Now–What with Squirrels and All," *Washington Star*, May 27, 1955.

69. Statement reprinted in "We've Been Labeled Bandits Too Long," *Fra Noi*, Chicago, December 1963.

70. Fourth Report of the National Anti-Defamation Committee, May 28, 1955, box 3, folder 11, Order Sons of Italy in America, Pennsylvania Grand Lodge Collection, Immigration History Research Center Archives, University of Minnesota (hereafter OSIA–PA Grand Lodge Collection).

71. Fourth Report of the National Anti-Defamation Committee, May 28, 1955, box 3, folder 11, OSIA–PA Grand Lodge Collection; Joseph Errigo, OSIA National Defamation Committee Chairman, to Francis Walter, March 30, 1955, and April 7, 1955, box 3, folder 11, OSIA–PA Grand Lodge Collection; and Joseph Errigo, OSIA National Defamation Committee Chairman, to President Eisenhower, April 11, 1955, box 3, folder 11, OSIA–PA Grand Lodge Collection. See numerous OSIA chapter appeals to President Eisenhower, General File, GF 9, July–September 1959, box 179, folder Corsi Dismissal Con, Dwight D. Eisenhower Central Files, Dwight D. Eisenhower Presidential Library.

72. George Spatuzza to President Eisenhower, April 1955, box 3, folder 11, OSIA–PA Grand Lodge Collection.

73. OSIA–Michigan to President Eisenhower, General File, GF 9, July–September 1959, box 179, folder Corsi Dismissal Con, Dwight D. Eisenhower Central Files, Dwight D. Eisenhower Presidential Library.

74. Francis Walter to Joseph Errigo, April 5, 1955, and John Hanes Jr., Special Assistant to Secretary Dulles, to Joseph Errigo, box 3, folder 11, OSIA–PA Grand Lodge Collection; and Fourth Report of the National Anti-defamation Committee, May 28, 1955, box 3, folder 11, OSIA–PA Grand Lodge Collection.

75. For individual and organizational letters, see box 23, Corsi Papers; and General File, GF 9, July–September 1959, box 179, folder Corsi Dismissal Con, Dwight D. Eisenhower Central Files, Dwight D. Eisenhower Presidential Library.

76. "Corsi Refuses Dulles Job Offer," *New York Times*, April 11, 1955; Columbian League, New York, to President Eisenhower, General File, GF 9,

July–September 1959, box 179, folder Corsi Dismissal Con, Dwight D. Eisenhower Central Files, Dwight D. Eisenhower Presidential Library.

77. Max Corvo, Chairman of the Connecticut Non-Partisan Committee Pro Edward Corsi, to President Eisenhower, April 12, 1955, box 12, folder 15, Alberto Cupelli Papers, Immigration History Research Center Archives, University of Minnesota (hereafter Cupelli Papers).

78. William Affatigato to Angela Rossi, box 75 Port and Dock Committee General Correspondence, folder 1955, Italian Welfare League Records, Center for Migration Studies (hereafter IWL Records); and Fourth Report of the National Anti-defamation Committee, May 28, 1955, box 3, folder 11, OSIA–PA Grand Lodge Collection.

79. Joseph Martorana telegram, April 11, 1955, General File, GF 9, July–September 1959, box 179, folder Corsi Dismissal Con, Dwight D. Eisenhower Central Files, Dwight D. Eisenhower Presidential Library.

80. "Lettera Aperta a Congressman Walter," *Il Progresso Italo-Americano*, April 10, 1955. For similar articles, see "What's behind Corsi Firing," *Michigan Catholic*, April 28, 1955, box A15, folder Detroit Chapter Correspondence, American Committee on Italian Migration–National Office, New York City Records, Center for Migration Studies (hereafter ACIM–National).

81. A. Philip Randolph to Eisenhower, General File, GF 9, July–September 1959, box 179, folder Corsi Dismissal Con, Dwight D. Eisenhower Central Files, Dwight D. Eisenhower Presidential Library.

82. Joseph Lichten of B'nai B'rith to Joseph Errigo, April 15, 1955, box 3, folder 11, OSIA–PA Grand Lodge Collection; Hyman Hayes to Edward Corsi, June 10, 1955, box 12, folder 15, Cupelli Papers; "National Jewish Leader Raps Corsi Firing as Aid to Reds, Surrender to McCarranists," *Italian News*, Boston, April 19, 1955; and "Refugee Act Hold to Be Sabotaged," *New York Times*, May 9, 1955.

83. Memo, April 19, 1955, Special Assistants Chronological Series, box 7, folder April 1955, Dulles Papers; Voluntary Agencies to John Foster Dulles, April 15, 1955, and Memo, April 19, 1955, box 3, folder Corsi (Edward) (4), Dulles Papers; and "Nine Relief Groups Protest on Corsi," *New York Times*, April 12, 1955.

84. See, for example, Senator Herbert Lehman Press Release re: Corsi Dismissal, April 9, 1955, box 3, folder NCNC Publications, 1953–1959, American Immigration and Citizenship Conference Records, Social Welfare History Archive, University of Minnesota (hereafter AICC Records); and "Corsi Ties Ouster to His Liberalism on Refugee Act," *New York Times*, April 10, 1955.

85. Corsi interview; "The Administration: 90 Day Wonder," *TIME Magazine*, April 25, 1955; and "New York: Change of Course," *TIME Magazine*, May 2, 1955.

86. "The Corsi Affair," *New York Herald Tribune*, April 11, 1955.

87. Corsi interview.

88. McLeod Senate Testimony, 2–33.

89. McLeod Senate Testimony, 3–4. For appropriate RRP processing times, see Bon Tempo, *Americans at the Gate*, 50–51.

90. McLeod Senate Testimony, 3–4.

91. McLeod Senate Testimony, 19.

92. Corsi Senate Testimony, 35–58.

93. Corsi Senate Testimony, 35–58.

94. *Senate Committee on the Judiciary, Investigation on Administration of Refugee Relief Act: Hearings before a Subcommittee of the Committee on the Judiciary, United States Senate*, 84th Cong., 1st Sess., April 13–May 27, 1955, 108 (statement of Francis E. Walter, Member of the House of Representatives from the 15th Congressional District of the State of Pennsylvania) (hereafter Walter Senate Testimony).

95. McLeod suggested that the RRA would be more appropriately called the "Emergency Migration Act" in that it more directly addressed population pressures and economic concerns in Europe rather than a refugee crisis. McLeod Senate Testimony, 81.

96. Walter Senate Testimony, 109.

97. Walter Senate Testimony, 114–15.

98. Thirty percent of visas allocated under the Displaced Persons Act were reserved for agricultural workers as a recognition of labor shortages in American agriculture but also to limit the number of Jewish refugees who were eligible for visas as most European Jews had traditionally been barred from landownership and thus agricultural professions. Loescher and Scanlan, *Calculated Kindness*, 20.

99. Walter Senate Testimony, 118–19.

100. Walter Senate Testimony, 118–19.

101. Walter Senate Testimony, 118–19.

102. Francis F. Walter to John Foster Dulles, March 14, 1955, entered into the record and quoted in Walter Senate Testimony, 110–11.

103. "Corsi Denounces Security Gang," *New York Times*, April 21, 1955; and "Corsi and Jenner Clash at Hearings," *New York Times*, April 22, 1955.

104. Corsi Senate Testimony, 192.

105. Glen Jeansonne, *Gerald L. K. Smith—Minister of Hate* (New Haven, Conn.: Yale University Press, 1988).

106. *Senate Committee on the Judiciary, Investigation on Administration of Refugee Relief Act: Hearings before a Subcommittee of the Committee on the Judiciary, United States Senate*, 84th Cong., 1st Sess., April 13–May 27, 1955, 317–21 (statement of Gerald K. Smith, Christian Nationalist Crusade, Tulsa, Oklahoma).

107. Jeansonne, *Gerald L. K. Smith*, 115–29.

108. "Rabb Testimony on Corsi Barred," *New York Times*, April 23, 1955.

109. "Rabb Testimony on Corsi Barred," *New York Times*, April 23, 1955.

110. David E. Rowe and Robert Schulmann, eds., *Einstein on Politics: His Private Thoughts and Public Stands on Nationalism, Zionism, War, Peace, and the Bomb* (Princeton, N.J.: Princeton University Press, 2007).

111. "President Bars Rabb as Witness on Corsi Case," *New York Times*, April 23, 1955.

112. Zolberg, *Nation by Design*, 323–24.

113. "Corsi Firing Reopens Immigration Debates," *New York Times*, April 17, 1955.

114. Following the Corsi Affair, Lehman introduced S.B. 1794. Accompanying legislation was introduced in the House. The reform bills allowed immigrant aid organizations to sponsor refugees in lieu of individual sponsors. Herbert Lehman Papers, Rare Books and Special Collections, Columbia University; Legislative Files, Displaced Persons and Immigration, drawer 362, folder 13 Refugee Relief Act Amendments and Hearings (1955–1956), William Welsh Papers, Rare Books and Special Collections, Columbia University; "Lehman Suggests Ouster of McLeod," *New York Times*, April 25, 1955; "Lehman Bid Senate Revamp Relief Act," *New York Times*, April 26, 1955; and "Corsi Asks Haste in Refugee Help," *New York Times*, April 27, 1955.

115. CBS News Radio analysis of affair, April 8, 1955, box 47, folder Research Data re Corsi-Dulles Dispute, Corsi Papers; "The Corsi Controversy, a Review of Political Repercussions: Party Chiefs Split on Effect of Ouster," *New York Times*, April 22, 1955; and "Corsi Controversy Seen as Vital Issue Affecting '56 U.S. Election," *Italian News*, Boston, April 29, 1955, box 44, folder Corsi Material, Maxwell Rabb Papers, Dwight D. Eisenhower Presidential Library.

116. "The Corsi Controversy, a Review of Political Repercussions: Party Chiefs Split on Effect of Ouster," *New York Times*, April 22, 1955.

117. Roderic O'Connor Memo to John Foster Dulles, Re: Refugee Relief Program, March 14, 1955, box 3, folder Corsi (Edward) (2), Dulles Papers.

118. "Message from the President of the United States Recommending Certain Changes in the Refugee Relief Act of 1953," House of Representatives, Committee on the Judiciary, 84th Cong., 1st Sess., May 27, 1955, box 8, folder Refugee Relief Act 1953–1956, AICC Records; and "10 Refugee Law Changes Asked by Eisenhower to Speed Entry," *New York Times*, May 27, 1955.

119. "Message from the President of the United States Recommending Certain Changes in the Refugee Relief Act of 1953," House of Representatives, Committee on the Judiciary, 84th Cong., 1st Sess., May 27, 1955, box 8, folder Refugee Relief Act 1953–1956, AICC Records. The most significant proposals included liberalizing the definition of the term *refugee*, increasing the number of refugee visas available, allowing oversubscribed nations to utilize quotas

from undersubscribed countries, repealing the practice of performing a two-year background check for a refugee to obtain security clearance, and waiving passport requirements for escapees.

120. Memo, Maxwell Rabb to Roderic O'Connor, April 27, 1955, box 3, folder Corsi (Edward) (2), Dulles Papers.

121. Applicant Files, box 3, folder Corsi (Edward) (2–4), Dulles Papers.

122. Carl Bon Tempo has produced the most comprehensive study of the United States refugee policies in the twentieth century but states, "The reasons why Walter and McLeod acquiesced to the Gerety appointment, and to (effectively) McLeod's demotion, remain a mystery." Bon Tempo, *Americans at the Gate*, 56–57. The Corsi Affair clarifies these events.

123. "Lawyer Named to Refugee Post with Orders to Speed Entry," *New York Times*, June 10, 1955.

124. Loescher and Scanlan, *Calculated Kindness*, 47. Zolberg also notes that Eisenhower began to shift toward a more liberal stance on immigration in 1956; Zolberg, *Nation by Design*, 323.

125. Bon Tempo, *Americans at the Gate*, 56.

126. Harley M. Kilgore, "Report on Efforts to Ascertain Eisenhower Administration's Position on Immigration," Senate Judiciary Subcommittee on Immigration Report, 84th Cong., 1st Sess., July 30, 1955; and "Summary of Testimony before Senate Judiciary Subcommittee on Immigration and Naturalization (Kilgore Committee)," November 21–December 1, 1955, box 10, folder Materials Sent to Members 1954–1955, AICC Records.

6. FROM REFUGEE RELIEF TO FAMILY REUNIFICATION

1. Mae Ngai, *Impossible Subjects: Illegal Aliens and the Making of Modern America* (Princeton, N.J.: Princeton University Press, 2004), 227–64; and Daniel J. Tichenor, *Dividing Lines: The Politics of Immigration Control in America* (Princeton, N.J.: Princeton University Press, 2002), 176–218.

2. G. Calvin Mackenzie and Robert Weisbrot, *The Liberal Hour: Washington and the Politics of Change in the 1960s* (New York: Penguin Books, 2008); James Patterson, *Grand Expectations: The United States, 1945–1974* (New York: Oxford University Press, 1996); and John Patrick Diggins, *The Proud Decades: America in War and in Peace, 1941–1960* (New York: W. W. Norton and Company, 1988).

3. Ngai, *Impossible Subjects*, 227–64.

4. Box E44, folder Washington, American Committee for Italian Migration–National Office, New York City Records, Center for Migration Studies (hereafter ACIM–National); and Joseph Jordan, ACIM Public Relations Director, "U.S. Has Moral Obligation to Reunite Families Kept Apart by Immigration Barriers, Say Migration Group Officials," Press Release, March 18, 1957, box E49, folder Legislation Statement March 18, 1957, ACIM–National.

5. Box E34, folder Reallocations 1955, ACIM–National; ACIM National Headquarters to Chapter Officers and Priest Consultants, box 1, folder 4, American Committee on Italian Migration, Chicago Chapter, Immigration History Research Center Archives, University of Minnesota (hereafter ACIM–Chicago); "Applications for Italian Visas in Refugee Act Now Exceed 60,000 Quota," *Dispatch*, February 1956; box D, ACIM–National; and "Bills Introduced for Eisenhower's Proposals on Immigration," *Dispatch*, March 1956, box D, ACIM–National.

6. ACIM to U.S. Congressmen and Senators re: Amendment of Refugee Relief Act of 1953 or other Immigration Legislation, July 18, 1956, box 1, folder 4, ACIM–Chicago. There is very little literature on Greek American activism on immigration in this period. For a start on the American Hellenic Educational Progressive Association, see Rachel Rains Winslow, *The Best Possible Immigrants: International Adoption and the American Family* (Philadelphia: University of Pennsylvania Press, 2017), 48–69.

7. For general views on what liberals thought of extensions to refugee relief, see Aristide Zolberg, *A Nation by Design: Immigration Policy in the Fashioning of America* (Cambridge, Mass.: Harvard University Press, 2006), 293–336; and Carl Bon Tempo, *Americans at the Gate: The United States and Refugees during the Cold War* (Princeton, N.J.: Princeton University Press, 2008). Neither author discusses this particular issue at great length.

8. "Big Rise Is Urged in Refugee Quota," *New York Times*, June 13, 1955.

9. Tichenor, *Dividing Lines*, 176–218; and ACIM National Headquarters Memo to Chapter Officers and Priest Consultants, August 2, 1956, box 1, folder 4, ACIM–Chicago.

10. ACIM National Headquarters to Chapter Officers and Priest Consultants, June 8, 1956, box 1, folder 4, ACIM–Chicago; "Immediate Action Urged on Langer and Walter Bills," ACIM *Dispatch*, June 1956, box D, ACIM–National; Italian Hour, WJLB radio, Detroit, June 1956, box 1, folder ACIM 1956 Miscellaneous, Carolyn Sinelli Burns Papers, Bentley Historical Library, University of Michigan (hereafter Sinelli Burns Papers); Piemontese Social Club (Detroit) to Congresswoman Martha Griffith Re: Amendments to Sheepherders' Bill (H.R. 6888), July 18, 1956, box 1, folder 1956 Miscellaneous, Sinelli Burns Papers; Memo Carolyn Sinelli Burns to ACIM Officers Michigan and Detroit Chapters, June 20, 1956, box 3, folder 1956 Miscellaneous, Sinelli Burns Papers; and Memo Carolyn Sinelli Burns to ACIM Officers Michigan, Re: Sheepherders' Bill H.R. 6888, July 21, 1956, box 3, folder 1956 Miscellaneous, Sinelli Burns Papers.

11. ACIM National Headquarters Memo to Chapter Officers and Priest Consultants, August 2, 1956, box 1, folder 4, ACIM–Chicago.

12. Tichenor, *Dividing Lines*, 206–7. Walter continued to block or alter bills to extend refugee relief legislation from 1956 through 1959. Marchisio and

Walter Correspondence, 1959, box E66, folder Legislation, ACIM–National; and "The Controversial Congressman and Controversial Issue," *Patriot News*, April 14, 1957, box E49, folder Legislation Background, ACIM–National.

13. Joseph Jordan, "U.S. Has Moral Obligation to Reunite Families Kept Apart by Immigration Barriers, Say Migration Group Officials," Press Release, March 18, 1957, box E49, folder Legislation Statement March 18, 1957, ACIM–National.

14. ACIM Memo, Re: Separation of Families, December 1, 1955, box 1, folder 3, ACIM–Chicago.

15. "Reunion Visas Issued in Italy Now Nearly 20,000," ACIM *Dispatch*, October 1958, box D, ACIM–National. For another example, see Francesco Buscema to ACIM, box E22, folder Immigration Cases July–Dec. 1954, ACIM–National.

16. Joseph Jordan, "U.S. Has Moral Obligation to Reunite Families Kept Apart by Immigration Barriers, Say Migration Group Officials," Press Release, March 18, 1957, box E49, folder Legislation Statement March 18, 1957, ACIM–National.

17. Joseph Jordan, "U.S. Has Moral Obligation to Reunite Families Kept Apart by Immigration Barriers, Say Migration Group Officials," Press Release, March 18, 1957, box E49, folder Legislation Statement March 18, 1957, ACIM–National; "Red Gains Linked to U.S. Alien Laws," *New York Times*, March 18, 1957; and ACIM petitions sent to President Eisenhower and members of the Senate and House Judiciary Committees on Immigration, box A20, folder Chicago Chapter Correspondence 1957, ACIM–National.

18. Kenneth Keating, "Statement to Extend the Refugee Relief Act of 1953," Congressional Record, June 4, 1957, 8328, series 2, box 480, folder 81, Kenneth B. Keating Papers, Rare Books and Special Collections, University of Rochester; Juvenal Marchisio Memo to Chapter Chairmen and Officers, June 17, 1957, box 1, folder 6, ACIM–Chicago; and "ACIM Sets Legislative Goals for 1957," ACIM *Dispatch*, February 1957, and "Kennedy, Keating, Walter, Introduce Bills Containing ACIM Objectives," ACIM *Dispatch*, May–June 1957, box D, ACIM–National.

19. Juvenal Marchisio Memo to Chapter Chairmen and Officers, June 17, 1957, box 1, folder 6, ACIM–Chicago.

20. "Kennedy, Keating, Walter, Introduce Bills Containing ACIM Objectives," ACIM *Dispatch*, May–June 1957, box D, ACIM–National; and box A20, folder Detroit Chapter Correspondence 1957, ACIM–National.

21. June and July 1957 Correspondence, box 1, folder 6, ACIM–Chicago.

22. Juvenal Marchisio, Action Memo to All Chapter Chairmen and Officers, June 17, 1957, box 1, folder 6, ACIM–Chicago; box E49, folder Congressional Correspondence, ACIM–National; and box E49, folder Legislative Background, ACIM–National. The Italian American Labor Council and the

International Ladies' Garment Workers' Union were especially active in lobbying. Box E45, folder ILGWU-Luigi Antonini, ACIM–National.

23. ACIM statement, *New York Times*, March 18, 1957.

24. Marchisio testimony before Congress on August 9, 1957, in favor of legislation and chapter lobbying for legislation, box E48, folder legislation, ACIM–National; and box E48, folder Chapter Responses from Senators on Congressional Appeals, ACIM–National.

25. "ACIM Reunion of Families Goal Attained," ACIM *Dispatch*, October 1957, box D, ACIM–National. ACIM sometimes referred to the legislation as the Family Reunion Act.

26. Pub. L. No. 85-316; Helen F. Eckerson, "United States and Canada Magnets for Immigration," *Annals of the American Academy of Political and Social Science* 316 (March 1958); Juvenal Marchisio Memo to All Chapter Chairmen and Officers, Re: New Legislation, September 30, 1957, box 1, folder 6, ACIM–Chicago; and "ACIM Reunion of Families Goal Attained," ACIM *Dispatch*, October 1957, box D, ACIM–National.

27. Frank Traverso, "1957 Annual Report of the Committee on Immigration and Naturalization," December 3, 1957, box 37, folder Immigration Reports, Italian Welfare League Records, Center for Migration Studies (hereafter IWL Records).

28. Marchisio Memo to All Chapter Chairmen and Officers, Re: New Legislation, September 30, 1957, box 1, folder 6, ACIM–Chicago; and "ACIM Reunion of Families Goal Attained," ACIM *Dispatch*, October 1957, box D, ACIM–National.

29. Kennedy to Caesar Donanzan, November 7, 1957, Senate Files, box 695, Papers of John F. Kennedy, Presidential Papers, John F. Kennedy Presidential Library.

30. Juvenal Marchisio Memo to All Chapter Chairmen and Officers, Re: New Legislation, September 30, 1957, box 1, folder 6, ACIM–Chicago.

31. Geir Lundestad, *The United States and Western Europe since 1945* (New York: Oxford University Press, 2009); Paul Ginsborg, *A History of Contemporary Italy: Society and Politics, 1943–1988* (New York: Palgrave, 2003), 212–53; and Lucia Ducci, Stefano Luconi, and Matteo Pratelli, *Le relazioni tra Italia e Stati Uniti, Dal Risorgimento all consequenze dell'11 settembre* (Rome: Carocci, 2012), 127–42. For the impact of economic recovery on Italian emigration, see Michele Colucci, *Lavoro in movimento, l'emigrazione italiana in Europa, 1945–1957* (Rome: Donzelli, 2008).

32. Robert Fleegler, *Ellis Island Nation: Immigration Policy and American Identity in the Twentieth Century* (Philadelphia: University of Pennsylvania Press, 2013), 161–90; and Zolberg, *Nation by Design*, 323–24.

33. The Jewish American Congress to ACIM, 1957, box E49, folder Legislative Background, ACIM–National.

34. Janice Alberti Russell, "The Italian Community in Tunisia 1861–1961: A Viable Minority" (PhD diss., Columbia University, 1977).

35. Donna Gabaccia, *Italy's Many Diasporas* (Seattle: University of Washington Press, 2000).

36. Migrants' continuing identification as "Italians" has been attributed to fascist policies and financial support that encouraged the maintenance of Italian "colonies" abroad. Ruth Ben-Ghiat, *Fascist Modernities: Italy 1922–1945* (Berkeley: University of California Press, 2001); Mark Choate, *Emigrant Nation: The Making of Italy Abroad* (Cambridge, Mass.: Harvard University Press, 2008); and Russell, "Italian Community in Tunisia."

37. Saul Kelly, *Cold War in the Desert: Britain, the United States and the Italian Colonies, 1945–52* (New York: St. Martin's Press, 2000); Russell, "Italian Community in Tunisia"; and Juvenal Marchisio, "Tunisian Report," box E75, folder Tunisian Report: Working Sheets, ACIM–National.

38. A number of those French nationals were in fact ethnic Italians who had recently claimed French citizenship. Fifteen thousand Italians had already migrated to Italy by the end of 1959. More than a thousand Italians left Egypt under similar circumstances for Italy by 1960. Box E65, folder Refugees of Egypt and Tunisia, ACIM–National.

39. Southerners made up most of the initial wave of "pioneer" colonizers in Italy's scramble for Africa. In the fascist period, colonists from overpopulated northern regions were encouraged to settle in Africa as part of the regime's racial propaganda and modernization projects. Many southern Italian migrants therefore sought alternative destinations such as French Tunisia. Francesca Locatelli, "La comunita' italiana di Asmara negli anni Trenta tra propadanda, leggi razziali e realta' sociale," in *L'Impero fascista: Italia ed Etiopia (1935–1941),* ed. Riccardo Bottoni (Bologna: Il Mulino, 2008).

40. Juvenal Marchisio, "Tunisian Report," box E75, folder Tunisian Report: Working Sheets, ACIM–National.

41. Russell, "Italian Community in Tunisia," 413–18; Marchisio, "Tunisian Report."

42. Of this total number of refugees, 16,254 lived in state-controlled refugee camps and 18,942 lived at or below the poverty line outside of camps. Marchisio, "Tunisian Report."

43. Marchisio, "Tunisian Report."

44. Marchisio, "Tunisian Report."

45. Bon Tempo, *American at the Gate.*

46. Legal scholars have suggested that alien "membership" in a society does entitle individuals to certain citizenship rights. See arguments regarding the position of unauthorized immigrants in a receiving state. Hiroshi Motomura, *Immigration Outside of the Law* (New York: Oxford University Press, 2014).

47. Form letter to Congressmen and List of Recipients, box E74, folder Tunisian Report, ACIM–National; Juvenal Marchisio, NCWC Press Release, March 4, 1960, box E75, folder Tunisian Refugees–General, ACIM–National; ACIM Board of Directors Meeting Minutes, 1960, box 1, folder 1960 ACIM Miscellaneous, Sinelli Burns Papers; and "Congress Stirred by Marchisio Report on Tunisia Refugees," and "Action on Refugees from Tunisia Urged by ACIM," ACIM *Dispatch*, May–June 1960, box D, ACIM–National.

48. Bon Tempo, *Americans at the Gate.*

49. Alessandro Brogi, *L'Italia e l'egemonia Americana nel Mediterraneo* (Florence: La Nuova Italia, 1996); Salim Yacub, *Containing Arab Nationalism: The Eisenhower Doctrine in the Middle East* (Chapel Hill: University of North Carolina Press, 2004); and Douglas Little, *American Orientalism: The United States and the Middle East since 1945* (Chapel Hill: University of North Carolina Press, 2004).

50. Marchisio also met with American ambassadors in both nations and Italian officials including the Italian foreign minister, the undersecretary of foreign affairs, and staff members of the Ministry of Foreign Affairs and the Ministry of the Interior. Juvenal Marchisio, "Address Regarding Tunisian Problem," box E75, folder Tunisian Report: Working Sheets, ACIM–National; and "Marchisio Surveying Plight of Tunisian Refugees," ACIM *Dispatch*, February 1960, box D, ACIM–National.

51. Marchisio, "Tunisian Report."

52. Marchisio, "Tunisian Report."

53. Marchisio, "Tunisian Report."

54. "Expropriated Italians in Tunisia Facing Starvation, Moral Degradation," ACIM *Dispatch*, March–April 1960, box D, ACIM–National.

55. "Expropriated Italians in Tunisia."

56. "Plight of Italian Refugees in Tunisia and Egypt Serious," "Letter from Tunisia," "Marchisio Surveying Plight of Italian Refugees," "Expropriated Italians in Tunisia Facing Starvation, Moral Degradation," "Congress Stirred by Marchisio Report on Tunisian Refugees," "Italian Refugee Family Resettled in Bay Ridge by ACIM Group," and "Action on Refugees from Tunisia Urged by ACIM," ACIM *Dispatch*, April 1959, January–June 1960, box D, ACIM–National.

57. Letters to Italian American organizations, Catholic groups, and Italian American politicians and government officials, box E74, folder Tunisian Report, ACIM–National.

58. "Italian Festa and Buffet in Rochester Benefits Italians," ACIM *Dispatch*, October 1960, box D, ACIM–National.

59. Italian American Labor Council, "Resolution on Racialism in Tunisia," April 26, 1960, box E74, folder Legislation-Refugees, ACIM–National.

60. ACIM National Conference in Washington, D.C., Panel on Refugees, May 18, 1959, box 1, folder ACIM 1959 Washington D.C. Symposium, Sinelli

Burns Papers; and "Resolution on Fourth Preference and Italian Refugees Adopted," ACIM *Dispatch*, May–June 1959, box D, ACIM–National.

61. Celler introduced H.R. 12029 calling for five thousand refugee relief visas for Italian migrants from Tunisia and Rodino introduced similar legislation in H.R. 12071. Senators Keating and Pastore also introduced bills. Box E74, folder Legislation-Refugees, ACIM–National; and "Congress Stirred by Marchisio Report on Tunisia Refugees," ACIM *Dispatch*, May 1960, box D, ACIM–National.

62. Peter Gatrell, *Free World? The Campaign to Save the World's Refugees, 1956–1963* (New York: Cambridge University Press, 2011); and ACIM National Conference in Washington D.C., Panel on Refugees, May 18, 1959, box 1, folder ACIM 1959 Washington D.C. Symposium, Sinelli Burns Papers.

63. Hope for Italian Refugees through World Refugee Year, ACIM Pamphlet, folder 10, ACIM–Chicago; and William Consedine, Director National Catholic Welfare Conference, to Caesar Donanzan, June 13, 1960, box E74, folder Legislation-Refugees (Egypt-Tunisia), ACIM–National.

64. "Slow Motion on Refugees," *New York Times*, April 12, 1960; "House Votes Bill on Refugees," "Congress Stirred by Marchisio Report on Tunisia Refugees," and "Action on Refugees from Tunisia Urged by ACIM," ACIM *Dispatch*, March–June 1960, box D, ACIM–National; Gatrell, *Free World?*; Bon Tempo, *Americans at the Gate.*

65. Giuseppe Messina to ACIM, December 12, 1959, reprinted "Letter from Tunisia," ACIM *Dispatch*, January 1960, box D, ACIM–National; Original Messina letter (circulated to other Italian American groups), box E75, folder Tunisian Refugees, ACIM–National; and Form letter to Congressmen and List of Recipients, box E74, folder Tunisian Report, ACIM–National. Italian American anxieties about Tunisian migrants' racial status were compounded by long-standing views, prevalent even in Italy, about the racial inferiority of southern Italians to northern Italians. See John Dickie, *Darkest Italy: the Nation and Stereotypes of the Mezzogiorno, 1860-1900,* (New York: St. Martin's Press, 1998).

66. "Letter from Tunisia," ACIM *Dispatch*, January 1960, box D, ACIM–National.

67. "Expropriated Italians in Tunisia Facing Starvation," ACIM *Dispatch*, March–April 1960, box D, ACIM–National.

68. Juvenal Marchisio to Congressmen and List of Recipients, box E74, folder Tunisian Report, ACIM–National; and Juvenal Marchisio, Press Release, National Catholic Welfare Conference, March 4, 1960, box E75, folder Tunisian Refugees-General, ACIM–National. For settler colonialism, see Ruth Ben-Ghiat and Mia Fuller, eds., *Italian Colonialism* (New York: Palgrave Macmillan, 2005); and Caroline Elkins and Susan Pedersen, eds., *Settler Colonialism in the Twentieth Century: Projects, Practices, and Legacies* (London: Routledge, 2005).

69. Bon Tempo, *Americans at the Gate*; Penny Von Eschen, *Race against Empire: Black Americans and Anticolonialism, 1937–1957* (Ithaca, N.Y.: Cornell University Press, 1997); and Odd Arne Westad, *The Global Cold War* (New York: Cambridge University Press, 2007).

70. The only tangible results it yielded was a symbolic gesture. Eisenhower appointed Marchisio as director of the US Committee for Refugees (a group that had no discernible impact on policy). "Expropriated Italians in Tunisia Facing Starvation," ACIM *Dispatch*, March–April 1960, box D, ACIM–National.

71. Yuki Oda, "Family Unity in U.S. Immigration Policy, 1921–1978" (PhD diss., Columbia University, 2014), 232–37.

72. Frank Traverso, "1957 and 1958 Annual Reports of the Committee on Immigration and Naturalization," box 37, folder Immigration Reports, IWL Records.

73. Robert McCollum, Deputy Administrator, Office of Refugee and Migration Affairs, U.S. Department of State, Remarks, "Italian Immigration and American National Interest," Symposium Report, 1959, box 7, folder 57, ACIM–Chicago.

74. By June 1959, 64,453 Italians (brothers, sisters, and unmarried adult children of American citizens) were waiting for fourth preference visas, followed by Greece with only 4,500 fourth preference cases. In Italy's case, where first, second, and third preference visas were also oversubscribed, fourth preference candidates faced a projected wait of upward of ten years. INS Ann. Rep. (1957–1959).

75. "ACIM Launches Drive for Reunion of Fourth Preference Cases," *Dispatch*, February 1958, box D, ACIM–National.

76. Immigration Case Files, box 1–95, folders Immigration Cases, ACIM–National; and box E54, E55, folder Fourth Preference Cases, ACIM–National.

77. Immigration Case Files, box E1–95, folder Immigration Case Files, ACIM–National; and Refugee Relief Files, box F1–5, ACIM–National.

78. "Appeals for Help on 4th Preference Cases Increase Daily," *Dispatch*, November 1958, box D, ACIM–National.

79. "ACIM Launches Drive for Reunion of Fourth Preference Cases," "ACIM Flooded with Requests to Help Resolve 4th Preference Problem," "Appeals for Help on 4th Preference Cases Increase Daily," *Dispatch*, February, October–November 1958, box D, ACIM–National.

80. Eight bills of this kind were introduced in the 82nd Congress (1951–1952), one in the 83rd Congress (1953–1954), and one in the 85th Congress (1957–1958). Edward P. Hutchinson, *Legislative History of American Immigration Policy, 1798–1965* (Philadelphia: University of Pennsylvania Press, 1981), 299, 321, 333.

81. Caesar Donanzan Memo to Chapter Chairmen, Officers, and Priest Consultants, October 7, 1958, box 1, folder 7, ACIM–Chicago; and "Proposal

to Resolve a Problem of Good Will in the American National Interest," box 1, folder 7, ACIM–Chicago.

82. "Italian Immigration and American National Interest," Symposium Report, 1959, box 7, folder 57, ACIM–Chicago.

83. Other lawmakers in attendance included members of the House Subcommittee on Immigration and Naturalization, Michael Feighan (D-OH), Peter Rodino (D-NJ), and Victor Anfuso (D-NY). President Eisenhower was far less forthcoming in expressions of support for ACIM's goals. "Nine Months of Experience with the 'Reunion of Families' Legislation," "Interest in ACIM Symposium Runs High," April 1959, and "First ACIM Symposium a Success," *Dispatch*, May–June 1959. For a full list of attendees, see "Italian Immigration and American National Interest," Symposium Report, 1959, folder 57, ACIM–Chicago.

84. Caesar Donanzan Memo to Chapter Chairmen, Officers, and Priest Consultants, October 7, 1958, box 1, folder 7, ACIM–Chicago; "Fourth Preference Clean-Up Bill Introduced by Keating," and "Address by Senator Kenneth B. Keating," *Dispatch*, January, May–June 1959, box D, ACIM–National; and "Kennedy Bill Would Admit 150,000 Relatives Annually," *Dispatch*, April 1959, box 1, folder 1959 ACIM *Dispatch*, Sinelli Burns Papers.

85. Walter Correspondence, January–July 1959, box E66, folder Legislation HR 5896, ACIM–National.

86. Walter Correspondence.

87. Walter Correspondence; Caesar Donanzan Memo to Juvenal Marchisio, September 16, 1959, box E66, folder Legislation 4th Preference 1959, ACIM–National; and Action Memo, Caesar Donanzan to All Chapter Chairmen and Officers, June 5, 1959, box 1, folder 8, ACIM–Chicago.

88. Changes included the addition of unmarried sons and daughters of American citizens over twenty-one years of age to the second preference quota (moved up from the fourth). It made unmarried sons and daughters of legal resident aliens over twenty-one years of age eligible for third preference visas (they had no status before). And it allowed spouses and unmarried minor children to accompany fourth preference visa holders when they migrate (so long as they are also eligible for visas). Caesar Donanzan Memo to ACIM Chapter Officers and Priest Consultants, September 30, 1959, box 1, folder 9, ACIM–Chicago.

89. "Eisenhower Signs Bill to Reunite Families," *Dispatch*, September 1959, box D, ACIM–National.

90. "New Walter Bill Passed by House," *Dispatch*, January 1960, box D, ACIM–National. For further legislation, see Pub. L. No. 87-301 (1961), and Pub. L. No. 87-885 (1962).

91. Hutchinson, *Legislative History*, 315–16.

92. Catherine Lee, *Fictive Kinship: Family Reunification and the Meaning of Race and Nation in American Immigration* (New York: Russel Sage Foundation,

2013), 74–98; Fleegler, *Ellis Island Nation*, 161–90; and Carolyn Wong, *Lobbying for Inclusion: Rights Politics and the Making of Immigration Policy* (Stanford, Calif.: Stanford University Press2006), 44–63.

93. Zolberg, *Nation by Design*, 324–33; and Hutchinson, *Legislative History*, 337.

94. "Senator Kennedy Announces 7-Point Immigration Bill," Press Release, Office of Senator Kennedy, February 19, 1959, box E65, folder Legislation, ACIM–National. For similar statements on the need for comprehensive immigration reform from Kennedy, see John F. Kennedy remarks to the American Jewish Congress, National Congress Week, November 17, 1957, box 10, folder AIC Materials Sent to Members, Oct 1957–Sept 1958, American Immigration and Citizenship Conference Records, Social Welfare History Archive, University of Minnesota (hereafter AICC Records).

95. "Senator Kennedy Announces 7-Point Immigration Bill," Press Release, Office of Senator Kennedy, February 19, 1959, box E65, folder Legislation, ACIM–National.

96. "A Nation of Immigrants" originated as a series of pamphlets and was later published as a book posthumously in 1964. Kennedy also published the pamphlet "Let the Lady Hold Up Her Head: Reflections on American Immigration Policy" in August 1947 for the American Jewish Committee. Box 10, folder AIC Materials Sent to Members, Oct 1956–Oct 1957, AICC Records.

97. "With Clean Hands and a Clear Conscience," *Saturday Evening Post*, October 3, 1964.

98. Matthew Frye Jacobson, *Roots Too: White Ethnic Revival in Post-civil Rights America* (Cambridge, Mass.: Harvard University Press, 2006), 11–71.

99. The party's immigration plank and Kennedy's campaign linked immigration reform to the civil rights movement. Tichenor, *Dividing Lines*, 207–11; Zolberg, *Nation by Design*, 324–33; MacKenzie and Weisbrot, *Liberal Hour*, 57, 104; and Fleegler, *Ellis Island Nation*, 147–60. For the emergence of an Italian American support for President Kennedy see Betty Santangelo, *Lucky Corner: The Biography of Congressman Alfred. E. Santangelo and the Rise of Italian Americans in Politics* (New York: Center for Migration Studies, 1999), 119, 141–44, 170–89.

100. Tichenor, *Dividing Lines*, 207–11; and Zolberg, *Nation by Design*, 324–33.

101. See lobbying activity, box 2, folder 12, ACIM–Chicago; "Resolution on Immigration," United Italian-American Labor Council, December 5, 1959, printed in *American Immigration and Citizenship News*, January 29, 1960, box 18, folder vol. 6, AICC Records; and Zolberg, *Nation by Design*, 327.

102. "A Statement to Lawmakers," *Dispatch*, May 1962, box D, ACIM–National.

103. "A Statement to Lawmakers," *Dispatch*, May 1962, box D, ACIM–National.

104. Zolberg credits ethnic constituency pressure as the most important factor in the amendment's passage. Zolberg, *Nation by Design*, 327.

105. Juvenal Marchisio correspondence with Francis Walter, August 1962, box E85, folder 1962 Legislation, ACIM–National; Caesar Donanzan Memo to Chapter Officers Re: The Shameful Record of the 87th Congress on Immigration, October 17, 1962, box 2, folder 12, ACIM–Chicago; Pub. L. No. 87-301 (1961); and Pub. L. No. 87-885 (1962).

106. Tichenor, *Dividing Lines*, 176–218; and Zolberg, *Nation by Design*, 293–336.

107. Ngai, *Impossible Subjects*, 227–64.

7. THE END OF THE NATIONAL ORIGINS SYSTEM AND THE LIMITS OF WHITE ETHNIC LIBERALISM

1. Rena C. Trevor (née Marcello) Obituary, *Chicago Tribune*, February 11, 2014; and Deborah Baurac, "Rena Trevor's Commitment to Others Bloomed Early in Life," *Chicago Tribune*, December 8, 1999.

2. Rena Trevor, "The Negro Has Rights Too," *Fra Noi*, Chicago, October 1963. For a similar commentary on liberalism, see Carolyn Sinelli Burns to Mrs. Frank Schaden, Committee on International Relations, National Council of Catholic Women, July 22, 1956, box 4, folder Conference of Catholic Women 1956, Carolyn Sinelli Burns Papers, Bentley Historical Library, University of Michigan (hereafter Sinelli Burns Papers).

3. Edward P. Hutchinson, *Legislative History of American Immigration Policy, 1798–1965* (Philadelphia: University of Pennsylvania Press, 1981), 357–68.

4. Catherine Lee, *Fictive Kinship: Family Reunification and the Meaning of Race and Nation in American Immigration* (New York: Russel Sage Foundation, 2013), 1–18, 74–98; Daniel J. Tichenor, *Dividing Lines: The Politics of Immigration Control in America* (Princeton, N.J.: Princeton University Press, 2002), 176–218; David Reimers, *Still the Golden Door: The Third World Comes to America* (New York: Columbia University Press, 1985), 61–91; and Carolyn Wong, *Lobbying for Inclusion: Rights Politics and the Making of Immigration Policy* (Stanford, Calif.: Stanford University Press, 2006), 44–63.

5. Hutchinson, *Legislative History*, 357–68; Maddalena Marinari, "Americans Must Show Justice in Immigration Policies Too: The Passage of the 1965 Immigration Act," *Journal of Policy History* 26, no. 2 (2014); Reimers, *Still the Golden Door*, 61–91; Tichenor, *Dividing Lines*, 176–218; and Aristide Zolberg, *A Nation by Design: Immigration Policy in the Fashioning of America* (Cambridge, Mass.: Harvard University Press, 2006), 293–336.

6. For the most compelling critique of the 1965 act, see Mae Ngai, *Impossible Subjects: Illegal Aliens and the Making of Modern America* (Princeton, N.J.: Princeton University Press, 2004), 227–64.

7. G. Calvin Mackenzie and Robert Weisbrot, *The Liberal Hour: Washington and the Politics of Change in the 1960s* (New York: Penguin Books, 2008); Carol

Anderson Horton, *Race and the Making of American Liberalism* (New York: Oxford University Press, 2005), 121–66; Gary Gerstle, *American Crucible: Race and Nation in the Twentieth Century* (Princeton, N.J.: Princeton University Press, 2001), 268–310; Julian Zelizer, *The Fierce Urgency of Now: Lyndon Johnson, Congress, and the Battle for the Great Society* (New York: Penguin Books, 2015); and James Patterson, *Grand Expectations: The United States, 1945–1974* (New York: Oxford University Press, 1996).

8. In her discussion of interwar cultural pluralism, Selig refers to this phenomenon as the "immigrant gifts" movement. In his discussion of American ethnic politics at midcentury, Fleegler uses the term "contributionism." Diana Selig, *Americans All: The Cultural Gifts Movement* (Cambridge, Mass.: Harvard University Press, 2008); and Robert Fleegler, *Ellis Island Nation: Immigration Policy and American Identity in the Twentieth Century* (Philadelphia: University of Pennsylvania Press, 2013). I use both terms almost interchangeably.

9. For commentaries on liberalism's limitations, see Gerstle, *American Crucible*; Wendy Wall, *Inventing the "American Way": The Politics of Consensus from the New Deal to the Civil Rights Movement* (New York: Oxford University Press, 2008); Selig, *Americans All*; Horton, *Race and the Making of American Liberalism*.

10. Joseph DeSerto to representative officials, February 19, 1964, box 5, folder 41, American Committee on Italian Migration, Chicago Chapter, Immigration History Research Center Archives, University of Minnesota (hereafter ACIM–Chicago); and Frank Cavaioli, "Chicago's Italian Americans Rally for Immigration Reform," *Italian Americana* 6, no. 2 (Spring/Summer 1980).

11. Daniel Corelli Speech, Immigration Rally, Chicago, December 15, 1963, box 5, folder 40, ACIM–Chicago.

12. ACIM Introductory Letter, April 1953, box A2, folder Chicago Chapter, American Committee on Italian Migration–National Office, New York City Records, Center for Migration Studies (hereafter ACIM–National); and "ACIM Fact Sheet," box 2, folder 1962 ACIM Miscellaneous, Sinelli Burns Papers.

13. Ngai, *Impossible Subjects*, 228–29.

14. *Senate Committee on the Judiciary, Subcommittee on Immigration and Naturalization, Hearings to Amend the Immigration and Nationality Act*, 89th Cong., 1st Sess., 404–27 (March 8–August 3, 1965) (statement of Joseph Errigo, Order Sons of Italy in America) (hereafter Errigo Testimony).

15. *Senate Committee on the Judiciary, Subcommittee on Immigration and Naturalization, Hearings to Amend the Immigration and Nationality Act*, 89th Cong., 1st Sess., 515–32 (March 8–August 3, 1965) (statement of Mario Biaggi, Grand Council of Columbia Associations in Civil Service).

16. Tichenor, *Dividing Lines*, 176–218; Zolberg, *Nation by Design*, 293–336; and Ngai, *Impossible Subjects*, 228–64.

17. The Kennedy administration's bill was introduced one month after Congressman Walter's death. Tichenor, *Dividing Lines*, 208–11.

18. Quoted in Tichenor, *Dividing Lines*, 209.

19. Joseph DeSerto, "Italian Immigration and American National Interest," Symposium Report, 1959, box 7, folder 57, ACIM–Chicago.

20. For ACIM, OSIA, and the Italian Catholic Federation's participation in a Los Angeles Conference on Immigration (January 1965) in which they worked with Chinese, Japanese, Korean, Mexican, Filipino, and Jewish organizations, see box 2, folder 17, ACIM–Chicago. Members of ACIM–Chicago participated in the Interethnic Midwest Conference (Spring 1965) with Jewish, Chinese, Japanese, and Serbian groups and in The Committee for a Just Immigration Law by the early 1960s. Box 2, folder 17, ACIM–Chicago.

21. Box E18, folder American Immigration Conference, ACIM–National. The AICC was formed in 1960, merging the National Council on Naturalization and Citizenship (est. 1930) and the American Immigration Conference (est. 1954). American Immigration and Citizenship Conference Finding Guide, Social Welfare History Archive, University of Minnesota.

22. Box E18, folder American Immigration Conference, ACIM–National. Similarly, the American Immigration Conference called for the National Origins System's replacement by "a humane and rational immigration plan consonant with our firm and undeviating opposition to racial, ethnic, and religious discrimination." American Immigration Conference, Committee on Legislation, Memorandum re: Major Legislative Recommendations, January 15, 1957, box 7, folder Papers and Correspondence 1957, American Immigration and Citizenship Conference Records, Social Welfare History Archive, University of Minnesota (hereafter AICC Records).

23. Box 1, folder Annual Meetings, 1954–1960, AICC Records; and box 9, folder AIC Annual Meetings, 1955–1959, AICC Records. Members of the Italian Welfare League were more actively involved in both the AICC and the National Council on Naturalization and Citizenship, but they did not set the agenda for the broader Italian American immigration reform lobby, nor did they have ACIM's political influence. Box 2, folder NCWC–Legislation Committee, 1950–1960, AICC Records.

24. "Recommendations for Amending Certain Provisions of the Immigration and Nationality Act," Report prepared by the Committee on Legislation, AICC, October 1958, box 10, folder AIC Materials Sent to Members, Oct 1958–April 1959, AICC Records. In December 1960, ACIM endorsed an AICC statement of principles to be sent to President-elect Kennedy urging the president to lead in developing a "non-discriminatory, humanitarian immigration policy," but that was a rather level modest level of participation in AICC's activities. ACIM endorsed a second similar statement by the AICC again in July 1961. Box 14, folder Statement of Principles re: American Immigration Policy and Second Statement, AICC Records. But in 1961, ACIM still pursued a legislative agenda that primarily benefitted Italians.

25. AICC memo to all member organizations, October 25, 1962, box E85, folder Legislation 4th preference lists and background material, ACIM–National; box E88, folder AICC, ACIM–National; and box E94, folder AICC, ACIM–National.

26. *House of Representatives Committee on the Judiciary, Hearings to Amend the Immigration and Nationality Act, United States Congress*, 88th Cong., 2nd Sess., 639–63 (August 6, 1964) (statement of Juvenal Marchisio, American Committee for Italian Migration) (hereafter Marchisio Testimony 1964); *Senate Committee on the Judiciary, Subcommittee on Immigration and Naturalization, Hearings to Amend the Immigration and Nationality Act*, 89th Cong., 1st Sess., 494–514 (March 8–August 3, 1965) (statement of Juvenal Marchisio, American Committee for Italian Migration) (hereafter Marchisio Testimony 1965); and Errigo Testimony.

27. Mary Dudziak, *Cold War Civil Rights: Race and the Image of American Democracy* (Princeton, N.J.: Princeton University Press, 2000); and Thomas Borstelmann, *The Cold War and the Color Line: American Race Relations in the Global Arena* (Cambridge, Mass.: Harvard University Press, 2001). For the limits of accepted racial agitation in Cold War liberalism, see Penny Von Eschen, *Race against Empire: Black Americans and Anticolonialism, 1937–1957* (Ithaca, N.Y.: Cornell University Press, 1997).

28. Marchisio Testimony 1964 and 1965.

29. Errigo Testimony 1965.

30. George Spatuzza to Senator Everett Dirksen, May 18, 1965, box 3, folder 20, ACIM–Chicago.

31. Caesar Donanzan, "ACIM's Immediate and Ultimate Goals," "Proceedings, ACIM's Second Symposium on Italian Migration," 1961, Rome, box 7, folder 58, ACIM–Chicago.

32. "Resolution #1 United States Immigration Policy and Italy's Needs," "Proceedings, ACIM's Second Symposium on Italian Migration," 1961, Rome, box 7, folder 58, ACIM–Chicago.

33. Caesar Donanzan, "Opening Remarks," "Proceedings, ACIM's Third Symposium on Italian Migration," 1963, Washington, D.C., box 7, folder 59, ACIM–Chicago.

34. "Proceedings, ACIM's Third Symposium on Italian Migration," 1963, Washington, D.C., box 7, folder 59, ACIM–Chicago. Similar sentiments are also reflected in L. H. Pasqualicchio's remarks to fellow OSIA members on Columbus Day in 1963 when he called for "more human [*sic*] and liberal laws" and encouraged Italian Americans to "band together and insist for equal rights for the sake of humanity." Leonard Pasqualicchio, Remarks on Columbus Day, Arlington, Virginia, October 13, 1963, box 1, Leonard Pasqualicchio Papers, Immigration History Research Center Archives, University of Minnesota.

35. Copies of Speeches from December 15, 1963, Immigration Rally, Chicago, box 5, folder 40, ACIM–Chicago.

36. Copies of Speeches from December 15, 1963, Immigration Rally, Chicago, box 5, folder 40, ACIM–Chicago.

37. Those seven churches were St. Anthony's, Our Lady of Pompei, Our Lady of Mt. Carmel, St. Michael's, St. Callistus, Sta. Lucia, and Sta. Maria Incoronata. Joseph DeSerto to representative officials, February 19, 1964, box 5, folder 41, ACIM–Chicago; and List of contributors, box 5, folder 40, ACIM–Chicago.

38. Kevin M. Schultz, *Tri-Faith America: How Catholics and Jews Held Postwar America to Its Protestant Promise* (New York: Oxford University Press, 2011); Jonathan Herzog, *The Spiritual-Industrial Complex: America's Religious Battle against Communism in the Early Cold War* (New York: Oxford, 2011); and Stephen J. Whitfield, *The Culture of the Cold War* (Baltimore: Johns Hopkins University Press, 1991), 77–100.

39. I discuss Italian Americans who are active in the immigration reform movement and who self-identified as Catholic or who were influenced by Catholic philosophies. I do not attempt to address the official position of the Catholic Church in America. For scholarship on that subject see Grainne McEvoy, "Justice and Order: American Catholic Social Thought and the Immigration Question in the Restriction Era, 1917–1965" (PhD diss., Boston College, 2014); and Todd Scribner, "Negotiating Priorities: The National Catholic Welfare Conference and United States Migration Policy in a Post–World War II World, 1948–1952," *American Catholic Studies* 121, no. 4 (2010).

40. The main concern of *Pacem in Terris* was nuclear nonproliferation, but that argument was made within a broader context about moral law. Charles E. Curran, *Catholic Moral Theology in Dialogue* (Notre Dame, Ind.: University of Notre Dame Press, 1976).

41. Burns left unusually detailed records her activity in ACIM and Catholic lay groups, as well as extensive personal writings reflecting on her religious beliefs and the role of Catholicism in her life.

42. Burns was a member of the Italian American Professional Women's Association and the Piemontese Social Club, a mutual aid society and club devoted to the preservation of Piemontese culture. Box 2, folder Piemontese Ladies Club 1954–1968, Sinelli Burns Papers.

43. Among many other issues, the National Conference of Catholic Charities was concerned with material and social aid to displaced persons, immigration policies, and international relations. Rev. Msgr. John O'Grady, "Present Objectives of National Conference of Catholic Charities," September 13, 1952, box 3, folder National Conference of Catholic Charities, Sinelli Burns Papers; Burns' Devotional Journals, box 5, folder Religious Material Personal Retreats 1943–1965, Sinelli Burns Papers; and Detroit Archdiocesan Council of Catholic Women, Committee on International Relations, March 13, 1956, box 3, folder ACIM 1956 Miscellaneous, Sinelli Burns Papers.

44. "Catholic Women and International Affairs," National Conference of Catholic Women Yearbook, 1962, box 4, folder National Conference of Catholic Women, 1962, Sinelli Burns Papers.

45. "Catholic Women and International Affairs," National Conference of Catholic Women Yearbook, 1962, box 4, folder National Conference of Catholic Women, 1962, Sinelli Burns Papers.

46. Carolyn Burns, Remarks to the Piemontese Ladies Social Club, 18th Annual Banquet, May 22, 1960, box 2, folder Piemontese Ladies Club 1960, Sinelli Burns Papers; and Detroit Archdiocesan Council of Catholic Women, Committee on International Relations, March 13, 1956, box 3, folder ACIM 1956 Miscellaneous, Sinelli Burns Papers.

47. "Personal Service," National Conference of Catholic Charities, Annual Meeting, Cleveland, Ohio, September 13, 1952, box 3, folder National Conference of Catholic Charities, Sinelli Burns Papers.

48. Yuki Oda, "Family Unity in U.S. Immigration Policy, 1921–1978" (PhD diss., Columbia University, 2014).

49. "Draft of Marchisio Proposed Remarks on Cleveland's TV Panel," 1952, box E24, folder Marchisio Articles, ACIM–National.

50. Nicholas Petruzzelli, "Morality of Immigration Restrictions by the U.S.," *OSIA News*, August 1950.

51. Present Objectives of National Conference of Catholic Charities, Annual Meeting, Cleveland, Ohio, September 13, 1952, box 3, folder National Conference of Catholic Charities, Sinelli Burns Papers.

52. Five of the eight speakers were members of the clergy and one layperson was the president of the International Catholic Migration Commission. "Proceedings, ACIM's Second Symposium on Italian Migration," 1961, Rome, box 7, folder 58, ACIM–Chicago.

53. Rev. Louis Donanzan, "Press Release Re: Immigration Legislation," August 15, 1961, box 4, folder 28, ACIM–Chicago.

54. Juvenal Marchisio, speech to Buffalo archdiocese, May 1962, box E70, folder Biographies, ACIM–National.

55. Rev. Caesar Donanzan, Speech at ACIM Symposium, Washington, D.C., 1963, box 2, folder ACIM 1963 Washington D.C. Symposium, Sinelli Burns Papers; and Caesar Donanzan, "Opening Remarks," "Proceedings, ACIM's Third Symposium on Italian Migration," 1963, Washington, D.C., box 7, folder 59, ACIM–Chicago.

56. A similar address was delivered by Rev. Edward E. Swanstrom of the NCWC, who also elaborated on the teachings of Pope Pius XII and John XXIII regarding the right of migration, state governance, Christian charity, and brotherhood. Rev. Edward E. Swanstrom Speech at ACIM Symposium, Washington, D.C., 1963, box 2, folder ACIM 1963 Washington D.C. Symposium, Sinelli Burns Papers.

57. "Migration: Natural, Inalienable Right," ACIM *Dispatch*, May 1962, box D, ACIM–National.

58. Marchisio Testimony 1964 and 1965.

59. Samuel Moyn, *Christian Human Rights* (Philadelphia: University of Pennsylvania Press, 2015), 25–100.

60. Martin Luther King Jr.'s "Letter from Birmingham Jail" in 1963 might be the most famous example of religious or Christian rhetoric used in the civil rights movement. See also Robert Weisbrot, *Freedom Bound: A History of America's Civil Rights Movement* (New York: W. W. Norton, 1990).

61. The religious roots of human rights discourse had both domestic and international applications. Weisbrot, *Freedom Bound*; Patterson, *Grand Expectations*; Michael Barnett, *Empire of Humanity: A History of Humanitarianism* (Ithaca, N.Y.: Cornell University Press, 2013), 97–160; and Moyn, *Christian Human Rights*.

62. Daniel Corelli Speech, December 15, 1963, Immigration Rally, Chicago, box 5, folder 40, ACIM–Chicago.

63. Resolution on Immigration, box 5, folder 40, ACIM–Chicago. Copies of resolutions sent to lawmakers, box 5, folder 41, ACIM–Chicago.

64. Gerstle, *American Crucible*; Selig, *Americans All*; Wall, *Inventing the "American Way"*; and Philip Gleason, "Americans All: World War II and the Shaping of American Identity," *Review of Politics* 43, no. 4 (1981).

65. Fleegler, *Ellis Island Nation*, 161–90.

66. John F. Kennedy, *A Nation of Immigrants* (New York: Popular Library, 1964).

67. Gerstle, *American Crucible*; Wall, *Inventing the "American Way"*; Schultz, *Tri-Faith America*; Fleegler, *Ellis Island Nation*; Selig, *Americans All*; and Ngai, *Impossible Subjects*, 227–64.

68. Joseph DeSerto, Open Letter to Everett Dirksen, *Fra Noi*, Chicago, June 1965, box 3, folder 21, ACIM–Chicago.

69. Joseph DeSerto, Open Letter to Everett Dirksen, *Fra Noi*, Chicago, June 1965, box 3, folder 21, ACIM–Chicago.

70. For similar statements, see Frank Annunzio comments, "H.R. 2776—Repeal of National Origins Immigration Quota System," *Congressional Record*, April 6, 1965, 6888–89.

71. *Why We Fight: War Comes to America*, directed by Frank Capra (U.S. War Department, 1945). See also Wall, *Inventing the "American Way."*

72. Lizabeth Cohen, *Making a New Deal: Industrial Workers in Chicago, 1919–1939* (New York: Cambridge University Press, 1990); Lizabeth Cohen, *A Consumer's Republic: The Politics of Mass Consumption in Postwar America* (New York: Alfred A. Knopf, 2003); Wall, *Inventing the "American Way"*; and Victoria de Grazia, *Irresistible Empire: America's Advance through 20th Century Europe* (Cambridge, Mass.: Harvard University Press, 2005).

73. For just a few examples, see the physical and economic ghettoization of Chinese people in Nyan Shah, *Contagious Divides: Epidemics and Race in San Francisco's Chinatown* (Berkeley: University of California Press, 2001), or for laws against Japanese ownership of land, see Roger Daniels, *The Politics of Prejudice: The Anti-Japanese Movement in California and the Struggle for Japanese Exclusion* (Berkeley: University of California Press, 1999).

74. Ellen Wu, *The Color of Success: Asian Americans and the Origins of the Model Minority* (Princeton, N.J.: Princeton University Press, 2014); Madeline Hsu, *The Good Immigrants: How the Yellow Peril Became the Model Minority* (Princeton, N.J.: Princeton University Press, 2015); and Charlotte Brooks, *Alien Neighbors, Foreign Friends: Asian Americans, Housing, and the Transformation of Urban California* (Chicago: University of Chicago Press, 2009).

75. Fleegler, *Ellis Island Nation.*

76. Rev. Theodore McCarrick, "Italian Contributions to American Culture," June 1963, American Committee on Italian Migration's Third Annual Symposium, Washington, D.C., box 7, folder 59, ACIM–Chicago.

77. Marchisio Testimony 1964 and 1965.

78. Marchisio Testimony 1964 and 1965.

79. For examples of contributionism similar to Marchisio's testimony, see Resolution #4 "Contributions of Italians," ACIM 1961 Symposium, Rome, box 7, folder 58, ACIM–Chicago; and Fleegler, *Ellis Island Nation,* 104–36, 161–90.

80. Errigo Testimony 1965, 422.

81. Emphasis in the original text. Daniel Corelli Speech, December 15, 1963, Immigration Rally, Chicago, box 5, folder 40, ACIM–Chicago. Similar language was common in speeches Italian Americans delivered on Columbus Day in the postwar period. Statements criticizing the racist provisions of American immigration laws were usually followed by qualifiers including "People from [southern and eastern] Europe are considered inferior to some other people, less worthy to enter our shores, and less worthy to embrace the rights and duties of citizenship." George Spatuzza, "1952 Columbus Day Speech," box 13, folder 5, George Spatuzza Collection, Immigration History Research Center Archives, University of Minnesota (hereafter Spatuzza Collection). Other speakers claimed the McCarran-Walter Act was "framed for the sole purpose of practically eliminating immigrants from Southern and Eastern Europe." John Guarino, Columbus Day Speech, Worcester, 1958, OSIA newsletter, January 1958, box 13, folder 5, Spatuzza Collection.

82. Resolution on Immigration, box 5, folder 40, ACIM–Chicago; and Copies of resolutions sent to lawmakers, box 5, folder 41, ACIM–Chicago.

83. Emphasis in original text. Daniel Corelli, Speech, December 15, 1963, Immigration Rally, Chicago, box 5, folder 40, ACIM–Chicago.

84. The chronology here is important to note as much scholarship focuses on white ethnic grievances articulated in the wake of the civil rights move-

ment. Matthew Frye Jacobson, *Roots Too White Ethnic Revival in Post-civil Rights America* (Cambridge, Mass.: Harvard University Press, 2006); and Horton, *Race and the Making of American Liberalism*, 139–222.

85. Copy Frank Annunzio, Immigration Statement before House Subcommittee on Immigration and Nationality, April 6, 1965, Annunzio to Joseph Deserto, box 2, folder 19, ACIM–Chicago.

86. John Guarino Columbus Day Speech, Worcester, 1958, OSIA newsletter, January 1958, box 13, folder 5, Spatuzza Collection.

87. John Guarino Columbus Day Speech, Worcester, 1958, OSIA newsletter, January 1958, box 13, folder 5, Spatuzza Collection. See similar conclusions in George Spatuzza, "1950 Columbus Day Speech," box 13, folder 5, Spatuzza Collection.

88. Frank Gigliottti to George Spatuzza, January 15, 1954, box 1, folder 46, Spatuzza Collection.

89. Juvenal Marchisio, Columbus Day Speech, St. Paul, Minnesota, 1954, box K1, folder Marchisio Speeches 1954–1955, ACIM–National.

90. Joseph Errigo, Columbus Day Speech, 1962, box 2, folder OSIA Speaking Engagements, Joseph Errigo Papers, Immigration History Research Center Archives, University of Minnesota (hereafter Errigo Papers).

91. George Spatuzza, "1955 Columbus Day Speech," box 13, folder 5, Spatuzza Collection; and John Guarino, Columbus Day Speech, Worcester, 1958, OSIA newsletter, January 1958, box 13, folder 5, Spatuzza Collection.

92. George Spatuzza, "1949, 1950, 1951, 1952, 1955, 1956 Columbus Day Speeches," box 13, folder 4 and 5, Spatuzza Collection; and Joseph Errigo, Columbus Day Speech, 1962, box 2, folder OSIA Speaking Engagements, Errigo Papers.

93. John Guarino, Columbus Day Speech, Worcester, 1958, OSIA newsletter, January 1958, box 13, folder 5, Spatuzza Collection.

94. George Spatuzza, "1952 Columbus Day Speech," box 13, folder 5, Spatuzza Collection.

95. George Spatuzza, "1954 Columbus Day Speech," box 13, folder 5, Spatuzza Collection.

96. George Spatuzza, "1952, 1954, 1956 Columbus Day Speeches," box 13, folder 5, Spatuzza Collection; and Juvenal Marchisio Speech, Verrazano Day Ceremonies, Battery Park, New York City, April 12, 1957, box K1, folder Marchisio Speeches 1956–1957, ACIM–National. Marchisio noted that minimizing Verrazano's "discovery" of New York eighty-five years before Henry Hudson "gives fuel to those bigots who are relegated the powers to control immigration to this country with prejudiced mentalities transmuted into law. These people would like to bury the great accomplishments of other Italians in the founding and growth of our great nation."

97. George Spatuzza, "1954 and 1956 Columbus Day Speeches," box 13, folder 5, Spatuzza Collection. In 1949, Spatuzza called Columbus "a true and

dedicated Catholic who began the missionary movement in the Americas."
George Spatuzza, "1949 Columbus Day Speech," box 13, folder 4, Spatuzza
Collection. Spatuzza also noted (in 1954) that like other "pioneers," Columbus
"did not let adversity stop him" and praised Columbus's "indominable spirit."

98. Dominick M. Alberti, "Hymn to Cristopher Columbus," Alberti and
Associates, Chicago, 1961, box 82, folder 15, Order Sons of Italy in America,
National Grand Lodge Collection, Immigration History Research Center
Archives, University of Minnesota.

99. Philip Mazzei was said to have influenced Thomas Jefferson and Ben-
jamin Franklin. Spatuzza outrageously argued that America's founding fathers
and Christopher Columbus shared similar political philosophies—philosophies
that were eventually codified in the Bill of Rights. George Spatuzza, "1954 and
1956 Columbus Day Speeches," box 13, folder 5, Spatuzza Collection.

100. Joseph Errigo, Columbus Day Speech, 1962, box 2, folder OSIA
Speaking Engagements, Errigo Papers.

101. Juvenal Marchisio, Columbus Day Speech, St. Paul, Minnesota, 1954,
box K1, folder Marchisio Speeches 1954–1955, ACIM–National.

102. George Spatuzza, "1950, 1952, 1954, 1955 Columbus Day Speeches,"
box 13, folder 5, Spatuzza Collection.

103. "Order's Statement on Immigration," July 1965, *OSIA News*.

104. George Spatuzza, "1950, 1952, 1954, 1955 Columbus Day Speeches,"
box 13, folder 5, Spatuzza Collection.

105. George Spatuzza, "1955 Columbus Day Speech," box 13, folder 5,
Spatuzza Collection.

106. George Spatuzza, "1954 Columbus Day Speech," box 13, folder 5,
Spatuzza Collection.

107. Frank Annunzio, Open Letter re: 1963 ACIM Chicago Immigration
Rally, November 13, 1968, box 5, folder 39, ACIM–Chicago.

108. Fleegler, *Ellis Island Nation*, 161–90; Ngai, *Impossible Subjects*, 227–64;
Zolberg, *Nation by Design*, 328–33; and Tichenor, *Dividing Lines*, 207–18.

109. Ngai, *Impossible Subjects*, 227–64.

110. Schultz argues that Catholic and Jewish struggles for social equality in
the late 1940s and early 1950s "helped soften the ground for the Civil Rights
movement of the 1960s." Schultz, *Tri-Faith America*, 8.

111. Wall, *Inventing the "American Way"*; and Fleegler, *Ellis Island Nation*.

112. Thomas Sugrue, *The Origins of the Urban Crisis: Race and Inequality in
Postwar Detroit* (Princeton, N.J.: Princeton University Press, 1996); Cohen,
*Consumer's Republic*; Cybelle Fox, *Three Worlds of Relief: Race, Immigration, and
the American Welfare State from the Progressive Era to the New Deal* (Princeton,
N.J.: Princeton University Press, 2012); Schultz, *Tri-Faith America*; and Rob-
ert . Self, *American Babylon: Race and Struggle in Postwar Oakland* (Princeton,
N.J.: Princeton University Press, 2003).

113. David Roediger, *Working toward Whiteness: How America's Immigrants Became White, the Strange Journey from Ellis Island to the Suburbs* (New York: Basic Books, 2005).

114. Moreover, white ethnic and religious organizations never found ways to work effectively with African American organizations, nor did they fully incorporate African Americans into pluralist paradigms. Selig, *Americans All*; Wall, *Inventing the "American Way"*; Ngai, *Impossible Subjects*; and Fleegler, *Ellis Island Nation*.

CONCLUSION: THE DEEP ROOTS OF WHITE ETHNICITY, 1965 AND BEYOND

1. *Public Papers of the Presidents of the United States: Lyndon B. Johnson, 1965*, vol. 2 (Washington, D.C.: Government Printing Office, 1966), entry 546, 1037–40.

2. Only months earlier (in May 1965), Johnson called for adding Ellis Island to the Liberty Island National Monument. A bill to that effect was approved by Congress in August 1965 (Pub. L. No. 89-129).

3. Rosenthal also commented that both locations "would give too much of a DAR-type [Daughters of the American Revolution] cast." Jack Rosenthal, Director of Public Information, to Bill Moyers, Special Assistant to the President, Memo re: Immigration Bill Signing, August 31, 1965, box 1, folder The Signing at Liberty Island, Legislative Background Files Immigration Law 1965, Lyndon Baines Johnson Presidential Library.

4. James Greenfield to Bill Moyers, Memo re: Immigration Bill Signing Ceremony, September 26, 1965, box 1, folder The Signing at Liberty Island, Legislative Background Files Immigration Law 1965, Lyndon Baines Johnson Presidential Library.

5. U.S. Congress, House of Representatives, *Subcommittee No. 1 of the Committee on the Judiciary, Immigration Hearings*, 88th Cong., 2nd Sess., 412.

6. U.S. Congress, House of Representatives, *Subcommittee No. 1 of the Committee on the Judiciary, Immigration Hearings*, 88th Cong., 2nd Sess., 412.

7. "Draft of Remarks for the President on Signing of the Immigration Reform Act," box 1, folder The Signing at Liberty Island, Legislative Background Files Immigration Law 1965, Lyndon Baines Johnson Presidential Library.

8. *Public Papers of Lyndon B. Johnson*, entry 546, 1037–40.

9. Gabriel Chin would argue the latter point, whereas most other scholars accentuate the Eurocentric focus and shortsighted views of lawmakers on this subject. Gabriel Chin, "Were the Immigration and Nationality Act Amendments of 1965 Antiracist?" in *The Immigration and Nationality Act of 1965: Legislating a New America*, ed. Gabriel Chin and Rose Cuizon Villazor (New York: Cambridge University Press, 2015); David Reimers, *Still the Golden Door: The Third World Comes to America* (New York: Columbia University Press, 1985),

61–91; and Mae Ngai, *Impossible Subjects: Illegal Aliens and the Making of Modern America* (Princeton, N.J.: Princeton University Press, 2004), 246.

10. U.S. Senate, Subcommittee on Immigration and Naturalization of the Committee on the Judiciary, Washington, D.C., February 10, 1965, 1–3.

11. Michael Novak, *The Rise of the Unmeltable Ethnics: Politics and Culture in the Seventies* (New York: MacMillian, 1972); Andrew Greeley, *Why Can't They Be Like Us? America's White Ethnic Groups* (Boston: E.P. Dutton, 1971); and Nathan Glazer and Daniel Patrick Moynihan, *Beyond the Melting Pot: The Negroes, Puerto Ricans, Jews, Italians, and Irish of New York City* (Cambridge, Mass.: Harvard University Press, 1963).

12. Matthew Frye Jacobson, *Roots Too: White Ethnic Revival in Post-civil Rights America* (Cambridge, Mass.: Harvard University Press, 2006); Joshua Fishman, "The Rise and Fall of the 'Ethnic Revival' in the USA," *Journal of Intercultural Studies* 4, no. 3 (1983); and Rudolph Vecoli, "Return to the Melting Pot: Ethnicity in the United States in the Eighties," *Journal of American History* 5, no. 1 (Fall 1985).

13. Jacobson, *Roots Too*, 19–22. Jacobson also credits the Black Power movement and other minority rights movements that followed with helping to legitimize notions of group pride and group rights in the United States. However, there needs to be more critical analysis of those claims. Black nationalism largely rejected participation in mainstream American politics and culture. It argued for a vastly different conception of citizenship in America for whites and nonwhites. It also drew upon and contributed to anticolonial discourse and consequently argued for a more transnational identity for nonwhite groups of Americans.

14. Jacobson, *Roots Too*, 19–20. Elsewhere, Jacobson argues that white ethnics' "inchoate sense of social grievance needed only the right vocabulary [taken from the civil rights movement] to be mobilized." Matthew Frye Jacobson, "A Ghetto to Look Back To: World of Our Fathers, Ethnic Revival, and the Arc of Multiculturalism," *American Jewish History* 88, no. 4 (December 2000), 465.

15. Kevin M. Schultz, *Tri-Faith America: How Catholics and Jews Held Postwar America to Its Protestant Promise* (New York: Oxford University Press, 2011).

16. Jacobson, *Roots Too*, 19–22; Carol Anderson Horton, *Race and the Making of American Liberalism* (New York: Oxford University Press, 2005), 121–89; Nathan Glazer, *Affirmative Discrimination: Ethnic Inequality and Public Policy* (New York: Basic Books, 1975); and Novak, *Rise of the Unmeltable Ethnics*. For just a few examples demonstrating how white ethnics benefitted from white privilege and social welfare programs in the twentieth century, see Lizabeth Cohen, *A Consumer's Republic: The Politics of Mass Consumption in Postwar America* (New York: Alfred A. Knopf, 2003), 112–256; David Roediger, *Working toward Whiteness: How America's Immigrants Became White, the Strange Journey from Ellis Island to the Suburbs* (New York: Basic Books, 2005); and Cybelle Fox, *Three*

*Worlds of Relief: Race, Immigration, and the American Welfare State from the Progressive Era to the New Deal* (Princeton, N.J.: Princeton University Press, 2012).

17. Jacobson characterizes these political and social trends almost exclusively in terms of a white backlash to Leftist reforms and racial politics in the 1960s. Jacobson, *Roots Too.*

18. Horton, *Race and the Making of American Liberalism*, 134–37, 167–73. This view is supported by Jonathan Rieder's ethnographic work. Jonathan Rieder, *Canarsie: The Jews and Italians of Brooklyn against Liberalism* (Cambridge, Mass.: Harvard University Press, 1985).

19. Roediger, *Working toward Whiteness*; and Matthew Frye Jacobson, *Whiteness of a Different Color: European Immigrants and the Alchemy of Race* (Cambridge, Mass.: Harvard University Press, 1998). Even though Guglielmo asserts European immigrants' claims to whiteness "on arrival," he characterizes Italian immigrants and ethnics moving from transnational or ethnic identifications to a white mainstream identity by World War II. Thomas Guglielmo, *White on Arrival: Italians, Race, Color, and Power in Chicago, 1890–1945* (New York: Oxford University Press, 2003).

20. In their 1963 study, *Beyond the Melting Pot*, Glazer and Moynihan argue for the durability of certain Euro-American ethnic identifications in the postwar period that persisted even under the pressures of assimilation. Similar works followed, including Novak, *Rise of the Unmeltable Ethnics*, and Greeley, *Why Can't They Be Like Us?*, but those publications occurred after 1965.

21. For a rich consideration of Euro-American ethnicity/ethnic identification in this period, see Roediger, *Working toward Whiteness*; and Richard Alba, *Ethnic Identity: The Transformation of White America* (New Haven, Conn.: Yale University Press, 1990). Jordan Stanger-Ross argues for the saliency of ethnic identification at midcentury in *Staying Italian: Urban Change and Ethnic Life in Postwar Toronto and Philadelphia* (Chicago: University of Chicago Press, 2009). However, Stanger-Ross is mostly focused on the 1960s and later.

22. Along with the civil rights movement, Black nationalism, and other minority rights movements that followed, Jacobson also identifies a "current of antimodernism," involvement in homeland politics, and academic and public endorsements of cultural pluralism as other factors that helped to promote a surge of white ethnic revivalism after 1965. He gives no consideration, however, to postwar immigration. Jacobson, *Roots Too*, 11–71.

23. Stanger-Ross, *Staying Italian*; Salvatore LaGumina, *From Steerage to Suburb: Long Island Italians* (New York: Center for Migration Studies, 1988); and Laura Ruberto and Joseph Sciorra, eds., *New Italian Migrations to the United States*, vol. 1, *Politics and History since 1945* (Urbana: University of Illinois Press, 2017).

24. Frank Cavaioli, "Patterns of Italian Immigration to the United States," *Catholic Social Science Review* 13 (2008). From 1940 to 1980, there were

nearly four million documented European immigrants out of a total of just over eleven million documented immigrants. U.S. Census Bureau, Statistical Abstract of the United States, 1999, http://www.census.gov/prod/99pubs/99statab/sec31.pdf.

25. For an excellent study of this nature, see Mary Patrice Erdmans, *Opposite Poles: Immigrants and Ethnics in Polish Chicago, 1976–1990* (University Park: Pennsylvania State University Press, 1998). Erdmans provides an important counterpoint to Herbert Gans's understanding of late twentieth century white ethnicity as largely symbolic. See Herbert Gans, "Symbolic Ethnicity: The Future of Ethnic Groups and Cultures in America," *Ethnic and Racial Studies 2*, no. 1 (January 1979).

26. Hiroshi Motomura, *Immigration Outside of the Law* (New York: Oxford University Press, 2014), 235.

BIBLIOGRAPHY

*Archival Materials*

BENTLEY HISTORICAL LIBRARY, UNIVERSITY OF MICHIGAN

Carolyn Sinelli Burns Papers

CENTER FOR MIGRATION STUDIES, NEW YORK

American Committee on Italian Migration–National Office, New York City
    Records
Intergovernmental Committee for European Migration Collection
Italian Welfare League Records
Juvenal Marchisio Papers
National Catholic Welfare Conference Collection
National Catholic Welfare Conference Addendum Collection
Victor Anfuso Papers
War Relief Services, National Catholic Welfare Conference

COLUMBIA UNIVERSITY, RARE BOOKS AND SPECIAL COLLECTIONS

Herbert Lehman Papers
William Welsh Papers

DWIGHT D. EISENHOWER PRESIDENTIAL LIBRARY, ABILENE, KANSAS

Dwight D. Eisenhower Central Files
John Foster Dulles Papers
Maxwell Rabb Papers

IMMIGRATION HISTORY RESEARCH CENTER ARCHIVES, UNIVERSITY OF MINNESOTA

Alberto Cupelli Papers
American Committee of Italian War Relief of St. Paul Collection

American Committee on Italian Migration, Chicago Chapter
George Quilici Papers
George Spatuzza Collection
Giuseppe D. Procopio Papers
Howard E. Molisani Papers
Immigration and Refugee Services of America
Italian American Newspaper Collection
Italians in Chicago, Oral History Collection
Joseph Errigo Papers
Leonard Pasqualicchio Papers
Maurice Marcello Papers
Order Sons of Italy in America Joseph Gorrasi Papers
Order Sons of Italy in America, National Grand Lodge Collection
Order Sons of Italy in America, Pennsylvania Grand Lodge Collection

JOHN F. KENNEDY PRESIDENTIAL LIBRARY, BOSTON, MASSACHUSETTS

Papers of John F. Kennedy. Presidential Papers.

LYNDON BAINES JOHNSON PRESIDENTIAL LIBRARY, AUSTIN, TEXAS

Legislative Background Files Immigration Law 1965

NEW YORK PUBLIC LIBRARY, RARE BOOKS AND SPECIAL COLLECTIONS

Boys' Town of Italy, Inc. Collection

SENATOR JOHN HEINZ HISTORY CENTER, PITTSBURGH, PENNSYLVANIA

Post-WWII Italian American Oral Histories, Italian American Collection

SOCIAL WELFARE HISTORY ARCHIVE, UNIVERSITY OF MINNESOTA

American Immigration and Citizenship Conference Records

SYRACUSE UNIVERSITY, RARE BOOKS AND SPECIAL COLLECTIONS

Edward Corsi Papers

TAMIMENT LIBRARY, ROBERT F. WAGNER LABOR ARCHIVES, NEW YORK UNIVERSITY

Italian American Labor Council Collection

UNIVERSITY OF ROCHESTER, RARE BOOKS AND SPECIAL COLLECTIONS

Kenneth B. Keating Papers

*Manuscripts*

Alba, Richard. *Ethnic Identity: The Transformation of White America*. New Haven, Conn.: Yale University Press, 1990.

———. *Italian Americans: Into the Twilight of Ethnicity*. Englewood Cliffs, N.J.: Prentice Hall, 1985.

———. "Social Assimilation among American Catholic National Origin Groups." *American Sociological Review* 41 (December 1976): 1030–46.

Alba, Richard, and Victor Nee. *Remaking the American Mainstream: Assimilation and Contemporary Immigration*. Cambridge, Mass.: Harvard University Press, 2005.

Audenino, Patrizia, and Maddalena Tirabassi. *Migrazioni Italiane, Storia e storie dall'Ancien regime a oggi*. Turin, Italy: Bruno Mondadri, 2008.

Auker, Theodore Buchanan. "American Immigration Policy during the Eisenhower Administration." Master's thesis, Washington State University, 1973.

Bach, Morten, and Korcaighe Hale. "'What He Is Speaks So Loud That I Can't Hear What He's Saying': R.W. Scott McLeod and the Long Shadow of Joe McCarthy." *Historian* 72, no. 1 (Spring 2010): 67–95.

Baily, Samuel. *Immigrants in the Land of Promise: Italians in Buenos Aires and New York City, 1870 to 1914*. Ithaca, N.Y.: Cornell University Press, 1999.

Barkan, Elazar. *The Retreat of Scientific Racism*. New York: Cambridge University Press, 1992.

Barnett, Michael. *Empire of Humanity: A History of Humanitarianism*. Ithaca, N.Y.: Cornell University Press, 2013.

Bedani, Gino. *Politics and Ideology in the Italian Workers' Movement: Union Development and the Changing Role of the Catholic and Communist Subcultures in Postwar Italy*. Oxford, UK: Berg Publishers, 1995.

Ben-Ghiat, Ruth. *Fascist Modernities: Italy 1922–1945*. Berkeley: University of California Press, 2001.

Ben-Ghiat, Ruth, and Mia Fuller, eds. *Italian Colonialism*. New York: Palgrave Macmillan, 2005.

Benton-Cohen, Katherine. *Inventing the Immigration Problem: The Dillingham Commission and Its Legacy*. Cambridge, Mass.: Harvard University Press, 2018.

Bernardi, Emanuele. *La riforma agraria in Italia e gli Stati Uniti. Guerra fredda, Piano Marshall e interventi per il Mezzogiorno negli anni del centrismo degasperiano*. Bologna: Il Mulino, 2006.

Biagi, Ernest L. *The Purple Aster: A History of the Order Sons of Italy in America*. New York: Veritas Press, 1961.

Bodnar, John. *The Transplanted: A History of Immigrants in Urban America*. Bloomington: Indiana University Press, 1985.

Bon Tempo, Carl. *Americans at the Gate: The United States and Refugees during the Cold War*. Princeton, N.J.: Princeton University Press, 2008.

Bonifazi, Corrado. *L'Italia delle migrazioni*. Bologna: Il Mulino, 2013.

Borgwardt, Elizabeth. *A New Deal for the World: America's Vision for Human Rights*. Cambridge, Mass.: Harvard University Press, 2007.

Borstelmann, Thomas. *The Cold War and the Color Line: American Race Relations in the Global Arena*. Cambridge, Mass.: Harvard University Press, 2001.

Bosniak, Linda. *The Citizen and the Alien: Dilemmas of Contemporary Membership*. Princeton, N.J.: Princeton University Press, 2006.

Bottiglieri, Bruno. *La politica economica dell'Italia centrista (1948–1958)*. Milan: Comunità, 1984.

Brayer, G. Sheldon. *A Temple of Fine Tailoring: The Hickey-Freeman Story*. Rochester, N.Y.: Hickey-Freeman Company, Inc., 1999.

Briggs, John W. *An Italian Passage: Immigrants to Three American Cities, 1890–1930*. New Haven, Conn.: Yale University Press, 1978.

Brinkley, Alan. *The End of Reform: New Deal Liberalism in Recession and in War*. New York: Vintage Books, 1995.

———. "The New Deal and the Idea of the State." In *The Rise and Fall of the New Deal Order, 1930–1980*, edited by Steve Fraser and Gary Gerstle, 85–121. Princeton, N.J.: Princeton University Press, 1989.

Broadwater, Jeff. *Eisenhower and the Anti-Communist Crusade*. Chapel Hill: University of North Carolina Press, 1992.

Brogi, Alessandro. *Confronting America: The Cold War between the United States and the Communists in France and Italy*. Chapel Hill: University of North Carolina Press, 2011.

———. *L'Italia e l'egemonia Americana nel Mediterraneo*. Florence: La Nuova Italia, 1996.

Brooks, Charlotte. *Alien Neighbors, Foreign Friends: Asian Americans, Housing, and the Transformation of Urban California*. Chicago: University of Chicago Press, 2009.

Brubaker, Rogers. "The 'Diaspora' Diaspora." *Ethnic and Racial Studies* 28, no. 1 (January 2005): 1–19.

Cahn, Susan. *Sexual Reckonings: Southern Girls in a Troubling Age*. Cambridge, Mass.: Harvard University Press, 2007.

Canaday, Margot. *The Straight State: Sexuality and Citizenship in Twentieth-Century America*. Princeton, N.J.: Princeton University Press, 2009.

Cancian, Sonia. *Families, Lovers, and Their Letters: Italian Postwar Migration to Canada*. Winnipeg: University of Manitoba Press, 2010.

Candeloro, Dominic. *Chicago's Italians: Immigrants, Ethnics, Americans*. Chicago: Arcadia Publishing, 2003.

Cannistraro, Philip V. *Blackshirts in Little Italy: Italian Americans and Fascism, 1921–1929*. New York: Bordighera Press, 1999.

Cannistraro, Philip, and Elena Aga Rossi. "La Politica Etnica e il Dilemma dell' Antifascismo negli Stati Uniti: Il Caso di Generoso Pope." *Storia Contemporanea* 17, no. 2 (1986): 217–43.

Capuzzi, Lucia. *La frontier immaginata, Profilo politico e sociale dell'-immigrazione italiana in Argentina nel secondo dopoguerra.* Milan: Franco-Angeli, 2006.

Carnevale, Nancy. *A New Language, a New World: Italian Immigrants in the United States, 1890–1945.* Urbana: University of Illinois Press, 2009.

———. "No Italian Spoken for the Duration of the War: Language, Italian American Identity and Cultural Pluralism in the World War II Years." *Journal of American Ethnic History* 22, no. 3 (Spring 2003): 3–33.

Cassamagnaghi, Silvia. *Operazione spose di guerra: Storie d'amore e di emigrazione.* Milan: Feltrinelli, 2014.

Cavaioli, Frank. "Chicago's Italian Americans Rally for Immigration Reform." *Italian Americana* 6, no. 2 (Spring/Summer 1980): 142–56.

———. "Patterns of Italian Immigration to the United States." *Catholic Social Science Review* 13 (2008): 213–29.

Chin, Gabriel. "Were the Immigration and Nationality Act Amendments of 1965 Antiracist?" In *The Immigration and Nationality Act of 1965: Legislating a New America,* edited by Gabriel Chin and Rose Cuizon Villazor. New York: Cambridge University Press, 2015.

Chin, Margaret M. *Sewing Women: Immigrants and the New York City Garment Industry.* New York: Columbia University Press, 2005.

Choate, Mark. *Emigrant Nation: The Making of Italy Abroad.* Cambridge, Mass.: Harvard University Press, 2008.

Chopas, Mary Elizabeth Basile. *Searching for Subversives: The Story of Italian Internment in Wartime America.* Chapel Hill: University of North Carolina Press, 2017.

Cinel, Dino. *The National Integration of Italian Return Migration, 1870–1929.* Cambridge: Cambridge University Press, 1991.

Cinotto, Simone. *The Italian American Table: Food, Family, and Community in New York City.* Chicago: University of Illinois Press, 2013.

Cohen, Gerard Daniel. *In War's Wake: Europe's Displaced Persons in the Postwar Order.* New York: Oxford University Press, 2012.

Cohen, Lizabeth. *A Consumer's Republic: The Politics of Mass Consumption in Postwar America.* New York: Alfred A. Knopf, 2003.

———. *Making a New Deal: Industrial Workers in Chicago, 1919–1939.* New York: Cambridge University Press, 1990.

Cohen, Miriam. *Workshop to Office: Two Generations of Italian Women in New York City, 1900–1950.* Ithaca, N.Y.: Cornell University Press, 1993.

Colucci, Michele. *Lavoro in movimento, l'emigrazione italiana in europa, 1945–1957.* Rome: Donzelli, 2008.

Cooper, Fredrick, and Rogers Brubaker. "Identity." In *Colonialism in Question: Theory, Knowledge, History,* by Frederick Cooper, 59–90. Berkeley: University of California Press, 2005.

Corsi, Edward. *In the Shadow of Liberty.* New York: Arno Press, 1969.

Cullather, Nick. *The Hungry World: America's Cold War Battle against Poverty in Asia*. Cambridge, Mass.: Harvard University Press, 2010.

Curran, Charles E. *Catholic Moral Theology in Dialogue*. Notre Dame, Ind.: University of Notre Dame Press, 1976.

D'Agostino, Peter. "Craniums, Criminals, and the 'Cursed Race': Italian Anthropology in American Racial Thought, 1861–1924." *Comparative Studies in Society and History* 44, no. 2 (April 2002): 319–43.

———. "The Scalabrini Fathers, the Italian Emigrants Church, and Ethnic Nationalism in America." *Religion and American Culture* 7, no. 1 (Winter 1997): 121–59.

Daniels, Roger. *Guarding the Golden Door: American Immigration Policy and Immigrants since 1882*. New York: Hill and Wang, 2004.

———. *The Politics of Prejudice: The Anti-Japanese Movement in California and the Struggle for Japanese Exclusion*. Berkeley: University of California Press, 1999.

———. *Prisoners without Trial: Japanese Americans in World War II*. New York: Hill and Wang, 1993.

De Castro, Diego. *La questione di Trieste: L'azione politica e diplomatica italiana dal 1943 al 1954*. Trieste, Italy: LINT, 1981.

De Clementi, Andreina. *Il Prezzo della ricostruzione. L'emigrazione italiana nel secondo dopoguerra*. Rome: Laterza, 2010.

Degler, Carl. *In Search of Human Nature: The Decline and Revival of Darwinism in American Social Thought*. New York: Oxford University Press, 1991.

de Grazia, Victoria. *Irresistible Empire: America's Advance through 20th Century Europe*. Cambridge, Mass.: Harvard University Press, 2005.

Devoto, Fernando. *Storia degli italiani in Argentina*. Rome: Donzelli, 2006.

Dickie, John. Darkest Italy: The Nation and Stereotypes of the Mezzogiorno, 1860–1900. New York: St. Martin's Press, 1998.

Diggins, John Patrick. *Mussolini and Fascism: The View from America*. Princeton, N.J.: Princeton University Press, 1972.

———. *The Proud Decades: America in War and in Peace, 1941–1960*. New York: W. W. Norton and Company, 1988.

DiStasi, Lawrence. "War within War: Italian Americans and the Military in World War II." In *Una Storia Segreta: The Secret History of Italian American Evacuation and Internment during World War II*, edited by Lawrence DiStasi, 271–89. Berkeley, Calif.: Heyday Books, 2001.

Divine, Robert A. *American Immigration Policy, 1924–1952*. New Haven, Conn.: Yale University Press, 1957.

Ducci, Lucia, Stefano Luconi, and Matteo Pratelli. *Le relazioni tra Italia e Stati Uniti, Dal Risorgimento all consequenze dell'11 settembre*. Roma: Carocci, 2012.

Dudziak, Mary. *Cold War Civil Rights: Race and the Image of American Democracy*. Princeton, N.J.: Princeton University Press, 2000.

Eckerson, Helen F. "United States and Canada Magnets for Immigration." *Annals of the American Academy of Political and Social Science* 316 (March 1958): 34–42.

Ekbladh, David. *The Great American Mission: Modernization and the Construction of an American World Order*. Princeton, N.J.: Princeton University Press, 2010.

Elkins, Caroline, and Susan Pedersen, eds. *Settler Colonialism in the Twentieth Century: Projects, Practices, and Legacies*. London: Routledge, 2005.

Endy, Christopher. *Cold War Holidays: American Tourism in France*. Chapel Hill: University of North Carolina Press, 2004.

Enyeart, John. "Revolutionizing Cultural Pluralism: The Political Odyssey of Louis Adamic, 1932–1951." *Journal of American Ethnic History* 34, no. 3 (Spring 2015): 58–90.

Erdmans, Mary Patrice. *Opposite Poles: Immigrants and Ethnics in Polish Chicago, 1976–1990*. University Park: Pennsylvania State University Press, 1998.

Falco, Nicholas, ed. *A Guide to the Archives: Records of the Italian Welfare League Inc*. Staten Island, N.Y.: Center for Migration Studies, 1988.

Fieldston, Sara. *Raising the World: Child Welfare in the American Century*. Cambridge, Mass.: Harvard University Press, 2015.

Filippelli, Ronald. *American Labor and Postwar Italy, 1943–1953: A Study of Cold War Politics*. Stanford, Calif.: Stanford University Press, 1989.

Finkelstein, Monte S. "The Johnson Act, Mussolini, and Fascist Emigration Policy: 1921–1930." *Journal of American Ethnic History* 8, no. 1 (Fall 1988): 38–55.

Fishman, Joshua. "The Rise and Fall of the 'Ethnic Revival' in the USA." *Journal of Intercultural Studies* 4, no. 3 (1983): 5–46.

Fitzgerald, David, and David Cook-Martin. *Culling the Masses: The Democratic Origins of Racist Immigration Policies in the Americas*. Cambridge, Mass.: Harvard University Press, 2014.

Fleegler, Robert. *Ellis Island Nation: Immigration Policy and American Identity in the Twentieth Century*. Philadelphia: University of Pennsylvania Press, 2013.

———. "'Forget All Differences until the Forces of Freedom Are Triumphant': The World War II–Era Quest for Ethnic and Religious Tolerance." *Journal of American Ethnic History* 27, no. 2 (Winter 2008): 59–84.

Formagioni, Guido. *La Democrazia cristiana e l'alleanza occidentale (1943–1953)*. Bologna: Il Mulino, 1998.

Fox, Cybelle. *Three Worlds of Relief: Race, Immigration, and the American Welfare State from the Progressive Era to the New Deal*. Princeton, N.J.: Princeton University Press, 2012.

Fox, Stephen. *The Unknown Internment: An Oral History of the Relocation of Italian Americans during World War II*. Boston: Twayne Publishers, 1990.

Gabaccia, Donna. *Foreign Relations: American Immigration in a Global Perspective*. Princeton, N.J.: Princeton University Press, 2012.

———. *From the Other Side: Women, Gender, and Immigrant Life in the U.S., 1820–1990*. Bloomington: Indiana University Press, 1994.

———. *Italy's Many Diasporas*. Seattle: University of Washington Press, 2000.

Gans, Herbert. "Symbolic Ethnicity: The Future of Ethnic Groups and Cultures in America." *Ethnic and Racial Studies* 2, no. 1 (January 1979).

Garcia, Maria Cristina. *Havana USA: Cuban Exiles and Cuban Americans*. Berkeley: University of California Press, 1996.

Gardner, Martha. *The Qualities of a Citizen: Women, Immigration, and Citizenship, 1870–1965*. Princeton, N.J.: Princeton University Press, 2009.

Garland, Libby. *After They Closed the Gates: Jewish Illegal Immigration to the United States, 1921–1965*. Chicago: University of Chicago Press, 2014.

Gatrell, Peter. *Free World? The Campaign to Save the World's Refugees, 1956–1963*. New York: Cambridge University Press, 2011.

———. *The Making of the Modern Refugee*. New York: Oxford University Press, 2013.

Gerber, David. *Authors of Their Lives: The Personal Correspondence of British Immigrants to North America in the Nineteenth Century*. New York: New York University Press, 2006.

Gerstle, Gary. *American Crucible: Race and Nation in the Twentieth Century*. Princeton, N.J.: Princeton University Press, 2001.

———. "The Protean Character of American Liberalism." *American Historical Review* 99, no. 4 (1994): 1043–73.

Ginsborg, Paul. *A History of Contemporary Italy: Society and Politics, 1943–1988*. New York: Palgrave, 2003.

Glazer, Nathan. *Affirmative Discrimination: Ethnic Inequality and Public Policy*. New York: Basic Books, 1975.

Glazer, Nathan, and Daniel Patrick Moynihan. *Beyond the Melting Pot: The Negroes, Puerto Ricans, Jews, Italians, and Irish of New York City*. Cambridge, Mass.: Harvard University Press, 1963.

Gleason, Philip. "Americans All: World War II and the Shaping of American Identity." *Review of Politics* 43, no. 4 (1981): 483–518.

Greeley, Andrew. *Why Can't They Be Like Us? America's White Ethnic Groups*. Boston: E.P. Dutton, 1971.

Green, Nancy L. *Ready-to-Wear and Ready-to-Work: A Century of Industry and Immigrants in Paris and New York*. Durham, N.C.: Duke University Press, 1997.

Guglielmo, Jennifer. *Living the Revolution: Italian Women's Resistance and Radicalism in New York City, 1880–1945*. Chapel Hill: University of North Carolina Press, 2010.

Guglielmo, Jennifer, and Salvatore Salerno, eds. *Are Italians White? How Race Is Made in America*. New York: Routledge, 2003.

Guglielmo, Thomas. *White on Arrival: Italians, Race, Color, and Power in Chicago, 1890–1945*. New York: Oxford University Press, 2003.

Guterl, Matthew Pratt. *The Color of Race in America, 1900–1940*. Cambridge, Mass.: Harvard University Press, 2001.

Gutierrez, David. *Walls and Mirrors: Mexican Americans, Mexican Immigrants and the Politics of Ethnicity*. Berkeley: University of California Press, 1995.

Hahamovitch, Cindy. *The Fruits of Their Labor: Atlantic Coast Farmworkers and the Making of Migrant Poverty, 1870–1945*. Chapel Hill: University of North Carolina Press, 1997.

———. *No Man's Land: Jamaican Guest Workers in America and the Global History of Deportable Labor*. Princeton, N.J.: Princeton University Press, 2012.

Harper, John Lamberton. *America and the Reconstruction of Italy, 1945–1948*. New York: Cambridge University Press, 1986.

Hart, Justin. *Empire of Ideas: The Origins of Public Diplomacy and the Transformation of U.S. Foreign Policy*. New York: Oxford University Press, 2013.

Herzog, Jonathan. *The Spiritual-Industrial Complex: America's Religious Battle against Communism in the Early Cold War*. New York: Oxford University Press, 2011.

Higham, John. *Strangers in the Land: Patterns of American Nativism, 1860–1925*. New York: Atheneum, 1963.

Hirota, Hidetaka. *Expelling the Poor: Atlantic Seaboard States and the Nineteenth-Century Origins of American Immigration Policy*. New York: Oxford University Press, 2017.

Hogan, Michael. *The Marshall Plan: America, Britain, and the Reconstruction of Europe*. New York: Cambridge University Press, 1987.

Hoganson, Kristin. *Consumers' Imperium: The Global Production of American Domesticity, 1865–1920*. Chapel Hill: University of North Carolina Press, 2007.

Horton, Carol Anderson. *Race and the Making of American Liberalism*. New York: Oxford University Press, 2005.

Hsu, Madeline. *The Good Immigrants: How the Yellow Peril Became the Model Minority*. Princeton, N.J.: Princeton University Press, 2015.

Hsu, Madeline, and Ellen Wu. "Smoke and Mirrors: Conditional Inclusion, Model Minorities, and the Pre-1965 Dismantling of Asian Exclusion." *Journal of American Ethnic History* 34, no. 4 (Summer 2015): 43–65.

Hutchinson, Edward P. *Legislative History of American Immigration Policy, 1798–1965*. Philadelphia: University of Pennsylvania Press, 1981.

Iacovetta, Franca. "Ordering in Bulk: Canada's Postwar Immigration Policy and the Recruitment of Contract Workers from Italy." *Journal of American Ethnic History* 11, no. 1 (Fall 1991): 50–80.

———. *Such a Hardworking People: Italian Immigrants in Postwar Toronto*. Montreal: McGill-Queen's University Press, 1993.

Idini, Fabiana. "L'accordo di emigrazione assistita tra Italia e Australia (29 marzo 1951)." *Altreitalie* 45 (2012): 74–94.

Jacobson, Matthew Frye. "A Ghetto to Look Back To: World of Our Fathers, Ethnic Revival, and the Arc of Multiculturalism." *American Jewish History* 88, no. 4 (December 2000): 463–74.

———. *Roots Too: White Ethnic Revival in Post-civil Rights America*. Cambridge, Mass.: Harvard University Press, 2006.

———. *Whiteness of a Different Color: European Immigrants and the Alchemy of Race*. Cambridge, Mass.: Harvard University Press, 1998.

Jaroszynska-Kirchmann, Anna. *The Exile Mission: The Polish Political Diaspora and Polish Americans, 1939–1956*. Athens: Ohio University Press, 2004.

Jeansonne, Glen. *Gerald L. K. Smith: Minister of Hate*. New Haven, Conn.: Yale University Press, 1988.

Kanstroom, Daniel. *Deportation Nation: Outsiders in American History*. Cambridge, Mass.: Harvard University Press, 2007.

Kelly, Saul. *Cold War in the Desert: Britain, the United States and the Italian Colonies, 1945–52*. New York: St. Martin's Press, 2000.

Kennedy, John F. *A Nation of Immigrants*. New York: Popular Library, 1964.

Kessner, Thomas. *The Golden Door: Italian and Jewish Immigrant Mobility in New York City, 1880–1915*. New York: Oxford University Press, 1977.

King, Desmond. *Making Americans: Immigration, Race, and the Origins of the Diverse Democracy*. Cambridge, Mass.: Harvard University Press, 2000.

King, Russel. *Land Reform: The Italian Experience*. London: Butterworth & Company, 1973.

Klein, Christina. *Cold War Orientalism: Asia in the Middlebrow Imagination, 1945–1961*. Berkeley: University of California Press, 2003.

Kraly, Ellen Percy. "U.S. Refugee Policies and Refugee Migration." In *Immigration and U.S. Foreign Policy*, ed. Robert W. Tucker, Charles B. Keely, and Linda Wrigley. Boulder, Co.: Westview Press, 1990.

Kraut, Alan. *Silent Travelers: Germs, Genes and the Immigrant Menace*. Baltimore: Johns Hopkins University Press, 1995.

LaBanca, Nicola. *Oltremare: Storia dell'espansione coloniale italiana*. Bologna: Il Mulino, 2002.

LaFeber, Walter. *America, Russia, and the Cold War, 1945–2000*. 9th ed. New York: McGraw-Hill, 2008.

———. *The American Age: U.S. Foreign Policy at Home and Abroad*. New York: W. W. Norton, 1994.

LaGumina, Salvatore. *From Steerage to Suburb: Long Island Italians*. New York: Center for Migration Studies, 1988.

———. "In Search of Heroes: Italian Americans in World War II." *Italian Americana* 20, no. 1 (Winter 2002): 87–95.

———. *New York at Mid-Century: The Impellitteri Years*. Westport, Conn.: Greenwood Press, 1992.

Lee, Catherine. *Fictive Kinship: Family Reunification and the Meaning of Race and Nation in American Immigration*. New York: Russell Sage Foundation, 2013.

Lee, Erika. *At America's Gates: Chinese Immigration during the Exclusion Era, 1882–1943*. Chapel Hill: University of North Carolina Press, 2003.

Lee, Jessica Harriet. "To the Seventh Generation: Italians and the Creation of an American Political Identity, 1921–1948." PhD diss., Columbia University, 2016.

Little, Douglas. *American Orientalism: The United States and the Middle East since 1945*. Chapel Hill: University of North Carolina Press, 2004.

Locatelli, Francesca. "La comunita' italiana di Asmara negli anni Trenta tra propadanda, leggi razziali e realta' sociale." In *L'Impero fascista: Italia ed Etiopia (1935–1941)*, edited by Riccardo Bottoni, 369–91. Bologna: Il Mulino, 2008.

Loescher, Gil, and John Scanlan. *Calculated Kindness: Refugees and America's Half-Open Door, 1945–Present*. New York: Free Press, 1986.

Luconi, Stefano. "Anticommunism, Americanization, and Ethnic Identity: Italian Americans and the 1948 Letters to Italy Campaign." *Historian* 62, no. 2 (Winter 2000): 285–303.

———. "Contested Loyalties: World War II and Italian Americans' Ethnic Identity." *Italian Americana* 30, no. 2 (Summer 2012): 151–67.

———. *From Paesani to White Ethnics: The Italian Experience in Philadelphia*. Albany: State University of New York Press, 2001.

———. "Generoso Pope and Italian American Voters in New York City." *Studi Emigrazione* 38, no. 142 (2001): 399–422.

———. "I giornali italo-americani degli Stati Uniti e le elezioni politiche italiane del 1953." *Archivo Storico Emigrazione Italiana* (November 2006).

———. "Italian Migrations and Diasporic Approaches: Historical Phenomena and Scholarly Interpretations." In *The Cultures of Italian Migration: Diverse Trajectories and Discrete Perspectives*, edited by Graziella Parati and Anthony Julian Tamburri, 153–68. Teaneck, N.J.: Fairleigh Dickinson University Press, 2011.

———. "Italy, Italian Americans, and the McCarran-Walter Act." In *New Italian Migrations to the United States*. Vol. 1, *Politics and History since 1945*, edited by Laura Ruberto and Joseph Sciorra, 33–58. Urbana: University of Illinois Press, 2017.

———. *La "diplomazia parallela": Il regime fascista e la mobilitazione politica degli italo-americani*. Milan: Franco Angeli, 2000.

Lundestad, Geir. *The United States and Western Europe since 1945*. New York: Oxford University Press, 2009.

Maccari Clayton, Marina. "'Communists of the Stomach': Italian Migration and International Relations in the Cold War Era." *Studi Emigrazione* 41, no. 155 (2004): 575–97.

Mackenzie, G. Calvin, and Robert Weisbrot. *The Liberal Hour: Washington and the Politics of Change in the 1960s*. New York: Penguin Books, 2008.

Marinari, Maddalena. "Americans Must Show Justice in Immigration Policies Too: The Passage of the 1965 Immigration Act." *Journal of Policy History* 26, no. 2 (2014): 219–45.

———. "Divided and Conquered: Immigration Reform Advocates and the Passage of the 1952 Immigration and Nationality Act." *Journal of American Ethnic History* 35, no. 3 (Spring 2016): 9–40.

———. "In the Name of God . . . and in the Interest of Our Country: The Cold War, Foreign Policy, and Italian Americans' Mobilization against Immigration Restriction." In *New Italian Migrations to the United States*, edited by Laura Ruberto and Joseph Sciorra, 59–79. Urbana: University of Illinois Press, 2017.

———. "Liberty, Restriction, and the Remaking of Italians and Eastern European Jews (1882–1965)." PhD diss., University of Kansas, 2009.

Martinez, C. Edda, and Edward Suchman. "Letters from America and the 1948 Elections in Italy." *Public Opinion Quarterly* 14, no. 1 (Spring 1950): 111–25.

May, Elaine Tyler. *Homeward Bound: American Families in the Cold War Era.* New York: Basic Books, 1988.

McCarthy, Patrick. *The Crisis of the Italian State: From the Origins of the Cold War to the Fall of Berlusconi.* London: Palgrave MacMillan, 1995.

McEvoy, Grainne. "Justice and Order: American Catholic Social Thought and the Immigration Question in the Restriction Era, 1917–1965." PhD diss., Boston College, 2014.

McGreevy, John T. *Catholicism and American Freedom.* New York: W. W. Norton, 2003.

Meyer, Gerald. *Vito Marcantonio: Radical Politician, 1902–1954.* Albany: State University of New York Press, 1989.

Mikolji, Boris. "Ethnic Groups in America: The Italians of Rochester." *Il Politico* 36, no. 4 (December 1971): 660–82.

Miller, James Edward. *The United States and Italy, 1940–1950: The Politics of Diplomacy and Stabilization.* Chapel Hill: University of North Carolina Press, 1986.

Mills, Nicolaus. *Winning the Peace: The Marshall Plan and America's Coming of Age as a Superpower.* Hoboken, N.J.: Wiley and Sons, 2008.

Moloney, Dierdre. *American Catholic Lay Groups and Transatlantic Social Reform in the Progressive Era.* Chapel Hill: University of North Carolina Press, 2002.

Moore, Deborah. *B'nai B'rith and the Challenge of Ethnic Leadership.* Albany: State University of New York Press, 1981.

Morandi, Elia. *Governare l'emigrazione: Lavoratori italiani verso la Germania nel secondo dopoguerra.* Turin, Italy: Rosenberg & Seller, 2011.

Motomura, Hiroshi. *Americans in Waiting: The Lost Story of Immigration and Citizenship in the United States.* New York: Oxford University Press, 2006.

———. *Immigration Outside of the Law*. New York: Oxford University Press, 2014.

Mountjoy, Alan B. *The Mezzogiorno*. New York: Oxford University Press, 1973.

Moyn, Samuel. *Christian Human Rights*. Philadelphia: University of Pennsylvania Press, 2015.

———. *The Last Utopia: Human Rights in History*. Cambridge, Mass.: Harvard University Press, 2010.

Neils Conzen, Kathleen, David A. Gerber, Ewa Morawska, George E. Pozzetta, and Rudolph J. Vecoli. "The Invention of Ethnicity: A Perspective from the U.S.A." *Journal of American Ethnic History* 12, no. 1 (Fall 1992): 3–39.

Neuman, Gerald. *Strangers to the Constitution: Immigrants, Borders, and Fundamental Law*. Princeton, N.J.: Princeton University Press, 1996.

Ngai, Mae. *Impossible Subjects: Illegal Aliens and the Making of Modern America*. Princeton, N.J.: Princeton University Press, 2004.

Ninkovich, Frank. *The Wilsonian Century: U.S. Foreign Policy since 1900*. Chicago: University of Chicago Press, 1999.

Novak, Bogdan C. *Trieste, 1941–1954: The Ethnic, Political, and Ideological Struggle*. Chicago: University of Chicago Press, 1970.

Novak, Michael. *The Rise of the Unmeltable Ethnics: Politics and Culture in the Seventies*. New York: Macmillan, 1972.

Oda, Yuki. "Family Unity in U.S. Immigration Policy, 1921–1978." PhD diss., Columbia University, 2014.

Orchowski, Margaret Sands. *The Law That Changed the Face of the Nation: The Immigration and Nationality Act of 1965*. New York: Rowman & Littlefield, 2015.

Orsi, Robert. *The Madonna of 115th Street: Faith and Community in Italian Harlem, 1880–1950*. New Haven, Conn.: Yale University Press, 1985.

Parker, Kunal. *Making Foreigners: Immigration and Citizenship Law in America, 1600–2000*. New York: Cambridge University Press, 2015.

Pasto, James S. "Immigrants and Ethnics: Post–World War II Italian Immigration and Boston's North End (1945–2016)." In *New Italian Migrations to the United States*. Vol. 1, *Politics and History since 1945*, edited by Laura Ruberto and Joseph Sciorra, 105–31. Urbana: University of Illinois Press, 2017.

Patterson, James. *Grand Expectations: The United States, 1945–1974*. New York: Oxford University Press, 1996.

Perlmann, Joel. *Italians Then, Mexicans Now: Immigrant Origins and Second-Generation Progress, 1890 to 2000*. New York: Russell Sage Foundation, 2005.

Pope Leo XIII. *Rerum Novarum*. Encyclical Letter of Pope Leo XIII on the Conditions of Labor (1891). *Historical Catholic and Dominican Documents*, book 13. http://digitalcommons.providence.edu/catholic_documents/13.

Pope Pius XII. *Exsul Familia*. In *The Church's Magna Charta for Migrants*, translated and edited by Reverend Giulivo Tessarolo. Staten Island, N.Y.: St. Charles Seminary, 1962.

Pretelli, Matteo. *Il fascismo e gli Italiani all'estero*. Bologna: CLUEB, 2010.

*Public Papers of the Presidents of the United States: Lyndon B. Johnson, 1965*. Vol. 2. Washington, D.C.: Government Printing Office, 1966.

Pugliese, Enrico. *L'Italia tra migrazioni internazionali e migrazioni interne*. Bologna: Il Mulino, 2002.

Rabel, Roberto G. *Between East and West: Trieste, the United States, and the Cold War, 1941–1954*. Durham, N.C.: Duke University Press, 1988.

Reeder, Linda. *Widows in White: Migration and the Transformation of Rural Italian Women, Sicily, 1880–1920*. Toronto: University of Toronto Press, 2003.

Reimers, David. *Still the Golden Door: The Third World Comes to America*. New York: Columbia University Press, 1985.

Rieder, Jonathan. *Canarsie: The Jews and Italians of Brooklyn against Liberalism*. Cambridge, Mass.: Harvard University Press, 1985.

Rinauro, Sandro. *Il cammino della Speranza, l'Emigrazione clandestine degli Italiani nel Secondo Dopoguerra*. Turin, Italy: Einaudi, 2009.

———. "Politica e geografia dell'emigrazione italiana negli anni della ricostruzione." In *L'Italia alla meta del XX secolo: Conflitto sociale, Resistenza, construzione di una democrazia*, edited by Luigi Ganapini, 247–84. Milan: Guerini e Associati, 2005.

Roediger, David. *Working toward Whiteness: How America's Immigrants Became White, the Strange Journey from Ellis Island to the Suburbs*. New York: Basic Books, 2005.

Romero, Frederico. *Emigrazione e integrazione europea 1945–1973*. Rome: Edizioni Lavoro, 1991.

Rosoli, Gianfasto. "L'emigrazione italiana nel secondo dopoguerra." In *Emigrazione: memorie e realta*, edited by Casimira Grandi, 444–50. Trento, Italy: Provincia Autonoma di Trento, 1990.

Rosoli, Gianfausto, ed. *Un secolo di emigrazione italiana, 1876–1976*. Rome: Centro Studi Emigrazione, 1978.

Rowe, David E., and Robert Schulmann, eds. *Einstein on Politics: His Private Thoughts and Public Stands on Nationalism, Zionism, War, Peace, and the Bomb*. Princeton, N.J.: Princeton University Press, 2007.

Ruberto, Laura, and Joseph Sciorra, eds. *New Italian Migrations to the United States*. Vol. 1, *Politics and History since 1945*. Urbana: University of Illinois Press, 2017.

Rubin, Barry. *Secrets of State: The State Department and the Struggle Over U.S. Foreign Policy*. New York: Oxford University Press, 1985.

Russell, Janice Alberti. "The Italian Community in Tunisia 1861–1961: A Viable Minority." PhD diss., Columbia University, 1977.

Salvemini, Gaetano. *Italian Fascist Activities in the United States.* New York: Center for Migration Studies, 1977.

Santangelo, Betty. *Lucky Corner: The Biography of Congressman Alfred E. Santangelo and the Rise of Italian Americans in Politics.* New York: Center for Migration Studies, 1999.

Schrag, Peter. *Not Fit for Our Society: Immigration and Nativism in America.* Berkeley: University of California Press, 2010.

Schrecker, Ellen. *Many Are the Crimes: McCarthyism in America.* Boston: Little, Brown, and Company, 1998.

Schultz, Kevin M. *Tri-Faith America: How Catholics and Jews Held Postwar America to Its Protestant Promise.* New York: Oxford University Press, 2011.

Scribner, Todd. "Negotiating Priorities: The National Catholic Welfare Conference and United States Migration Policy in a Post–World War II World, 1948–1952." *American Catholic Studies* 121, no. 4 (2010): 1–25.

———. *A Partisan Church: American Catholicism and the Rise of Neoconservative Catholics.* Washington, D.C.: Catholic University Press of America, 2015.

Self, Robert O. *American Babylon: Race and Struggle in Postwar Oakland.* Princeton, N.J.: Princeton University Press, 2003.

Selig, Diana. *Americans All: The Cultural Gifts Movement.* Cambridge, Mass.: Harvard University Press, 2008.

Shah, Nyan. *Contagious Divides: Epidemics and Race in San Francisco's Chinatown.* Berkeley: University of California Press, 2001.

Shepard, Ben. *The Long Road Home: The Aftermath of the Second World War.* New York: Anchor Press, 2012.

Soyer, Daniel, ed. *A Coat of Many Colors: Immigration, Globalization, and Reform in New York City's Garment Industry.* New York: Fordham University Press, 2005.

Spanoglo, Carlo. *La stabilizzazione incompiuta. Il piano Marshall in Italia (1947–1952).* Rome: Carocci, 2001.

Sparrow, James. *Warfare State: World War II Americans and the Age of Big Government.* New York: Oxford University Press, 2011.

Stanger-Ross, Jordan. *Staying Italian: Urban Change and Ethnic Life in Postwar Toronto and Philadelphia.* Chicago: University of Chicago Press, 2009.

Sterba, Christopher. *Good Americans: Italian and Jewish Immigrants during the First World War.* New York: Oxford University Press, 2003.

Stern, Alexandra Minna. *Eugenic Nation: Faults and Frontiers of Better Breeding in America.* Berkeley: University of California Press, 2005.

St. John, Rachel. *Line in the Sand: A History of the Western U.S.–Mexico Border.* Princeton, N.J.: Princeton University Press, 2011.

Storrs, Landon. *The Second Red Scare and the Unmaking of the New Deal Left.* Princeton, N.J.: Princeton University Press, 2013.

Sugrue, Thomas. *The Origins of the Urban Crisis: Race and Inequality in Postwar Detroit.* Princeton, N.J.: Princeton University Press, 1996.

―――. *Sweet Land of Liberty: The Forgotten Struggle for Civil Rights in the North.* New York: Random House, 2008.

Tarrow, Sydney. *Peasant Communism in Southern Italy.* New Haven, Conn.: Yale University Press, 1967.

Thibault, Roberta, ed. *Edward Corsi: Inventory of His Papers.* Syracuse, N.Y.: Syracuse University Library, 1969.

Tichenor, Daniel J. *Dividing Lines: The Politics of Immigration Control in America.* Princeton, N.J.: Princeton University Press, 2002.

Tintori, Guido. "Italiani Enemy Aliens. I Civili residenti negli Stati Uniti d'America durante la Seconda Guerra Mondiale." *Altreitalie* 28 (January–June 2004): 83–109.

―――. "New Discoveries, Old Prejudices: The Internment of Italian Americans during World War II." In *Una Storia Segreta: The Secret History of Italian American Evacuation and Internment during World War II*, edited by Lawrence DiStasi, 236–53. Berkeley, Calif.: Heyday Books, 2001.

Ueda, Reed. *Postwar Immigrant America: A Social History.* Boston: Bedford/St. Martin's Press, 1994.

Vecoli, Rudolph. "The Making and Un-making of the Italian American Working Class." In *The Lost World of Italian American Radicalism: Politics, Labor, and Culture*, edited by Philip Cannistraro and Gerald Meyer, 51–76. Westport, Conn.: Praeger, 2003.

―――. "Return to the Melting Pot: Ethnicity in the United States in the Eighties." *Journal of American History* 5, no. 1 (Fall 1985): 7–20.

Vellon, Peter. *A Great Conspiracy against Our Race: Italian Immigrant Newspapers and the Construction of Whiteness in the Early 20th Century.* New York: New York University Press, 2014.

Venditto, Elizabeth. "Nation-Building and Catholic Assistance to Migrants in Italy's Transition from Land of Emigration to Immigration, 1861–1990." PhD diss., University of Minnesota, 2014.

Ventresca, Robert A. *From Fascism to Democracy: Culture and Politics in the Italian Election of 1948.* Toronto: University of Toronto Press, 2004.

Venturas, Lina, ed. *International "Migration Management" in the Early Cold War: The Intergovernmental Committee for European Migration.* Corinth, Greece: University of the Peloponnese, 2015.

Venturini, Nadia. *Neri e Italiani ad Harlem: gli Anni Trenta e la Guerra d'Etiopia.* Rome: Edizioni Lavoro, 1990.

Von Eschen, Penny. *Race against Empire: Black Americans and Anticolonialism, 1937–1957.* Ithaca, N.Y.: Cornell University Press, 1997.

Waldinger, Roger. *Through the Eye of the Needle: Immigrants and Enterprise in New York's Garment Trades.* New York: New York University Press, 1986.

Wall, Wendy. "America's Best Propagandists: Italian Americans and the 1948 Letters to Italy Campaign." In *Cold War Constructions: The Political Culture of*

*United States Imperialism, 1915–1960*, edited by Christian G. Appy, 89–109. Amherst: University of Massachusetts Press, 2000.

———. *Inventing the "American Way": The Politics of Consensus from the New Deal to the Civil Rights Movement*. New York: Oxford University Press, 2008.

Walzer, Michael. *Spheres of Justice*. New York: Basic Books, 1984.

Weisbrot, Robert. *Freedom Bound: A History of America's Civil Rights Movement*. New York: W. W. Norton, 1990.

Westad, Odd Arne. *The Global Cold War*. New York: Cambridge University Press, 2007.

White, Nicola. *Reconstructing Italian Fashion: America and the Development of the Italian Fashion Industry*. New York: Bloomsbury Press, 2000.

Whitfield, Stephen J. *The Culture of the Cold War*. Baltimore: Johns Hopkins University Press, 1991.

Winkler, Elizabeth. "Voluntary Agencies and Government Policy." *International Migration Review* 15, no. 1 (Spring–Summer 1981): 95–98.

Winslow, Rachel Rains. *The Best Possible Immigrants: International Adoption and the American Family*. Philadelphia: University of Pennsylvania Press, 2017.

Wong, Carolyn. *Lobbying for Inclusion: Rights Politics and the Making of Immigration Policy*. Stanford, Calif.: Stanford University Press, 2006.

Wright, Robert G. "Voluntary Agencies and the Resettlement of Refugees." *International Migration Review* 15, no. 1 (Spring–Summer 1981): 157–74.

Wu, Ellen. *The Color of Success: Asian Americans and the Origins of the Model Minority*. Princeton, N.J.: Princeton University Press, 2014.

Wyman, Mark. *DP: Europe's Displaced Persons, 1945–1951*. Ithaca, N.Y.: Cornell University Press, 1998.

———. *Round-Trip to America: The Immigrants Return to Europe, 1880–1930*. Ithaca, N.Y.: Cornell University Press, 1993.

Yacub, Salim. *Containing Arab Nationalism: The Eisenhower Doctrine in the Middle East*. Chapel Hill: University of North Carolina Press, 2004.

Yans, Virginia. "On 'Groupness.'" *Journal of American Ethnic History* 25, no. 4 (Summer 2006): 119–29.

Zanoni, Elizabeth. "'A Wife in Waiting': Women and the 1952 McCarran-Walter Act in *Il Progresso Italo-Americano* Advice Columns." In *New Italian Migrations to the United States*. Vol. 1, *Politics and History since 1945*, edited by Laura Ruberto and Joseph Sciorra, 80–104. Urbana: University of Illinois Press, 2017.

Zappia, Charles. "From Working-Class Radicalism to Cold War Anti-Communism: The Case of the Italian Locals of the International Ladies' Garment Workers' Union." In *The Lost World of Italian American Radicalism: Politics, Labor, and Culture*, edited by Philip Cannistraro and Gerald Meyer, 143–62. Westport, Conn. Praeger, 2003.

Zelizer, Julian. *The Fierce Urgency of Now: Lyndon Johnson, Congress, and the Battle for the Great Society*. New York: Penguin Books, 2015.

Zolberg, Aristide. *A Nation by Design: Immigration Policy in the Fashioning of America*. Cambridge, Mass.: Harvard University Press, 2006.

Zucker, Norman L. "Refugee Resettlement in the United States: Policy and Problems." *Annals of the American Academy of Political and Social Science* 467 (May 1983): 172–86.

Page references in *italics* indicate photos or illustrations.

Critical Studies in Italian America

SERIES EDITORS:
Nancy C. Carnevale and Laura E. Ruberto

www.ingramcontent.com/pod-product-compliance
Lightning Source LLC
Chambersburg PA
CBHW022132020426
42334CB00015B/865